From *Primitive* to *Postcolonial*
in Melanesia and Anthropology

From *Primitive* to *Postcolonial* in Melanesia and Anthropology

Bruce M. Knauft

Ann Arbor
THE UNIVERSITY OF MICHIGAN PRESS

Copyright © by the University of Michigan 1999
All rights reserved
Published in the United States of America by
The University of Michigan Press
Manufactured in the United States of America
⊚ Printed on acid-free paper

2002   2001   2000   1999   4   3   2   1

A CIP catalog record for this book is available from the British Library.

Library of Congress Cataloging-in-Publication Data

Knauft, Bruce M.
     From primitive to postcolonial in Melanesia and anthropology /
     Bruce M. Knauft.
        p.   cm.
     Includes bibliographical references and index.
     ISBN 0-472-09687-7 (acid-free paper)
     ISBN 0-472-06687-0 (pbk. : acid-free paper)
        1. Ethnology—Melanesia.   2. Melanesia—Social life and customs.
     3. Melanesia—Social conditions.   4. Ethnology—Melanesia—History.
     I. Title.
     GN668   .K53   1999
     305.8'00995—dc21   98-40153
                                                                  CIP

Contents

Illustrations

Acknowledgments

Since at least the late nineteenth century, the course of Melanesian anthropology has been wonderfully varied. Even during the last decade, while the present work was being configured, there have been important and sometimes momentous changes in Melanesian lifeways and in anthropologists' views of them. Located amid this stimulating and shifting current, the present work owes debts to many persons, places, and sources. My first debt is to the Gebusi, whose effervescent spirit and friendly indulgence afforded me a special perspective on a wonderfully alternative way of life. Though Gebusi are but one of many peoples dealt with in the following pages, they have had a strong impact on my attempts to understand Melanesian sensibilities.

I also owe a debt of gratitude to the many colleagues, students, and administrators who have stimulated my interests as a Melanesianist and provided me critical commentary and collegial support during one or more parts of the present project. I extend a warm thanks to James Baker, Peggy Barlett, Fredrik Barth, Eytan Bercovitch, Aletta Biersack, James Boon, Michael Brown, Philippe Descola, Donald Donham, James Ferguson, Robert Foster, Carla Freeman, Lawrence Hammar, Simon Harrison, Terence Hays, Gilbert Herdt, Jonathan Hill, Stephen Hugh-Jones, Margaret Jolly, Ivan Karp, Stuart Kirsch, Raymond Kelly, Corinne Kratz, Rena Lederman, Lamont Lindstrom, Michael O'Hanlon, Anton Ploeg, Joel Robbins, Alan Rumsey, Debra Spitulnik, Andrew Strathern, Marilyn Strathern, Holly Wardlow, James Weiner, and Geoffrey White. All shortcomings remain my own. The Anthropology Department at Emory University has been an exemplary home base for research and collegial support since 1985, and research support from the Harry Frank Guggenheim Foundation is gratefully acknowledged during 1985 through 1988 and 1990 through 1994. My research has also benefited from a fellowship year at the Center for Advanced Study in the Behavioral Sciences, Stanford, California, in 1991 through 1992 (funded by NSF Grant BNS-8700864), and a fellowship at the École des Hautes Études en Sciences Sociales, Paris, hosted most genially by Maurice Godelier in the spring of 1994. Special thanks are due Thomas

Gregor and Donald F. Tuzin for conceptualizing and organizing the Wenner-Gren conference "Amazonia and Melanesia: Gender and Anthropological Comparison," held in Mijas, Spain, September 7–15, 1996, which helped spawn chapter 4 of the present work.

I would like to thank the following for permission to reproduce substantial parts of previously published papers: Urzone, for "Bodily Images in Melanesia: Cultural Substances and Natural Metaphors," in *Fragments for a History of the Human Body, Part Three,* edited by Michel Feher, with Ramona Naddaff and Nadia Tazi, 198–279 (New York: Zone Books, 1989) copyright © 1989 Urzone, Inc.; Oceania publications, for "Melanesian Warfare: A Theoretical History," *Oceania* 60 (4): 250–311 (1990); and the Royal Anthropological Society, for "Gender Identity, Political Economy, and Modernity in Melanesia and Amazonia," *Journal of the Royal Anthropological Institute,* vol. 3, 233–59 (1997). These papers have all been edited, revised, and updated herein, where they form the core of chapters 2 through 4. The present book's map of Melanesia was originally published as the frontispiece to Gilbert H. Herdt's edited volume *Ritualized Homosexuality in Melanesia,* rev. ed. (Berkeley: University of California Press, 1992), copyright © 1984 The Regents of the University of California; permission for reprinting this map is gratefully acknowledged from Gilbert Herdt and the University of California Press.

A special thanks is due Susan B. Whitlock at the University of Michigan Press; it is rare for an editor to provide such consistently helpful advice and encouragement for the configuration and production of a book such as this. The figures in chapter 2 were drawn by Robin Mouat. A generous subvention from the Graduate School of Arts and Sciences at Emory University has made possible the publication of color photographs in the present book; special thanks and gratitude go to Associate Provost Eleanor C. Main for approving and overseeing this subvention. Credit for taking photographs 13 and 16, of New Guinea highlanders, goes to Michael D. P. O'Hanlon, whose generosity in permitting their publication here is gratefully acknowledged. Photograph 16 was originally published as plate 14 in Michael O'Hanlon's book *Paradise: Portraying the New Guinea Highlands* (London: The British Museum, 1993). Credit for taking the remaining photographs, of Gebusi, goes to my wonderful wife and partner, Eileen M. Cantrell. To her and my son, Eric, I owe my deepest debt and give my greatest thanks.

This book is dedicated to the peoples of Melanesia, to previous intrepid cohorts of Melanesian anthropologists, and to an emerging generation of new researchers who will help us appreciate this remarkable world area yet more fully in the years ahead.

Chapter 1

Melanesia as "Culture Area"

As an insular part of the southwest Pacific, Melanesia is a highly distinctive world region. Stretching from the French colony of New Caledonia in the southeast to the west half of New Guinea claimed by Indonesia, Melanesia additionally harbors at least three postcolonial nations—four if one includes Fiji in addition to Papua New Guinea, Vanuatu, and the Solomon Islands (see map 1). In political and geographic terms, Melanesia is certainly a patchwork, and it has even been debated if the contours of the region can be effectively delineated.[1]

Beyond its national and neocolonial lineaments, Melanesia is justifiably renowned for being the most culturally and linguistically diverse region on earth. Though Melanesia has a population of under eight million people, it includes an amazing one-quarter of the entire world's languages and associated cultures.[2] Approximately 80 percent of Melanesia's population—and an even greater proportion of its linguistic and cultural diversity—is found in New Guinea and its associated islands.[3] Accordingly, Melanesia—and New Guinea within it—has had a special place in the understanding of human cultural variation.

The present work is concerned with the diversity of Melanesian lifeways and also with the history of anthropological interest in them. Both of these are part of our knowledge of the peoples and cultures of this remarkable region. More generally, the chapters that follow are

---

1. For instance, see Thomas 1989; Sahlins 1990; cf. Chowning 1977; Brookfield and Hart 1971.

2. Melanesia contains approximately 750 Papuan and 400 Austronesian languages; collectively, these constitute 1,150 of the roughly 4,000 languages estimated to be spoken in the world as a whole (Wurm 1982a:7, 1982b, 1983; Finegan and Besnier 1989:296).

3. This statement pertains to the combined populations of Papua New Guinea and West New Guinea (Irian Jaya). These areas, along with the Solomon Islands and Vanuatu, are the principal foci of the present work. Information from New Caledonia and Fiji is also included, but more sporadically.

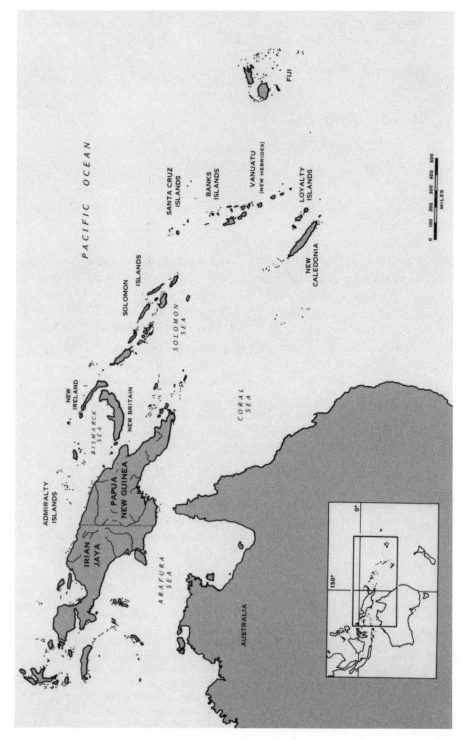

Map 1. Melanesia. (Reprinted from the frontispiece in Herdt 1984a [rev. ed.], by permission of Gilbert Herdt and the University of California Press.)

concerned with the ongoing relationship between Melanesia as a vibrantly changing world area and anthropology as a vibrantly changing discipline. The subjects and objects of Melanesian anthropology over the last century open a unique perspective upon larger developments. These include broad trajectories of sociocultural change in a shrinking world, and transformations within anthropology that have shifted perspective and emphasis from the "primitive" to the "post-colonial." How these issues have played out in and through Melanesia is particularly revealing given the region's cultural and historical distinctiveness.

Anthropology and Cultural Diversity

As is often noted, one of anthropology's key strengths is its attempt to comprehend the full range of human cultural diversity. This emphasis relates to the general value of social understanding by attempting to see the world through the lens of people different from ourselves. As discussed elsewhere (Knauft 1996: chap. 2), it is simple but still important to assert the passion and rigor of anthropology's desire to appreciate alternative ways of thinking and acting. Understanding cultural diversity remains a key means of combating ethnocentrism. Recent approaches that emphasize complexity and fragmentation—both in the world and in our understanding of it—do not undercut this importance so much as reemphasize it.

At its best, cultural anthropology considers other peoples not in rarefied terms, but as living agents whose knowledge, imagery, and experience broaden and enrich our own. Though it is questionable whether all humans are completely equal, and though it is doubtful whether understanding between peoples could ever approach completeness, it is important that humans have the ability to reach across cultural differences and comprehend alternative ways of life. Taking cultural distinctiveness seriously means embracing rather than suppressing differences in belief and practice. Because our understanding of these differences is always influenced by our own background and position, this endeavor also forces us to critically consider power relations and inequality, including how power is ingrained in different forms of belief and representation.

Broadened in this way, an appreciative understanding of cultural differences continues to widen our understanding of humanity, questions the limitations of our prior experience, and expands our under-standings of culture and power. Our interest and wonder at the range of human possibilities are increased. As such, cultural anthropology is not the search for an essential and foreign "thing out there," a radical Otherness that we project as the negative definition of ourselves. And it is not the Enlightenment desire to expose a single path through human variety toward moral or technical improvement. Rather, it is the late modern desire to illuminate a diversity of potential alternatives to appreciate and choose among. In the process, taken-for-granted assumptions about the naturalness of power and inequality can be pro-ductively challenged.

What's in a Region? The Changing Status of Melanesia as a Distinctive "World Area"

Given its cultural diversity, Melanesia has been extremely important to the development of social and cultural anthropology. Reciprocally, Melanesia has been more heavily "anthropologized" over the last hun-dred years than most other world areas. At the same time, the resulting diversity of anthropological attentions combines with Melanesia's own multiplicity to make generalizations about the region surprisingly dif-ficult to come by. The region's unity is its variety; circumstances are dif-ferent depending on the local cultural context. And this variation can be interpreted through any one of the myriad perspectives that anthro-pologists have developed in the study of Melanesian peoples.

Deeper questions concern the configuration of culture areas as contemporary "regions." What distinctions do individual regions retain as they are increasingly influenced by transnational networks and global interconnections? What is the relationship between local identity and the national aspirations of postcolonial states? Is Melane-sia becoming more like the rest of the world and losing its diversity? As an area for understanding cultural change in the context of global influ-ence, Melanesia certainly has continuing importance for anthropology. But in what ways does this understanding itself put in question the dis-tinctiveness of different world areas?

At this point, it is useful to step back and briefly review the concept of "world areas," which typically configure the world into geographic regions for purposes of course work and research specialization. The notion that the world is comprised of broad cultural areas has a venerable history in anthropology. As opposed to nineteenth-century attempts to trace the complex diffusion of cultural traits across and between major regions, anthropology through much of the twentieth century has emphasized how beliefs, practices, and cultural histories are distinct in different world areas and in specific locales within them. Originally associated with differences in physical artifacts and material culture, the idea of regional cultural areas grew during the twentieth century to include customs and beliefs that were widespread and transcended constituent political or linguistic units.

As more information has been gathered, the conceptualization of culture areas has become both richer and more diffuse. Especially when analyzing larger dimensions of cultural diversity and for teaching, it is common for anthropologists as well as political scientists or historians to speak of "sub-Saharan Africa," "the Mideast," "South Asia," "Latin America," "East Asia," and so on. Within regions, smaller areas are seen as sharing more specific characteristics amid more diffuse commonalities. Concerning New Guinea, for instance, it is common to designate areas such as "the core highlands," "the fringe highlands," "the Sepik," the "south lowlands," "the Massim," or other insular/coastal areas, though the boundaries between these areas can be fuzzy, even in scholarly discourse.[4]

Outside Melanesia, regional interests have taken on a much wider and more strategic importance—and with implications far beyond anthropology. During World War II, and especially in its wake of opposition between the West and the USSR, major non-Western culture areas were strategically important to the United States and other Western powers (see Rafael 1994). Relatedly, the study of culture areas garnered major research support in Western countries, especially during the 1960s, 1970s, and 1980s. Over this period, the connection between scholarship and political strategy—which had already been evident in the colonial era—helped spur the development of culture area programs, funding agencies, and associated area research institutes in major universities, especially in the United States.

Within area studies programs, of course, special import was attached to economic, political, or historical significance to the Western world—South Asia, Latin America, the Mideast, Africa, and so on—as

---

4. See Hays 1993; P. Brown 1978; Weiner 1988c; Gewertz 1983; Knauft 1993a; Leach and Leach 1983.

studied by the social sciences and humanities. Among these disciplines, anthropology was by no means preeminent. And, regions such
as Melanesia, which were seen as having little significance on a wider
world stage, were marginalized and were seldom given special areal
research support (except in Australia, where Melanesia's proximity
made it strategically important). For *anthropology*, however, Melanesia
came to have even greater importance given the apparent persistence
of its indigenous cultures and the relative inattention given the area by
the other social sciences and humanities. As implied previously, and as
discussed in chapter 5, Melanesia has been important to anthropology
for most of the twentieth century as the home of indigenous "tribal"
societies.

Now in the late twentieth century, however, the conceptualization
of cultural areas such as Melanesia has become problematic (see Trouillot 1991; Appadurai 1988). The notion of "tribes" is an anachronism. If
world areas have long been interconnected through travel, migration,
and exploration, this interconnection now occurs more quickly, more
intensely, and with greater complexity than before. Cultures are not just
local, they appropriate ideas and goods and images that travel widely
across space and into the most remote areas (e.g., Appadurai 1996).
Across anthropology, cultural studies, and the social sciences and
humanities more generally, there is heightened attention to transnational, hybrid, and globalizing processes. Given this focus, the question
of what a culture area is, or what significance it has, can be uncertain.

This question is particularly important for Melanesia, which
gained scholarly distinctiveness for the very reason that it was seen as
relatively isolated from outside influences. The current interest in
transnationalism gives greatest attention to the sites of greatest political
significance and economic activity, such as East and Southeast Asia, the
Mideast, Latin America, Eastern Europe, and diasporic populations
that complicate ideologies of Western national homogeneity. In this climate, however, contemporary Melanesian societies should become all
the more significant; they reorient us in a fresh way to the complexities
of cultural diversity and dynamic change.

The Importance of Regional Perspectives

For all the recent and deserved emphasis on global interconnection, it is
equally important to continue detailed scholarship of specific world

regions. Steeping oneself in the ethnography and history of a world area provides depth and breadth of understanding that is afforded by neither global analysis nor single case studies. The current tendency to consider the relation between the "global" and the "local" often neglects those key features of regional distinctiveness that lie in between. The argument that regional understandings are "untheoretical" (e.g., Shea 1997) belies the fact that any theoretical argument requires a discernible field of application. "Regions" do not determine theoretical orientations, but they provide an analytic context that can be rigorous, responsive to cultural differentiation, important in geographic scope, and conducive to broader comparisons. If networks are global, it is important to find ways that our analysis can hold them still or bracket their flow. As Marilyn Strathern suggests in her article "Cutting the Network," "[i]nterpretation must hold objects of reflection stable long enough to be of use" (1996:522). Regional analysis is one way, among others, that this can be done.

Under present conditions, regional analysis faces special challenges. Gaining mastery of regional ethnography or history is not just a lost art; it is almost impossible. The range of relevant sources skyrockets. Geographical as well as disciplinary markers blur as they get scrutinized. And the very idea of "mastery" goes against the current sense that scholarship should be supple and positional, that it should create hybrids of intellectual connection and make boundaries problematic rather than defining or defending them. Again, however, there is no reason why such intellectual agendas—and others—cannot benefit from and reinforce regional scholarship. Regional understandings inform and provide empirical grounding for many kinds of theoretical perspectives, including those that emphasize networks and interconnection. A regional purview mediates almost intrinsically between "diversity-within-similarity," on the one hand, and "similarity-within-diversity," on the other. To say that regional understandings are complemented by interregional or global influences, and by local particulars, is to underscore rather than undercut their importance.

History and Culture in Melanesia

Melanesia's regional significance has long been configured by the historical relationship between Westerners and Melanesians as well as by the intrinsic features of Melanesians' customs and beliefs. Though some coastal areas of Melanesia were explored by Europeans as early as the 1500s, Westerners had little direct contact with Melanesians from interior areas until well into the twentieth century. Combining tropical rain forests, precipitous mountain terrain, swamps, and hazardous coastlines, Melanesia has been viewed by Westerners as among the most inhospitable, least economically profitable, and most logistically difficult regions of the inhabited world to access or exploit. Unfortunately, Melanesians themselves were often disparaged in early accounts as being unattractive, violent, unscrupulous, and immoral.

Changes were brought to many parts of insular and coastal Melanesia through trade goods, disease, labor trade, and other intrusions that included sporadic gold rushes, the mining of nickel in New Caledonia, and sugar plantations in Fiji. But until recent decades, the bulk of Melanesian peoples have been less dramatically impacted by outside influences than those in many other world areas. This pattern persisted despite and in some senses because of the nominal colonial control in Melanesia by various Western powers in the nineteenth century.[5] The ostensibly benign and paternalistic colonialism of Melanesia has often attempted to pacify and sometimes to Christianize Melanesia peoples without attempting to alter their subsistence economy or social organization.

Of course, colonial pacification and attempts at missionization—in addition to labor recruitment in a number of areas—had a substantial and sometimes dramatic impact. These influences have been strong in coastal and insular eastern parts of Melanesia since late in the nineteenth century. But the impact of colonialism has been variable depending on the specific region of Melanesia, the historical time frame, and the goals of the colonial power in question. In general, direct influence was least where there was least profit to be taken. And

---

5. Exceptions are provided by continuing French control of New Caledonia and British influence in Fiji until 1970, among selected other examples. The British also held the Solomon Islands until 1978 and, in a joint governance with France, the New Hebrides—since renamed Vanuatu—until 1980. The Dutch held West New Guinea from the nineteenth century until it was transferred to Indonesia in 1963. Northeast New Guinea was held by Germany from 1884 until World War I, when it was ceded to Australian control. Following its earlier annexation by the British, southeast New Guinea (Papua) was controlled by Australia from early in the twentieth century; Australia subsequently held this area in addition to northeast New Guinea until both regions were combined in the independent country of Papua New Guinea in 1975.

Melanesia was, in general terms, unprofitable. Compared to most other parts of the colonial world, then, outside commercial influence has been relatively sparse in Melanesia until recent decades. In many areas, a relative lack of Western social and economic presence was far out-stripped by the escalating desire for Western goods and associated ideas among Melanesians themselves. Historically, this has often been reflected in Melanesian desires for *greater* foreign influence, especially in terms of business development, education, and material infrastructure. For various reasons, and as discussed in chapter 5, the strident anticolonialism that has been prominent in many of the world's post-colonies has been slow to develop an academic or scholarly tradition in Melanesia—possibly excepting in New Caledonia, which is still under French control.[6]

For most of the twentieth century, the great importance of Melanesia to anthropology has been directly related to the region's relative marginality to the West in political and economic terms.[7] Though now belied by more current developments, Melanesia was less attractive to Western profit-takers and less thoroughly transformed by colonial development—again, with the exception of New Caledonia and some other insular eastern areas—than most other parts of the colonial world. Conversely, Melanesia has historically been a hotbed of ethnographic fieldwork. And within Melanesia, those locales that were the most remote, unexploited, and "unacculturated" have received the lion's share of anthropological attention. That many of these societies were highly decentralized or "tribal" made them all the more interesting to anthropologists.

Melanesian peoples have often had elaborate religious beliefs and ritual practices and distinctive political, military, and gendered or sexual customs. The documentation of these by professional anthropologists has been particularly important for understanding the range of human cultural diversity. Until fairly recently, those features of Melanesian societies that have been most strongly foregrounded include:

---

6. This can be contrasted to the proliferation of Melanesian creative writing and popular fiction (see bibliography in Elliston 1997).

7. Notable exceptions to this lack of economic and strategic importance include the geographic significance of Melanesia in the Pacific theater during World War II and the political significance to Australia of adjacent parts of Melanesia.

- Subsistence that combined decentralized horticulture of root crops (or sago palm harvesting) and hunting, fishing, or the domestication of pigs;[8]
- Decentralized residence in villages or dispersed hamlets;
- Political leadership that was aggressively achieved but highly decentralized, archetypally associated with "big men" or "great men";
- Cycles of competitive or ceremonial exchange, sometimes quite elaborate, that indicated the social relationship between groups and between individuals;
- Indigenous patterns of conflict and intergroup warfare that sometimes included large-scale killing and/or head-hunting and/or cannibalism;
- Pronounced patterns of gendered polarity or "sexual antagonism," including frequent beliefs concerning female pollution and customs that proscribed or prescribed a diverse array of heterosexual or homosexual practices;
- Complex systems of cosmological belief, myth, ritual, and/or magic that informed a wide range of initiation systems, sorcery practices, fertility rites, and ancestral ceremonies, often accompannied by elaborate body decoration, carvings, painting, and/or music.

Collectively, the documentation of these practices and beliefs has been tremendously important to anthropology's wider comprehension of diverse topics, including political organization, spiritual belief and ritual, gender and sexuality, subsistence intensification, socioeconomic exchange, and so on. At the same time, the details and the wider representation of these practices have led many nonacademic Westerners to see Melanesians as rather "primitive" or "exotic," if not bizarre. Anthropologists themselves have played an inextricable role in this emphasis. Among other things, the cultivation of Western interest in "primitive Others" was important for generating institutional and financial support for anthropological research in out-of-the-way places.

Over the last ten or fifteen years, however, Melanesian anthropology has seen a growing groundswell of interest in issues that are more

---

8. Among some insular or riverine groups, fish was traded to other groups for root crops or sago.

"contemporary" than "tribal," including the Melanesian experience of nationalism, Christianity, urbanization, crime or "raskolism," sexually transmitted diseases, economic development, mining and logging, and other dimensions of postcolonial or late colonial change. Concern with these issues was foreshadowed by earlier interests, including the documentation and analysis of so-called Melanesian cargo cults, which entailed spiritual and social responses to Western influence that troubled colonial sensibilities.[9] But interest in Melanesian social and cultural change has intensified remarkably in recent years.

In a larger sense, Melanesia as a known "world area" cannot be detached or decontextualized from its history, or even from its history as an object of study by anthropologists. If Melanesia has been important for anthropology, the region is also distinctive for having been represented to the world largely by the many sociocultural anthropologists who have worked there. By contrast, many other world areas—including Japan, China, India, Southeast Asia, the Mideast, Latin America, and some parts of Africa—have been prominently represented to Western understanding through the perspective of political scientists, economists, sociologists, historians, and scholars of business, law, or religion—or archeologists or paleontologists—as much as or more than they have been by cultural anthropologists.

Among other things, the "anthropologizing" of Melanesia means that many Westerners see the region in a way that foregrounds its cultural distinctiveness and diversity. In the context of Melanesia's special characteristics, this can make the region seem especially "uncivilized" relative to other areas, at the same time that it appears culturally remarkable and fascinating. Though many anthropologists of Melanesia have worked hard to combat the region's image as "primitive," their efforts have often been received within a restricted or exotic frame of perception. There is still inordinate media interest in the possibility of supposedly "lost tribes" or uncontacted peoples in Melanesia (see Kirsch 1997b). Relative to the growing importance of other non-Western areas to Western sensibilities, there is a distinct larger risk of "rediscovering" in Melanesia the very marginality that has been projected onto it. Such an attitude can easily be patronizing. In the process, the larger powers and inequalities that both intrude upon Melanesia and

---

9. See Worsley 1968; Burridge 1960; Schwartz 1963; Lawrence 1964; Knauft 1978; McDowell 1988; Keesing and Corris 1980; Lindstrom 1993.

arise within it are underemphasized in our knowledge and in our appreciation of this distinctive world area.

Within the field of anthropology, the study of Melanesia has multiple dimensions. As discussed in chapter 5, the classic ethnography of Melanesia was at the cutting edge of most of the principal theories of society and culture developed in anthropology over the twentieth century. These have included late-nineteenth and early-twentieth-century cultural diffusionism; the advent of modern fieldwork based on participant-observation; the functional study of social organization and exchange; key perspectives on ecological anthropology and cultural materialism; symbolic analysis and cultural interpretation; structural Marxism; and the study of male–female relations, gender, and sexuality. In all these regards, and others, the history of Melanesian ethnography has been deeply influential in the history of anthropology itself.

In contrast to the long-standing importance of Melanesia to anthropology, however, the region has a less distinctive relationship to the field's contemporary concern with power, history, and social complexity. Interest in these issues has become prominent if not dominant within cultural anthropology, especially in the United States. These also dovetail with critical perspectives on the politics of representation and authorship, including questions about anthropology's role in a world where peoples increasingly speak for themselves. Amid the concern with these issues, the importance of Melanesia for anthropology is now being creatively reconfigured.

Classic studies of Melanesian societies often focused on the local village or community as an indigenous and ostensibly autonomous or stable unit. Now, even as these assumptions are no longer tenable among anthropologists, their legacy is reflected in travel literature and mass media coverage of Melanesia. In a nationally televised evening news story—one of the very few to take people from this part of the world as its subject— Americans were told that people of New Guinea were "exotic, primitive, and fierce" and "shaped by prehistoric tribal customs, in some villages, even cannibalism" (*ABC Nightly News*, May 26, 1997).[10] Many introductory anthropology courses uncritically perpetuate this view; Melanesia is represented through anecdotes or case

---

10. The same news story was rebroadcast by ABC shortly thereafter in parts of the Pacific.

studies that suggest isolated tribes of "Stone Age peoples" living in "a land that time forgot."

Melanesians who consider themselves modern can resent such images. The following letter was written by an urban Papua New Guinean man, Jack Kagoi, and published by the P.N.G. national daily paper *The Post Courier* in 1995 (quoted in Foster 1996/97:3).

> The new Shell television commercial showing a Tari [Southern Highlands] man and his family dressed in traditional gear driving to a Shell station with a pig in the car, is in low taste, and portrays a very primitive P.N.G. society. In case Shell hasn't noticed, we Papua New Guineans do not walk or drive around in grass skirts carrying pigs with us. Maybe a small group of people up in the Highlands still do this, but the rest of us don't. To the expatriate executives of Shell, we Papua New Guineans are working very hard to take our place in the modern world. . . . Where I come from, which is the Momase region, we do not cheapen the value of our traditional clothes by using them to sell petrol.

Note here that Kagoi's assertion is not a simple rejection of indigenous traditions, but an awareness that Melanesians continue to value aspects of their indigenous life-style at the same time that they are working hard to attain "our place in the modern world."

As Errington and Gewertz (1995), Foster (1995a), Keesing (1992), the Carriers (1989, 1991), and many others have noted, it is shortsighted to polarize an "indigenous Melanesia" against "contemporary trends." Migration and diffusion, economic and political change, and changing dimensions of cultural value have been indigenous to Melanesia for thousands of years. In recent decades, these legacies have been influenced not just by colonialism but by major postcolonial developments. Melanesia's status as a region continues to evolve, both in itself and as a focus of scholarly interest, as its populations engage national identities and the cultural and economic dynamics of the global marketplace.

The present challenge for Melanesian anthropology, as for Melanesians themselves, is to recontextualize traditions of cultural distinction in a period of self-avowed modernity. Modernity in Melanesia includes a deeply internalized value placed on commodities and cash. Today, Melanesians want much more than steel axes, salt, beads, and matches.

They want a regular supply of tinned fish and packaged rice, Western clothes, trucks or motor-powered boats, refrigerators, Western-style houses, airplane tickets, cash reserves, and advanced schooling for their children. Along with other postcolonial possibilities, these wants intensify the desire of Melanesian landowners and governments to make money quickly. Increasingly, this dovetails with the contracting of Asian logging firms and multinational mineral and petroleum or gas corporations to exploit Melanesia's major timber and subterranean resources. The size and spread of these large-scale development projects now pose severe challenges and problems in many parts of Melanesia.

Rather than presenting a rupture with indigenous practices and beliefs, the dynamics of Melanesian economic aspirations are best seen as a permutation upon long-standing cultural patterns. These emphasize the giving and receiving of gifts and services—sometimes competitively—as key to personal prestige and community success. Indications of modern accomplishment—or the lack thereof—thus have distinctively Melanesian meanings and implications. These draw upon the distinctive "transactional" nature of Melanesian social relationships, which provide the basis for collective as well as individual identity (M. Strathern 1988). Reciprocally, Melanesian beliefs and practices proliferate as they confront the challenges, the occasional windfalls, and the many disappointments of a wider political economy and a lush but fragile environmental ecology. Through Melanesians' distinctive orientations, legacies of colonial control and postcolonial politics inform current features of personal, local, and national identity. The human importance and intellectual understanding of these developments is a central issue that begs deeper understanding of Melanesian cultural traditions and their relation to contemporary trends.

Reprise of the Regional, Revenge of the Local

Though it may go against the grain of academic trends, it is just when our concern with transcultural influences is greatest that it may be most important to re-appreciate cultural diversity and areal distinctiveness. Such appreciation has long been one of anthropology's major contributions. This impetus has often had to assert itself against intellectual approaches that are theoretically and globally reductive. In the history of anthropology, this problem has been associated with various forms of evolutionism, functionalism, structuralism, and politicoeconomic analysis.

Now, however, it is the transnational and globalizing perspectives that emerge as an "international" emphasis in political science, economics, and sociology that are often reductive. Ironically, the recent influence of cultural studies can also neglect cultural differences, at the same time that cultural studies importantly emphasize subaltern distinctions based on racial, gendered, sexual, ethnic, national, or religious positioning (see Knauft 1996: chaps. 3 and 8). Sometimes unwittingly, similar problems inflect approaches in cultural anthropology that emphasize ubiquitous networks of diasporic, postnational, or traveling cultural identifications.[11] Amid such innovative awareness, what remains regionally distinctive about cultural orientations is easily neglected or underplayed.

Regional scholarship provides a counterweight to global reduction. It also guards against an opposite problem: particularism and excessive relativism. In this instance, local circumstances, or even each voice or representation, may be portrayed narrowly without larger pragmatic context—sometimes to the point of utter uniqueness or confusion.

Past understandings certainly do need to be reevaluated through current sensibilities; our understanding and analysis of cultural diversity needs to be recuperated and revitalized by critical interventions. Correspondingly, the ways that Western stereotypes are projected onto non-Western others needs to be more rigorously and critically assessed. But in the process, ethnography based on previous decades of painstaking and often sensitive field research cannot be summarily dismissed; it needs to be carefully reanalyzed and put in fresh comparative perspectives. This goal is particularly important given current tendencies to reduce the past to the present and the local to the global.

It remains an enduring contribution of cultural anthropology to emphasize regional as well as local cultural diversity. In late modern conditions, this certainly does not mean reasserting an autonomy or homogeneity of presumably shared ways of life. What it does mean is carefully and critically combining an awareness of complexity, diversity, and fragmentation with an appreciation of cultural continuities and of widespread themes that permute as local distinctions. As a field

---

11. E.g., Clifford 1992, 1994; 1997; Hannerz 1996; Appadurai 1996; Marcus 1995.

of cultural and political friction, the tense relationship between what is regionally shared and what is locally distinctive provides a core dynamic of sociocultural change in many world areas and in Melanesia in particular.

The Present Book

The anthropological study of Melanesia now provides key perspective on some of the most important issues in the social sciences and humanities. How can we generalize about cultural themes and variations within world areas? How can we articulate an understanding of relatively "indigenous" beliefs and practices with the transnational impact of economic, political, and cultural influences? What is the relevance of a rich ethnographic record for the study of contemporary conditions? The present work explores these issues in the context of Melanesia. The answers provided are representative rather than definitive; they work by illustration rather than by recipe. As a set of excursions, they proceed inductively and from complementary vantage points. Often, they build critical awareness by taking a larger view of the wealth of ethnographic information that has been carefully collected in Melanesia during the last century. These excursions illustrate the process of being a late modern ethnologist: not of how to reach closure on an old world area, but how to use different analytic perspectives to articulate classic information with contemporary concerns. The book's chapters illustrate that indigenous and modernizing orientations in Melanesia are mutually defining rather than dichotomous. So too, different aspects of this relation may be emphasized for different purposes.

Chapter 2 considers themes and permutations of Melanesian customs that concern the human body. Scholars have long been intrigued by the amazing diversity of bodily beliefs and practices in individual Melanesian societies. It has proven more difficult, however, to consider this amazing panoply of variation in relation to larger regional terms.[12] Chapter 2 undertakes this project by reviewing and analyzing the life cycle of bodily and social development as configured in diverse areas of Melanesia and as punctuated by striking local examples. As quickly becomes evident, these practices and beliefs reveal remarkable larger ecologies that have at one and the same time been social, material, and

---

12. For a major exception, see M. Strathern 1988.

cosmological. The account aims to provide an understanding of Melanesian bodily traditions that is both expansive and sensitive to local diversity. Its larger goal is to appreciate the most basic legacies of lived cultural experience upon which Melanesian social change has been built.

Chapter 3 shifts perspective to the study of Melanesian warfare and violent conflict, which have been pronounced and of major interest to anthropologists since the nineteenth century. The chapter familiarizes the reader with a number of intersecting issues: the political and cultural history of conflict in Melanesia; how anthropologists have theorized and attempted to explain Melanesian warfare; and how ethnographic and historical evidence can be marshaled to critically assess larger contexts of collective violence in Melanesia. In contrast to chapter 2, the treatment of Melanesian warfare is fundamentally diachronic and developmental. The perspective develops as a kind of helix in which our understanding of Melanesian conflicts is dialectically related to the history of Western concerns and to Westerners' own violent or nonviolent interactions with Melanesians. Just as the account keeps Melanesian and Western histories in tension, so too a tension is maintained between taking Melanesian warfare as an object of study and considering it as a Western construction and projection. The chapter is a case example of how we can reinforce rather than undercut a productive relationship between critical historical analysis, ethnographic understanding, and theoretical evaluation. In this sense, the account combines "objectivizing" and "reflexive" or "deconstructive" moments of analysis.

Melanesian gender relations are the focus of chapter 4. Here, classic analyses of gender polarity and antagonism in Melanesia provide the point of departure for reconsidering the contemporary relation between gender identity, political economy, and modernity in Melanesia. This analysis is itself made comparative by viewing Melanesian trajectories of gendered development against those in another rainforested world area itself often associated with so-called tribal ways of life: Amazonia. The chapter analyzes developments in gender relations and politicoeconomic change in these two world areas and finds remarkable similarities—as well as poignant differences—between them. In the process, the account addresses an important larger issue: how long-standing asymmetries between men and women in various parts of the world are elaborated and recreated even as they become more ostensibly "modern." In comparative as well as temporal terms, the analysis draws on and yet fundamentally recasts our received understandings of Melanesian gender relations. In the process, it emphasizes the fundamental importance of gender and its cultural history for understanding contemporary developments in political economy and the pursuit of modernity.

The book's final chapter steps back and takes a reflexive look at the construction of Melanesia as a world area. This portrayal considers many theoretical contributions that Melanesian studies have made over the last century and compares these to the productive tensions that Melanesia as an ethnographic region now experiences in a late modern era. The relationship between world areas and anthropological scholarship is increasingly complex and politicized, including on the national and the local as well as at the international level. Given its long-standing importance to cultural anthropology, the field of Melanesian studies bears special scrutiny for the strengths and weaknesses of its historical trajectory and its future potentials. In this and other respects, Melanesian anthropology holds special promise for yielding cultural insights, theoretical contributions, and applied practical value.

As a tool for teaching, this book is intended to complement the ethnographic case studies and programmatic articles that typically form the backbone of area studies courses on Melanesian and Pacific peoples. Accordingly, it provides background on many significant features of Melanesian cultural variation, history, and development. However, I cannot pretend to provide a full or systematic introduction to Melanesia. The present study is in keeping rather than at odds with the various ways that world areas such as Melanesia have emerged and are now perceived. In this regard, the complementary perspectives developed in subsequent chapters can be played off each other to provide grist for discussion and student debate. These issues include the tensions of Western representation and voicing as well as the appreciative understanding of Melanesian practices, beliefs, and circumstances of change. How to deepen our respect for Melanesian distinctiveness—both as an object of rigorous analysis and as a subject of representation—is an important issue. In these and other respects, the present work intends a dialogue between ethnographic rigor and comparative generalization, on the one hand, and the need to be critically historical, on the other.

Each of this book's subsequent chapters is introduced by a head-note that contextualizes and reflects briefly on the substantive accounts that follow it. Since the chapters provide different perspectives on Melanesia, each has a dialogic and implicitly provocative relation to the others. Each was also first drafted at a slightly different point in my own understanding of Melanesia as a region. Since temporal development is intrinsic to the progression of knowledge and comprehension, the head-notes comment (in a limited and bracketed fashion) on the dynamics of knowledge construction in the course of each essay's presentation.

The day when one can write a definitive account of a world area seems to be past, if this was ever truly possible. But one can nonetheless configure ethnographically rich analyses of issues that are anthropologically significant, important to regional understanding, and valuable to the lives of people themselves. As I hope to show, Melanesian anthropology is particularly remarkable in these respects.

My own personal journey as an anthropologist makes it fitting to bring regional considerations of Melanesia and anthropology together at the present time. Following upon a deep fascination with Melanesian peoples and cultures as a graduate student during the late 1970s, my interests led me to extended fieldwork during 1980 through 1982 among the Gebusi of Papua New Guinea's Western Province. In the years following, I completed a monograph and articles concerning the Gebusi (1985 et seq.) and broadened my perspective to comparatively analyze the range of remarkable cultural groups that have spanned the south coast of New Guinea, from Papua New Guinea through Irian Jaya (1993a). During the late 1980s and early 1990s, I became both intrigued and provoked by new developments in cultural theory or antitheory, and I began to critically consider the relevance of these interdisciplinary influences for anthropology's understanding of cultural diversity. I brought this project together in a volume that engaged a range of contemporary theoretical issues with ethnographic analyses, many of which were drawn from Melanesia (1996). This work completed, I now contemplate the scintillating challenges and opportunities of another major period of fieldwork in New Guinea and with Gebusi, including the new round of subsequent interests that this can spawn. My hope for Melanesian studies is now paralleled by my personal hopes as I look forward to reconnecting with my Gebusi friends, whose lives have changed if not been transformed in recent years. Before embarking on this personal and professional experience, how-

ever, it has seemed appropriate to first bring together a more composite view of my understandings of Melanesia as a whole.

Like many compositions, the present one has mosaic designs. It
weaves together a larger relationship between Melanesia and anthropology via comparative details and ethnographic renderings. The
remarkable humanity that informs these details is the larger and deeper
foundation of Melanesia that my account portrays but can only approximate.

Chapter 2

Bodily Images in Melanesia: Cultural Substances and Natural Metaphors

Against the brilliant diversity of cultural orientations in regions such as Melanesia, recent authors have sometimes questioned anthropology's documentation of indigenous beliefs and practices. For one thing, practices that have been taken as traditional have often been influenced by outsiders, sometimes quite fundamentally or over significant periods of time. What was initially reported as pristine may be influenced by our own tendency to see in other peoples those "primitive" aspects that we either lack or fear in ourselves.

Such arguments are important and cannot be ignored by any anthropologist who seriously contemplates working in the twenty-first century. But world areas also retain deep-seated cultural influences that have long historical roots. Often, these have been highlighted by a venerable tradition in anthropology that stresses the respectful documentation and detailed understanding of cultural diversity, including customs that were less explicitly configured against outside domination. The beliefs and practices of people from different world areas are more than local responses to global cultural influence or the history of capitalist imperialism.

How can anthropology continue to appreciate the radical nature of cultural differences? How do we reinvigorate anthropology's commitment and its rigor for documenting the full scope of cultural diversity? One answer is that a world of cultural variation is continually rediscovered in relation to changing intellectual and political agendas—both our own and those of the people we study among.[1] *Likewise, as the history of anthropology's own scholarship grows, we rediscover previous ethnographic accounts and draw upon their record in new ways. Even as we acknowledge criticisms of anthropology's past, there are many important uses to which its treasure trove of ethnography can be put. The question is not whether previous works become gradually out of date; of course they do. It is rather how to assemble and critically use a range of accumulated information to enlarge its frame of reference and, in the process, increase our appreciation of cultural variation. As such, we can link the ethnographic record to larger and more current concerns.*

In 1987, I was asked by Michel Feher to contribute an essay on the diverse range of Melanesian bodily practices and beliefs for his enormous project Fragments for a History of the Human Body. *Published in 1989 in three large and colorful volumes, this series included contributions from historians, social scientists, and a range of other authors. Their portrayals documented the startling variety of bodily practices and beliefs across human space and time, including in Western history.*

Western scholarship has a long historical legacy of putting together large compendiums of ethnographic and historical information. Such projects were prominent among nineteenth-century researchers, some of whom are now considered as precursors to comparative anthropology or sociology.[2] *But these Victorian scholars often viewed foreign or historical customs to be a rude past against which Western beliefs and practices marked a distinct "advancement"; whites were considered "civilized" while many people from foreign lands were considered "primitive." As the culmination of human development, European culture was seen as the most evolved and enlightened of all.*

Michel Feher's project was based on a different if not contrary principle. Rather than illustrating a path of progress and development, bodily practices from different times and places were viewed as diverse alternatives that we ourselves should learn from. In the process, our own history of looking at others' bodies was critically reassessed. Following Michel Foucault, the idea was

---

1. Appadurai (1996: chaps. 1, 7) suggests that culture should now be thought of as a self-consciously created phenomenon rather than one that is exposed by outside researchers. Along this line of reasoning, "culture" is best considered a self-avowed minority status, for instance, as configured by subordinate groups in relation to dominant ones within a nation-state.

2. See, for instance, Pritchard 1836–47; Latham 1859; Spencer 1873–81; see overviews in Stocking 1987.

that we should expand beyond our traditional assumptions and blind spots, bequeathed from Western traditions of knowledge and power, about what is "appropriate" bodily practice and belief.[3] As Foucault emphasized, the scope of human possibility is more tightly constrained by our own categories of thinking than we usually realize. As a result, alternative possibilities remain "unthought" and "unsaid." To widen this envelope, it is important and valuable to seek out greater variation in human plasticity and innovation. Indeed, it is often at the extremities of human experience and diversity that we have most to learn.

Drawing upon Foucault, Feher's goal was neither to fit bodily practices into a grand theoretical or historical plan, nor to uniformly survey their possibilities. By design, his project was particularist rather than synthetic or encyclopedic. The rough and unusual diversity of bodily practices—the way they irritate rather than harmonize with our own assumptions about proper bodily conduct—was itself the point. This agenda casts a new and contemporary light on the understanding of traditional bodily practices in a region such as Melanesia.

From a Western perspective, Melanesians have developed a wealth of alternative bodily customs and beliefs. Though early observers often disparaged or castigated these practices, the anthropological sentiment was increasingly that these customs should be appreciated in their own cultural context. Even during the early part of this century, anthropological perspectives tended to be "progressive" (and sometimes even radical) relative to then-prevalent and much more pejorative Western attitudes about indigenous peoples. Like all orientations, however, anthropology's perspectives have housed their own unintended biases, and these have played themselves out over time. Among others, these have included three assumptions that are now considered problematic: (1) that cultural practices and beliefs are stable or static over fairly long periods; (2) that culture is shared in a relatively uniform manner among a population of same-speaking people; and (3) that culture can be investigated most successfully by restricting the researcher to an intensive study of single village or community. These assumptions were influential in anthropology—and particularly strong in the anthropology of Melanesia—until fairly recently. And they influenced, at least in part, my own primary research among Gebusi in interior Papua New Guinea in 1980 through 1982. Histori-

---

3. See Foucault 1980, 1984, 1985, 1986.

cally, however, a positive side to this emphasis has been its strong dedication to detailed local fieldwork. This emphasis has been particularly productive in Melanesian anthropology. Though topically limited to issues of indigenous culture, the classic ethnography of Melanesia has, as a whole, been richer and more detailed than that of most other world areas.

To adequately convey the beauty, trauma, and richness of Melanesian bodily practices and beliefs is, ultimately, an impossible task. And yet it is important to make an attempt. It is still important to draw on traditional ethnography, to recuperate others' histories, to configure understandings of regional diversity, and to make problematic some of our own most deeply embodied assumptions.

This chapter foregrounds Melanesian beliefs and practices that were well established prior to Western intrusion. In some cases, these images and customs have persisted until quite recently, but in others they have not. Today, Melanesia is comprised largely of independent South Pacific countries, some of which have democratically elected governments and robust constituencies as third world states. This current reality, however, should not prevent us from appreciating beliefs and customs that have had a longer history in Melanesia, particularly given their rich variety. The people we ourselves studied with, the Gebusi of South New Guinea, were proud of their cultural heritage and eager that others know of it; most of the photographs accompanying this chapter are of them. Across a gap of differences, an honest respect for cultural diversity is indispensable. The following chapter offers a glimpse of some of the things we can learn to appreciate in bodily beliefs and customs that may at first appear unusual or exotic.

If anthropology attempts to provide through other cultures a mirror to ourselves and to humanity as a whole, it is as if in Melanesia this mirror has been configured into a mosaic of intricate inversions and permutations—a structuralist panoply. To order the facets of this gem would require the genius of a Lévi-Strauss,[4] a task that for Melanesia remains as yet unfulfilled. For the present, we attempt to

---

4. Lévi-Strauss is the famous French structural anthropologist who analyzed an enormous corpus of myths from native North and especially South America. He considered myths and their episodes to present structural permutations on central dichotomies of human thought, such as the opposition between "nature" and "culture."

convey at least a few patterns of Melanesian bodily beliefs and cus-toms. In so doing, we steer always uneasily between the twin dangers of ethnographic exploitation—ripping the sensational out of con-text—and of ethnographic particularism—portraying many details from only a very few Melanesian cultures and culture areas, to the neglect of others.

The variety of bodily practices and beliefs in Melanesia has been enormous. In some societies elaborate body costuming was crucial in ritual and cosmology, especially as it represented spirit forms and sym-bolized cosmic regeneration or spiritual authority. Masculine bodily development and vitality were a major concern in many New Guinea cultures, and a number of Melanesian societies practiced ritualized male homosexuality—for instance, the "growing" of boys into men by inseminating them with semen as male life force. Heterosexuality in Melanesia has also exhibited myriad patterns, ranging from pro-nounced male fear of female menstrual pollution and sexual contami-nation to serial sexual intercourse with a young woman by men of her husband's clan to heighten her fertility and produce a life-giving elixir of commingled male and female sexual fluids. Violence to the body has been similarly diverse, ranging from traumatic male initiations, scarifi-cation, finger-lopping, and widow-strangulation to cannibalistic head-hunting, endocannibalism (eating one's own dead), the use of the corpse for divination, the smearing or drinking of its cadaveric fluid, or the use of parts of the skeleton as sacred relics. Warfare and killing of enemies were endemic in complex patterns throughout most of pre-colonial Melanesia, as discussed later in chapter 3. Perhaps conversely, costuming of the living body has been the primary art form of Melane-sia, with a diversity and beauty of decoration matched by the intricacy of local spiritual symbolism and ritual transformation. Status markers and insignia on the body have indicated diverse features of age, sex, and prestige. Concepts of the body's physical constitution and anatomy have also been widely variant, including elaborate local beliefs con-cerning what foods, events, and bodily substances induce conception, growth, maturation, sickness, senescence, and death.

How can the diversity of such body images and practices be understood? First, they must be understood within their larger cultural and regional contexts. What appear to be strange or exotic bodily prac-tices are meaningful dimensions of intricate cosmologies. Second, they need to be understood theoretically through processes of body-constitution that are common if not characteristic in Melanesia. The latter will be considered first, in their general aspect.

Cultural conceptualizations of the body, being so merged with the perception of bodily experience, *seem* uniquely natural and basic. While the body is eminently "natural," it is just this perception of naturalness that allows culturally variable beliefs about the body to be so fundamentally ingrained in the collective psyche. Including in our own culture,[5] images of the body embody cultural belief and social form.

In Melanesia, the growth and development of bodies are defined fundamentally through social and spiritual relationships. This notion is both important and sometimes difficult for the Western nonanthropologist to understand. Our own individualism and personal atomism are so taken for granted that the independence of the single body as a biological entity goes without saying; the conceptual isolation of the body and its identity with an individual self seem as natural to us as they do foreign in other cultures. Consider, in contrast, societies for which the body is at heart socially and collectively constituted. Its physical makeup, including its gender, is not deep-sealed at the moment of conception, but arises sequentially depending on the actions and thoughts of relatives, spirits, and the person him- or herself. The health and well-being of the newborn may be influenced by infelicitous actions of parents and others; do they follow required dietary and sexual taboos? Are adult men kept a safe distance from the infant—lest its prolonged contact with its mother's womb harm the man while his own masculine spirit overwhelms the newborn's weak soul? Does the growing child have its body-spirit nourished by the correct complement of social and spiritual forces? As the concrete physical embodiment of the social relations, nourishment, and spirits that have raised it, the body in Melanesia mobilizes these same entities and processes in its illnesses and difficulties. The person's field of social and spiritual relations are scrutinized and called into question when the body is sick; their misalignment produces sorcery, witchcraft, or ancestral vengeance, which can harm or kill the body. These same social and spiritual relationships are manipulated or ameliorated to cure the body and make it better; their positive reaffirmation makes bodies grow and mature. At death, this relational process continues; the soul of the deceased may become

---

5. For instance, see Martin 1994; Bordo 1993.

an ancestral spirit. As such, it can continue to exert social impact, for instance, by sending sickness or misfortune upon the living to punish their social or spiritual infractions.

The point here is not that "magical," let alone "nonrational" beliefs have often been present in Melanesia, but that the shaping of personal and even physical identity through social and spiritual experience is deeply recognized. There is a powerful relationship between body, social relationship, and belief—a relationship that we ourselves have frequently ignored. In Western cultures, the importance of social transaction to the constitution of the body and the self is a late annex to knowledge—a relatively recent academic "discovery," ranging perhaps from Husserl in phenomenological philosophy to labeling theory in psychology and sociology. In Melanesia, by contrast, it is a fundamental axiom of being that self and body are constructed transactionally through social relationships and through belief in spiritual forces.

For the present, then, we focus on the process of social and spiritual life through which bodies are created in Melanesian societies. This embodiment is grounded in the wonderful diversity of Melanesian symbol systems and actualized in each case through the praxis of social development and experience. Our perspective here is similar to that described in an African ethnographic context by Jean Comaroff.

> The body is the tangible frame of selfhood in individual and collective experience, providing a constellation of physical signs with the potential for signifying the relations of persons to their contexts. The body mediates all action upon the world and simultaneously constitutes the self and the universe of social and natural relations of which it is part. Although the process is not reflected upon, the logic of that universe is itself written into the "natural" symbols that the body affords. (1985:6–7)

Given this perspective, we shall find ourselves presented at every turn with myriad connections between bodily imagery and sociocultural orientation. Unfortunately, we cannot pretend to consider or systematize these connections for Melanesia in an exhaustive way. Each Melanesian culture entrenches the body in cultural meanings, spiritual beliefs, and political economies; while we trace the body as it enters a few such avenues, we must often pull ourselves back from specifics to retain a wider regional view. Hence, we cannot hope to draw the many connections important to Melanesian specialists in any given area. Practically, we present a collage of ethnographic vignettes, focusing on some of the more elaborate and distinctive bodily practices and beliefs from various Melanesian regions. In so doing, we attempt to create as if by illusion the semblance of larger bodily portraitures for Melanesia. A few organizational conventions are adopted in presenting this material. In particular, we adopt a life-cycle perspective and trace Melanesian bodily images through various stages from birth to death. For convenience, the present tense is often used to describe bodily practices that may have continued only selectively or in vestigial form to the present. Overall, we depict as much as possible the articulation of ontology and ontogeny—the play between cultural notions of being and their diverse bodily growths and developments in Melanesia.

Conception

Construction of the body in utero enjoins primal notions of being and can reflect important beliefs concerning gender, spirituality, and group organization. For instance, conception beliefs can reflect the intergenerational transfer of rights and group identity through either the male or the female descent line. The strongly patrilineal[6] Kaliai of New Britain assert that the fetus is composed exclusively of the father's semen, with the mother's role confined to providing a place of protective growth during gestation (Counts and Counts 1983). In contrast, Malinowski's famed Trobriand Islanders, who traced clan identification through female descent, held that the fetus was constituted in virtual entirety by the fertile substance of the mother. This substance was animated not so much by the semen of the father as through ethereal fertilization by *baloma* spirits who were also from the mother's descent line.[7] On one level, these divergent beliefs encode "conceptually" the patri- versus matricentric bias of their societies' descent and kinship systems—

---

6. *Patrilineal* indicates that identity in descent groups, such as clans or lineages, is passed on and traced through male descent. *Matrilineal,* in contrast, indicates that kin group identity is passed on and traced through females. Melanesian societies exhibit a plethora of descent-group variations, many of which crosscut or combine these polar analytic types. It is nowadays generally realized by Melanesianists that simple reference to "matrilineal" or "patrilineal" groups is too simplistic; the distinction is made primarily for didactic purposes in the present context.

7. See Malinowski 1916, 1927, 1929; cf. A. B. Weiner 1976; see Jorgensen 1983a.

whether preeminent kin group identity is passed down through males or females.

Such "clean" associations, however, are not pervasive in Melanesia and provide merely a point of departure into the complexity of substance and conception beliefs (Jorgensen 1983a). Among the strongly patrilineal Mae Enga of the New Guinea highlands, for instance, the fetus is believed to be formed largely by *maternal* blood. Indeed, the Enga "place little emphasis on the father's biological role" (Meggitt 1965a:163). However, the ancestral *spirits* of the father's clan are believed to be quite crucial for conception to occur, and the Enga are quite concerned "with the child's acquisition of a spirit and ultimately of a social identity as a consequence of his father's clan membership."[8]

A further variation is illustrated among the Kwoma of the Sepik (Williamson 1983). Kwoma hold that male semen and female blood are necessary to conceive a child, but that the anatomical derivatives of these substances are unfixed and highly variable. They recall our own notion of random genetic inheritance in averring that "any person can have a combination of parental characteristics," for instance, happening to be endowed with the height of one's father or the facial structure of one's mother (1983:15). Yet Kwoma also believe that conceptual transmission by prestigious patrilineal bush spirits is passed from a father to his eldest son. These individually owned spirits establish patrilineage seniority as well as protecting and punishing the members of the descent group and serving as a focus of ceremonial activity.

Perhaps the strongest contravention of descent by conception beliefs comes from the Northern Mandak of New Ireland, who are strongly matrilineal and yet claim that the fetus is anatomically constituted in its entirety by *male* procreative substance.[9] This apparent anomaly is comprehensible since it is the nurturing environment of the mother that is perceived to nurture and grow the child—first in utero, then through breast milk, and finally through the food contributions of her natal clansmen. Thus, while the father furnishes what might in some sense be the "seed," the social and biological viability of the child is tied to its mother and to those maternal kindred who are its clanmates.

As these examples collectively suggest, we are quickly forced to move beyond analysis of procreative substances as discrete symbols

8. Meggitt 1965a:163; see A. J. Strathern 1972:9–14; cf. J. F. Weiner 1982:9.

9. See Clay 1977: chap. 2; cf. Clay 1986.

and into the universe of social relations that shape bodily development in Melanesia. The first of these is gender.

Gender

In many if not most areas of Melanesia, distinct male and female sexual substances—such as male semen and female "blood"—are believed to join in forming the fetus. Each of these gender-linked substances, however, is commonly believed to exert an opposed antithetical effect on body formation. This polarity of sexual substances in conception reflects the fact that Melanesian men and women are domestically interdependent but often strongly divided by sexual polarity or antinomy in public relationships and behavior (see photos 1 and 2).[10] One belief common in New Guinea is that men are stronger, harder, or more steadfast and enduring in societal obligations, while women are considered weaker, softer, and more self-indulgent. This cultural assumption easily informs beliefs that male semen contributes bone and/or spirit—the hard or "enduring" portions of the fetus—while maternal blood or female fertile fluids generate the softer, wetter, and "weaker" parts of the infant, such as the blood and flesh. Perhaps correspondingly, a belief common in societies of highland New Guinea is that male semen "binds," congeals, and structures the woman's amorphous menstrual matter into a fetus. This seems to be an apposite gender metaphor where the substance and structure of "femaleness" are in fact effectively appropriated and circumscribed by men. In some highland areas, such sexual antinomy extends to misogyny or "sexual antagonism," in which women are subjected to assiduous male control and derogation, while men, conversely, harbor fears that they may be polluted and physically debilitated by the sexual or menstrual fluids of women.[11] Some have argued that such beliefs reflect men's guilt or worry that women oppose and undercut male domination.

We must be wary, however, of assuming that men are everywhere dominant, that clear-cut associations between gender and substance exist, or even that cultural notions of "masculinity" and "femininity" can be assigned to all men or women. Melanesian women can have

---

10. See this volume, chap. 4, and Poole and Herdt 1982.
11. See Meggitt 1964; Langness 1967, 1974; Read 1952, 1954.

important control over large and highly valued domains of social life.[12] And even where this influence is not evident, notions of personal identity may compete with those of biological gender, so that males who appear weak, indecisive, or "without spine" may be considered feminized, while women who exhibit more "masculine" characteristics are considered relatively more like men.[13]

In some cases these changes are themselves culturally mandated by recognition of gendered alteration over the course of the life cycle. For instance, where menstrual blood is thought to be feminizing and polluting, women are commonly thought to become relatively more like men when they become postmenopausal, that is, when they no longer harbor "menstrual contamination." Thus, for example, the Bimin-Kuskusmin, who maintain a rigid gender polarity, afford selective postmenopausal women roles and knowledge of great importance, including central participation in extremely secret and sacred male initiation rites (Poole 1981a). Conversely, in a number of New Guinea societies, the inability of men to rid themselves of polluting bodily blood—because they cannot menstruate—puts them at special risk of becoming feminized or debilitated. In many of these societies, particularly in the eastern highlands and Sepik regions of New Guinea, men regularly bleed themselves—usually from the penis or the nose—to release feminine blood and promote their masculine strength and well-being.[14] In a few societies, such as the Hua of the eastern highlands, men who do not bleed themselves sufficiently are believed to be capable of becoming physiologically pregnant—due to the coalescence of female blood which is said to bloat their stomachs.[15] This demonstrates the extent to which gender characteristics may be culturally defined. On the other hand, there are also societies, such as the Ankave of the south Anga region, who believe that blood-related substances rather than semen are the key to male growth and development (Bonnemère 1996). Indeed, the transformation of blood—sometimes even menstrual blood—into a potent beneficial substance has sometimes been a highly secret dimension of male initiation in Melanesia.[16]

The impact of sexually linked substances on personal identity and

---

12. See A. B. Weiner 1976; Feil 1978; Faithorn 1976.
13. This point has been developed by M. Strathern 1980, 1981, 1987, 1988.
14. E.g., Herdt 1982a, c; Read 1952; Hogbin 1970; contrast G. Lewis 1980.
15. See Meigs 1976, 1984, 1987.
16. See Allen 1967; Herdt 1982c.

development can be elaborate throughout the life cycle. Among the
Bimin-Kuskusmin, a complex balance of bodily substances must be
socially maintained even for the unborn child, whose viability depends
upon the attenuation and/or reversal of parents' male and female substances.

> While the woman is secluded [in the pregnancy/birth house],
> she must abandon certain female foods (such as sweet potatoes)
> and female food taboos, and must consume certain male foods,
> notably taro and pork. The *finiik* [masculine/clan essence] con-
> tained in these foods is said to counteract somewhat her highly
> polluted state and to strengthen and protect the child. In con-
> trast . . . her husband . . . may not enter a men's house, taro gar-
> den, or cult house, and must sleep in the forest or a garden hut.
> His male name, which he received at first initiation, may not
> be used. He is forbidden to hunt or to touch a bow. . . . He must
> avoid taro and pork (and other *finiik*-bearing male foods) and
> consumes only "soft" and "cold" female foods. (Poole 981a:138)

For the Bimin-Kuskusmin, this cultural manipulation of "natural" substance is only the beginning of a lifelong process. It is important to
attain the complement of male and female substances appropriate to
one's gender and age-status as these evolve over the course of the life
cycle.[17]

Copulation

In addition to nonsexual activities and beliefs, conception in Melanesia
encompasses a variety of beliefs about coital activity. In most New
Guinea societies, it is believed that several acts of sexual intercourse are
necessary to provide enough semen to form the male contribution to
the fetus. In many cases, however, this is crosscut by the belief that frequent sexual congress can be debilitating to men. Thus in some societies, including a number in the New Guinea highlands, men have used
sexual techniques or magic to minimize vaginal contact and/or reduce
their loss of ejaculate during coitus.[18] Among the Kaulong of New

---

17. See Poole 1981b, 1982a, b, 1983, 1984, 1985, 1986, 1987a–c.
18. E.g., Meggitt 1964; Newman and Boyd 1982.

Britain, fear of female sexual contamination was such that men did not marry until late in life, and there were a significant number of permanent bachelors. "Men looked on intercourse as something to take place late in life when they were old and ready to die, and even then they engaged in sex only to reproductively replace themselves."[19] More commonly in Melanesia, heterosexual intercourse has been considered inimical, if not to male health itself, then to male activities such as hunting or warfare. Commonly, these or other masculine pursuits are believed to require prior heterosexual abstinence in order to be successful.

Newlywed copulation practices among the Awa of the eastern highlands illustrate the strong tension between the need for coital repetition to induce fertility and the countervailing belief that this was dangerous or debilitating to men. On the one hand, Awa required that a newly married woman submit to "prolonged, serial copulation with as many of her husband's clansmen as wished to have sex with her" (Newman and Boyd 1982:281). However, since coital contamination posed a risk to men, serial intercourse was indulged in mostly by the older males of the clan; they were believed to be at reduced risk of impairing their reproductive future since they had typically fathered several children already. In Awan belief, the purpose of serial copulation was "to ready the young women for procreative activities by 'opening' the vagina and forcing out any bloody fluids that would harm their husbands and thereby impair successful reproduction" (281). From a more critical perspective, however, this could also be seen as an ideology that allowed senior men disproportionate rights to have sex with young women.

Serial copulation was also mandated in several south New Guinea cultures, but here fears of female sexual pollution were minimal or absent; the emphasis was on fertility in a more positive and general sense. Such was the case, for instance, for the *moguru*, or "life-giving ceremony," which was "the most secret, sacred, and awe-inspiring ceremony of the Kiwai people" who lived at the mouth of the Fly River (Landtman 1927:350). The central part of the ceremony entailed the preparation of mingled sexual fluids as life-giving "medicine" for gardens and people.

---

19. Goodale 1985:231–32; cf. also Keesing 1982b.

In groups, one after another, the men betake themselves to the
women's compartments, where soon a promiscuous intercourse is
in progress. All jealousy, all marriage rules, otherwise so strongly
emphasized, are laid aside, men exchange their wives, and any one
may choose any partner he likes, avoiding only his closest blood
relations. After the act the men empty the semen into the *baru* [a
palm-spathe bowl], and the women add in a similar way to the
production of the potent medicine. . . . Everybody seems to be
intent upon contributing as much as possible to the medicine, so
that the *baru* should be filled up, and a great number of men, sum-
moned from other villages, render assistance, their wives being
among the other women. . . . The debauchery lasts till early morning, when everybody goes and swims, afterwards drying themselves at a fire and putting on their usual covering. The people
then sleep most of the day. This part of the *moguru* goes on several
nights, in Waboda, so it is said, till some of the women show signs
of pregnancy. (1927:352)

The sexual "medicine" obtained from this general fertility rite could be
used to promote the fertility of sago palms (a primary food source) by
smearing it on the trunk or tree shoots, and it also could be mixed with
food and eaten to promote human growth and well-being.

In some Melanesian societies, conception was facilitated by a combination of sexual and nonsexual practices. The following description
of the Mekeo of southern Papua delineates "the details of newlywed
ritual where the expressed desire for conception of a child is most
urgent" (Mosko 1983:25).

The bride each day is fed enormous quantities of boiled plant food
along with the broth to increase the amount of womb blood in her
abdomen. This sustained engorging results in a few short weeks
with the bride becoming quite visibly fat. In indigenous terms, her
body is also wet with plenty of skin and blood. During this time
she does no work which would divert her blood away from her
abdomen. Instead she sits each day inside a mosquito net at the
virtual disposal of the groom. He visits her in seclusion as frequently as possible for the purpose of sexual intercourse, and with
each act deposits a quantity of male procreative blood or semen in
her abdomen. Since considerable quantities of both womb blood
and semen are thought necessary to assure conception and avert

menstruation, the bride's engorging and her regular intercourse with the groom are sustained for three months minimally. (Mosko 1983:25)

All this is not to suggest that beliefs about conception or procreative substance are highly elaborate throughout Melanesia. In some if not many Melanesian societies these notions are vague or apparently unimportant, with informants offering little clarity or consistency about how conception or bodily formation takes place. In some societies, as among the Telefol people, men's and women's views of conception may differ significantly from each other (Jorgensen 1983b). Such discrepancy reinforces Wagner's (1972, 1981) suggestion that "beliefs" do not have a uniform or single normative status within a culture; rather, they are constantly shaped and reinvented through creative use (cf. Barth 1975, 1987).

Basic notions of procreative conception—whatever their content or clarity—tend in Melanesia to link together the local culture's beliefs concerning gender, growth, nurturance, and productive labor. Correspondingly, the cultural understanding of conception or growth is often complemented by beliefs concerning substance depletion, senescence, and death.

Growth and Nurturance

In the dietary self-consciousness of contemporary Western cultures, "you are what you eat" is a popular concept (and one nicely symbolized in refrigerator posters of a human face or body made as a collage from different types of food). The literalness and validity of this idea is not wasted on Melanesians, whose daily tie to food production and subsistence labor is very strong. But for them, once again, material substance cannot be divorced from social and spiritual life; food is irrevocably tied to personal relationships and to unseen effects that may enhance or alter its potency. Social and spiritual relations form the precondition for nourishment and growth, and the body is conceptualized in terms of these.

Mothers

The newborn's preeminent social relationship is to its mother, epitomized through the process of nursing. This pattern is extremely common in human societies,[20] and it has a strong influence on images of bodily substance and development in Melanesia. The mother in many Melanesian cultures is symbolized and sometimes explicitly defined as "the woman who gave me breast milk," with the strong sense that "she grew me as a child," or "she gave herself bodily to make my own body." Nursing on demand is common in Melanesia until the child is three or four years old, and in some cultures, such as the Murik of the north New Guinea coast, nursing may persist for last-born children until they are six or seven (Meeker, Barlow, and Lipset 1986:39). Correspondent with prolonged nursing, there is an important cultural association in Melanesia between maternal sustenance and healthful bodily constitution. The larger implications are well developed among the Murik.

> [T]he most important qualities expressed by the nursing scene are the generosity, abundance, and security provided by the mother and the peace, pleasure, and almost intoxicated satiation of the infant. Besides the ideal of the nursing mother-infant, the good mother is also seen as a giver and feeder. A good mother feeds her children whenever they are hungry and indulges their requests for certain kinds of food. Closely related to feeding is the general association of mothers with giving. Each mother hopes that her children will remember her as a generous and abundant source of food. (Meeker, Barlow, and Lipset 1986:39; more generally, see Lipset 1997)

This orientation is pervasive and has many local variants in Melanesia (see photo 3).

Mother's Brothers

The indulgence and sustenance given the child by its mother is extended in many if not most Melanesian societies to a sense of bodily support and contribution by the mother's closest blood relatives, particularly her brother or her father and mother. The contribution of such persons is substantial—they have supported the mother herself and

---

20. West and Konner 1976; Konner 1981:30–32.

then given her to her husband in a connubial relationship. In this sense, maternal relatives have themselves underwritten the development of the woman's offspring.

In terms of bodily and social influence, the mother's brother in Melanesia often has a special affinity for the child, and this is commonly reflected in distinctive duties and ritual obligations between them. Very commonly, the mother's brother has a special role to play in the initiation, marriage, or funeral of his sister's son (see photo 4). Reciprocally, obligation and tangible repayment are often given by the child's father to its mother's brother or mother's father. In some societies, as among the Iatmul of the Sepik (Bateson 1936), these social and ritual relationships are very elaborate and complex.

The child's tie with maternal kin stands in potential opposition to its countervailing affiliation with its father and his kin, particularly in the majority of mainland New Guinea societies where preeminent rights of kin-group identity and/or spiritual essence are transmitted through the male line. This often leads to complementarity or divergence between paternal and maternal kin over their opposing claims on the child—a tension that can have far-reaching implications. For instance, Forge (1972:537) notes that "He [the mother's brother] and his clan sometimes literally own the blood or have a lien on the spirit of their sister's son and do not release him to his patriline [paternal kin] until they receive an often very substantial, final payment of valuables." Thus, the effective recruitment of a child to its father's clan can require compensatory payment to the child's maternal relatives to reciprocate, abrogate, or "pay off" their "blood" contribution to the child (see J. F. Weiner 1982:9–10). In some societies, this sense of blood payment is such that the mother's brother and his kin must be tangibly compensated whenever the blood of their sister's sons is accidentally or violently shed.

The importance of a child's maternal uncle is intriguingly illustrated among the Daribi of the southeastern New Guinea highlands. Here the mother's brother is considered "just the same as mother," since both of them were formed in the same womb and composed of the same maternal blood (Wagner 1967:64). Given that the child's tie to its mother's brother is irrevocable, the recruitment of a child to its father's group in this nominally patrilineal society is particularly problematic. Payments must be continually made by patrikin to the child's mother's brother to keep the uncle's "ownership" of the child's body at bay.[21] These payments, which are largely comprised of pork, are intriguingly linked to Daribi notions of conception, since the juices and fat from animals such as pigs are believed to replenish the supply of semen within the human male body (Wagner 1983). At one level, then, Daribi male procreative substance is given as pork to the mother's kin group in reciprocity for the female procreative substance of blood which the mother contributed to the formation of her child. In this respect, Daribi food and sexual transactions reciprocate and complement each other as idioms of bodily formation.

A pattern somewhat complementary to that of the Daribi is found among the Sabarl of the northern Massim (Battaglia 1985, 1990). The Sabarl are matrilineal, and here it is the "bone" contributed by the father rather than the "blood" contributed by the mother and mother's brother that must be compensated by the child's natal (matrilineal) clan. Among the Sabarl, this is especially evident at death, when axes that metaphorically represent the substance of the dead person are given back as valuables to his or her classificatory "father." Through such means, the bones of the dead person are "harvested" back by his or her patrilineal kin. This gift is but one part of the elaborate exchanges of "male" and "female" valuables and foods—exchanges through which kinship and gender are established and transacted.[22]

Initiation and Transition to Adulthood

The relationship between bodily substance, social nurturance, and growth is particularly pronounced in Melanesian initiations. Girls in Melanesia have sometimes been accorded significant and elaborate initiations.[23] In many other cases, however, girls are believed to mature "naturally," with little cultural manipulation or interference, even as the transition of the boy to adult male status can be considered dramatic and ritually marked.[24] In developmental terms, this reflects a tendency for early maternal influence to be seen as providing a natural

---

21. In the absence of sufficient payments by a boy's patrikin, the Daribi maternal uncle may curse the child—believed to cause him sickness or misfortune—or he may even take the child physically as his own.

22. Cf. Maschio 1994; Wagner 1986.

23. See Lutkehaus and Roscoe 1995; Newman and Boyd 1982; cf. A. B. Weiner 1976.

24. See Allen 1967; Herdt 1982c.

template for female gender socialization, whereas boys tend to be pulled outside the sphere of maternal identification as they establish their masculine identity.[25] In Melanesia, where gender role dichotomies and oppositions are strong, the resocialization of boys into men has often been deeply rooted in notions of bodily transformation. In several regions of New Guinea, it is believed that boys must be ritually resocialized or cosmologically "reconceived" through male initiations to become men. In some of the more extreme cases, this occurs through a traumatic purging of the boyish feminized self and arduous bodily reconstruction of him as a maturing man.

Common components of male initiation in New Guinea have included prohibition of heterosexual contact and the avoidance of "female" foods.[26] Often, male initiate novices are temporarily secluded bodily from women, and some of the taboos against female contact may last for years. During the period of their seclusion, boys may learn or practice skills of manhood, such as hunting and warfare techniques, and they may learn sacred lore or have cult secrets revealed to them. Frequently, they undergo ordeals of pain, obedience, or endurance designed to inculcate masculine strength and forbearance. In some parts of New Guinea, such as the Sepik, Mountain Ok, and eastern highlands regions, this process is linked with the ritual inducement of bodily changes by purging "female" substances such as blood from the novice, for example, by bleeding his nose or penis.[27]

Among the most traumatic initiation rites reported are those of the Bimin-Kuskusmin (Mountain Ok area), who indoctrinate boys nine to twelve years of age into the first of a lifelong series of initiation grades (Poole 1982a). The young novices are, among other things, (1) stripped naked, (2) forcibly washed, (3) deprived of sleep, food, and water, (4) harshly rubbed with nettles, (5) forced to eat and then vomit "female" foods, (6) beaten, (7) shaved and bled about the head, (8) pierced with bone daggers through their nasal septa, (9) told they are dying, (10) burned about their forearms with hot fat, (11) force-fed pus from bodily wounds, (12) forced to live in their own excrement, and (13) repeatedly deceived by initiators concerning the progression and termination

---

25. E.g., Herdt 1987a; Langness 1967.

26. We focus here largely on New Guinea; the subject of male initiation in Melanesia more generally is reviewed in M. R. Allen 1967; cf. Herdt 1982c.

27. See Tuzin 1980; Barth 1975; Poole 1982a; Langness 1967; Read 1965; Newman and Boyd 1982; Herdt 1982d.

of the ordeals. The general context in which these traumas are administered is one of antagonism and ridicule (Poole 1982a:122–23).

As Poole summarizes:

> [B]oys endure severe privation, extensive degradation, extreme
> fatigue, constant hunger and thirst, psychological shock, enor-
> mous pain, acute illness (including nausea, diarrhea and infec-
> tion), and other trauma. . . . In no instances are the boys given any
> warning of what is to happen. Deceptive, veiled threats often do
> not lead to what the boys fear or fully expect. And ritual violence
> erupts unexpectedly. . . . I have witnessed numbers of boys lapse
> into states of uncontrolled, pronounced physical and psychologi-
> cal shock, becoming unconscious or hysterical. . . . The ritual elders
> still maintain, nevertheless, that such stress, as long as it is accom-
> panied by knowledgeable control, is completely necessary to the
> desired efficacy of the *ais am* [first-stage initiation]. (Poole
> 1982a:138)

Obviously, here the body itself is a key focus of gender resocialization—as feminine substances and associations are purged and masculine ones strongly infused. Poole (1982a) found from interviews and
projective tests that novices did indeed change significantly in bodily
self-perception and gender identification as a result of the rites.

Bodily trauma in male and female initiation varies greatly in New
Guinea, both in type, severity, and/or relative absence. While first
stage initiation was typically traumatic in Mountain Ok, Sepik, and
eastern highlands societies, accession to manhood was relatively
benign in the Strickland-Bosavi and western highlands areas, where
initiate novices were older, usually in their late teens or even early
twenties. Among the Gebusi, the main ordeal for these young men was
the wearing of a bark wig (see photo 5). While the wig was heavy and
pulled tightly on the scalp, it was worn for only a few hours and was
discarded by the initiate novice at his own discretion. Among the
nearby Kaluli, there was little if any bodily trauma at the ceremonial
male seclusion lodge, from which the novices forayed to hunt (Schieffelin 1982). Kaluli novices both accumulated and consumed large quantities of game, and their main proscription was to maintain an attitude
of "ritual sobriety" with regard to heterosexual taunts and joking.

Among the Koriki of the Purari Delta along the New Guinea south coast, the *pairama* initiation rites entailed virtually no trauma. Despite the significance of warfare and cannibalism in Koriki society, the boys simply enjoyed themselves in the company of men while they learned aspects of mask-making and other male activities (Williams 1923a, 1924). Initiation in a number of the south New Guinea cults also appears to have been benign, with some exceptions among the Marind-anim.[28] In the central and western New Guinea highlands, several bachelor and other male cults emphasized male purification, beautification, and masculinization prior to marriage, with a relative absence of prolonged and traumatic ordeals.[29]

In many cases, transformation of the male body through initiation was as much cognitive as corporeal, with an emphasis on learning obligations, prohibitions, and ritual knowledge requisite for manhood. This was especially true in the more advanced stages of initiation cults, that is, in societies where initiation was a multileveled process persisting well into adulthood. Particularly in the Mountain Ok area, the Sepik, and regions of insular and eastern Melanesia, indoctrination into a series of male cults became a lifelong process of acquiring spiritual knowledge and authority.[30] In these cases, the cults often served as a preeminent focus of political or economic as well as spiritual life. First stage initiation into such elaborate hierarchies, however, often tended in New Guinea to entail prolonged seclusion from women, ritual bleeding of "female" blood, or the traumatic enforcement of obedience to male elders. At the end of the ordeals, novices were frequently dressed in elaborate body decoration that indicated their new status and their general beauty, vitality, and fertility. Decoration of initiates at higher cult stages has also been quite pronounced in some Sepik and insular sections of Melanesia. Such patterns of costuming and decoration will be considered further below.

Homosexuality and Bisexuality

In some sections of Melanesia, particularly the southern lowlands of New Guinea, parts of the southern highlands fringe, and sections of

---

28. See Knauft 1993a; F. E. Williams 1940; Landtman 1927; Zegwaard 1959; cf. van Baal 1966.

29. A. J. Strathern 1970, 1979a; Meggitt 1964; Reay 1959; Biersack 1982; cf. J. F. Weiner 1987.

30. E.g., Barth 1975; Gell 1975; Tuzin 1980, cf. 1997; Allen 1967.

Vanuatu, masculine development was abetted by homosexual insemination, that is, the direct transmission of semen as a life force from men
to initiate novices (Herdt 1992).[31] In different cultures, this insemination took place through fellatio, anal intercourse, or, less commonly, the
rubbing of masturbated semen on the boy's body. Among Gebusi of the
Strickland-Bosavi area, insemination rites were practiced even for male
toddlers, who might be given small amounts of their fathers' masturbated semen to ingest with their food (Cantrell pers. comm.). In most
regions where homosexuality was practiced, however, it was limited to
adolescence and early adulthood, culminating ultimately in bisexuality
or in exclusive heterosexuality for full adult men. In men's homosexual
relationships, junior boys were often subordinated by their elders,
though in other cases the relationship has been more voluntary and/or
mutually erotic.[32]

In regional terms, it would be tempting to contrast the south New
Guinea emphasis on homosexual growth with the highland New
Guinea emphasis on heterosexual depletion—asserting a lowland
"semen belt" of homophilia in contrast to a highlands "blood belt" of
heterophobia.[33] Such a highlands/lowlands contrast, however, is too
simple to fit the facts. Important areas of south New Guinea have not
practiced homosexuality and do not fall into either of these categories
(Knauft 1993a: chap. 3). Conversely, various parts of northern New
Guinea show fascinating permutations of homoerotic and/or het-
eroerotic custom.[34] In addition, there are several areas on the interven-
ing southern "fringe" of the New Guinea highlands (including Anga
and Strickland-Bosavi regions) that combine homoerotic and hetero-
phobic beliefs, for instance, the belief that masculinity is enhanced both
by homosexual insemination and by heterosexual avoidance, including, in some cases, initiatory bloodletting.

These orientations are elaborately combined among the Sambia of
the Anga-speaking region, who considered semen a crucial life force
that males obtained through homosexual insemination and the eating
of special foods. As Herdt (1984b, 1987a) documents, the acquisition,
retention, spending, and then replenishment of seminal fluid was a

---

31. Reports of female homosexuality in Melanesia have been rare and fragmentary
(Herdt 1984a:75 n.10).
    32. E.g., Ernst 1991; Knauft 1987a, 1993a: appendix.
    33. E.g., Lindenbaum 1984, 1987; Whitehead 1986a, b.
    34. E.g., Bateson 1936; Thurnwald 1916; Meeker, Barlow, and Lipset 1986.

continuing preoccupation of Sambian men, both in homosexual and in heterosexual relations. These concerns have been crosscut by high male anxiety over pollution and debilitation from female blood and by antagonistic gender polarity. Sambian male initiation rites reflected both these concerns, enjoining, among other things, radical separation from women, copious homosexual insemination, traumatic thrashings, harangues, fasting, food taboos, and severe nose-bleeding to purge, strengthen, and masculinize the boys.[35]

Among the Etoro of the Strickland-Bosavi area, homosexuality likewise found a complement in gender antinomy, but one that was focused more exclusively on male fears of contamination and depletion in the heterosexual act itself (Kelly 1976, 1993). The Etoro apparently did not have harsh initiation procedures, had little domestic gender antagonism, and had little belief in female menstrual pollution. Concern over heterosexual congress, however, led Etoro to prohibit coitus for between 205 and 260 days per year (Kelly 1976:43). The nearby Gebusi present a different permutation, by contrast; their strictures about the contaminating influence of female sexuality were more a source of hilarity than anxiety to Gebusi themselves. Indeed, Gebusi men seemed particularly prone to break their own rules of heterosexual and homosexual propriety.[36]

A much more elaborate pattern of bisexuality was found among the Marind-anim of south coastal New Guinea, among whom both homosexual and heterosexual contacts were ritually and socially prescribed.[37] Here, as among several other south coastal culture areas, semen was considered more an unlimited source of potency than a scarce bodily resource. Semen was used to "grow" young boys through regular anal intercourse from their maternal uncles (their *binahor-fathers*). More promiscuous homosexual intercourse occurred among Marind males at some rites. Nevertheless, semen was considered by the Marind to be an especially potent life force when it was mixed with, rather than separated from, the sexual fluids of women. Mingled semen and vaginal fluid were obtained by Marind through rites of serial heterosexual intercourse and were used for numerous life-enhancing purposes. Marind use of these mixed sexual fluids was more elaborate and

35. Herdt 1981, 1982a, b, 1987a, b; Godelier 1986; contrast more recent changes as documented in the anthropological film "Guardians of the Flutes" (G. Herdt, consultant).

36. Knauft 1985a, b, 1986, 1987a.

37. van Baal 1966, 1984; see extended summary and analysis in Knauft 1993a.

pronounced even than among the Kiwai, whose promiscuous sexual rites were described previously.[38] Among the Marind, sexual rites were particularly traumatic for the female participants, since numerous men of the resident clan copulated serially with only one or two of the young women present. The very frequent practice of these sexual rites and their attendant trauma to the women involved appear to have rendered a significant percentage of Marind women permanently sterile—from pelvic inflammatory disease caused by the chronic vaginal irritation of excessive coitus.[39] The overall result was thus the opposite of what Marind intended: fervent fertility rites significantly reduced the reproductive viability of Marind society. Indeed, the Marind population declined so significantly that they resorted to buying children from neighboring groups and to capturing them in large numbers during head-hunting raids.

Despite their sexual ordeals, however, Marind women were subject to few female pollution restrictions and participated in many activities that were under the exclusive control of men in many other Melanesian societies. Thus, for instance, Marind women exercised significant influence in choosing their spouses, were initiated into a series of initiation grades parallel to those of the men (including ritual insignia), took an active part in almost all of the major cult rituals, and even accompanied men on long-distance head-hunting raids (Knauft 1993a:93ff.).

These patterns are in some respects the antithesis of the highland patterns described before, in which women were socially and sexually inimical to men. Men from highlands areas who failed to take adequate purification and precautionary measures against female influence were liable to jeopardize male activities and to become sick or debilitated themselves, or to die. However, as previously mentioned, local patterns preclude simple dichotomies concerning areal types of sociosex-

---

38. The fertility of a young Marind-anim woman was thought to be directly tied to her frequency of serial sexual congress with the men of her husband's clan, both upon marriage and whenever she renewed menstruation following childbirth (van Baal 1966; Knauft 1993a: chap. 8). The mingled sexual fluids obtained from the rite were also applied directly to wounds and scarifications to help them heal, mixed with ceremonial food and ingested to enhance growth, placed on plant shoots to promote garden abundance, mixed with sorcery potions to empower them, mixed with other substances to blacken the teeth, and, more generally, used to ensure the potency and success of numerous ritual performances and social activities.

39. South Pacific Commission 1955; see Knauft 1993a: chap. 8.

ual domination or insecurity. In both sexual complexes, for instance, men who were truly strong and energetic were believed potent enough to engage in increased heterosexual activity without suffering adverse effects. While such beliefs in highland areas only moderately increased the amount of heterosexual activity (e.g., for politically vigorous polygynists), such belief was extended much more broadly and confidently to men in general along much of the New Guinea south coast. A more evenly balanced tension between these poles is evident in several societies of the fringe highlands in north and south New Guinea, in which male pursuit of heterosexuality could be quite active and yet strongly hedged with ambivalence concerning debilitation.[40]

In many of the preceding cases, bodily substances are active metaphors that engender and reflect wide ranges of social action. Sometimes, a very concrete "economy" of bodily substances is envisaged, with specific practices mandated to mediate the transmission, depletion, replenishment, and/or complementarity of these fluids.[41] Such a pattern can be illustrated as well among some matrilineal societies, for example, the Wamira of Milne Bay, among whom blood transmitted through females creates clan identity and essence but also causes women to gradually wither and die, as they lose this vital substance through menstruation and childbirth (Kahn 1986:100). More generally, Melanesian beliefs about bodily substance are highly variable in their degree of elaboration and their salience for concrete social action. Often, they articulate spiritual and cosmological orientations with features of social organization, productive energy, and gendered difference.

Sorcery and Witchcraft

Sorcery and witchcraft are, in a sense, the obverse or flip side of growth and nurturance. In most parts of Melanesia, bodily sickness and death have been believed to be brought about by social and spiritual agency rather than sickness or old age as "natural causes."[42] This is the nega-

---

40. E.g., R. C. Kelly 1976:41–44; Meigs 1984:16; Buchbinder and Rappaport 1976:20–22.

41. E.g., Herdt 1984b.

42. Melanesian sorcery and witchcraft are vast and intriguing topics. Principal sources include Fortune 1932; Stephen 1987, 1994; Knauft 1985a; Forge 1970; Young 1983a; Zelenietz and Lindenbaum 1981; Patterson 1974. For a brief and trenchant overview, see Glick 1973.

tive aspect of the social and cultural construction of the body; in the same way that positive or rejuvenating social and spiritual action can grow and nurture the body, malevolent action can cause it sickness and death. In a number of Melanesian societies, as alluded to before, bodily demise, particularly among men, was associated with sexual or menstrual pollution from women (see Brown and Buchbinder 1976). In addition, however, nefarious actions upon the leavings or exuviae of a person—their food scraps, excrement, spittle, or items that had been in contact with them—could be used in an attempt to cause them harm. In some societies, renowned sorcerers cultivated elaborate knowledge of spells and magic for the practice of their craft (e.g., Stephen 1994; see Fortune 1932). In cases of witchcraft, an intrinsically evil force within the body of the evildoer is believed to cause sickness or death to the victim.

Suspicions of sorcery or witchcraft in cases of illness or death have been widespread in Melanesia. In some areas, including the Strickland-Bosavi area of interior south New Guinea, elaborate divinations have been held to uncover the ostensible identity of the sorcerer or witch—even though there is little evidence that individuals actually attempted to send sickness by these means. In many of these cases, the person targeted was scapegoated, publicly accused, and eventually executed and cannibalized.[43] In cultural perception, the life of the sorcerer or witch was extinguished and their body consumed in reciprocity for the depletion and death that they were believed to have sent against the sickness victim. In most parts of Melanesia, by contrast, suspicions or fears of sorcery have not resulted in the frequent killing of suspects, even though belief in the power of social and spiritual malevolence continues to be widespread, and violence may sometimes erupt against those suspected of sending illness and death.[44]

Food and Bodies

The linkage between food and exchange in Melanesia informs bodily practices and beliefs across many different contexts. Perhaps most basically, those whose food you consume are those whose labor, land, and essence constitute your own being. Melanesians appreciate quite concretely the physical energy used in subsistence cultivation and the way

43. See Knauft 1985a, 1987b; Schieffelin 1976; R. C. Kelly 1976, 1993.
44. See Zelenietz and Lindenbaum 1981; Stürzenhofecker 1995, 1998.

this is converted into bodily substance to maintain health and vitality. Sometimes the spiritual essence of a clan ancestor or cult spirit permeates or otherwise influences the food that grows on "its" land. This spiritual force can correspondingly infuse or reproduce itself in the bodies of those who eat it.

In the sharing or giving of food, its force or influence is transferred to another person. This makes a gift of food a gift of oneself in a fundamental way. Since food in Melanesia is typically shared, notions of physical and spiritual force link the growth and development of the individual body almost intrinsically to the growth and development of the wider social group. James Weiner (1982:27) suggests for highland New Guinea that the frequent sharing of food is culturally equated with the sharing of biogenetic substance. In a sense, this is an alimentary dimension of more direct transmission of bodily substances, for instance, during sexual intercourse. As we have seen before, transactions of food and bodily substances relate to each other in important ways, for example, the consumption of sexual substances may be a special form of nourishment, while, conversely, the eating of particular foods can augment the supply of particular sexual substances.

As might be expected, Melanesian food gifts—including the type, quality, and quantity of food—symbolize in myriad ways the social relationship between the giver and the receiver. Food-giving in Melanesia has often been subject to elaborate culturally specific conventions concerning who may share food with whom, what kinds of foods may be given, and under what conditions certain foods may or may not be eaten. In short, food is a central link between the body and wider social and cosmological relationships (see photo 6).

Even in its internal characteristics, food is subject to a wide range of Melanesian symbolism and belief. Often, important foods are "gendered," with different edible species considered "masculine" or "feminine" based on metaphoric associations of the food's hardness, color, texture, shape, or pattern of growth. For instance, milky or greasy foods may be considered to be "like semen," while red pandanus may be considered "like women's blood"; hard or dried foods may be considered relatively "male," while soft, fleshy, or watery foods may be considered "female," thus mirroring the body characteristics associated with men and women. According to their culture-specific associations, certain foods may be proscribed or prescribed for consumption depending on sex, age, initiation grade, marital status, or totemic or ritual affiliation of the person intending to eat them. For instance, some species of plants or animals may be proscribed during initiatory seclusion, others during periods of bereavement or mourning. Such dietary strictures explicitly or implicitly bring one's body into physical and mental alignment with the social role being adopted.

Beyond the "intrinsic" properties of a food, eating it also implies trust in the giver that it is healthful and untainted. This is particularly important given beliefs in many Melanesian societies that food may be poisoned or bespelled by polluting substances (such as menstrual blood) that can sicken or kill the person who eats it. Even healthy food may pose a danger in the presence of a deceitful guest, since, as we have seen, it is frequently believed that food scraps or bodily exuviae may be surreptitiously gathered and bespelled or burned by a sorcerer in order to harm the person from whom they were collected. Food thus connects the body and its substance to the world of social relationships, through which it is maintained or, alternately, maligned.

Competitive Exchange and Bodily Transaction

In its competitive mode, Melanesian food-giving can become an aspect of aggressive or ostentatious self-presentation. Here we encounter the famous exchange systems of highland and insular Melanesia, in which wealth valuables and/or enormous quantities of food—often live pigs or piles of tubers—are given to an individual or group as a show of force and challenge.[45] Large shell valuables, which can have a rich mythic history, may be exchanged and associated in memory with those who held or gave them in the famed inter-island *kula* exchanges of the Massim.[46] Even along the less populated regions of the New Guinea south coast, the size of food prestations could be prodigious; among the Keraki of the Trans-Fly, display racks presenting food could comprise up to two and one-half kilometers of fence-line heaped with produce, and even one of the less extensive feasting racks was esti-mated to hold at least twenty-five to thirty tons of yams (Williams 1936:231–35). The receiving group must reciprocate at a later time with

---

45. See, for example, A. J. Strathern 1971; Feil 1984; Meggitt 1974; Rappaport 1984; Lederman 1986; Young 1971; Oliver 1955; A. B. Weiner 1976, 1992; Malinowski 1922; Leach and Leach 1983; Clay 1986; Errington 1974; cf. P. Brown 1978; Rubel and Rosman 1978.

46. E.g., Malinowski 1922; Leach and Leach 1983; Damon 1990.

an equal or hopefully larger gift if they are to save face and maintain or increase their reputation. In some societies, status competition through food exchange has taken the place of exchanging casualties bodily in warfare, for example, among peoples such as the Kalauna of the Massim, who have come to "fight with food" (Young 1971).

In cases of aggressive food exchange, the link between social presentation and bodily discipline is quite explicit. To produce a surplus of food for others typically requires some degree of personal privation—minimizing one's food consumption—while undertaking countless hours of hard garden work. The cultural ideal in several insular societies of the Melanesian Massim is thus to have an empty belly but a full storehouse of food saved for competitive exchange. The corresponding corporeal ideal is a body that is lean, hard, "dry," and light—in other words, self-disciplined and unindulgent.[47] This image may be tied in part to gendered attributes of male strength and corporeal fortitude, since it is often senior men who publicly orchestrate the politics of food exchange, whose bodies are considered "hard and light," and who are seen to enforce the domestic value of personal privation and hard work. Against this, however, is the prominent fact that women often do the most tedious and backbreaking garden labor.

In a few areas of Melanesia, the controlled discipline and authority of adult men is channeled into the growing of special and prestigious crops raised by men alone. Archetypal here is the growing of long yams by men in parts of the Sepik in northern New Guinea and the growing of yams or taro in parts of the insular Massim and eastern Papua.[48] Sepik yams frequently contain important aspects of the group's patrilineal substance; in some areas each clan has its own distinct "seed line" of yams, which must be kept distinct and perpetuated over generations, analogous to the way that yam tubers are themselves thought to proliferate in subterranean genealogies (Tuzin 1972; Harrison 1982). The energies of older men in particular are infused in these long yams, which may grow up to twelve feet in length. In addition to hard work, the yams require elaborate magic and isolation of both grower and crop from female sexual contamination in order to propagate. The longest yams are given in the most prestigious of competitive food exchanges; their production is a central focus of adult men's lives. In some cases,

---

47. Young 1971, 1986; cf. Munn 1986; A. B. Weiner 1976; Kahn 1986.

48. Tuzin 1972; Harrison 1982; Kaberry 1971; Young 1971, 1986; Fortune 1932: chap. 2; Malinowski 1935; A. B. Weiner 1976; Kahn 1986; Schwimmer 1973.

the huge tubers may be ritually festooned and painted with human costuming appropriate to their owners, whom they literally embody. The ostentatious presentation of these yams puts the receivers in the vulnerable and tenuous position of having to self-present themselves later through counter-gifts of food equal to or larger than those obtained.

Perhaps the largest competitive gift-exchanges in Melanesia have been found in the New Guinea highlands, where scores of pigs and, in the postcolonial era, thousands of dollars (kina) and even trucks and motorcycles may be given away to a political rival in a massive show of a leader's prestige.[49] In this case, the leader is in a sense the body of the group—or rather, of the network of persons through which he has amassed items for exchange. To receive such a large gift, on the other hand, puts the recipient and his group under a crushing obligation to reciprocate it at a later time by orchestrating the help of his supporters. Here the idea of bodily self-presentation is bound up in the items given; these are a concrete manifestation of productive and political prowess. If men gain prestige in these exchanges, however, the labor of women is often backgrounded or effaced; though women raise the bulk of sweet potatoes and raise most of the pigs used in highland exchange, the giving of pigs (themselves fed on sweet potatoes) is generally a prerogative of a woman's husband or her brothers. Women have important behind-the-scenes influence in competitive exchanges and gain status "by association." In some cases, however, women have controlled their own exchange relationships, including some postcolonial instances in which money is amassed from the proceeds gained from selling coffee as a cash crop.[50]

Highlands exchanges are also accompanied by elaborate body decorations indicating self-enhancement.[51] These have sometimes become particularly innovative in a postcolonial era, including the use of Western goods or artifacts in ways unimagined by those who manufactured them. The issue of bodily decoration as an index of the self and the competitive group is one to which we shall return later. In the present context, however, it may be noted that food and wealth items are in many areas of Melanesia ceremonially exchanged for bodies them

---

49. See A. J. Strathern 1971; Meggitt 1974; and the ethnographic film "Ongka's Big Moka."

50. See Lederman 1986; Sexton 1986; Feil 1978, 1984; Weiner 1976.

51. O'Hanlon 1989; Strathern and Strathern 1971; M. Strathern 1979.

selves, notably, in marriage or homicide compensation (cf. M. Strathern 1988).

Bodily Exchanges—Marriage

In several areas of Melanesia, including some societies of north and south New Guinea, marriage ideally entails the reciprocal exchange of bodies between different groups—a woman is given in marriage from one kin group in direct reciprocity for one received in return. This true or classificatory "sister exchange" links bodily economy to social relations in a very direct way. In many other parts of Melanesia, however, including the New Guinea highlands, a woman's sexual, child-rearing, and labor capacities are largely transferred along with the woman herself to her husband's group when the latter make a material payment to the woman's natal kin. This payment or series of payments, termed *bridewealth,* was in precolonial times comprised largely of pigs, stone axes, and shell valuables (e.g., Glasse and Meggitt 1969).

In bridewealth, the wealth and productive embodiments of the husband's group are exchanged for the productive and reproductive powers of the wife. These exchanges are mutually informing aspects of a larger bodily ecology, since in-married wives work to augment the production of pigs—tending, provisioning, and even suckling them for the husband's group. At the same time, the natal kin of the out-married women receive bridewealth pigs and valuables that they themselves may use in the service of further exchanges, including the acquisition of new wives for themselves. As such, food, wealth, and women are transacted in an encompassing cycle.

This is not to say that women themselves are passive objects in marital or competitive exchange (there has been much debate in the literature about this issue).[52] Rather, the dominant ideology is that women and goods are exchanged as complements of one another. In many instances, the woman herself is elaborately adorned for marriage and "wears" a portion of her wealth, some of which she may individually keep. For some Melanesian societies, it has been effectively argued that the male exchange of valuables is cosmologically complemented

---

52. See Feil 1978; Lederman 1986; M. Strathern 1972, 1980, 1981, 1987; Faithorn 1976; Josephides 1983, 1985; Godelier 1986; Sillitoe 1985; Errington and Gewertz 1987a; Keesing 1985a; Young 1983b; Sexton 1986; cf. Mead 1935.

and socially balanced by the reproductive and regenerative value of
women (A. B. Weiner 1976, 1980). In other cases, it has been strongly
suggested that large elements of spiritual belief and gender ideology
promulgate male domination over women.[53]

Bodily Exchanges—Death

In precolonial Melanesia, the norm of bodily exchange between many
groups was one of violent revenge or predation; tribal warfare was
endemic in much of pre-pacification Melanesia (see chapter 3, this vol.).
In many cases, there was an explicit ethic of person-for-person
exchange, in which killings continued in a cycle of death-for-death reciprocity.[54] Relations of chronic raiding or warfare between groups
resulted in high homicide rates, especially for men, in many if not most
areas of precolonial Melanesia. Among the Mae Enga of the New
Guinea highlands, for instance, about 35 percent of all men died from
warfare (Meggitt 1977:110).

Cycles of killing could sometimes be attenuated, however, by the
payment of homicide compensation; in many parts of New Guinea, the
giving of pigs or wealth could serve to recompense the close kin of
those persons who had been killed. As such, material payments could
be used to end, at least temporarily, blood feuding and revenge
between enemy groups.[55]

In many cases, including that of the Mae Enga, killing, compensation, and other forms of exchange could themselves be linked together
in a temporal cycle. For instance, a truce could be arranged through the
payment of homicide compensation, and this compensation could then
itself provide the opening round of competitive material exchanges
between the two sides. These material exchanges could eventually lead
to bridewealth payments and marriage between the erstwhile enemy
groups. Indeed, the Enga themselves declared, "We marry the people
we fight." Eventually, however, relations between the intermarried
groups could deteriorate, and a pattern of enmity and reciprocal killing

---

53. E.g., Godelier 1986; Josephides 1985; Read 1952; Meggitt 1964; Langness 1974; cf.
Lindenbaum 1987; M. Strathern 1987.

54. E.g., Heider 1979; Meggitt 1977; Koch 1974; Langness 1972b; Hallpike 1977;
Berndt 1962, 1964.

55. In many cases this compensation was paid to kin of slain persons by their allies
who had started the war, rather than by the enemy group themselves.

would reemerge. A long-term cycle thus developed in which bodily exchanges went through phases of "positive" and "negative" reciprocity—that is, the exchanging of wealth, of wives, of killings, and of wealth once again.[56]

Cycles of Death and Regeneration

Cycles of reciprocity that linked killing with other forms of exchange were often connected to larger social and cosmological relationships in Melanesia. During the "negative" exchange of tit-for-tat killing, for instance, it was commonly believed that the group of the slain victim suffered spiritual as well as social loss. Accordingly, the ancestral spirits or ghosts of the victimized group would demand revenge. Spiritual anger that the killing was unavenged typically persisted until the demand for vengeance was satisfied (see photo 7). Conversely, the killers might celebrate or gloat over a victim's death. In a few cases, the corpse of the victim might be defiled or mutilated as a sign of ignominy for the deceased's relatives to discover, for instance, left with its genitals stuffed in its mouth (Meggitt 1977:76), the head of a rival leader displayed on a pike (Reay 1987:90), or the intestines of the victim tied together and strung up (Zegwaard 1959:1037). Among the Iatmul of the middle Sepik, boys of important households would make their first kill as a child; an enemy would be captured and held for the boy to spear. If the boy was too small to wield the spear effectively, his mother's brother would help him slay the victim (Bateson 1932:276). Commonly in Melanesia, attackers celebrated the killing of an enemy with celebrations or a festive dance, such as the Dani *edai*, the Daribi "mock funeral" festival, or the Purari rite of cannibal celebration.[57]

An adult man's status in precolonial Melanesia was sometimes linked importantly to his killing of others in warfare or raiding, and this was commonly reflected in bodily insignia. In some groups it was believed that killers gained or incorporated potent spiritual force from the slain victim. A group's gain or loss in battle casualties was thus articulated directly with beliefs about the spiritual or cosmological welfare of the group as a whole. Such beliefs were especially pronounced

---

56. D. Brown 1979; Schwimmer 1973; Whitehead 1986a, b; cf. Sahlins 1972b; Modjeska 1982.

57. See, respectively, Heider 1970, 1979; Wagner 1972:150ff.; Williams 1924: chap. 14.

in those societies where head-hunting and/or ceremonial killing of captives was practiced (see McKinley 1976). Among the Kwoma of the Sepik, for instance, the killer was believed to supplement his own spirit or *mai,* located in the head, with those spirits of as many persons as he had killed—to the pleasure of his group's own spirits.[58] This same head-spirit was embodied in insignia decorations worn by the killer and could be transferred to fertility cult statues, who as masked "heads" were likewise festooned with homicidal insignia.[59]

In some parts of Melanesia, especially in some coastal and insular areas, persons killed in warfare were butchered, brought home, and eaten by the victors. Among many peoples of the New Guinea south coast, head-hunting and cannibalism were associated quite dramatically with spiritual regeneration. Among the Purari delta peoples, enemies were on occasion ambushed and slain so that their bodies or heads could be ritually fed into the mouths of large wicker spirit-monsters, kept in the sacred rear section of the men's cult house (see fig. 1). These wicker spirits, termed *kaiemunu,* embodied the spiritual force of the victorious group. The "feeding" of *kaiemunu* with a human head was a crucial part of Purari male initiation and group rejuvenation rites (see Williams 1922, 1924).

Among the Asmat of the southwest New Guinea coast, bodies of victims were cannibalized and their skulls highly valued and carefully prepared as ritual sacrae. Indeed, disputes over possession of a recently taken head could lead to severe fights among the victors themselves. The heads figured prominently in elaborate male initiation rites.[60] During one ritual stage, the secluded novice initiate held the victim's head against his genitals for a prolonged period; as such, he absorbed the life force of the victim as part of his symbolic rebirth into manhood. Through complex rituals enacting death, rebirth, and growth, the Asmat novice was imbued with the spiritual identity of the headhunt victim. At the end of the rites he received the headhunt victim's name as his own adult appellation, and he was closely associated with him

---

58. Williamson 1983:16; Bowden 1983:99, 105, 110, 165; cf. also Bateson 1936:137ff.

59. The Kwoma statues were closely linked in cult usage with spiritual power in growing yams, fertility, and protection of the group in warfare (Bowden 1983:105ff., 115–17). Indeed, only persons who had killed enemies were believed capable of growing yams, and they alone were automatically permitted to join the most prestigious fertility cult, the *nowkwi* (16, 105).

60. Zegwaard 1959; cf. Konrad, Konrad, and Schneebaum 1981; contrast Schneebaum 1988.

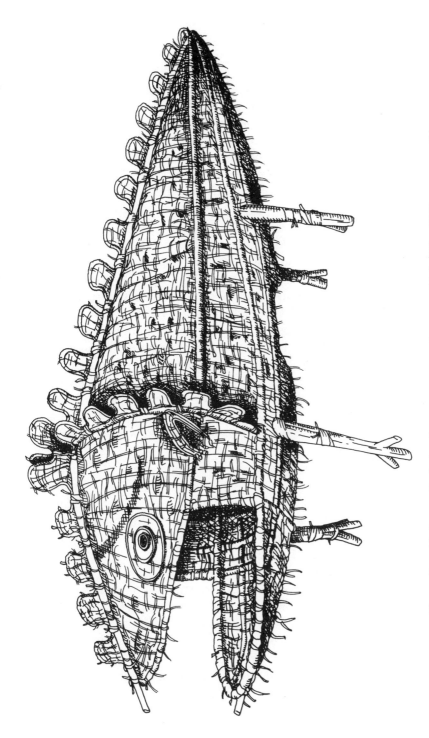

Fig. 1. Purari *kaiemunu*. Lashed and woven cane; 3.5 m long × 2 m high. (After Williams 1923a:376.)

for the rest of his life. This identity transformation was so great that the initiated man was even immune to attack from the headhunt victim's own relatives, who were now his "kin"; indeed, he could be greeted and feasted by them as their lost relative! Among some Asmat groups, the body of the victim provided spiritual energy for elaborately carved *bis*-poles (see fig. 2). The blood from fresh heads was used to anoint and sanctify the pole, and various body parts of the victim were placed in the canoe that was sometimes carved at the base of it. The *bis*-pole was subsequently planted in the sago forest, where its spiritual force infused the starch of the sago palm and was transferred as strength and fearlessness to those who ate it.[61] As such, bodily life force was taken to augment the vitality of the killer's group, the masculinity of its initiates, the fertility of their land, and the potency of their food.

Among the Bimin-Kuskusmin of the Mountain Ok area, the ritual torture and elaborate cannibalism of a captured enemy were the focus of the major public ritual of societal rejuvenation—the great pandanus rite. "In the great pandanus rite . . . the ritual strength that was transferred to the victim through ritual adornment, sacrifice, and endurance of a slow and painful death is said to have been incorporated in all . . . ritual elders" (Poole 1983:21). Consuming the potent spiritual essence of a corpse's genital tissue appears to have been particularly important in the process of Bimin-Kuskusmin spiritual regeneration. Mortuary rites articulated richly with Bimin-Kuskusmin beliefs concerning gender and bodily substance previously alluded to.

A somewhat different permutation is found among the Kiwai of the New Guinea south coast. Among them, "the penis of a slain foe [was] sometimes cut off, threaded on a stick and dried. Before a fight a small piece of it mixed with banana [was] given to the young warriors to swallow, and this [made] them successful in catching and killing male enemies" (Landtman 1927:151).

In some societies, the incorporation of or accession to others' spiritual force was accompanied by serial copulation, as a further aspect of societal regeneration. Among the Purari, mentioned before, the wife of a successful headhunter was placed at the coital disposal of men in the village, who paid material compensation to her husband in return for their sexual access to her (Williams 1923a).

Melanesian groups from various lowland, coastal, and insular

---

61. See Eyde 1967:347; Kuruwaip 1984; Renselaar and Mellema 1956.

Fig. 2.   Asmat *bis*-pole. Wood, paint, fiber; 6 m high. (After Rockefeller and Gerbrands 1967:302–11.)

areas demonstrate diverse linkages between the taking of life force, copulation, and regeneration, on the one hand, and loss of life force and depletion, on the other. The former association was found in Trobriand mortuary copulation customs in association with the death of in-group members. During the mortuary wake (*yawali*), which took place immediately after a man's death, people from surrounding communities congregated and took part in the songs and ceremonies. Toward the end of the night, as the visitors returned home, it was the custom for some of the girls to remain behind to sleep with boys of the bereaved village—without interference by their usual lovers (Malinowski 1929:219). This is perhaps an aspect of female regeneration that was pronounced more generally in Trobriand mortuary rites and exchanges (A. B. Weiner 1976).

The countervailing association—between warfare, copulation, and depletion—is seen among the Murik of north coast New Guinea. Among Murik, women married to members of the junior moiety grade of the war cult were enjoined to copulate with those of the elder grade to facilitate the transmission of the latter's spiritual authority. When the members of the elder grade had all been successfully seduced, their war-making prowess was symbolically depleted and relinquished, and their authority was officially transferred to the erstwhile junior grade (Meeker, Barlow, and Lipset 1986; Lipset 1997). The belief that copulation is inimical to warfare or long-distance trade was pronounced in many areas of Melanesia, including much of highland and northern New Guinea.

In a few cases, the slaying of outsiders had important practical as well as symbolic and cosmological dimensions. The Marind-anim, to the east of the Asmat, were among the most inveterate and wide-ranging headhunters in Melanesia (van Baal 1966; see Knauft 1993a: chap. 8). Head-hunting raids were undertaken, as among the Asmat, to obtain "head names" for Marind children, but they also occasioned the systematic capture and adoption of victims' orphaned children, who were brought back to Marind territory and raised as full Marind adults. The capture of these children was of such great magnitude that perhaps one-sixth of all adult Marind were in fact children of foreign headhunt victims. This large-scale incorporation of outsiders was demographically important since, as mentioned before, many Marind women were rendered permanently sterile by the excessive heterosexual coitus enjoined in Marind rituals. The influx of captive children thus countered what was widely recognized to be a very low Marind birth rate. Indeed, the inflow of children was great enough to make the Marind-anim a culturally and territorially expanding group despite their negative internal growth rate. Ultimately, of course, it was Marind spirit beliefs themselves that motivated and intensified this extraordinary cycle of hypersexuality, infertility, violence, and demographic replenishment. These connections are strikingly evident in elaborate Marind myth and ritual cycles, which emphasize impaired copulation, head-hunting, and rebirth.[62]

Spiritual Reincorporation from Death in the Community

If the essence of slain outsiders was often considered a powerful force, so too the spiritual force of those who died from natural causes within the community was potent and might be reincorporated by the living. While, as discussed later, the primary mortuary emphasis in many Melanesian societies has been how to keep ghostly wrath at bay, the positive power of the deceased is sometimes also harnessed. Mortuary rituals often facilitate the amalgamation of the deceased's spirit to the more undifferentiated realm of ancestral spirits, who tend to be the ultimate protectors and overseers of the group's sacred knowledge and success. Selected societies in most of the major areas of Melanesia kept parts of the skeleton, particularly the skull of deceased adult men, as relics.[63] In many societies, skeletal relics were carefully preserved as important sacrae in cult houses or at sacred sites, sometimes as part of elaborate ritual proceedings or displays.

In the southeast highlands fringe of New Guinea, there was particularly strong emphasis on the physical reincorporation of deceased group members. In some of these groups, members of the community who died were eaten by their female kin and coresidents. This consumption was undertaken as an act of sorrow, and it prevented the escape and dispersal of the deceased's spiritual force. Among the Gimi, this endocannibalism was extensive; the entire body of the deceased was eaten by women, with each woman later receiving a portion of a pig corresponding to the part of the corpse she had eaten. Associated

---

62. See van Baal 1966, 1984; see summary in Knauft 1993a: chap. 8.

63. These areas include parts of the Sepik, south New Guinea, Mountain Ok, insular eastern Melanesia, and the New Guinea highlands.

cultural beliefs were emphatic: "Come to me so you shall not rot on the ground. Let your body dissolve inside me!"[64] Gimi endocannibalism initiated a process of mortuary regeneration. During the year after death and consumption of the corpse, the skull and jaw of a deceased man were commonly worn by the deceased's mother; thereafter, the bones were placed in rock and tree crevices said to be "like vaginas" in clan hunting grounds and at the borders of the deceased's garden. Eventually, the spirit was reincarnated as a bird of paradise, which continued to reside in Gimi territory. Gimi endocannibalism was thus "the first stage in a process to regenerate the dead, part of the means to maintain the continuity of existence by transferring human vitality to other living things" (Gillison 1983:39).

Bereavement

As may be expected, Melanesian funerary and mortuary procedures have been widely variant. When a person dies from illness (or when the body of a slain victim is recovered), the corpse is usually the focus of grief-stricken mourning among close kin. This often includes attempts to mollify the spirit of the deceased and/or facilitate its passage to the world of the unseen. Violence to the bodies of the living was often part of this process. Meggitt summarizes for the Mae Enga of the New Guinea Highlands:

> Relatives attending the initial mourning are expected to demonstrate the extent of their sorrow. Male affines and distant kinsmen tear their hair and beards. A few slice their earlobes so that blood flows over their shoulders. Some of the closest kin of both sexes cut off the tops of fingers. This action also placates the ghost of the deceased, which comes into being at the moment of death when the agnatic spirit leaves the corpse. (1965a:182)

Lopping off finger joints from female relatives of the deceased was particularly pronounced among the Dani of the Irian Jaya highlands. By adulthood, many Dani women had by this means lost many or most of their distal finger joints on both hands (Heider 1979:124ff.). Among the Kaulong of New Britain, the widow of a deceased was strangled to

---

64. Gillison 1983:43; cf. 1980, 1987.

death shortly following her husband's demise. This custom appears to have been adhered to fairly consistently among Kaulong in precolonial times (Goodale 1980, 1985). Much more commonly in Melanesia, men and particularly women in mourning wailed and keened for prolonged periods (see photo 8). The kin of the deceased were usually subjected to mourning restrictions; these could variously include a taboo on sex and on the eating of various kinds of foods, restriction of bodily adornment, the wearing of mourning capes or smearing the body with mud or clay, and circumscription of social activity. The severity of mourning procedures usually varied depending on the sex and age of the mourner as well as the social importance of the deceased; mourning was often greatest for adult women after the death of husbands or brothers and less arduous following the demise of women or children.

Treatment of the Corpse

The treatment of the corpse was also commonly influenced by the status of the deceased. Often, the corpse of an important man was dressed in his full complement of ritual finery and the insignia of his status. Among the Iatmul of the Sepik, the death of a renowned man occasioned an elaborate mortuary display, at which his various accomplishments in warfare, ritual, knowledge, and exchange were iconically portrayed (Bateson 1936). Techniques of corpse divination—to ascertain the cause of death and the identity of the sorcerer or witch responsible—also varied depending on the status of the person who died. In significant parts of the New Guinea interior, corpses were inspected before or during decomposition to ascertain the circumstances of death.

Among Gebusi of the Strickland-Bosavi area, the corpses of almost all adults who died from sickness were subject to divinatory procedures (Knauft 1985a: chaps. 2 and 4). After the bloating corpse of the deceased had been mourned for one or more days, the primary sorcery suspects were enjoined to shake the decomposing body in a display of their grief. If the eyes of the corpse burst (due to intracranial pressure) or if cadaveric fluid suddenly flowed out of the body cavity, it was taken as a tangible sign that the suspect was indeed guilty of having killed the person through sorcery. In such cases, the suspect could then be legitimately killed on the spot by the aggrieved parties without retaliation by the suspect's own kin. The executed sorcerer was then steam-cooked with sago and distributed in a cannibalistic feast in a manner similar to the cooking and distribution of game animals such as pigs or cassowaries. This act was considered appropriate reciprocity for the sorcerer's own actions. The killing of sorcery suspects within the community led to a very high Gebusi homicide rate.[65]

A rather different permutation of corpse divination was emphasized among the nearby Etoro and Kaluli peoples, who also had a high homicide rate from the execution of witches.[66] Here it was the person who had been killed for practicing witchcraft whose corpse was examined for divination. His or her heart was cut out and exhibited on a stake; a "bright" or "yellowish" heart was thought to indicate that the slain person had indeed been a witch. The rest of the body might be consumed thereafter.

The Wola, further to the east, believed that the spiritual essence of the sickness-victim's body was transferred to pork, the eating of which was accompanied by omen-taking in which the consumers proclaimed their innocence with respect to the deceased's death (Sillitoe 1987). Among the Marind-anim of the New Guinea south coast, the cadaveric fluid of the corpse itself facilitated divination; this fluid was drunk by a close relative of the deceased as he or she lay next to the corpse in the grave. During the mourner's ensuing "sleep," his or her dreams were believed capable of disclosing the identity of the sorcerer responsible for the death (van Baal 1966:772). The Marind believed that shamanic power was also transmitted through cadaveric fluid. Novice shamans were enjoined to ingest cadaveric fluid in substantial quantities—the liquid being administered orally, nasally, and into their eyes until they became delirious. Through this ordeal and its accompanying indoctrination, the novice shaman risked death itself to attain the "vision" necessary to see accurately into the world of the spirits and into the world of death (van Baal 1966:888). Cadaveric fluid was also smeared on the bodies of female mourners as a sign of their grief in some interior New Guinea societies; among Gebusi and adjacent Bedamini, close female relatives rubbed the skin off the corpse for this purpose and could also be coated with cadaveric fluid as they sat under burial platforms constructed for deceased young men.

An important objective of many mortuary practices and taboos was to encourage the ghost of the deceased person to depart for the

---

65. See Knauft 1985a, 1987b; cf. 1987c.
66. See R. C. Kelly 1976, 1993; Schieffelin 1976.

world of the dead. This process was facilitated by entreaties or demon-strations of grief by the living. In the absence of such entreaties—and even sometimes when they were carefully followed—the spirit of the deceased was frequently believed to be angry over its worldly death. As such, it might harbor ghostly malice and cause misfortune or sick-ness among his or her own living relatives. The various means by which corpses were disposed of reflected, in part, different beliefs con-cerning the proper departure of the deceased's spirit. In some societies, such as the Dani (Heider 1970, 1979), the corpse was cremated on a funeral pyre. In others, such as the Mae Enga (Meggitt 1965a, b), it was quickly buried, while in many other cases it was mourned for several days before burial.

In a large number of Melanesian societies, ranging from at least the Marind-anim in Irian Jaya to the Kwaio in the Solomon Islands,[67] the corpse was buried and later exhumed, whereupon the bones were dec-orated and reburied again. In many other societies, the corpse was left to decompose partially or totally above ground, in part so its spirit could disperse into the clan's ancestral land.

A specific case study illustrates how several of these funerary cus-toms could be combined. Among Daribi, who live on the southern fringe of the New Guinea highlands, "[t]he mourning of the dead con-stitutes the most powerful ideological expression in Daribi culture" (Wagner 1972:145). The Daribi corpse was first keened by patrikin, spouses, and coresidents. Uterine kin of the dead person then arrived and reproached the deceased's clanspeople, accusing them of negli-gence in allowing the person to die. In precolonial times, the visitors might vent their anger by cutting down food-bearing trees, chopping at houseposts, or attacking their opponents by beating them with sticks or slashing at them with axes. The corpse was then left in the residential house for six to ten days, during which time body parts were taken as relics by close descent group and family members:

> While the body is still in the house, parts of it, such as the hands, feet, or scalp, are occasionally cut off as relics. These are dried over the fire and then pressed beneath a sleeping mat, after which they are worn around the neck as an expression of sorrow. Horobame, of Kurube, wore the dried skin of her son's footsole in this way

---

67. Van Baal 1966; Keesing 1982b.

"because she couldn't see him anymore, he couldn't walk around anymore." (Wagner 1972:147)

After relics were obtained, the closest kin were persuaded to relinquish the remainder of the body, which was placed at midday in an open exposure coffin which also served as a dripping pit for decomposition. The body was removed again at sundown, when remaining portions of its flesh were eaten. The decomposing corpse flesh was steam-cooked and eaten by the same people whom the deceased "shared meat with" in life, though not by his or her closest family members. The final remains of the corpse were then returned to the burial rack, securely covered, and tied down with bark. After the corpse had totally decomposed, the bones were recovered and kept in a special "bone house" of pandanus leaves. When this bone house began to disintegrate, the clansmen of the deceased hunted between ten and twenty marsupials, the bones of which they burned under the structure in order that the wafting smoke provide a last "sharing of food" with their deceased relative. This act was also believed to reduce ghostly malice. After the ceremony, the bones were taken from the tiny house, put in a new string bag, and hung in the central corridor of the longhouse. When, much later, the string bag itself began to disintegrate, the bones were removed and deposited, permanently, in a burial cave or rock shelter. The importance of this process is illustrated in the Daribi belief that ghosts, particularly of those who die unmourned in the bush, may come back and cause sickness. To alleviate this, the Daribi staged *habu* ceremonies which "bring the ghost back to the house." This results in a competitive confrontation between a group of men impersonating the ghost and other men and women acting as longhouse residents. The ghost is ultimately appeased and a communal feast held.

Mortuary Feasts

Particularly in seaboard and insular eastern Melanesia, the staging of mortuary rituals to commemorate the dead was an important occasion of wealth distribution and political competition.[68] In economic terms,

---

68. See Wagner 1986; Battaglia 1990; Damon and Wagner 1989; Foster 1995a; Maschio 1994; Keesing 1983; Clay 1986; Goodale 1995; Lutkehaus 1995; Lipset 1997.

the death of a powerful political leader ruptured the extensive ties of wealth exchange he had established. The reformulation or extension of these exchange relations, undertaken symbolically in commemorative mortuary rituals, allowed new and old leaders to vie in amassing and distributing wealth. By this means, the politicoeconomic continuance of society was linked to its spiritual perpetuation and rejuvenation following death, particularly the death of leaders. In some matrilateral groups, such as the Trobriand Islanders, much of this process was under the economic and spiritual control of women (A. B. Weiner 1976), while in others, it was under the more general control of men.[69]

Among the most artistically elaborate mortuary commemorations were the Malanggan of northwestern New Ireland. Closely associated with these ceremonies were elaborate fretted wood masks and other carvings of clan emblem designs.[70] These masks and sculptures, also termed Malanggan, were a genre of commissioned artistic rivalry in which prestige depended upon the Malanggan of a clan's mortuary ceremony being more inventive, elaborate, and spectacular than those of others. The intricate meanings of the designs were owned and most fully understood by the clan elders, who commissioned and directed the carvers as well as sponsoring the mortuary feasts at which they were prominently displayed. The Malanggan artwork was itself left to decay when the ceremonies were over.

Developed mortuary feasts also appear to be prominent in some societies of Irian Jaya[71] and include elaborate ancestral statues or fretwork in both north and south parts of the region, for example, among the Asmat in the south and the Geelvinck Bay area in the north.[72] Spirit house and totemic art have been particularly developed in the Sepik area of northern New Guinea.[73] In most of these cases, elaborate carvings or paintings simultaneously commemorate, incarnate, and reembody the spiritual force of ancestors and ancestral spirits.

In general, New Guinea mourning practices reflect the tension

---

69. Keesing 1982b; Wagner 1986; Clay 1986; Errington 1974; Salisbury 1966; Goodenough 1971.

70. Küchler 1997; Kramer 1925; Wingert 1962:46ff., 234–39; cf. Meyer and Parkinson 1895; Nevermann 1933; Groves 1935:353–60, 1936.

71. E.g., Heider 1979; Serpenti 1977 [1965].

72. E.g., Konrad, Konrad, and Schneebaum 1981; Schneebaum 1985; Rockefeller and Gerbands 1967; Wingert 1962:193ff.; cf. Chauvet 1930.

73. E.g., Greub 1985; cf. Forge 1966.

between three themes: the culturally appropriate expression of grief, the appropriation or retention of the deceased's spiritual force or essence, and the assertion of difference and antipathy between the world of the living and that of the dead.

The Body in Its Prime: Spiritual Embodiment and Rejuvenation

Because Melanesian bodies are so deeply defined through social and spiritual relationships, the most spectacular displays of bodily beauty tend also to be those that reaffirm the social and cosmic rejuvenation of the group as a whole. Customs and beliefs of bodily conception, nurturance, productive growth, and death articulate closely with ceremonies that promulgate or promote the strength, vitality, maturation, and regeneration of individuals and their communities (Whitehead 1986a, b).

Even in nonceremonial contexts, Melanesian bodies have exhibited a wide range of clothing and ornamentation styles. Noseplugs and earplugs, tattoos, scarification, teeth-blackening, penis gourds, and casual ornamentation that uses leaves, fur, or feathers complement in different cultures the scant traditional coverings of loincloths, "ass-grass," fiber skirts, or even total nakedness (traditional in parts of the Sepik). Hairstyles ranged from a shaved head—sometimes at mourning—to intricate long braids or elaborate wigs, as among the Huli of the southern highlands. Daily clothing styles or insignia often provided clear indices of the sex, age, marital status, and political achievements of the individual—what initiation grade they had attained, how many people they had killed, how many large exchanges they had transacted, whether they were in mourning, if they belonged to a special ritual or leadership cult, and so on.

In ceremonial contexts, the body was more greatly transformed, often with great symbolism and rich artistry. In most of Melanesia, the decorated body itself was the preeminent form of art (Kirk 1981). Ritual costuming took forms as diverse and creative as Melanesian cultures themselves. Typically, they were celebratory icons of a vital self and a wider sociocultural and spiritual vitality.

Costuming and Spirit Impersonation— South Coastal New Guinea

In many south coast New Guinea cultures, spectacular body costumes and masks were associated with mythical beings or ancestral spirits—

spirits whose form and force the wearer of the costume embodied or incarnated (Lewis-Harris 1996). These spirits often took on unusual or composite animal forms, as was the case for the *horiomu* spirits commemorated by Kiwai islanders (see fig. 3).

The Marind-anim, to the west of the Kiwai, employed a particularly elaborate array of decorative costumes, which presented various aspects of mythical *dema*-spirits (van Baal 1966). These costumes were employed in an exceedingly complex ritual cycle through which the travels and activities of the *dema* were elaborated, reenacted, and/or revealed to initiates. One of the accompanying costumes was the *garia* sky-image, a bright semicircular body ornament extending like an enormous fan six feet over the head and to each side of the wearer. "The ornament is fan-shaped, made of the very light kernel of sago-leaf ribs. The thin, long strips, radially arranged, are lashed together and then painted in various colors, among which white dominates" (see fig. 4; van Baal 1966:356).

The use and meaning of Marind *dema* costumes was predictably elaborate. The following passage describes the appearance of *Sosom,* one of the principal *dema:*

> The neophytes are brought to the festive grounds and made to sit under the platform, with their backs to the entrance. Some sort of removable fence encloses the place. *Sosom* has donned an enormous headgear made of thin reeds covered with white down. His face is hidden behind the *batend* mask [of scarlet bowerbird feathers], his breast is covered with fiber, and a heavy red-brown skirt folds around his limbs. A garland of bright croton-leaves is draped over his shoulders and down his back hang the long strands of his hairdo. Surrounded by men dancing and swinging their bullroarers, *Sosom* proceeds to the festive grounds. . . . Suddenly the structure moves to and fro, as if a gigantic monster had leapt upon it. A hideous black something descends upon the neophytes: the tail of a monster. The thundering noise has stopped. An eerie silence prevails when the fence is taken away and the uncles and fathers of the boys grasp their arms and drag them out of the enclosure to meet the *dema.* At the same time a hardwood pole [*Sosom's* phallus] is set up and as soon as it stands upright the ordeal starts anew. . . . At last the *dema* kneels down and in front of the boys his decorations are taken off him. The *dema* is revealed to the boys as an ordinary man. (van Baal 1966:481)

Fig. 3.   Kiwai *horiomu* costume. Wood, grass, vines, feathers, turtle shell mask. (After Landtman 1927:339.)

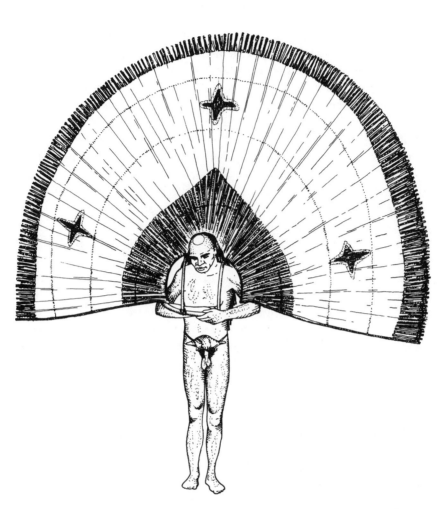

Fig. 4.   Marind-anim *gari* sunburst costume. Sago leaf ribs, vines, paint, wood;
2.5 m × 2.5 m. (After Wirz 1928, plate 100.)

The use of body costumes to represent diffuse spiritual or ancestral forms—revealed to initiates as real men—was pronounced across much of lowland south as well as north New Guinea. Among the Elema of the central south coast, initiation into the wearing of spectacular totemic and spirit-associated masks was both benign and a major social event (see fig. 5; Williams 1940). The largest body masks, the *hevehe,* combined in their meaning and symbolism aspects of sea spirits, ancestral spirits, totemic and clan affiliations, and considerable artistic elaboration. The masks were made of a light cane and palm-wood frame across which bark cloth was stretched and sewn, painted with intricate inherited designs, and fitted at the bottom with a face and gaping sculptured mouth. The masks when worn could stretch twenty-five feet in the air, and yet each was mobile enough to be paraded extensively by a single wearer around the village and on adjoining beaches. Huge vaulted longhouses were built to house the masks, and the elaborate twenty-year cycle of preparing them was a preeminent dimension of Elema sociopolitical as well as religious life. In the ultimate display, well over one hundred different *hevehe* emerged from their single house for over a month of celebration and feasting. This event was the epitome of Elema spiritual and politicoeconomic effervescence.

Costuming and Spirit Impersonation—The Sepik

In the Sepik area of north New Guinea, the embodiment of spirits as men with elaborate effigies, masks, or noise-making instruments was a crucial aspect of initiatory ordeals and cult revelations. Women and children were told that the embodiments were truly those of spirits, though the initiation ordeals ultimately revealed to male novices exactly how they were in fact produced and worn or used by men. Spirit images were linked to elaborate mythical lore and ritual enactments; typically, these were associated with traumatic male initiation rites, as in the Tambaran cult (Tuzin 1980). The plaited mask depicted on the cover of the present book, for example, was worn by initiate novices in the middle Sepik Iatmul village of Kanganaman at the festival ending the seclusion phase of the initiation cycle (Wirz 1959: 38, 76, fig. 44; Greub 1985: text after plate 101).

The intricacies of this process cannot be detailed here; a single example must suffice. In the ritual climax of the Ilahita Arapesh *Nggwal Benafunei,* the initiating elders dress in spectacular costumes and

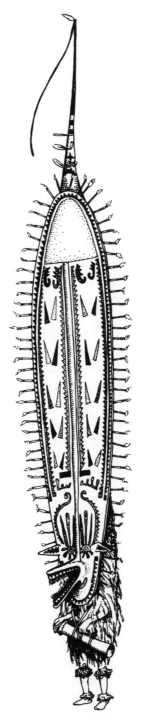

Fig. 5.   Elema *hevehe* mask. Bark cloth, wood, cane grasses, feathers, fiber, thread; 6–7 m high. (After Williams 1940, plates 28, 38, 51, 55.)

parade themselves in public prior to bestowing their ritual knowledge and its accompanying social status to the next class of initiates (who are themselves already adult men). Tuzin (1980:221–22) describes the initiators' costumes.

> Except for his eyelashes, all the dancer's facial hair has been removed, and his hairline has been shaved back to expose the front half of his scalp. A yellow oil (*akwalif*) applied to his face gives his skin a much-admired golden glow and uniform texture. . . . At the center of the artificial hairline a spot of magical red paint (*noa'w*) is applied. Concealed under layers of cosmetic trapping, the *noa'w* is the final, mystic agent of ritual beauty. Its existence is known only to cult members, but its effects are reputedly felt by all. . . . [T]he decorators exploit virtually every type of pleasing material known to them—feathers, natural fabrics, colorful and/or aromatic leaves, berries, blossoms, shells and sundry other items—to create a costume so striking that the audience will be spellbound by its transcendent beauty. The *pièce de resistance* is a tall, pointed headdress rising from its point of attachment at the back of the man's head. . . . The dancer is transformed into a being akin to the Tambaran itself; and, indeed, numerous myths tell of this event permanently changing the mortal protagonist into a spirit entity. The rites of this and the following two days must be judged, then, the climax of Arapesh religious culture.

In the rites themselves, the elder initiators—having previously displayed their transcendent beauty—berate and beat the adult novices. These "initiates" are shoved down a human tunnel into the longhouse. "As each novice disappeared into the dark doorway a sickening thud was heard from within—the wretch's head being crushed under the heel of the Tambaran. By now many of the women [observing from the outside] were sobbing uncontrollably" and the awaiting men were "visibly fearstricken" (Tuzin 1980:236). The "killing," however, was a typical Tambaran ruse:

> As his fear abated and his eyes adjusted to the darkness, the novice beheld the lavishly decked interior: on the right, the gallery wall of spirit paintings running the entire length of the house and festooned with decorated cassowary daggers, mounted birds of par-

adise, and a multitude of shell arrangements; on the left, filling the larger portion of the outer sanctum, a towering line of impassive spirit effigies, and at their feet another line of sculptures in dignified repose. All the remaining floor area was crammed with shells, feathers and daggers. (238)

In essence, these adult novices were "seeing for the first time the master works of an artistic tradition whose very existence had been unknown to them"—the artwork associated with the Nggwal Tambaran class into which they were being initiated. This art was of course extremely secret and could not be seen by women or by those men who had not been initiated into this final Tambaran stage. Subsequent phases of the ritual involved the revelation of varieties of sacred flutes and drums, and a two- to three-month seclusion in which much good food was consumed. At the conclusion, a huge coming-out ceremony was staged at which the new initiates paraded in public the same spectacular costume previously worn by their initiators. A major transfer of ritual knowledge and status was thus enacted.[74]

In some cases, the social and cultural dominance of senior cult members was concretely enacted and reinforced by donning masks of spirits who were angry and vengeful. Through their impersonators, these spirits could mete out social control within their community. In its more extreme forms, this spiritual antagonism could be extremely violent, involving several variants of ritual murder. The *Nggwal Benafunei*, previously alluded to so artistically, could serve in this alternate capacity on other occasions. Another such Tambaran, *hangamu'w*, was revealed to novices during first-stage initiation:

Of the 214 *hangahiwa* recorded in Ilahita village, about ten percent have a reputation for murder. Their trappings include crimped cordyline leaves as homicide badges and . . . the skulls of their victims hung in grisly display around their necks. By donning one of the *hangamu'w* masks, it is said, the wearer becomes possessed of the indwelling spirits of its victims; wild with their passion of revenge, he is likely to kill any living thing that crosses his path. Upon doing so, he supposedly recovers his senses, returns the

74. Tuzin (1980:223) asks, "What does this bestowal entail? Nothing less than renewal of the grand conditions of existence: human and natural fertility, physical security, social harmony, and cultural meaning."

mask to its place among the others in the spirit house, and, concealing his guilt, joins in the general distress that is agitated when
the victim's body is discovered. Moral responsibility is deflected
onto the Tambaran itself, which is credited with another killing as
evidence of its insatiable appetite. (Tuzin 1982:339)[75]

In general, the violent power of Tambaran and totemic spirits was
seen as enjoining public adherence to ritual traditions, taboos, and the
requirements of exchange prestation. Tambarans also promoted successful male development and facilitated eminence and success in
politicoeconomic relations and warfare. One of the deepest secrets of
the Tambaran initiations was that the spirits were in fact impersonated
and controlled by men (Tuzin 1974, 1976, 1980, 1982). Correspondingly,
Tambarans expressed diverse desires and personalities, ranging from
the beautiful or the extremely violent to the hilarious and ludic. The
importance of the Tambaran to social order and meaning among the
Ilahita Arapesh has been underscored more recently by the disruption
and gender antagonism that have arisen since the demise of the cult
and the public revelation of the cult secrets to women, children, and
younger men (Tuzin 1997).

In many parts of the Sepik and south New Guinea, as well as insular Melanesia, some costumed cult figures were designed to be outra-
geously disheveled or clumsy; as bogeymen or buffoons, they could
terrorize residents but were also potent sources of humor and enter-
tainment. In many cases there was a variable or ambiguous boundary
between the humor and the danger that such spiritual enactments
could provoke.[76] The extremes of this tension are evident in the traditional initiation to the *tansa* society on Nissan in the Solomon Islands
(Nachman 1982). Here the grand initiator decorated his penis with yellow, red, and white stripes, and—as a central aspect of initiatory revelation—dramatically exposed his penis to the novices. Such behavior
was thought to be both outrageous and very funny. At the initiation
itself, however, any boys who smiled or laughed were held to be highly

---

75. Tuzin (1982:339) describes the hangamu'w costume itself as follows: "a full-
body costume consisting of a woven helmet mask, a shoulder area fashioned from coiled
strands of bright orange fruits, and a concealing body curtain of yellow sago fibers. The
women are told the half truth that these are spirits incarnate, rather than being merely
men disguised as such."

76. See Bateson 1936; Lipset 1997: chap. 6.

disrespectful; custom held that they could in fact be killed, cooked, and eaten by their initiators.

Costuming and Political Achievement— Insular Melanesia

In diverse Melanesian societies, the right to wear or possess powerful spirit masks or insignia was, as in the Sepik, gained through a progressively restrictive process of initiation or political accession. These bodily markers were both symbols of eminent status and the embodiment of spiritual power and authority.[77] In the Tami-Huon area of northeast New Guinea, for instance, special wooden and bark-cloth masks were, like the Tambaran, symbols of "precarious ancestor-spirit beneficence."[78] These beings were in control of the secret society and of social propriety in general.

In many insular areas east of New Guinea, political hierarchy was even more closely tied to rights over elaborate masks or bodily decorations. Rights to make and/or wear masks or insignia were purchased and exhibited ceremonially at lavish feasts, the staging of which was the hallmark of the man's political success. In Northeast New Britain and the Duke of York Islands, the aspirant's spiritual and political life revolved around the purchase and control of *tubuan* or *dukduk* body masks at mortuary feasts. At these feasts, the deaths of important ancestors or relatives were commemorated.[79] At such occasions, the society as well as the key individuals at its apex were symbolically regenerated and reconstituted in political and spiritual well-being, as concretely symbolized in the elaborate masks themselves. In many societies of insular and northern Melanesia, as in the Sepik above, the owners of the masks or their henchmen could exercise considerable power and social control when wearing the masks or acting in their name. Thus, for instance, they could attack rivals of lower standing or extort their compliance in matters of political support or exchange

---

77. While this dimension of masked costuming is most pronounced in insular Melanesia, discussed later, and in the Sepik, it was also present in parts of south New Guinea. Among the Purari peoples, for instance, men of stature could be initiated into several cults, which conveyed on them legitimate knowledge and use of various spirit-masks (Williams 1923a, 1924). These rites were paid for by the initiate and culminated in major feasts.

78. See Wingert 1962:212; cf. Meyer and Parkinson 1895; Nevermann 1933.

79. See Errington 1974; cf. Danks 1887, 1892; Parkinson 1907; Salisbury 1966, 1970.

prestation. In New Caledonia, control of elaborate body masks and an associated mythology of ancestral descendance were tied to chiefly rivalry and authority (Guiart 1966).

The combination of political and spiritual authority established through the control of bodily insignia and decoration was particularly developed in the restrictive secret or public graded cults of New Britain and Vanuatu in eastern Melanesia.[80] Allen summarizes the general characteristics of the graded cult society:

> Wherever the graded society occurs, it consists of a number of ranked grades, entry into which is gained by the performance of ritual based on the sacrifice of pigs with artificially developed tusks, the transfer of payments for insignia and services, and the performance of elaborate dances. Members of the various grades are marked off from one another by their exclusive right to certain insignia, titles and ritual privileges. For the lower grades the complications are minimal and take no heavy toll on the resources or ability of the aspirant. For the higher grades the requirements become progressively more complex and more expensive. . . . Men who attain the highest rank are believed to acquire or gain access to supernatural powers which they can then utilize in their attempts to control the political aspirations of those beneath them. (Allen 1984:33)

The sociopolitical and body-decoration ramifications of public and more secret ritual societies are effectively recounted in Allen's description of a North Vanuatu island:

> On the tiny island of Mota, with a diameter of less than three kilometers and a population of about 500 persons, Rivers (1914:2: 87–129) recorded the existence of no less than seventy-seven secret societies when he visited the community in 1912. Many of these societies had permanent cult buildings in the bush where the members kept their regalia and elaborate headdresses and where they frequently slept and ate. . . . Each society took great pride in its own unique insignia, masks, dances, and taboos, and each

---

80. Allen 1984; Meyer and Parkinson 1895; Rivers 1914; Deacon 1934; Layard 1942; M. R. Allen 1981; cf. Chowning and Goodenough 1971.

strove to gain members at the expense of the others. Any male of consequence found it imperative to belong to numerous societies—imperative both to advance in the public graded society, and hence aspire to influence and leadership, and as a necessary means of property protection. . . . The societies displayed numerous Tammany-Hall-style characteristics, including political assassination and general terror tactics. A leader who held high rank in the public graded society and was also a member of powerful secret societies was provided with a degree of institutional support and legitimation not commonly available to Melanesian Big Men. (Allen 1984:32)

It is obvious here that political, economic, and religious aspects of Melanesian culture come together through a panoply of powerful and diverse bodily markers.

Costuming and Societal Rejuvenation—
Fringe New Guinea

The political import of bodily insignia and spiritual enactment does not negate the public embrace and enjoyment of spectacular costuming; it typically symbolizes the vitality, power, and beauty of the larger group or society. This dimension of ritual enhancement is present across Melanesia and is pronounced in those regions where status differentials among men are less competitive or invidious. In fringe areas of the New Guinea highlands, elaborate ritual enactment promulgates health, rejuvenation, and/or the overcoming of death for the collectivity at large. For instance, the *habu* ritual previously described for the Daribi publicly dispels ghostly influence; it both combats the specter of death and promotes life.

A similar theme is found among the cult and ritual practices of the Foi people living near Lake Kutubu to the west of the Daribi.[81] As opposed to traumatic male initiation, the Foi practiced a myriad of curing cults and organized ritual feasts during mortuary rites as a way of promulgating general fertility. As J. F. Weiner (1987:274) suggests in elaboration of Williams (1977): "The prevention of sickness and its implicit converse, the promotion of general fertility is a theme of male

---

81. See F. E. Williams 1977; J. F. Weiner 1984, 1986, 1987, 1988a, 1993, 1995.

definition throughout the southern fringe area of the highlands of New Guinea." Among the Kaluli, to the west, the spectacular *gisaro* ritual poignantly evoked the memory of the dead and simultaneously asserted the emotional passion of the living.[82] In the successful *gisaro*, elaborately costumed dancers visiting from other settlements sang songs about the hosts' forest lands and deceased relatives. In response, audience members burned the dancers severely about their shoulders and back—for having aroused such intense grief and sorrow among them. However, the performers continued their dancing and singing unabated. Indeed, they themselves paid compensation to the hosts at the conclusion of the ritual the following morning, in recompense for the emotional anguish that their exquisite performance had evoked. In all, the *gisaro* was a preeminent assertion of Kaluli aesthetic power and reciprocity.

Themes of otherworldly evocation and emotional passion reach a more exuberant and sexual expression further to the west, among the lowland Gebusi. The Gebusi *gigobra* is a general rite of well-being, typically including a generous feast, an all-night dance, and much singing and joking (Knauft 1985a, b). The dancers embody on their person the beauty and harmony of the Gebusi spiritual universe (see photo 9). Costume parts worn on the upper half of the body signify spirit-creatures of the upper world, and those on the lower body spirit-forms of the underworld. Thus, for instance, the drum presents a large open-mouth fish or crocodile—the incarnate form of elder male spirits who live in the larger streams and rivers. The top half of the *gigobra* costume, in contrast, presents the world above. The large halo of white headdress feathers comes from the egret, a bird incarnating "male" qualities; the forehead band is fur from the cuscus, a tree-dwelling marsupial spirit-form; and the pearl-shell sliver under the chin is said to present a crescent moon.

The Gebusi dancer as a whole, moving and swaying slowly to the beat of his drum, enacts in his person the beauty, attractiveness, and coordinated harmony of Gebusi spirits in their various forms. This is an apt metaphor for the social purpose of the dance itself, which promotes healing, conflict resolution, and friendly camaraderie. More erotically, the dance is also a context for exuberant public joking and for private attempts to initiate homo- and heterosexual liaisons. This dimension of

---

82. Schieffelin 1976, 1979, 1980; Feld 1982.

the ritual is also visually encoded in the symbolism of the dance costume, which is said as a whole to present the red bird of paradise (*Paradisaea raggiana*). This bird is the incarnate form of the beautiful and alluring Gebusi spirit-woman and is a general image of vitality, beneficence, and strong erotic attraction. The brilliant red plumage of this bird is portrayed in the red body paint of the dancer and in sprays of red bird of paradise feathers at the dancer's back and inside his white halo headdress. The dark head and gold banding of the bird are reflected in the black eye mask of the dancer, ringed in yellow, and in the black ribbing lined in gold on his trunk and legs.

A further visual semiotic among Gebusi may be illustrated in the costume of the male initiates, also said in general to be an embodiment of the red bird of paradise (see photo 10). In this costume, the decorative elements have been presented as gifts by men and women of different settlements who have helped sponsor the initiate. The initiate's costume thus displays the craftsmanship of his allies and his ties of social and political support to settlements throughout Gebusi territory. The costume also has a pronounced sexual dimension. This is reflected not only in the general red bird of paradise imagery but in the long phallic leaf, said to present the initiates' enlarged penises (see also photo 11). This sexual emphasis is particularly appropriate since the young men at the time of their initiation have been liberally inseminated through fellatio and have been exhorted to avoid sexual contact with women. As such, they are believed to be at the peak of their physical growth and sexual potency. The term for male initiation is itself "child become big" (*wa kawala*). After initiation, the initiates' much-vaunted virility is released bisexually, first, in homosexual insemination of uninitiated boys, and second, in the active quest for women as sexual and marital partners (Knauft 1987a). These same activities are also pursued at the initiation festivities themselves by the visitors and hosts in attendance. When the half dozen or more age-grade initiates process and line up in identical costume, they collectively embody not only the harmony of various spirit forms, but the fertility and interconnection of the Gebusi people as a whole (see photo 12). Initiation festivities are the largest and most artistically elaborate events in Gebusi society.

As Gebusi costuming illustrates, decorative symbolism can be both complex and polysemic. This multivalence is especially apposite for articulating complex cultural themes of sexual potency, vitality, and societal rejuvenation. A similar panoply can be seen in a different cultural context among the Umeda of West Sepik Province, to the north of the New Guinea highlands.[83] Among Umeda, elaborately costumed dancers convey processes of biological growth, sexuality, reproduction, and spiritual regeneration over the course of a night-long ritual. The initial dancers are symbolically associated with cassowaries—large flightless birds—and with elder men, whose active sexuality is indicated by large penis gourds. These phallic adornments are flapped up and down and clack loudly during the dance. The ritual proceeds amid many embellishments through a series of painted performers, including sago dancers and sexual buffoons. The rite culminates with the brief dance of red bowmen (*ipele*), who symbolize, among other things, youthful initiates whose penises are bound and who are potent and successful in hunting. Overtly, the ritual is staged to facilitate the growth and fertility of sago (a principal palm-food), but as an ethnographer, Gell shows its messages to be much richer, including poignant portrayals of gender complementarity, of "natural" reproduction, and of spiritual regeneration as it is transferred from one initiation grade to the next. Ultimately, the ritual employs a sequence of spectacular costuming to enact the rejuvenation and reproduction of Umeda society itself.

Costuming as Personal Enhancement and Seduction—Massim and the New Guinea Highlands

The symbolization of beauty, sexuality, and vitality is not limited in Melanesia to fringe and coastal societies of New Guinea. In numerous areas, highly costumed male initiates or dancers are believed capable of attracting women as wives. As occurs in much of the New Guinea highlands, young men emerging from initiation-grade or bachelor-cult seclusion are festooned in ritual finery appropriate to their sexual attractiveness or marriageability. In both the New Guinea highlands and the Melanesian Massim, themes of bodily attraction are extended to economic or political activities as well. For the Massim in particular, beauty magic and enhanced appearance increase the individual's abil-

---

83. See Gell 1975; cf. Juillerat 1986, 1992.

ity to attract wealth as well as lovers.[84] Such beautification can be important for men who wish to initiate successful wealth exchanges and induce exchange partners to relinquish their most prized wealth items, such as the famed *kula* valuables.[85] *Kula* valuables are themselves forms of body decoration—arm shells and necklaces. However, these valuables are so important that they take on personalities and lives of their own. The history of their exchange and the stages of their possession by inhabitants of various islands is well-known lore, making them a transcultural repository of renown across the region as a whole. Appropriately, many of the prized valuables are too large and/or important to be worn; they dwarf the bodies that would wear them.

A different permutation of decorative self-actualization is found in the New Guinea highlands. Here costuming is used especially in the context of group status rivalry and display, for example, when large competitive gifts of wealth are given. The stature of participants is justly enhanced by their elaborate decorations—long-plumed head-dresses, elaborate face-painting, wigs, shells, and other accoutrements.[86] Such decoration has been prominent throughout the New Guinea highlands, where the linkage between decoration and deeper aspects of self-enhancement are effectively evident. In some highlands societies, the status of an elaborate wig worn at important events was taken as a de facto index of a person's social relations. Among Wahgi peoples of the western highlands, special wigs were configured by maternal relatives, or from materials given by them (see photo 13). The beauty—or imperfection—of these wigs was taken to indicate the status of the wearer's matrilateral relations in festivities that otherwise strongly emphasized the prowess and accomplishments of the patriclan. As O'Hanlon (1992) suggests, such wigs "come out" like a kind of "maternal second-skin." The persistence of this decorative form is evident in contemporary highlands celebrations such as the Wahgi Pig Festival. Unmarried women as well as men can occasionally be decorated with these special wigs, as shown in photo 13. In this case, the base of the wig has been overlain with women's cloth blouse material (painted red), in lieu of the traditional bark cloth. This, in addition to

---

84. E.g., A. B. Weiner 1976: chap. 5; Munn 1986:101–18.

85. Malinowski 1922; Leach and Leach 1983.

86. See Strathern and Strathern 1971; Kirk with Strathern 1981; A. J. Strathern 1975; M. Strathern 1979; O'Hanlon 1989, 1992.

the one-kina coins tied to the base of the wig, illustrates the persistence of indigenous decorative motifs even as they incorporate modern materials and associated meanings.

The features of highland body decoration among Wahgi peoples and in Mount Hagen are delineated by O'Hanlon (1989) and by Strathern and Strathern, who suggest:

> In Hagen, thought, material success, and physical health are alike expressed in a man's bodily condition. A person should be well filled-out, with a gleaming skin, and oiling the body contributes to it a desired, glossy appearance. Hageners also say that one of the aims of decorating is to make the dancers appear larger: at festivals, where they wear a whole range of ornaments, their enhanced size goes with increased attractiveness; in warfare it makes them impressive and frightens the enemy. (Strathern and Strathern 1971:134)

Not surprisingly, the most impressive and expensive bodily decorations were often worn by or at the direction of the so-called big-men, those leaders who by dint of personal assertiveness compete effectively at the upper rungs of the shifting status hierarchy. Some bodily insignia specified particular aspects of the big-man's economic or military achievements. Such, for instance, is the *omak*, a set of bamboo tally sticks laced side by side and hung from the wearer's neck—a bit like a broad but stiff necktie. Among the Melpa, the number of tally sticks— and hence the length of the *omak*—is determined by how many times the man has given away a set of eight or ten major shells in *moka* wealth exchange (Strathern and Strathern 1971).

The term *big-man* is frequently itself a literal gloss of vernacular terms, and big-men *were* sometimes physically big—an association not unrelated to their effectiveness and eminence in warfare (Watson 1971). However, the "largeness" of the big-man, particularly as he reached his prime, was equally if not more evident in economic exchanges, feasting, and elaborate oratory; he embodied forcefulness, aggression, and incisive vitality.[87] In many Melanesian societies, such aspects of leadership were dispersed among different individuals with different skills

---

87. E.g., Read 1959; Sahlins 1963; Salisbury 1964; Watson 1971; A. J. Strathern 1966, 1971, 1979b; Meggitt 1971; cf. Keesing 1985b.

and abilities rather than cohering into a single leader as "big-man." The term *great man* has sometimes been used by anthropologists for leaders in the many more decentralized societies outside the core highland areas of New Guinea.[88]

Just as the big-man or great man is in a sense the embodiment of his group, his accomplishments also accrue to his followers and his kin group as a whole; they have contributed their own wealth as part of his gift-giving display and their own effort to his political or military eminence. Accordingly, all men and women can, on appropriate occasions, decorate themselves elaborately. Commonly, groups of dancers from a given clan dress elaborately in near-identical costumes as an indication of their similarity and solidarity. At the same time, there can also be much room for individual creativity. When combined with choice costume parts, this creativity can promote special recognition of the wearer's individuality and power in self-presentation. Individual variation in costuming has had great aesthetic and social force in most Melanesian societies.

While subject to personal discretion, the appropriateness of an individual's and a group's choice of costume is—even in the realpolitik of the New Guinea highlands—also ultimately underwritten by spiritual sanction.

> A clan can achieve success only if it has the active support of its ancestral ghosts. . . . At a festival, a demonstration that an individual or a group is prosperous and healthy itself indicates ghostly blessing. Conversely, failure or disaster is a sign that the ghosts have become angry at some wrong and have withdrawn their help. (Strathern and Strathern 1971:130)

This spiritual sanction enforces the conformity of costuming with the degree of self-enhancement that the individual or group can legitimately claim. It is in this sense that "the whole act of self-decoration is a kind of omen-taking" (134).

These themes reflect the more general highlands linkage between spiritual force, bodily vitality, attractiveness, and cultural well-being (M. Strathern 1979; O'Hanlon 1989).

---

88. See Godelier 1986; Godelier and Strathern 1991.

In the most general terms, it may be said that presentation of the decorated body in Melanesia is a celebration of social and cultural vitality in
its myriad local dimensions. That this decoration focuses on or about
the skin is particularly appropriate, as the skin is the boundary, media-
tor, and index of relationship between the internal self and the social
collective.[89] Through its decorations, the body both establishes and
indicates self–other relations, particularly in spheres of production and
reproduction, substance and spirit. The body in Melanesia is a multifaceted icon that is particularly rich and varied—a performative that
binds people together in intricate webs of meaning and experience (see
photo 14).

Conclusion

The body in Melanesia is intricately tied to cycles of fertility, depletion,
and regeneration. These include the "natural" cycles of change in the
physical environment, the biological patterns of development within
the individual body, and the social and spiritual cycles through which
interpersonal relationships grow, mature, and deteriorate. We in
postindustrial Western societies tend to divorce these cycles from one
another; we tend to assume that our bodily, social, and spiritual worlds
are largely separate—that they operate along separate orders of causa-
tion. In Melanesia, by contrast, these processes tend to be linked as
complementary parts of a cosmological universe made manifest
through bodily ecology.

This is not to suggest that Melanesian patterns of symbolism or
meaning form integrated wholes; Melanesian cultures have always
grown and changed in dialectical and inconsistent fashion. Certainly,
too, an overarching bodily ecology has been subject to much greater
cultural elaboration in some Melanesian societies than in others. It can
be argued, however, that Melanesians recognize the natural world, the
anatomical self, and the world of social and spiritual relationships to be
connected in ways that Westerners largely deny or fail to appreciate.

This reflects more general differences. Though Melanesian cosmologies are full of tensions and contradictions—particularly with
respect to gender and male status competition—they do not harbor the

---

89. Turner 1980; cf. A. J. Strathern 1975; M. Strathern 1979; O'Hanlon 1989.

anxieties of ontological doubt that gnaw the West in matters of mind, symbol, and belief. There is little of the radical epistemological schism that we in the West harbor so uneasily—the scientific versus the religious versus the pragmatic versus the personal. Such fragmentation of understanding has been largely foreign to Melanesia. As was so clearly recognized by the great anthropologist Gregory Bateson (1936, 1972, 1979), the symbolic, social, and environmental dimensions of life are equally real and intrinsically interconnected. As Bateson also suggested, we neglect an awareness of this holistic ecology to our own peril and impoverishment. In this respect, Melanesian cosmologies present a major advance over our own.

From this perspective, the relationship between the present account and other forms of inquiry comes into clearer view. Certainly it would have been possible to analyze Melanesian bodily beliefs and practices as art—or as artifacts—in and of themselves. However, this leaves out the indigenous meanings of art and aesthetics; it leaves behind their significance as well as their connection to other aspects of Melanesian life and cosmology.

It would also be possible to forward causal or functional arguments as to why certain Melanesian bodily customs and beliefs exist in the form they do. Living in a richer biotic environment than we, it is perhaps "natural" that Melanesians have taken basic processes of growth, maturation, and death as more poignant and pervasive cultural metaphors than we have. More specifically, it could perhaps be argued that cultural concern with food, disease, or bodily privation is foregrounded in those areas of Melanesia where the environment is harsher or morbidity higher; that cannibalism is common where people are plentiful but other sources of protein are not; that male socialization is most arduous where resource competition, social organization, or warfare place a premium on collective male toughness and aggression. Correspondingly, competition or restrictiveness over bodily insignia may be greater where material resources, population densities, and/or political hierarchies heighten conflict. Perhaps as well, the tendency for adolescent girls to mature more quickly than boys could provide some explanation of male anxiety and ritualization of physiological development vis-à-vis women.

These arguments cannot be dismissed out of hand. Indeed, our understanding of bodily meanings and practices in Melanesia remains sadly divorced from the sparse comparative information available on subsistence ecology, nutrition, and human physiology in this part of the world. However, it is undeniable that Melanesian bodily beliefs and practices also have a cultural life of their own. The elaborateness, intricacy, and incredible diversity of Melanesian bodily customs are far greater than any explanation on the basis of genetic, ecological, or sociological predicates can reasonably comprehend. A model of interaction between "natural" ecology and the ecology of cultural belief is probably the best that can be hoped for in this respect.

In a regional perspective, our account suggests that certain areas of Melanesia have placed relatively greater stress on different parts of a life cycle that connects bodily and cosmological processes. An emphasis on sexual vitality and sexual celebration seems especially great along coastal and adjacent lowland areas of south New Guinea. Conversely, a stress on the body's material productivity through labor and its transaction through gift-giving and exchange has seemed particularly elaborate in highland areas of New Guinea and some areas of insular Melanesia. Emphasis on masculine bodily maturity through stages of ranked ritual hierarchy or secret society initiation are particularly emphasized in parts of insular eastern Melanesia, as they also are—sometimes on a smaller political scale—in fringe highland and Sepik areas of New Guinea. In many parts of these areas and especially insular Melanesia (as well as parts of Irian Jaya), there has been a notable emphasis on mortuary rites and associated practices to commemorate ancestors. The latter have been prominently connected with the taking of enemy life force along much of the New Guinea south coast and in parts of the Sepik. Across most of Melanesia, cultural emphasis on one or another stage of bodily and cosmological cycles is reflected in elaborate body costuming at rituals, ceremonial feasts, or exchanges associated with that dimension of bodily and cosmic progression.

Amid broad regional associations, it would be mistaken to distinguish areas too specifically or assign them neatly to different bodily or cosmological emphases; there are diverse permutations upon cycles of bodily and cosmic fertility throughout Melanesia. Exceptions to areal trends, sometimes dramatic, have been evident from virtually all major areas of Melanesia. Conversely—and at least as importantly—there is a complex linkage and reinforcement between phases of bodily and cosmological cycles. Alternate stages or themes are frequently evoked as

Photo 1.　Gebusi man. (Photograph by Eileen Cantrell.)

Photo 2.   Gebusi woman. (Photograph by Eileen Cantrell.)

Photo 3.   Mother and child. (Photograph by Eileen Cantrell.)

Photo 4.   A young man undergoing initiation is decorated by his classificatory mother's brother. (Photograph by Eileen Cantrell.)

Photo 5. Initiate wearing a heavy bark wig. (Photograph by Eileen Cantrell.)

Photo 6. Men preparing a collective sago oven for a community feast. (Photograph by Eileen Cantrell.)

Photo 7. His face blackened in anger, a man waits to vent his aggression over a kinsman's death at a funeral fight. (Photograph by Eileen Cantrell.)

Photo 8. Woman mourning the death of her husband. (Photograph by
Eileen Cantrell.)

Photo 9.   Embodying the harmony of the spirits: dancer at a ritual feast. (Photograph by Eileen Cantrell.)

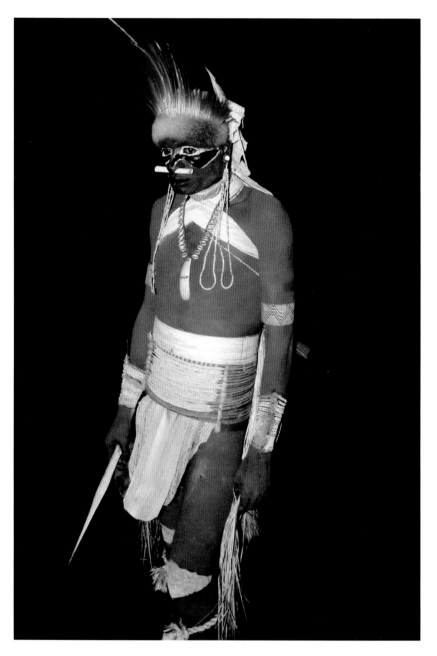

Photo 10.   Male initiate in full regalia: the cultural expression of beauty and effervescence. (Photograph by Eileen Cantrell.)

Photo 11. Male initiate in yellow transitional decoration, with phallic leaf. (Photograph by Eileen Cantrell.)

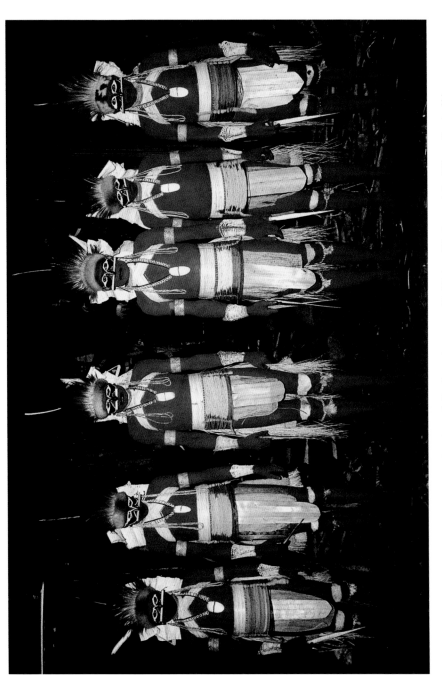

Photo 12.   Unity in collectivity: formal display of costumed initiates. (Photograph by Eileen Cantrell.)

Photo 13. Unmarried Wahgi girl decorated with maternally derived wig—a kind of "second skin." (Photograph by Michael O'Hanlon.)

Photo 14.   Self-styled decoration. (Photograph by Eileen Cantrell.)

Photo 15. Principal antagonists in a funeral fight make peace by sharing tobacco over the deceased's grave. (Photograph by Eileen Cantrell.)

Photo 16.   Western highlands man with contemporary fighting shield, painted with the South Pacific beer logo. (Photograph by Michael O'Hanlon.)

aspects of one another; clear division between them is contrary to their own idioms of interconnection.

In a different vein, we may consider Melanesian bodily belief against the emphasis on reflexivity and the relativity of ethnographic perspectives.[90] Prominent here is the problematic relationship between the viewer and the thing being viewed—between the ostensible objectivity of the author and the more authentic subjectivity of his or her subject. The assumptions that underlie our portrayals can be critically examined, as may the assumption that beliefs or customs are "entities" that can be summarily characterized or generalized about. Has our account adopted a masculinist bias and perpetuated a view of bodies that privileges men? Or have we simply documented the gendered bodily emphases evident among Melanesians themselves? Have we emphasized traditional norms at the expense of current variations, or do these customs provide an important history with its own rich legacies for the present? It must be admitted, at the very least, that our account has not adequately represented the many different areas of Melanesia, due to the selective nature of the available literature and the personal limitations of the author.[91]

Despite limitations of ethnographic writing, we have tried to make substantive characterizations concerning bodily belief and custom in early colonial Melanesia. In a sense, however, we cannot do otherwise. However filtered or relative our accounts may be, we must at some point rely on our best sources and our best abilities, bracket ontological questions, and take the leap of faith that assumes a real world of social and symbolic attributes that we can at least partly understand and approximate in our accounts. To refuse this leap of faith would be to keep other cultures in the dark while shining the light of inquiry indulgently on ourselves.

90. E.g., Marcus and Fischer 1986; Clifford and Marcus 1986; Clifford 1988; Tyler 1988.

91. For instance, we have paid relatively less attention to Irian Jaya and particularly to areas of insular eastern Melanesia. In these respects, the account is restricted by my own knowledge and language abilities, and by the relatively fewer rich ethnographic accounts of indigenous practices from these regions (but see Guiart 1956, 1963a, b, 1966; Leenhardt 1979 [1947]; Layard 1942; Deacon 1934; Harrisson 1937; Allen 1981; Keesing 1982b; Oliver 1955, 1971; Hogbin 1964; Blackwood 1935; Powdermaker 1979 [1933]; Parkinson 1907; Speiser 1991; Oosterwal 1961; van Baal 1966; Serpenti 1977 [1965]; Heider 1970, 1979; Koch 1974; Pospisil 1958, 1963a, b; for a West New Guinea bibliography, see van Baal, Galis, and Koentjaraningrat 1984).

It is only a sketch of comparative bodily pastiche that we have attempted here for Melanesia. One of the greatest strengths of Melanesian ethnography is the detail and rigor of its published accounts. To Melanesia belongs the rich diversity of indigenous beliefs and customs themselves. Our intent has been more to whet the appetite for appreciating this cultural diversity than to prematurely attempt its grand explanation.

Chapter 3

Warfare and History in Melanesia

As a topic, warfare has loomed large in the Western understanding of Melanesia. For one thing, the populations of Melanesia seemed to explorers more prone to fighting—both with whites and among themselves—than the peoples they encountered in Polynesia, Micronesia, or Australia. In addition, the political organization of Melanesian societies was viewed in terms of opposition or enmity between locally autonomous groups. Even as these notions have been critically reconsidered, the evidence still suggests that armed conflict among Melanesians was often an important and sometimes pivotal aspect of cultural orientation and social practice.

For explorers and then anthropologists, this violence raised several issues. Perhaps most pragmatic was the fact that the observer's own safety or survival could be at risk unless protected by a mantle of colonial authority or pacification. Early anthropologists depended implicitly or explicitly on their status as powerful outsiders to help immunize themselves from local conflicts and violence. But beyond this, most anthropologists had a strong desire to investigate local customs, including warfare, in order to understand them. The larger hope was that finding the causes of warfare in simpler societies could help uncover the causes of warfare and human violence more generally—and the features that might control or reduce human suffering. Understanding warfare in Melanesia was also important to colonial officials, who wished to pacify and extend their control over indigenous populations. In the colonial encounter, these governmental and scholarly agendas tended to be complementary, even though there were often tensions between them.

The scope of literature on Melanesian warfare has grown enormously over the decades, and it peaked particularly with the ethnographic study of the New Guinea highlands in the late 1950s, 1960s, and 1970s. A wide range of competing theories has been adduced to explain armed conflict in this part of the world. Indeed, the cultural diversity of violence in Melanesia has often been viewed as a natural laboratory or conceptual testing ground for theories of aggression and warfare.

When I was asked to review and evaluate this literature for the sixtieth anniversary issue of Oceania, *the redoubtable journal of Pacific anthropology, my first thought was how difficult it would be to take stock of all this material and its competing claims about warfare in Melanesia. Gradually, however, this concern was shadowed by another that was equally compelling: my increasing sense of how much had not been investigated in the anthropology of warfare in Melanesia. Among other things, some of the most significant armed conflicts that have occurred in Melanesia over the last century were between Melanesians and Westerners, and between Westerners and Japanese during World War II. The ethnographic topic of "Melanesian warfare" tended to neglect these conflagrations. So too, the armed conflict in independent Melanesian states between ethnic minorities and state governments, sometimes involving the tacit or active role of state-affiliated multinational corporations, has been considered a separate topic of investigation.*

Anthropologists have been very keen and effective in looking at local-level conflict that seemed indigenous. But they have, historically, paid less attention to spheres of political power, contention, and dispute at the colonial, national, and international levels. Over the years, these contexts have proven increasingly important for understanding collective violence in Melanesia.

Apart from these larger developments, anthropologists' views of indigenous warfare have themselves changed dramatically over the course of the last century. Given the impact of these developing views on the information collected, it is difficult to evaluate theories about warfare derived from one ethnographic period or Melanesian locale against information collected through a different perspective from a different part of Melanesia at a different point in time. It is just these kinds of problems that have led some cultural anthropologists to give up on sifting evidence, making regional generalizations, or evaluating hypotheses. Along this line of reasoning, the ethnographic record is just too bound up in our own changing Western interests, projections, and assumptions to be viewed as "objective" in a comparative sense. It seems evident, however, that this view itself harbors an inflexible rather than a supple or contextual standard of objectivity. After carefully considering the assumptions and predilections of a given intellectual viewpoint, it is still possible to make reasoned assessments about its associated ethnography. It is important to productively reassess the great wealth of ethnographic information about Melanesian conflict that has been carefully collected over many decades. This information strikingly illuminates both the history of Melanesian violence and that of changing Western interests and influences in this part of the world. It also affords us the opportunity to evaluate several of the most commonly adduced theories of warfare in decentralized societies.

The following study of Melanesian warfare proceeds by way of two complementary perspectives. On the one hand, I consider the changing interests and representations of Western scholarship and the way these reflect and inform the colonial and postcolonial history of Melanesia. On the other, I bracket these assumptions at points to pursue a more refined empirical evaluation of theories of warfare themselves. If the concepts we use are themselves relative, the larger goal is to use our awareness of this relativity to make better and more rigorous assessments.

With each passing year, the study of "indigenous warfare" in Melanesia becomes increasingly historical. Conversely, the collective violence that now occurs in the region no longer fits easily under this label. At present, features of national dispute and international influence are increasingly important to the occurrence of violent conflict in this world area. The postcolonial era is now in or approaching its third decade for the independent nations Papua New Guinea, the Solomon Islands, Vanuatu, and Fiji. Armed conflicts have erupted between indigenous and Indian political factions in Fiji, between the Papua New Guinea Defense Force and rebel forces on the island of Bougainville, in the highlands of New Guinea, and between selected political factions or groups in the Solomon Islands and Vanuatu. The persistence of Indonesian hegemony in West New Guinea and French colonialism in New Caledonia carries ever deeper repercussions for local rebellions and movements of resistance.

In the spring of 1997, the government of Papua New Guinea arranged for international mercenaries to kill off the main forces of the Bougainville Republican Army (BRA) and neutralize their followers and sympathizers. Though this operation was exposed and forestalled through political and military opposition in Port Moresby (leading to a government crisis and resignation of the Prime Minister), it involved a secret contract for U.S. $36 million with "Executive Outcomes, Inc.," a South African army-for-hire corporation. The military operation was to have *attacked rebels by means of helicopter gunships and fixed-wing aircraft as well as ground combat and electronic warfare (Sandline 1997; Murdoch 1997a, b).*

If the research for the following chapter were to be redone today, such national and international potentials for "Melanesian warfare" would undoubtedly take a larger profile. The conflictual relation between state control and local identity—which the chapter historicizes and ultimately makes contemporary—looms increasingly large in Melanesia. So too, collective violence in Melanesia is increasingly impacted by the growth of criminal gangs of raskols, on the one hand, and local disgruntlement against multinational logging or mining corporations, on the other.[1] Meanwhile, on the other side of this relationship, foreign corporate interests affiliate increasingly with national governments. As parts of a larger power structure, these partners of financial convenience can find themselves in mutual opposition to elevated local desires for economic development and monetary compensation.

It might be tempting to consider such recent trends as separate from anthropologists' understanding of Melanesian warfare in its more "traditional" sense. To trade one of these perspectives in for the other, however, would be a mistake. If the ethnographic study of tribal conflict was narrow, it was richly attuned to local strategies, motives, and aspirations. These orientations have a key, continuing, and underappreciated legacy for contemporary conflicts in many if not most parts of Melanesia. By contrast, the current emphasis on national and multinational interests, local rebellions, and movements of resistance—as deeply important as these certainly are—has its own shortcomings. Documented especially by journalists, political scientists, and sociologists, our understanding of these developments often lacks in cultural depth what it gains in economic and political scope. The goal is not to polarize a rich understanding of local cultural pasts against a thin understanding of more widespread political and economic tensions in the present. It is rather to combine the strengths of these perspectives: the local dispositions and deeper suppositions through which conflicts are pursued, and the wider forces that condition, cultivate, and constrain them. Apart from their inherent interest, the legacies of Melanesian warfare for the present are far from being history.

---

1. E.g., Goddard 1992, 1995; Dinnen 1997; Hyndman 1994.

In a world historical perspective, the indigenous populations of Melanesia have been among the last to be contacted and then pacified by Western colonial powers. Particularly true of hinterland areas and New Guinea, this circumstance has been due to Melanesia's geographical remoteness from European colonial powers and a dearth of resources that could be easily exploited during the colonial era (e.g., Bitterli 1989: chap. 7). This legacy has been reflected in Melanesia's relatively peripheral status in the global political economy until relatively recently.[2] One result of this situation is that indigenous warfare in Melanesia persisted longer than in many other world areas. In the process, warfare has been relatively accessible to detailed ethnographic study and has been of major concern to anthropologists of Melanesia as well as to Melanesians themselves. Accounts of armed conflict in interior New Guinea in particular have provided among the most detailed and comprehensive accounts of indigenous warfare from any world area. The resurgence or transformation of Melanesian warfare in some of these same areas in the postcolonial era makes this issue of continuing interest (see photo 15).

A wide range of social structural, ecological, political, and psychological theories have been adduced concerning Melanesian warfare. However, a critical review of this work brings several neglected features to light. First, the respective strengths and weaknesses of various theories have rarely been addressed beyond the assertion of singular criticisms and polar contrasts. Second, theories of Melanesian warfare have seldom been considered against historical trajectories of colonialism and postcolonialism. These trajectories are important: they have frequently provided the conditions if not the impetus for the ethnographic study of warfare itself. Third, and relatedly, Melanesian warfare over the last century and a half arguably includes conflicts between indigenes and whites as well as among Melanesians themselves, yet this dimension of collective conflict has seldom been addressed in studies of Melanesian warfare. The present essay has two interrelated objectives. On one hand, I assess the value and validity of various explana-

---

2. See Brookfield 1972; Brookfield with Hart 1971: chap. 8; contrast Wolf 1982; Wallerstein 1989.

tions of Melanesian warfare with respect to extant ethnographic data;
on the other, I assess the historical influences that have shaped these
anthropological perspectives and influenced their past and present trajectory.

Warfare

As collective armed conflict, warfare has been a topical focus of
Melanesian ethnography for over a century.[3] Particularly in the
British anthropological tradition, warfare is virtually intrinsic to
political organization, since political units have often been defined by
their ability to adjudicate internal conflict and cohere in hostility
against outsiders. As Langness (1972a:925) put it in the Melanesian
context, "The public affair most widely used by anthropologists to
define the largest polities has been warfare." As proposed further
below, this notion harbors Hobbesian assumptions that warfare is a
state of nature that must be overcome through societal contract. Such
assumptions have informed the study of Melanesian violence virtually to the present.[4]

Though such problems might lead one to dismiss the concept of
"warfare" altogether, this would too hastily throw out the ethnographic object of study as available in written sources. "Warfare" as an
ethnographic category has an antiquity that makes for fruitful historical and comparative analysis even as the concept seems narrow in the
context of more recent additions and embellishments—the proliferat-
ing dimensions of contemporary collective violence in Melanesia. With
this recognized caveat, the term "warfare" will be used as commonly
accepted by Melanesianists to denote collective armed conflict between
putatively autonomous political groups. Even within the strictures of
this definition, however, collective armed conflict between Melanesians and members of state polities—both colonial and postcolonial—
flirts with inclusion as "warfare." Acknowledging this, I consider published perspectives on Melanesian warfare from the precolonial,
colonial, and postcolonial eras, critically evaluating their strengths and
weaknesses and tracing their trajectory to the present. Of correspond-

---

3. E.g., Codrington 1890; Haddon 1891.
4. See key counterexamples to this generalization by Harrison 1989a, 1993.

ing importance are the cultural and theoretical suppositions through which physical violence is ethnographically reported, emphasized, or minimized.

Before the Anthropologists

Hundreds of years ago the country which is called New Guinea was shaded black on the map and called the Islands of the Bad People. (Beaver 1920:40)

Anthropological perspectives on warfare in Melanesia were first influenced by the violent interactions that quickly followed European discovery and exploration.[5] In contrast to romantic portrayals of neighboring Polynesia,[6] early images of Melanesia were more in accordance with Eurocentric projections prevalent since the Middle Ages: of barbarism, cannibalism, and monstrosity assumed to exist beyond the peripheries of civilization.[7] Melanesians were seen as "wild, cruel, black savages" (Beaver 1920:41, citing Janz 1605). It was even believed into the late nineteenth century by some that interior New Guinea might harbor humanoid races with webbed feet or tails.[8]

Beyond perceptions, reciprocating violence between Melanesians and whites was extremely common in nineteenth-century coastal Melanesia. In many if not most areas, reciprocating armed conflict followed quickly after initial tenuous contacts (e.g., Rodman and Cooper 1983). Violence was pronounced in both the sandalwood trade, from approximately 1830 to 1865 (Shineberg 1967), and the labor trade, in which more than 61,000 Melanesians from insular areas were taken for three- to five-year terms of plantation work in Fiji, New Caledonia, and especially Queensland between 1863 and 1911.[9] Mortality was high among Melanesians who toiled in the labor trade, and depopulation was greatly accentuated by epidemic diseases introduced by Euro-

---

5. E.g., Beaglehole 1968: chap. 3; Jack-Hinton 1969; Bennett 1987: chap. 5.
6. Cf. Bitterli 1989: chap. 7; Aldrich 1990:7ff.
7. Hodgen 1964; J. B. Friedman 1981; Bernheimer 1952; see Tuzin and Brown 1983.
8. E.g., Murray 1912:107; Beaver 1920:17; cf. Webster 1984:343–46.
9. Scarr 1967, Corris 1968, 1971, 1973; Wawn 1893; Rannie 1912.

peans.[10] To these deaths must be added the killing of Melanesians in the course of trading and recruiting activities; these were effectively outside the reach of official supervision until the last decade and a half of the nineteenth century.[11]

The alternation between violence and trade in the early colonial encounter melded easily with Melanesians' indigenous cycles of "gifts and blows" between adjacent political groups in many areas.[12] With the large-scale introduction of the repeating rifle, beginning in the 1860s, the terms of this relationship became more asymmetrical: legitimate control of violence was gradually ceded by Melanesians to Western intruders (see Shineberg 1971).

With the advent of formal colonial administration of Melanesia by British, French, German, and Dutch in the latter nineteenth century, European–Melanesian warfare developed in the stricter sense of collective and orchestrated conflict between political units (cf. Cooper 1983). Conflict typically progressed from reciprocated raids to more unilateral and asymmetric punitive expeditions by whites, which commonly entailed burning villages, shelling coastal settlements from man-of-war ships, and killing any enemy encountered. Such warfare was quite pronounced in German New Guinea, parts of the Solomon Islands, Vanuatu (New Hebrides), and particularly New Caledonia.[13] In parts of Vanuatu and especially the Solomon Islands, a virtual firestorm of internal Melanesian violence was fueled by large-scale introduction of guns as trade items.[14] In New Caledonia, the scale of Western violence became more quickly overwhelming and devastating for the indigenous population.[15]

In coastal West New Guinea, nineteenth-century warfare was characterized by endemic slave raids led by fire-armed forces of Islamicized "rajahs." These leaders were tacitly supported by Dutch policies of indirect rule, which vested political power in the vassal sultan of

---

10. E.g., Shlomowitz 1987, 1988; Firth 1983:155; Harrisson 1937:197–207, 261–80; Rivers 1922.

11. E.g., Harrisson 1937: chap. 4; Docker 1970; see Drost 1938; Dunbabin 1935; Paton 1913.

12. See D. Brown 1979; see Seligmann 1910: chaps. 9, 41; Wedgwood 1930.

13. Firth 1983; Harrisson 1937; Bennett 1987: chap. 5; Guiart 1983; Latham 1974; Priday 1944; Thompson and Adloff 1971; Aldrich 1990.

14. E.g., Keesing and Corris 1980; Zelenietz 1983; cf. Howe 1974.

15. Guiart 1983; Weitzman 1985.

Tidore and in his presumed local agents in West New Guinea.[16] In the Vogolkop Peninsula or "Bird's Head" region, indigenous leaders had long orchestrated the procurement and trade of Papuan slaves for valued cloths, articulating with southeast Asian trade further west (Miedema 1988a, b).

Even in Papua, where colonial control was, in relative terms, more benign, Lieutenant-Governor William MacGregor declared in 1898 at the end of his ten years in British New Guinea that "[a]s a matter of simple fact the administration has practically had to subdue by force almost every district now under control" (quoted in Griffin, Nelson, and Firth 1979:15–16). Accordingly, Baden-Powell's (1892:175–209) chapter account, titled "New Guinea Warfare," pertains during this period primarily to lethal confrontation between whites and Melanesians (cf. Mayo 1973). The imposition of colonial governance through violence is not exceptional on a world historical scale; as Anthony Giddens (1987:223) notes, "British armies were involved in fifty major colonial wars between 1803 and 1901."

Irrespective of whether armed conflict between Melanesians and whites was caused by one side or the other, the nineteenth-century Western attitude was generally that Melanesians were dangerous and bloodthirsty savages. The prevailing view is rendered succinctly in 1898 by Caley-Webster, who had explored extensively in insular Melanesia and along sections of the New Guinea coast.

> They are one and all cannibals, frightfully cruel and terribly treacherous. Headhunting seems to be their only occupation, and the practice of offering up human sacrifice on even the most trivial occasion prevails throughout. (1898:135)

The moral overtones of such assessment are clear. As enunciated by the trader Andrew Cheyne (1971 [1842]:53), "The Natives are extremely cruel, void of affection, and are truly wretches in every sense of the Word, degraded beyond the power of conception."

The European fascination as well as repulsion with such savagery

---

16. Bone 1964; van Baal, Galis, and Koentjaraningrat 1984:43f.; see Miklouho-Maclay 1874, 1881; Strachan 1888: chaps. 10–15.

rebounded upon the travel and adventure literature, which catered to such appetites. Hence, for random instance, a 1929 book—in fact a quite placid if not yawning depiction by Land Commissioner S. G. C. Knibbs of his time in the Solomons—entitled *The Savage Solomons as They Were and Are: A Record of a Head-Hunting People Gradually Emerging From a Life of Savage Cruelty and Bloody Customs, With a Description of Their Manners And Ways and of the Beauties and Potentialities of the Islands*. Such imagery moved like a shadow preceding colonial pacification through insular Melanesia to the coast of New Guinea and finally to its interior.

The cause of violence in nineteenth-century Melanesia was nonetheless a source of significant disagreement even among whites. Traders tended to attribute the cause of bloodshed to atrocities perpetrated by the Melanesians themselves, for example, the gratuitous killing and cannibalism of ships' crews. Along this reasoning, Europeans had little choice but to forcefully prevent and punitively respond to such wanton action.[17]

But this image of the ruthless Melanesian was strongly contested by pacifist missionaries, who countered it with the image of the savage European—that is, the unscrupulous and un-Christian labor recruiters and traders, who were the most pervasive conduits of nineteenth-century Western influence in insular Melanesia.[18] In the missionary perspective, Melanesian violence was a retaliatory response to the precipitating violence of uncouth Europeans, who brought trade goods, diseases, and guns, while taking profits, sexual favors, and Melanesian bodies and lives. Missionaries argued vehemently that Melanesians were not intrinsically hostile but undertook punitive revenge on Europeans after having themselves been subject to violent attack (e.g., Bishop Tyrrell, cited in Whiteman 1983:112).

Though influential among the scholarly and incipient anthropological audience, the missionary perspective was ultimately as one-sided as its unlettered counterpart, begging the dynamics of violence both within indigenous Melanesian cultures and in the Western encounter.[19] The difficulty of holding so tenaciously to the pacifist position was underscored by missionaries' own susceptibility to violent

---

17. E.g., Wawn 1893; Powell 1883:262ff.

18. E.g., Fison 1872–73; Inglis 1872; Macdonald 1878; Markham 1873; Palmer 1871; Paton 1913; Drost 1938; Dunbabin 1935; Miklouho-Maclay 1881.

19. E.g., Shineberg 1967: chap.14; cf., for Polynesia, Borofsky and Howard 1989:266.

intimidation and martyrdom at Melanesian hands and by their own ultimate recourse to armed response in many instances. Violent retaliation against Melanesians was undertaken by some of the most pacifist and pro-native missionaries, including Reverends James Chalmers,[20] John Paton,[21] and George Brown.[22]

In hindsight, the competing views of traders and missionaries can be seen as complementary dimensions of a reciprocating cycle of violence between insular Melanesians and Europeans in the nineteenth century. Traders and recruiters frequently did disregard Melanesian lives, but they were also themselves attacked by Melanesians in the latter's frequent desire to obtain trade goods, bodies, or heads for culinary/ceremonial purposes, or military glory. The cycle could be started by either side, and evidence could in many instances be interpreted variously to support the missionaries' or the traders' point of view. In current theoretical terms, it would take a good deal of a priori bias to uphold either a rigid Marxist accusation of unilateral colonial exploitation or an imperialist one of establishing law and order among wild indigenous peoples. The actual situation was more complex, demanding a reconsideration of anthropological evidence concerning nineteenth- and early-twentieth-century warfare in insular and coastal Melanesia.

Patterns of Precolonial Warfare: Insular Melanesia and Coastal New Guinea

Reconstructive accounts by contemporary anthropologists suggest indigenous warfare was quite prevalent in insular Melanesia and coastal New Guinea. Available information tends to be smoothed over and denuded of detail by nineteenth-century depictions or by the recesses of informant memories as jogged by twentieth-century anthropologists to recall distant events. This leads to generalized and "normative" accounts of warfare in insular and coastal Melanesia, with details limited to dramatic episodes of one or two particularly well-storied conflicts (which are often depicted in a way that puts the teller's own group in a favorable or victorious light). These tendencies notwithstanding, the weight of evidence suggests that precolonial war-

---

20. See Langmore 1974:28–31; Webster 1984:249–52.
21. See Harrisson 1937:174–82; Paton 1927.
22. See Powell 1883: chaps. 4–6, cf. Young 1977, 1980, 1989.

fare was common if not intense in at least parts of the following areas of insular Melanesia and coastal New Guinea:

the Admiralty Islands (e.g., Schwartz 1963; Moseley 1877; Parkinson 1907)

New Ireland (Bell 1934a, b; Clay 1986:192; Romilly 1886: chap. 3)

northern New Britain (e.g., Brown 1910: chap. 6; Parkinson 1907: 124ff., 263f., 401f.; Salisbury 1962:334f.; Powell 1883: chap. 4.; Chowning and Goodenough 1971:150–55, 158–61)

interior southern New Britain (Fenbury 1968)

Bougainville (e.g., Thurnwald 1910:115–29; Oliver 1955: chap. 12, 1971)

Choiseul Island (e.g., Scheffler 1964a, b, 1965:223–39)

New Georgia (e.g., Zelenietz 1983; Hocart 1931)

Malaita (e.g., Keesing 1985b; White 1983; Ivens 1927: chap. 14, 1930: chap. 10)

San Cristoval (e.g., Fox 1925: chap. 24)

Vanuatu [New Hebrides] (e.g., Rodman and Cooper 1983; Allen 1981, 1984; Deacon 1934: chap. 8; Guiart 1956:79–85, 94–103; Layard 1942: chap. 23; Humphreys 1926:54–60, 148–50; Harrisson 1937)

New Caledonia (e.g., Leenhardt 1930: chap. 3; Guiart 1963a; Cheyne 1971 [1842]:105–6 ; Ta'unga 1968, 1982; see Douglas 1992

Fiji (e.g., Clunie 1977; Vayda 1976; Sahlins 1983, 1990)

The same is true on and near the New Guinea coast, for example, concerning warfare for:

parts of coastal West New Guinea (e.g., Strachan 1888: chaps. 10–15; Redlich 1876; Miklouho-Maclay 1874; Webster 1984: 120, chap. 7)

parts of the New Guinea north coast (e.g., Lipset 1985, 1997; Moresby 1876:273f.; Webster 1984:189–90; Lutkehaus 1984)

the north Papuan coast (Williams 1930: chap. 11)

the Massim (e.g., Seligmann 1910: chaps. 41, 42; MacIntyre 1983; Malinowski 1920; Roheim 1946)

the Port Moresby area of the New Guinea south coast (e.g., Seligmann 1910: chap. 9; Chalmers 1887; Abel 1902)

Finally, for the south New Guinea coast, warfare in association with head-hunting was particularly pronounced and well documented among:

the Purari [Namau] (Williams 1924: chap. 9; Maher 1961: chap. 2, 1967; Holmes 1924: chap. 21)

the Kiwai (Landtman 1927: chap. 9; 1917: chap. 13; Riley 1925: chap. 22)

the Trans-Fly peoples (Williams 1936: chap. 15; Beaver 1920: chaps. 6–9)

the Marind-anim (van Baal 1966: chap. 12; Haddon 1891; Wirz 1933; Ernst 1979)

the Kolopom (Serpenti 1966, 1977)

the Jacquai (Boelaars 1981: chaps. 9–12)

the Asmat (Zegwaard 1959; cf. Eyde 1967)

There are a few areas of coastal Melanesia where warfare is reported to have been relatively infrequent and unimportant, such as parts of the northeast New Guinea coast[23] and northeastern Guadalcanal (Hogbin 1934:246)—though in the latter case head-hunting for ritual purposes was also noted. And it can be difficult to distinguish among (1) areas where warfare might have been infrequent, formalized, or nonintensive; (2) areas in which warfare was largely a product of European presence; or (3) areas where there has been little anthropological research at all or in which postpacification research does not significantly address the topic of preceding warfare. Conversely, given that warfare tends to be sporadic, it is difficult to know if early accounts based on quite short experience are a reliable guide to more general patterns in the area.

All this notwithstanding, the dominant sense one gets from available accounts, primary ones as well as contemporary reconstructions, is that warfare was indeed quite prominent if not endemic in most coastal and insular areas of Melanesia at the time these regions were first regularly contacted by Europeans. In this respect, one is inclined to agree with Sillitoe's (1978:252) more general assessment

---

23. E.g., Moresby 1876:292; Jenness and Ballantyne 1920: chap. 7; Webster 1984.

that warfare was a commonplace feature of life throughout Melanesia, and that it occurred regularly in a large number of different societies and in a bewildering variety of cultural guises and social contexts.

As Chowning (1977:42) and many others have noted, the generally small scale of Melanesian polities and the shifting characteristics of competitively achieved Melanesian leadership led easily to violent clashes within and between unstable political units (though ranked leadership hierarchies were common in eastern Melanesia).[24] Accordingly, there were great variations in the local characteristics and intensity of warfare in coastal/insular Melanesia; traders and missionaries frequently noted just such variations.

In most coastal areas of Melanesia, there was significant demarcation between local groups or settlements that were allies or enemies of one another. In the course of conflict, large-scale slaughter of enemy villagers sometimes occurred, while in others, ritualized battle led to few or no casualties and to prolonged political and military standoffs. In most cases, however, attacking forces in coastal areas of precolonial Melanesia mounted surprise strikes with the purpose of avenging past losses. The goal of most such raiding parties was to capture and/or kill one or more enemies in retribution for previous killing. It was usually of little consequence if the person(s) were men, women, or children. Frequently, the raiders would try to surprise their target village or obtain victims unaware on its periphery. Ideally a victim could be obtained without raising the general alarm, thus allowing the raiders to return successfully to their own territory without resistance. In many cases, the killing of a single victim by the attacking force (without themselves sustaining a loss) was tantamount to a "victory." The killing of several or even a large number of enemy victims might occur on those rarer occasions when circumstances permitted, for instance, when a large surprise strike was organized, or when political and military asymmetries grew to the point where a ritual standoff could be transformed into a major route.

24. One must be careful not to overgeneralize the competitive individualism of Melanesian leadership (e.g., Sahlins 1963). Particularly in insular Melanesia, hereditary chiefdomship and rank societies were also important, and in many parts of Melanesia control of ritual or magical knowledge was highly salient to leadership (see Douglas 1979; Chowning 1979; Lindstrom 1984; Hau'ofa 1983; Godelier 1982, 1986; Sahlins 1990; Vayda 1976).

Many coastal groups extended the treatment for enemies to any stranger who was sighted unarmed or unprotected. Obviously, this practice boded particularly ill for shipwrecked sailors and for Westerners who found themselves too far away from their ship or unarmed away from their compatriots. In many areas of coastal and insular Melanesia, the fate of persons captured or killed was decapitation or cannibalism. Head-hunting was particularly developed along the New Guinea south coast, in the middle Sepik of north New Guinea, and in much of the Solomon Islands. Cannibalism in different permutations was widespread, being practiced:

> along the New Guinea gulf coast (excepting the Elema), the south coast of Papua, and the southern Massim (passim and Seligmann 1910: chaps. 9, 41, 42)
> large sections of the north Papuan coast (Williams 1930:171ff.)
> parts of the northeast New Guinea coast (Webster 1984:198)
> the Admiralty Islands (Lewis 1945 [1932]:38; Romilly 1886:61; Webster 1984:233f.)
> northern New Britain (G. Brown 1910: chap. 5; Powell 1883:90ff.)
> New Ireland (Romilly 1886: chap. 3; Bell 1934a; Powdermaker 1931:28)
> many parts of the Solomon Islands (e.g., Codrington 1891:343; Ivens 1927: chap. 14, 1930: chap. 10; Fox 1925: chap. 24; Zelenietz 1983)
> northern New Hebrides (e.g., Codrington 1891:343f.; Layard 1942: chap. 23)
> large areas of New Caledonia (Leenhardt 1930:41; Ta'unga 1982)
> Fiji (Fison 1907:xxxvi–xlv; Sahlins 1983; Clunie 1977)

In interior New Guinea, cannibalism occurred particularly in:

> the southeast highlands (Berndt 1962, 1971; Gillison 1983; Lindenbaum 1979)
> parts of northeast New Guinea and the Sepik (Harrison 1993: 27–28; Firth 1983:99; Reed 1943:53–54; cf. Bateson 1936:137ff.; D'Amato 1979)
> the Strickland-Bosavi area (Kelly 1976; Schieffelin 1976; Knauft 1985a; cf. A. J. Strathern 1982a)
> the Star Mountains of West New Guinea (Koch 1974)

ritually in parts of the Mt. Ok area (Poole 1983; see more generally,
Brown and Tuzin 1983)

In many areas, head-hunting and cannibalism were in complementary distribution; where one was prominent, the other was often
unemphasized or absent. However, both practices appear developed
among groups such as the Purari of the New Guinea south coast, the
Avatip of the Sepik, and in parts of the Solomon Islands.[25] In some
cases, ritual cannibalism of only selected body parts was practiced; in
others whole-body cannibalism was the norm; and, in a few cases in
insular Melanesia, indigenous flesh-markets existed. Cannibalism or
head-hunting had strong ritual and cosmological significance in many
of the societies that practiced it, with the incorporation of enemies' life
force promoting strength and well-being, spiritual rejuvenation,
and/or initiatory rebirth. In other cases, cannibalism was considered
more as a culinary treat or simply as a means of ravaging the homicidal
trophy. Like so many other Melanesian customs, the treatment of slain
enemies could be subject to structural permutation or what Schwartz
(1975) has called "ethnic totemism" between groups: polar oppositions
in certain key customs became markers of local cultural identity and
interethnic differentiation. Hence, there could be significant variations
in emphasis, for example, with some groups conspicuously abstaining
in a region where cannibalism or head-hunting was otherwise avidly
practiced.[26]

The emotional spirit of warriorhood in insular Melanesia is captured well by Geza Roheim (1946:227) in chants from Normandy Island,
where torture and cannibalism of victims were highly relished.[27] The
following chant, which metaphorically links the warrior with a wasp,
was sung into the navel of young men to make them good fighters.[28]

Wasp gaping. Where Ho! Wasp gaping in its gully.
Wasp gaping. Wasp gaped there. I became a wasp gaping.

---

25. See, respectively, F. E. Williams 1924: chap. 9; Harrison 1993:27–28; Codrington
1891:343ff.

26. For instance, see Layard (1942:619) concerning Malekula, and Williams (1940:90)
concerning Elema of the New Guinea south coast.

27. Roheim 1946:231f.; cf. Bromilow 1929:97.

28. The following is a free translation from Roheim's morphemically translated
original.

*Wasp angry with them. My anger, Wasp their muddy, my stomach
muddy. His mind gets boiling, inside became muddy. Anger turns
even to kin.*

*My thinking turns; war thoughts get angry for them.
My mind becomes a whirlpool. Liver thoughts turning.
My victim, bald. My victim, big woman. My victim, children.*

As here reflected, precolonial warriorhood in coastal areas of Melanesia archetypally combined a gushing sense of anger, individual and collective embracement of rage, and the projection of violence onto an external object as negative Other against which self and group are victoriously defined. Corresponding is the joy and prestige associated with the successful taking of enemy life.

*My man, bald one; his liver I take back. Strong thoughts his.
His liver I roll it up. His leg I roll it up.
His image I roll it up. His bones I roll it up.
His liver gets thin. His liver broken.
Thoughts become swinging to and fro.
My leg sole, they bring back. My hand palm, fat.*

(Roheim 1946:227)

In many cases, war cults had as a key feature the emotional dissociation and transfiguration of the warrior into a virulent persona of enragement, with complementary symbolic transformations reducing the enemy to fearful passivity, open to attack and dismemberment (cf. Harrison 1989a:589; 1993).

That such sentiments and practices were alien to Western sensibilities may seem so obvious as to need little explanation. However, the particular horror of Melanesian practices to whites was based on key underlying differences in European and Melanesian cultural orientations to violence. European valuation of the free and autonomous individual was directly at odds with Melanesian assumptions of collective identity and corollary beliefs that retribution was justified against any enemy, regardless if the person had initiated previous violence against one's own people. Likewise, Victorian European ideals of male honor, courage, and propriety in war were particularly inimical to Melanesian guerrilla tactics of hit-and-run, killing women and children, eulogizing deeds that entailed little risk, and taking delight in the dismemberment and/or sufferings of enemy victims. That these practices could take place in a context that seemed to Europeans devoid of larger military, political, or sometimes even economic objectives made them seem particularly inhuman and threatening. On the other side, what was cowardly and savage to Europeans was to Melanesians both cosmologically and strategically rational—maximizing the physical and emotional cost to one's enemy, asserting a sense of utter domination, disregard, and cultural/cosmological superiority, and minimizing the cost to one's own side.[29] This difference in nineteenth-century perspective was of course particularly threatening to Westerners when they did not themselves have the armaments or manpower to subjugate Melanesians in warfare.

The failure of early accounts to comprehend Melanesian warfare is not surprising given European intellectual dispositions and pragmatic concern with their own dominion over native populations. Paramount here were the commercial entrepreneurs, who wanted to appropriate Melanesian material resources and bodies, and the Christian missionaries, who wanted to appropriate Melanesian souls. Of their competing views, previously discussed, it was the more educated, liberal, and well-published perspective of the pacifist missionaries that exerted greatest influence in the latter nineteenth century and which became paramount toward the end of this period; their books, pamphlets, and sermons reached significant elements of the churchgoing population in Australia and England, and their publications were both much more numerous and much more respected than those of the South Pacific traders, labor recruiters, and beachcombers.[30] As discussed previously, the preponderant tendency in missionary accounts was to minimize and downplay the extent of violence in "traditional" Melanesian societies while emphasizing the violence visited upon Melanesians by traders and labor recruiters or "blackbirders."[31] This viewpoint had a significant impact on the developing scholarly community in England from which Melanesian ethnology emerged in the late nineteenth century.

---

29. One might note by comparison Europeans' own increasing recourse to maximal destruction, killing of innocents, torture, and ultimate genocide in subsequent decades during World War I and particularly World War II.

30. Shineberg 1967:208–9; Tippett 1956:101–9.

31. Cf. Macdonald 1878; Steel 1880; Fison 1871, 1872–73.

Warfare in Early Melanesian Ethnography

In several respects, mission perspectives found a natural complement in the assumptions of Victorian anthropology, viz., that cultural evolution occurred through social progress and moral improvement (see Stocking 1987). South Pacific missionaries and early British ethnologists shared an Enlightenment vision of savages as civilized people in the rough, full of potential but yet to experience higher cultural advance (Stocking 1987; cf. Langmore 1989: chap. 5). Thus, while early Melanesian survey ethnologists such as A. C. Haddon, W. H. R. Rivers, and A. B. Lewis studied the slow processes of diffusion that naturally informed evolutionary change, missionaries worked as change agents to catapult their subjects in moral and social advancement. These objectives were seen as different ends of a single developmental continuum; hence the easy linkage between them by early Melanesian missionary-anthropologists such as R. H. Codrington (1891).

As Whiteman (1983:110) notes, a second theme common to both early anthropology and missionization in Melanesia was the searching out and "salvaging" of natives who were largely "untouched" by previous contact. Ethnologists wanted to preserve such persons for their cultural knowledge, while missionaries wanted to preserve them for their authentic conversion to Christianity. From both perspectives, the influence of Western commercial interests upon "natives" was seen as contaminating and unfortunate, if not evil. Scholars and missionaries thus joined hands in attacking the excesses of labor recruiters and traders, and both tended to ally with colonial administrators in promoting what were seen as more civilized means of controlling native peoples, that is, by formal governance and spiritual enlightenment.[32]

Like the missions, most early scholarship concerning Melanesian societies emphasized indigenous customs that countered the dark emphasis on "native savagery." In this context, accounts of Melanesian warfare and violence are quite noticeable by their cursory treatment and relative absence in the large early compendiums of ethnography by Codrington (1891), Rivers (1914), and Haddon.[33] This lack of emphasis on warfare is thrown into relief by the extensive and often rich documentation in these works—running to hundreds of pages—

---

32. E.g., Langmore 1989: chap. 9; Romilly 1886:242; MacGregor 1897a: chap. 15; Rivers 1922.

33. E.g., Haddon 1897, 1901–35, 1920; Haddon and Wilken 1904.

concerning social organization, religion, material culture, and many other topics. Conversely, it is as disembodied material artifacts that warfare is most frequently considered in these works, viz., physical description and sometimes elaborate drawings or plates of weapons and related paraphernalia, especially as objects of technical sophistication or aesthetic beauty.[34] By contrast, little mention is made of the social context of weapon use and much less still of the political, psychological, and social or religious features of warfare, either in general or in specific cases.[35]

Certainly some of the downplaying and/or neglect of indigenous warfare during this early ethnographic period was a salutary caution, particularly with respect to insular Melanesia. Dependable information on violence was scarce in a climate of rumor and story. Not only were warfare practices difficult if not unethical to observe directly, but ethnologists tended for their own safety to operate out of Western outposts that had been rendered at least nominally peaceful through previous contact and pacification. Further, the *Notes and Queries* style of early ethnography promulgated by A. C. Haddon—which was based on lists of questions about disparate customs—left treatment of many topics, including warfare, as synoptic, conceptually isolated, and unelaborated. Finally, the relative omission of indigenous warfare in scholarly accounts could be a tacit safeguard against undue military response on the part of colonial authorities.

These caveats notwithstanding, the neglect of warfare in the published Melanesian ethnography from 1890 to the late 1920s is striking

---

34. E.g., Codrington 1891:304–13, cf. 1890; Rivers 1914 (1):329f., MacGregor 1897a: chap. 9; Comrie 1877:112; Haddon 1910, 1912, 1923; Hugel 1906, 1908; Edge-Partington 1902, 1906; Riley 1923; Lewis 1945 [1932]:104–16.

35. Among the greatest exceptions to this tendency are chapter-length accounts of warfare along the Papuan coast and the southern Massim compiled by C. G. Seligmann (1910: chaps. 9, 41, 42), including material from Abel (1902) and Chalmers (1887; cf. also Fox 1925: chap. 24 for the Solomon Islands). Landtman's Kiwai folktales volume (1917: chap. 13) contains rich indigenous views of precolonial warfare, including intriguing case stories of the politics of ethnic encroachment on neighboring "bushmen" and the dynamics of intersettlement rivalry and displacement among Kiwai themselves. Buried in a large volume of narratives, this information has been largely neglected by scholars (cf. Landtman 1970 [1927]). Other scattered information on Melanesian warfare gathered during the 1900s through 1920s includes an article by Hocart (1931) and monograph chapters by Williamson (1912: chap. 11), Ivens (1927: chap. 14, 1930: chap. 10), Fox (1925: chap. 24), Williams (1924: chap. 9), Riley (1925: chap. 22), Holmes (1924: chap. 21), Brown (1910: chap. 6), and Jenness and Ballantyne (1920:82–89). One of the earliest case-specific contributions is by Haddon (1891; cf. 1908).

given the high visibility of violence in less scholarly accounts, the rich ethnography of this period concerning many other indigenous practices, and the general agreement among contemporary Melanesianists that precolonial violence was endemic and still smoldering if not active in much of the region.[36] In this regard, anthropologists as well as missionaries carried on the lettered tradition of counteracting the assertions of traders and labor recruiters in Melanesia. Bitterli (1989:177) suggests, "The South Sea missionaries of the nineteenth century deserve credit for taking the islanders' side against most of the excessively ruthless commercial or political intervention by Americans and Europeans."

This opposition eventually resulted in governmental restriction of labor recruiting in eastern Melanesia and virtual preclusion of it in Papua, where regulations also effectively restricted the activities of traders and planters. Though in ways self-interested, the missionaries in particular were influential in reducing the level of violence directed against Melanesians by whites. As Lewis (1945 [1932]:33) puts it, "missionaries have always stood between the natives and unjust aggression on the part of certain European elements . . ." The tendency of missionary and early ethnology accounts to minimize the extent and intensity of indigenous Melanesian warfare in their published works must be understood with this important countervailing factor in mind.

The Rational Savage: Classic Functionalism and the Problem of Social Order

The rationalist defense of the primitive became more clearly enunciated in anthropology with the rise of Malinowskian functionalism and

---

36. Perhaps the most intensely studied instance of indigenous Melanesian warfare during the nineteenth century is the exception that illuminates the rule: the raids of the Marind-anim across the New Guinea border from Dutch into British New Guinea (see Haddon 1891; MacGregor 1893, 1897b; Murray 1912:83–86; cf. Wirz 1933; van Baal 1966: chap. 12). As reflected in colonial reports and the writings of explorers such as Strachan (1888:130–34, chap. 3), it was the international boundary preventing British retaliation against the Marind that gave British and Australians both the opportunity and the impetus to document Marind predations into English colonial territory. Gaining information about Marind raids was important to English-speakers both to pressure Dutch authorities into action and to convince the British that greater imperial expenditures were necessary—as Australians had long been insisting. Where indigenous raiding was not seen as a pestilence safeguarded by an international boundary, it was either left on its own or quelled with less ink spilled but more blood.

Radcliffe-Brown's structural-functionalism.[37] These theoretical approaches were strongly influential and indeed preeminent in the English-language ethnography of Melanesia from about 1920 through the 1950s. In the early functionalist perspective, indigenous warfare was rational and purposeful, limited in its disruption and actually therapeutic in the orderly management of disputes and the integration of society. By contrast, the blood, emotion, and destruction of warfare were greatly downplayed. Neither were violence or warfare in the colonial encounter given theoretical or analytic examination; the focus was rather on the ordered course of conflict management and resolution. Elizabeth Colson's acknowledgment of this functionalist legacy in the African context rings true for Melanesia as well.

> In the past, and probably for good reasons, including the protection of human subjects, we downplayed the violence, cruelty, and unhappiness existing in the areas where we worked. One reason may have been the belief that such actions were momentary departures from cultural norms that generated long-term harmony, but whatever the reason, by doing so, we falsified the record. (1989:3)

The tendency to downplay indigenous violence is clearly evident in Wedgwood's influential discussion of Melanesian warfare in the first issue of *Oceania* (1930). Whereas both Malinowski (1920, 1926) and Radcliffe-Brown (1922:84f., 133ff.) had considered the problem of political conflict as a functional one, it was Wedgwood—having had contact with both men early in her career (Elkin 1956:174)—who systematically applied these concerns to the comparative study of Melanesian warfare.[38] Reviewing a significant portion of the existing scholarly literature, mostly from insular Melanesia, Wedgwood fitted the scattered accounts of conflict into a coherent functional model in which warfare served to integrate the fighting community and intensify kinship. Warfare was correspondingly suggested to diminish potential disruption to the larger society so that "the wider unity is never lost sight of" (Wedgwood 1930:32).

In selectively portraying various warfare rules and restrictions, Wedgwood did insightfully foreground the connection between con-

---

37. E.g., Malinowski 1926, 1948; Radcliffe-Brown 1948, 1952.
38. See Wedgwood 1930; Lutkehaus 1995; cf. Malinowski 1920, 1926; Radcliffe-Brown 1922:84f., 133ff.; see Elkin 1956:174.

flict severity and social distance, on the one hand, and the inverse if somewhat tautological relationship between conflict regulation and superordinate political control, on the other. More specifically, she divided warfare into a series of escalating conflict types related to increasingly inclusive units of political membership. The closer the kin, the smaller the size of opposing groups, the more informal the conflict, and the less important it was likely to be. Between persons who were more distantly related or were unrelated, conflict became less uncontrolled, the groups larger, and the risk of violence and the need to control it both greater.[39]

Countering her structural insights is Wedgwood's relegation of war to a rational and impersonal handmaiden of political structure. War as she paints it is emotionally bloodless and devoid of spiritual, much less cultural, significance or motivation. Rather, the overarching hand of society allows in warfare a cathartic expression of basic competitive anger and aggression: "The expression of . . . anger, in fighting, relieved it; the discomfort and irritation which was disquieting the community was brought to an end, and thus a sense of well-being was restored" (1930:33). This fits uneasily with dominant patterns of reciprocating blood revenge and continuing retaliation in Melanesian warfare. However, Wedgwood's echoing of the liberal missionary and rationalist perspective does lead her to recognize, in passing, the violence of European impact (33). Her account is further well-intentioned in implying that use of colonial force against indigenous populations is frequently needless or unwarranted.

One of Wedgwood's more lasting legacies was her selective emphasis on highly formalized or ritualized battles that lead to conflict mediation and peace-making (see photo 15). Ritualized confrontations that ended in peace-making or feasting were not uncommon in Melanesia. And they became if anything more accentuated under conditions of colonial pacification, which tended to preclude more unrestrained forms of conflict. In the precolonial era, however, formalized encounters could also easily be a prelude to more destructive engagements, as some of the best data on New Guinea highlands warfare attests.[40] Many

---

39. This analytic scheme has frequently been adopted by Melanesianists to foreground the relationship between warfare types and social structural or kinship relations, and is reflected, for instance, in classic monographs on New Guinea highlands warfare by Koch (1974) and Meggitt (1977).

40. E.g., Meggitt 1977; Heider 1979.

of Wedgwood's sources in fact document a continuum if not a direct escalation from more restrained to more unrestrained warfare. Like all social action, warfare can be said to be "regulated" in the sense that it is socioculturally constituted and organized, but this regulation need imply neither that armed conflict is infrequent nor that it is low in casualty rates.

Mission influence and the Rivers–Haddon style of ethnography themselves predisposed primary accounts that emphasized topical synopsis and generalized description of rights, rules, and obligations. These descriptions then appeared to fit naturally with functional interpretations, which could then be viewed as independently confirmed by the ethnographic account. A typical example is C. B. Humphreys's (1926) little book on the southern New Hebrides; its sparse synopsis of warfare types and political institutions makes conflict almost intrinsically well-organized and politically neat. Humphreys gives little attention to case accounts of violence or to its social ramifications, but forwards cryptic rules of preparation, engagement, and peace-making. As a result, "the actual fighting" on Tanna becomes "more or less perfunctory" despite the fact that "it seems to have been going on pretty constantly in the old days" including looting of villages, destruction of gardens, and significant loss of life (1926:58, 59).[41] Guiart's (1956) more critical perspective reveals a remarkably tumultuous Tannese political history of rivalry, disruption, and violent displacement over a century and a half.

As Oliver (1989:I:471) notes generally for Melanesia, "battles intended to be game-like often ended up as exterminating ones." For instance, Wedgwood (1930:15) cites Romilly's (1886: chap. 3) eyewitness account of an indigenous battle on the New Ireland coast, emphasizing that the intruders were given a fair chance to embark from their canoes, that enemy fighters were ranged in lines of formal opposition, and that harangues were delivered and followed by the fighting of individual duels. What is neglected is the fervency and scale of unrestrained hostility that follows these preliminaries, including a full-scale rout and death-dealing pursuit of one side of several hundred warriors, glorification in the dismemberment of the dead bodies, and a quite fer-

---

41. Perhaps the most ethnographically explicit and deeply revealing elaboration of Wedgwood's thesis during this period was published as chapter 23 in Layard's massive 1942 monograph *Stone Men of Malekula*, based on fieldwork conducted in 1914–15 on the Small Islands off the coast of Malekula in Vanuatu.

vent cannibal feast. By contrast, New Ireland warfare is reduced by Wedgwood upon reconsideration to "a grand sort of barbarous Homeric scolding match" (1930:16, citing Paton 1907:93, 137).

Though the dynamics of political alliance configuration vary in the many cases discussed by Wedgwood, the precolonial tendency for formalized encounters to later devolve into more unrestrained war is evident in many if not most of the specific primary accounts she draws upon.[42] In some cases large numbers of dead could be carried away even in continuing "rule-governed" encounters.[43] Fox (1925:305–6) states for San Cristoval that rule-governed warfare on a regular battleground was crosscut by "sudden temporary war" in which "everyone was killed and eaten if possible." Contractual death alliance and deception were common, and in one case "400 bushmen were killed by the people of Ubuna and Tawaatana in an ambush to which they had been led by treachery" (311). None of this denies the presence and significance of rule-governed engagements in many Melanesian societies, but it does underscore the functionalist gloss on the extent and intensity of precolonial violence.

The functionalist underpinnings of early accounts of warfare by Melanesian anthropologists are perhaps best exemplified in Malinowski's article on Trobriand warfare, cited by Wedgwood in support of her thesis. Beginning with the formalized call to arms and the clearing of a battleground, Malinowski describes Trobriand fighting in which opponents ranged themselves in lines 30 to 50 meters apart and threw spears at each other (1920:11). When one party became overmatched, however,

> the road to its villages was open, and the enemy would rush on killing men, women, and children indiscriminately, burning the village and destroying the trees. The only remedy for the defeated party was to abandon their villages and fly for life into another district. (1920:11)

Rather than giving credence to this destructive reality, Malinowski continues directly with the non sequitur that defenseless victims were

---

42. E.g., Fox 1925: chap. 24; Thurnwald 1910; Malinowski 1920; Parkinson 1907; Romilly 1886; Powell 1883; Humphreys 1926.

43. E.g., Cheyne 1971:105–6 [1842].

allowed to escape and that the warfare was thus "lenient and conventional."[44]

Colonial pacification itself could encourage the staging of formal display in lieu of more unrestrained combat. F. E. Williams (1930:31) describes in his study of the north Papuan Orokaiva how a period of violent Western pacification forced indigenous warfare to give way to formal and ritualized displays of aggression.[45] Under such conditions, functional assessments of "controlled" indigenous conflict dovetailed neatly if unadmittedly with the imposition of colonial law and order itself.

In general, information on Melanesian warfare during the 1920s, 1930s, and 1940s followed the early lead of Seligmann, Haddon, and Rivers in being descriptive and largely atheoretical, often buried in large monographs, and backgrounded relative to issues such as social organization and religion.[46] The desire to safeguard indigenous populations from undue interference was likely a continuing subtext of such treatment. In more extreme accounts, such as Malinowski's (1941) synthesis, indigenous violence in insular Melanesia is deemed to have been so divorced from large-scale violence as to exclude it from being considered "warfare" at all. Using a definition of warfare as "an armed contest between two independent political units, by means of organized military force, in the pursuit of a tribal or national policy," Malinowski continues:

---

44. A similar bias regarding Kiriwina war is evident in Sidney Ray's editing for publication of a governmental dispatch by Le Hunte (Le Hunte 1901); the summary provides a detailed account of a Kiriwina peace-making ceremony but makes no mention of the preceding warfare.

45. Cf. Newton 1983; see Young 1971.

46. The most well-known other papers on Melanesian warfare from this period are perhaps those by Fortune (1939) on Arapesh warfare and discussion of headhunting in south coastal New Guinea by Williams (1936: chap. 15, 1924: chaps. 9, 17; cf. Holmes 1924: chap. 21), Landtman (1927: chap. 9; cf. Riley 1925: chap. 22); Wirz (1933; cf. 1922–25, cf. Haddon 1891), and van der Kroef (1952). Accounts of warfare in other parts of Melanesia during this period include articles or chapters by Bell (1934a, b) for the Tanga (off the New Ireland coast), Hocart (1931) for Eddystone Island (Solomon Islands), Fox (1925: chap. 24) for San Cristoval, Hopkins (1928) and the missionary Ivens (1927: chap. 14, 1930: chap. 10) for Malaita, Leenhardt (1930:39–45) for New Caledonia, Williams (1930: chap. 9) for the Orokaiva, Jenness and Ballantyne (1920:82–89) for the northern D'Entrecasteaux, G. Brown (1910: chaps. 5, 6) for northern New Britain, and Deacon (1934: chap. 8), as edited by Wedgwood, for Malekula. During this period, coastal and insular Melanesia was already pacified, while the ethnography of the interior of New Guinea was just beginning in earnest and not yet widely published. There was little theoretical advancement in the study of Melanesian warfare during this time.

It is necessary to remember that organized fighting at higher stages of savagery or barbarism does not always present this politically significant character. Most of the fighting at this stage belongs to an interesting, highly complicated, and somewhat exotic type: raids for head-hunting, for cannibal feasts for victims of human sacrifice to tribal gods. Space does not allow me to enter more fully into the analysis of this type of fighting. Suffice it to say that it is not cognate to warfare, for it is devoid of any political relevancy; nor can it be considered as any systematic pursuit of intertribal policy. (1941:538)

Beneath such atheoreticism lay the assumption that, in fact, "tribal warfare" constituted a conflictual adjustment within wider schemes of societal organization. This orientation is implicit in the organizational format of monographs that topicalize warfare as an aspect of law and order. Thus, one finds the intrepid ethnographer F. E. Williams (1930:161) having to note apologetically that "Although the title of this chapter is warfare, the following pages will deal with indiscriminate fighting."

During the 1940s, Europeans and Australians were preoccupied with their own world war. Few Melanesian warfare studies were published during this period, but White and Lindstrom (1989) have produced an important volume on Melanesian recollections of World War II.[47]

Taken collectively, anthropologists' accounts of Melanesian warfare through about 1955 tended to protect populations from undue interference while also echoing the larger paternalism of the colonial order. First, collective violence was taken as functional in the establishment and maintenance of social order. Second, neither indigenous nor colonial violence was criticized openly or assessed as being particularly bloody. And third, both indigenous violence and that of the colonial encounter were viewed as small and separate topical niches, neither having much impact or legacy in the ethnographic present.

---

47. The exceptions, which tend to be descriptive, include accounts published by Fortune (1947a, b, cf. 1960) and Vicedom and Tischner (1943–48 vol.2:140–51) on New Guinea highlands warfare on the basis of mid-1930s field experiences, and a wonderful paper by Roheim (1946) on Normanby Island war chants and mythology based on fieldwork done in 1930. Roheim's Normanby Island notes have been acquired by the Melanesian archives at the University of California at San Diego and contain further rich information.

Structure, Function, and Political Economy in the Study of New Guinea Highlands Warfare

The opening of the New Guinea highlands to Western contact in the 1930s through 1950s was particularly relevant for the anthropological study of Melanesian warfare. Although colonial rule was established by lethal force and enforced by threats of imprisonment and forced labor, a general state of warfare between whites and highlanders did not ensue. Several factors combined to produce a relatively brief and relatively nonviolent "pacification" of one of the larger and latest-contacted indigenous populations on earth. Salient elements of this pacification included (1) the capacity of sophisticated mid-twentieth-century rifles to put the control of lethal violence almost entirely in the hands of small Western exploratory patrols; (2) the ability and willingness of Westerners to bring in large quantities of trade goods, such as steel axes and pearlshells, that were coveted by indigenous peoples; and (3) the pressure of Commonwealth liberalism and international demands for "native policies" that were considered progressive and conducive to later decolonization.[48] Highlanders *were* forced to "discover the gun," as Paula Brown (1995: chap. 4) suggests, and they suffered multiple deaths in a number of violent clashes with armed exploratory patrols (see Connolly and Anderson 1987). But relative to indigenous populations in North America, South America, Africa, Southeast Asia, and other parts of Oceania, the percentage of highlanders who died in the colonial encounter was low, the duration of active colonial control was relatively short—in many cases, from the 1950s to the 1970s—and the amount of land alienated from indigenous use was relatively small.

The lateness of colonial pacification combined with Australian and indeed worldwide scholarly fascination to encourage intensive anthropological study of New Guinea highlanders—including their patterns of warfare—at early stages of outside influence. Dovetailing with this circumstance, the aura of wealth, authority, and firepower that devolved from whites' first contacts with highlanders lent early ethnographers a certain immunity from being attacked themselves, even when they worked unarmed in areas only recently or partially pacified. As a result, professional anthropologists had a special opportunity to investigate practices such as indigenous warfare in the midst of and in some cases before pacification. Just as important, this research took

---

48. See Connolly and Anderson 1987; Nelson 1982.

TABLE 1. Publications on Melanesian Warfare by Anthropologists (after Ferguson and Farragher 1988:346–57)

1890s	3	1910s	4	1930s	8	1950–54	2	1960s	35	1980–86	30
1900s	4	1920s	2	1940s	2	1955–59	14	1970s	66		

place in a climate not rife with large-scale lethal combat between indigenous population and agents of colonialism themselves. The more complete accounts of Melanesian warfare from this period provide some of the best information on tribal fighting available from any world ethnographic area.

Collectively, these works reveal an intensity and ferocity of indigenous violence in interior New Guinea that was almost unimagined—both ethnographically and theoretically—in previous work by professional Melanesianists. This attracted an academic explosion of new research on New Guinea highlands warfare during the late 1950s, 1960s, and 1970s (see table 1).

Not surprisingly, the initial thrust of this work reflected the British structural-functionalism of the 1930s through 1950s. The theme enunciated by Wedgwood in 1930 was of special interest, that is, how warfare was organized so that social order was maintained. In the context of colonialism, the larger if often unstated question was how the functions of social control that were ostensibly served by warfare could be effectively reallocated to governmental supervision and regulation under conditions of pacification.[49]

Social Control or Its Absence?

The question of social order is particularly prominent in two of the first monographs frontally concerned with warfare in New Guinea highlands societies: Ronald Berndt's *Excess and Restraint: Social Control among a New Guinea Mountain People* (1962, cf. 1964) and Klaus Koch's *War and Peace in Jalemo: The Management of Conflict in Highland New*

---

49. In a wider Oceanic purview, it may be noted that publications on Australian and Polynesian warfare as listed by Ferguson diverge significantly from the New Guinea pattern, showing much less increase in recent decades:

	1890s	1900s	1910s	1920s	1930s	1940s	1950s	1960s	1970s	1980–86
Australia	0	0	0	1	3	1	2	2	1	0
Polynesia	1	5	4	7	6	1	14	11	13	8

Guinea (1974, cf. 1978, 1983). Concerned with unpacified or only nominally pacified populations on the highlands periphery, both books harbor a tension between the titles' emphasis on social control and rich
case studies depicting collective violence to be frequent, highly disruptive, and cannibalistic. Conflict in both cases flares like the lighting of
match-box tinder, easily escalates to lethal violence, and results in
seemingly interminable chains of reciprocal retaliation and blood
revenge. The potential for violence permeates all but the closest kinship
relations, and there is a palpable ethos of preemptive if not hair-trigger
aggression—marked by both public bravado and deep underlying fear
(cf. also Langness 1972b).

In both books, the scale of brutality and violence quickly swamps
the theoretical edifice of control and order designed to conceptually
contain it: there is plenty of "Excess" but little "Restraint," plenty of
"War" but little "Peace," "Management," or "Control." Koch's work
attempts to address this manifest theoretical problem by suggesting
that war in Jalemo results from the relative absence of crosscutting affil-
iative ties, leading to the conclusion that war will be present where
there is an "absence or inefficiency of third-party authorities" to mediate disputes (1974:170). This negative explanation of Jalemo warfare as
an instance of failed conflict mediation borders on tautology, since
armed conflict itself indicates lack of alternative mechanisms to resolve
dispute. As Koch himself reasons, "All warfare—whatever the cause
. . . follows from an absence or breakdown of peaceful means to settle
the dispute" (1974:173–74).

The great strength of Berndt's and Koch's work lies in their commitment to rich and detailed ethnography of violence and warfare—no
mean feat given their early fieldwork conditions. In Berndt's case, the
value of reported accounts is significantly diminished by an absence of
larger ethnographic context and, in a few instances, by indigenous narratives presented as fact but which are so extreme as to perhaps have
been fabricated or rendered fancifully as stories by informants.[50] The

---

50. For instance, Berndt relates as fact a story of a man who becomes so preoccupied
copulating for a second time with the corpse of a female enemy—while also cutting off
her breasts—that a woman also butchering the corpse grows disgruntled and proceeds to
cut off the man's engaged penis. According to the account, the woman blamed the man
for the incident and, to punctuate her feelings, "removed the end of the penis she had cut
off, popped it into her mouth, and ate it, and then continued with the cutting" (Berndt
1962:283). As related, there was apparently no male protest to or retribution for this
action. Cautious cross-checking would be necessary before assuming the factual accuracy
of such stories.

larger weakness of both works is their guiding functionalist assumption that violent propensities must be socially controlled so that order be maintained. If anything, however, the societies in question appear to have been surviving quite vigorously despite a great intensity of relatively unrestrained violence.

A more ambivalent and in some ways more theoretically sophisticated concern with the relationship between strident conflict and social order in the New Guinea highlands can be found in Marie Reay's *The Kuma*, subtitled *Freedom and Conformity in the New Guinea Highlands* (1959), and Anton Ploeg's *Government in Wanggulam* (1969). Again complementing the Papua New Guinea and West New Guinea highlands, these monographs focus on functional integrity and conflict management but show greater criticism of structural-functionalist orientations, albeit from within them. In particular, they show how tendencies toward endemic hostility and conflict escalation are deeply ingrained in their own right, and how they compete with the need for social order rather than being subsumed by it. Ploeg's volume in particular contains rich case analyses of political disputes involving lethal attacks.

Social Structure and Demography in Precolonial Highlands Warfare

In the late 1960s and the 1970s, the functionalist question of social order was progressively articulated with a focus on social structure and ecology: What social formations entail warfare as an integral part of societal structure? Does warfare occur, in Malthusian fashion, as a chronic response to ecological pressures such as land shortage or protein scarcity? Various answers to these questions were proposed. A point of departure is afforded by the now-classic studies of Mervyn Meggitt.

Meggitt's (1977) monograph on Mae Enga warfare built theoretically on his earlier meticulous study of Enga social structure (1965a). The latter work suggested that very high population density and attendant land pressure predisposed strong agnatic social structure, as reflected in strong patrilineal descent, tightly bounded patriclans, and segmentary lineage organization (cf. Meggitt 1971). In his subsequent monograph on warfare, Meggitt showed Enga conflict to be likewise strongly organized by both land pressure and the organization of strong patrilineages. The most common cause of Enga warfare has been land dispute—archetypally, a burgeoning clan's attempt to wrest territory from its neighbors (1977:13). Intensity of fighting has been correspondingly regulated by the degree of patrilineal connection, with strong constraints on fighting within the clan, but warfare that is increasingly unrestrained between groups who recognize no connections of ancestral "brotherhood" to one another. Armed conflict between adjacent clans of different phratries was thus the most frequent as well as the most severe form of Enga warfare; it entailed surprise attacks or invasions, maximal loss of life and property, and mutilation of fallen enemies.

The theoretical implication, though not stated so simplistically by Meggitt, is that patri-clanship and intense warfare are closely linked at the same time that they are each intensified if not caused by land pressure. This dovetails easily with fraternal interest group theories of feuding and warfare, that is, the notion that localized groups of related males are prone to feuding and the pursuit of warfare against other such groups.[51] Meggitt's argument also combines with ecological scarce-resource theories, for example, the notion that there is a direct linkage between land pressure and warfare competition (cf. Carneiro 1970). In short, land shortage, patrilineal descent, clan solidarity, and warfare against opposed clans are linked in a cycle of mutual reinforcement.

As might be anticipated, cracks have been found in the connections that tie this theoretical perspective together. In terms of kinship, it has been noted that Meggitt's "patrilineal descent" reflects fictive kinship over time—termed "cumulative patrifiliation" in this case (Barnes 1967)—rather than true genealogical relations. Individuals' "relatedness" is thus a social and cultural construct and not simply a biogenetic linkage.[52] In addition, the asserted connection between strength of agnatic principles and land pressure—that patrilineality is strongest where land is scarcest—has been shown by Kelly (1968) not to hold for many other highlands societies. The social structural correlates of land pressure vary even in core areas of the New Guinea highlands, and intense warfare does not correlate with strongly localized patri-clan organization. Warfare was also quite intense among groups such as the Simbu and the Huli, where residential affiliation was not based solely on patrilineal connection but was reckoned through a range of matrilateral and other cognatic as well as patricentric ties. This flexibility

---

51. E.g., Otterbein and Otterbein 1965; Otterbein 1968; van Velsen and van Wetering 1960.

52. Scheffler 1966, 1985; see A. J. Strathern 1972.

permitted individuals to relocate in areas where arable land was not quite as scarce.[53]

Though the kinship correlates of warfare are variable, evidence gives general support for the notion that those highlands populations with very high population densities had recourse to warfare, and that some of this warfare was related to perceived land scarcity. Rigorous study of this relationship is difficult, however, since, as Andrew Strathern (1977:141) has noted, "It is difficult to establish what population pressures were in the past, what carrying capacities were, how these are complicated by pig-herding, and whether people really fought to obtain conquests of land."

Warfare and Ecology in the Fringe Highlands

While land pressure and warfare appear related in some core highlands areas, a simple causal relation is belied by alternative patterns of warfare that were prominent in fringe areas of the New Guinea highlands. These areas had much lower population densities and ample land, and there was little if any emphasis placed on land acquisition. Yet their intensity of warfare was often quite high. While gross population density among the Mae Enga was 120 persons per square mile, it was only 33 per square mile among the south Fore, near the area where Berndt worked (Brown and Podolefsky 1976:214), where warfare was particularly virulent and unrestrained. Other groups with intense warfare but low population densities—and little other evidence of land pressure—include:

> the Anga-speaking populations (e.g., Godelier 1986:103–12; Herdt 1987a: chap. 2);
> the Kewa (e.g., Josephides 1985:2710) and the Wola (e.g., Sillitoe 1979:74–91);
> parts of the Mountain Ok area (e.g., Morren 1984, 1986; Barth 1971:175f.);
> the Huli (e.g., Glasse 1959, 1968); and
> the Maring (e.g., Rappaport 1984).

---

53. E.g., Brookfield and Brown 1963; P. Brown 1971, 1972; Glasse 1968. There *is* a direct correspondence between population density, agricultural intensity, group size, and individual land ownership (Brown and Podolefsky 1976). However, this configuration does not correlate with either social structural or residential patterns.

Morren (1984, 1986: chap. 10) reconstructs in detail the ecological difficulties posed in fringe highlands areas for ethnic expansion through
warfare, basing his account on the Miyanmin and Telefolmin of the
Mountain Ok area. Given the substantial protein resources available in
many of these fringe highlands areas,[54] it is difficult to maintain that
land pressure or competition over scarce material resources was a
major component of their warfare. A convincing empirical critique of
land shortage explanations of warfare in New Guinea has been compiled by Sillitoe (1977).

Of the fringe highlands groups, it is the Maring, on the northeast
edge of the Papua New Guinea highlands, who have been subject to the
greatest discussion concerning ecology and warfare. Rappaport (1984
[1968]) suggested that Maring warfare was part of a homeostatic cycle;
this cycle linked subsistence activity and demography with spiritual
beliefs, ritual behavior, and warfare in ways that kept Maring groups
effectively adapted to their biotic environment. Among other things,
Rappaport suggested that Maring warfare facilitated demographic
movement, adjusted man/land ratios, and, via spiritual beliefs, encouraged the raising and then slaughtering of pigs at feasts. Reducing the
herd kept large numbers of pigs from degrading the environment and
generated pork to compensate allies and supplicate spirits, which was
deemed necessary before another round of warfare could be pursued.
Warfare was thus part of an encompassing ecological cycle through
which conflict was managed and the population—both human and
porcine—was kept below the land's estimated carrying capacity.

Rappaport's argument has been very influential and has, correspondingly, attracted numerous critiques.[55] Although Maring warfare
tended in any particular engagement to be inconclusive and low in
casualties, the attrition of political alliance within one side over weeks
of desultory fighting risked leaving its remaining members significantly outnumbered on the battlefield. The larger enemy force could
then charge and rout its opponents, killing large numbers of them,
burning houses, destroying gardens, desecrating sacred places, and
forcing the vanquished to flee and live elsewhere (1984:139, 143ff.).
LiPuma (1988:20) mentions a Maring war in which the losing side is

---

54. E.g., R. C. Kelly 1977: chap. 2; Dwyer 1983, 1985a–c; Rappaport 1984; Morren
1986.

55. E.g., Friedman 1974; McArthur 1974; Bergmann 1975; Hallpike 1973; Peoples
1982; cf. also Vayda 1961, 1971, 1974, 1976, 1979, contrast Vayda 1989.

estimated to have suffered more than a hundred casualties, and Vayda (1989:166) notes one fight in which 23 persons of one side were killed, this being 8 percent of their total population. Healey (1985:23–27) documents many Maring killings in secret raids, ambushes into which the enemy had been unwittingly enticed, or surprise charges from the bush surrounding the battlefield. This violence puts a different, more critical perspective on Rappaport's claim that "sanctity is an alternative to political power among the Maring" (1984:237).[56] It has also been asked if the Maring ritual cycle (*kaiko*) would have appeared so regular and homeostatic if assessed over a longer period of time (cf. Rappaport 1984:156f.). Indeed, the Tsembaga group studied by Rappaport had by the time of his fieldwork been driven from their territory through warfare and subsequently was reinstated only with the support of the Australian patrol administration.[57]

The role of change rather than homeostatic maintenance is underscored by Healey (1985), who traces the history of warfare and settlement over almost a century for the Kundagai Maring, adjacent to the Tsembaga. Healey shows that the Kundagai expanded greatly over the last century and that their territory became more than twice the size of other Maring clan clusters. However, the Kundagai had one of the lowest population densities within the region (1985:14). Though this situation appears anomalous from a Malthusian perspective, it becomes more comprehensible as Maring cultural orientations are considered. LiPuma (1988) shows how Maring cosmological, spiritual, and bodily substance beliefs confer personal and collective identity through the food, labor products, and social transactions that derive from clan land. In warfare, attackers who rout their opponents ravage the land as they would their enemies' themselves. This renders the territory uninhabitable, including by the victors (212). Lingering spirits from the dispossessed group are believed to haunt the land, though after enough time, the spirits are believed to dissipate and the land may eventually be occupied by the new group (cf. Rappaport 1984:144ff.).

Given such beliefs and practices, the Maring population is often

------

56. Recently, Roscoe (1997) has forwarded an argument that additionally contests the cosmological determination of Sepik warfare. Forge (1990:168) discusses the reinforcing relationship between cultural and sociopolitical factors in the expansionist warfare of the Abelam in the Sepik. He estimates that approximately 30 percent of Abelam deaths were due to warfare in the precolonial era.

57. Rappaport 1984:145; Vayda 1989:166.

not dispersed equitably across arable land, as might otherwise be possible through land redistribution. LiPuma (1988:212f.) states that many Maring groups became more crowded as they absorbed kin and allies who had been displaced by warfare. Conversely, Healey's data independently document that the victorious and expansive Kundagai, who defeated the Tsembaga, were more land abundant than any of their neighbors; in essence, they inflated their body politic to possess much more land than they needed for subsistence, leaving groups such as the Tsembaga correspondingly crowded. Healey documents that Kundagai shifted flexibly within their large territory to maximize the ease of resource procurement, to minimize military harassment from enemies, and to keep their various land rights active (1985:13–14).

As the Maring case illustrates, residential relocalization and land redistribution are configured by motivations for cultural growth and reproduction that may work against the even distribution of arable land among a population. Population pressure and land redistribution thus seem inadequate explanations for Maring warfare (see also the recantation in Vayda 1989). This negative conclusion, does, however, demonstrate a larger contribution of Rappaport's work: his convincing demonstration that cultural beliefs and practices can have a dramatic impact on the strategic organization, frequency, and outcome of armed conflict. Political strategies are informed by cultural suppositions concerning worth, success, and spirituality in the context of sociodemographic and material opportunities and constraints. This does not suggest that availability of land or protein is an ultimate prime mover of Maring warfare, but it illustrates that cultural belief and human ecology are integrally related and mutually influential (see Rappaport 1984:337–44).

Taken collectively, the many research studies on ecology and warfare in interior New Guinea provide perhaps the most rigorous regional ethnographic illustration to date that the existence or intensity of warfare in pre-state societies cannot be predicted as a linear function of population density, population pressure, or protein scarcity.[58] The extensive materialist work in New Guinea can in this sense be said to have a major Popperian function in disproving single-cause materialist

---

58. R. C. Kelly (1985) provides a detailed refutation of similar arguments in an African context.

arguments concerning the presence or intensity of warfare. One can conclude that the presumed adaptiveness of pre-state warfare has much to do with stresses and adjustments of culturally mediated social, political, and spiritual relationships as well as with competition over biotic resources.

Of course, this does not mean that factors such as population pressure are totally irrelevant to warfare. As Sillitoe (1977) has noted, one need not adopt an ecological theory for all war to realize that ecological pressure can strongly influence cultural and political dispositions in some cases. In the more populous areas of the highlands, such as Enga and Simbu, the relationship between warfare and land pressure is pronounced in the sense that informants commonly say that disputes over land are an important cause of fighting. This connection reinforces rather than mitigates the importance of cultural response to land shortage, however, since, as seen previously, the perceptions of individual or group land scarcity—as well as the action believed necessary to alleviate the scarcity—are a function of cultural belief as well as ecological constraint (see also Burton-Bradley 1974). Meggitt (1977:183) notes this clearly when he writes that Enga "perceptions of scarcity . . . determined their relationship to the land no less significantly than did topography, the pattern of rainfall, or the range of indigenous plants. That is to say, ideas are also causally efficient components of human ecosystems."

Land Pressure and Resurgence of Warfare in the New Guinea Highlands

The perception of land shortage has been particularly important in the resurgence of warfare in core New Guinea highlands areas.[59] On the one hand, population densities have increased beyond indigenously high levels through sustained population growth (Cole 1993; cf. Agyei 1988). In some areas, and particularly among the Enga, the strong connection between clan identity and inherited land mitigates against population movement or outmigration as a means of redistributing or reducing land pressure. Land pressure is further exacerbated by strong

---

59. E.g., Gordon 1983; Gordon and Meggitt 1985; P. Brown 1982a, b, 1986; Westermark 1984, 1987; Podolefsky 1984; Strathern 1977; Meggitt 1977: chap. 9; Reay 1982.

desires to use land for cash crops such as coffee, which create more pressure on the remaining land for subsistence production.[60] Competition for land is thus intensified by sociocultural practices designed to maximize its value. This has helped make warfare in high density highland areas refractory to long-term eradication.[61]

Even in the eastern highlands, where population densities are lower and there has been less resurgence of warfare, disputes over land that can be used for cash-cropping have been a major source of violence-provoking conflict.[62] Other forms of violence are also impacted. Reay (1982:627) notes that Minj participation in the robbery activities of *raskol* (rascal) groups is strongly influenced by the increased number of siblings per family: lack of land for each son inhibits many of them from pursuing cash crop, pig-raising, or subsistence activities that would otherwise be a principal means of attaining economic stature and prestige.

As A. J. Strathern (1977:143) notes generally,

> The picture here supports the view of increasing land pressure on those areas in which (a) traditionally population densities were higher anyway, (b) political units are large, (c) the response to development opportunities has been keen, and (d) complex exchange systems also increase the pressure on resources.

The larger point, then, is that high population pressure can abet conflict, but whether and how demography facilitates warfare depends on the social organization of land distribution, the cultural valuations of what land should and should not be used for, the type(s) of technol-

---

60. A. J. Strathern 1977; P. Brown 1982a:535; Meggitt 1977:162.

61. A comparative example of created land shortage is evident precolonially among the Abelam—the one non-highlands group adduced by Sillitoe (1977) to have fought wars primarily for the sake of acquiring land (see Forge 1990). As noted by Tuzin (1976:13), the land-hungry expansion of the Abelam was predicated on their having "gone so far with slash-and-burn techniques that much of their territory lies unarable under a tough cover of tall sword-grasses. . . . [T]he progressive spread of the Sepik grassfields has produced severe land shortages . . . resulting in patterns of warfare based on territorial conquest."

62. See Westermark 1984; Strathern 1984:24. There appears to be less warfare resurgence in fringe highland as opposed to core highland areas, but Strathern's (1977:144) caveat is well-taken that "fighting and rumours of fighting are more common there [in Kainantu, eastern Highlands] than can be told from press's accounts, which concentrate on Chimbu."

ogy employed, and the sociocultural strategies used to deal with conflict. The articulation of such factors with national politics is discussed
later.

Politicoeconomic Intensification and Precolonial Warfare in the New Guinea Highlands

During the 1980s, the relationship between population pressure and
warfare in highland New Guinea was reconsidered in light of archeo-
logical evidence and ethnohistorical query: What promoted the development of high population density, intensive pig-husbandry and horticulture, elaborate ceremonial exchange, big-manship, and large-scale
warfare in core areas of the New Guinea highlands? In addressing
these questions, there was decreasing interest in the self-maintaining
relationship among ecology, economics, and warfare as propounded
by Rappaport (1984), and more interest in the evolutionary significance
of positive feedback and developmental change. This was consistent
with Melanesianists' melding of ecological and structural-functional
concerns with growing concern with Marxism and political economy
(see overview by Strathern [1982b]).

Numerous arguments bearing on highlands politicoeconomic
intensification have been advanced; for present purposes, a simple synopsis must suffice.[63] In general, it has been argued that political and
economic intensification in the New Guinea highlands resulted from a
cycle of mutual reinforcement among several factors:

1. increasing human population density;
2. increasing forest clearage;
3. declining wild food resources;
4. increasing need for supplementary protein;
5. increasing raising of domesticated pigs;
6. introduction of the sweet potato as the staple crop, thus facilitating major increases in pig production, human population,
   and forest clearage; and
7. increasing per capita pig holdings and surplus subsistence production.

---

63. See particularly Watson 1977; Modjeska 1982; Golson 1982; Feil 1986, 1987, 1995;
contrast R. C. Kelly 1988; cf. Ploeg 1988.

These features are considered to have directly impacted highlands politics and warfare by, for example,

8. increasing opportunities for conflict;
9. increasing need for conflict mediation;
10. increasing substitution of wealth for people in exchanges, including homicide compensation and bridewealth; and
11. increasing mediation of conflict by authoritative big-men and regional integration of exchange.

(after Modjeska 1982:56)

In this second part of the argument, increasing population density is suggested to increase the opportunities for both intragroup and intergroup conflict. This is reasoned to create pressure for more effective conflict resolution, such as the use of homicide compensation and bridewealth to forestall cycles of blood feuding and violent disputes over marriage. This increased rate of material transaction, in turn, is thought to have facilitated an efflorescence and elaboration of ceremonial exchange. The entire process is reasoned to have proceeded furthest in the most densely populated highlands groups, such as the Enga, Melpa, Simbu, and Dani—where big-manship and ceremonial exchange have been most elaborated.

This scenario has given rise to competing hypotheses concerning the specific effects of political and economic intensification on highlands warfare. On one hand, connections evident in Meggitt's earlier line of reasoning were extended across a range of sociocultural features by Healey (1978:202); he attributed a nexus of high population density and territorial expansion through warfare (as well as through elaborate ceremonial exchange) to western highlands societies such as the Mae Enga and Melpa. Implicitly in this model, exchange and land conquest through warfare work together to facilitate politicoeconomic intensification. (Correspondingly, on a state level, one might compare Carneiro's [1970] theory of demographic and economic intensification through intense warfare, leading to the origin of the state; cf. Roscoe and Graber 1988). Healey finds all these features to be absent in the societies of the fringe highlands, such as the Maring, which are less politically and economically "intensive."

In contrast, Feil (1987) has forwarded an argument that systematically opposes Meggitt's characterizations. In this model, warfare in the core areas of the New Guinea highlands was reduced and not increased. This reduction was accomplished by means of a well-organized structure of alliances and economic exchanges orchestrated by authoritative big-men to counteract political polarization and fragmentation. It is reasoned that the larger populations and more complex economies of this region have made a larger network of political and economic integration necessary. Feil suggests, correspondingly, that warfare was less intense and unrestrained in core highland areas and more virulent in the eastern highlands of Papua New Guinea, where subsistence intensification was less developed, population densities were lower, the authority of leaders diminished, and economic networks smaller and less complex. He thus divides the Papua New Guinea highlands into a western area where warfare is said to have been "restricted" by rules and regulations, and an eastern sector where warfare is said to have been "unrestricted," tending toward an "absence of rules" (1987:66–70; cf. Langness 1972a: 390). These characterizations are perforce relative rather than absolute, since most New Guinea highlands societies harbored a range of both more and less highly structured conflict types, for example, ritualized "little" or "nothing" fights as well as indiscriminate raids and major wars.

The best evidence available concerning conflict types does not appear to support Feil's thesis. For instance, Meggitt documents for the Mae Enga of the western highlands that the most ritualized form of fighting—"Great Fights" between phratries—was also the least common (only 2 of 84 engagements; Meggitt 1977:13).[64] By contrast, fighting that was unrestrained—including mutilation of enemies, wholesale destruction of property, killing of women and children, treachery, surprise raids, night attacks, and so on—was also the most common form of warfare among Mae Enga; it occurred more than twice as frequently as any other conflict type in Meggitt's sample (1977:13, 36–43).[65]

The principal quantitative evidence Feil uses to support his proposition is a supposedly higher rate of war casualties in eastern versus western and southern highland areas. However, these data are highly equivocal. For instance, battle deaths accounted for 35 percent of adult

---

64. Meggitt (20–21) cogently discusses the structural reasons for the relative rarity of such ritualized fights.

65. Evidence supplied by A. J. Strathern (1971:66f., 72–77) for Mount Hageners of the western highlands also suggests that major wars in this area could be unrestrained and minor wars sometimes quite destructive.

male mortality among the Mae Enga, which is the only western high-lands society in Feil's sample (Meggitt 1977:110). This is higher than casualty rates listed by Feil for the eastern highlands (1987:71).[66] For the southern highlands of Papua New Guinea, which Feil (1987:70f., 78f.) considers roughly consonant with the western highlands in regard to "restrained" warfare, the data are equally problematic. In his account of warfare among the Mendi of the southern highlands, Ryan (1959: 268) states that

> inter-clan fighting would seem to have been almost chronic . . . Apart from formal open battles, which were probably not very fre-quent, there was a constant series of sporadic guerrilla raids. The result of all this activity was that many clans were almost extermi-nated and the survivors driven off their land.

For the Huli, also of the southern highlands, Glasse (1959:285) notes, "The aim of warfare is general destruction: houses are burnt, gardens are destroyed, and men, women, and children are slaughtered without mercy." Glasse's (1968) monograph documents that Huli have a strong belief that anger should not be withheld or controlled but should be expressed as violence. Further,

> Huli have no idea of *lex talionis*. A man tries to inflict a greater injury than that which he has suffered. Moreover, the people who suffer as a result of vengeance do not accept their injuries as just or appropriate; they too seek counter-vengeance, and the conflict is unending. (1968:68)

As a result, "nearly every man nurses a grievance that can precipitate war" (88).

In general, then, available evidence does not support the claim that warfare was relatively restrained and less politically important

---

66. Though misciting the appropriate page for Meggitt's casualty figures, Feil (1987:71) appears to adopt Meggitt's (1977:110) textual discussion in which a liberal allowance is made for the possible greater remembrance of battle versus sickness deaths, whereupon Meggitt assesses that even in the most conservative estimate, at least 25 per-cent of Enga male deaths were battle casualties. Along this reasoning, a similar reduction would also have to be applied to the other data from the eastern highlands cited by Feil.

in the western highlands (and southern highlands) of Papua New Guinea. The same negative conclusion applies to politicoeconomically intensified areas of the Irian Jaya highlands, not considered by Feil, where ritual warfare articulated with catastrophic warfare as part of a larger cycle (cf. A. J. Strathern 1990). The periodic effects of such unrestrained warfare are highly evident among the Grand Valley Dani, the Ilaga Valley Dani, the Kapauku, and the Wanggulam.[67] Heider (1970:118f.) notes one Grand Valley war in which 125 persons were killed, and he calculates overall that 28.5 percent (100/350) of all male Grand Valley Dani deaths were due to warfare (Heider 1979:106). Within the Dani region, Ploeg (1988:516f.) assesses that warfare in the most intensively cultivated areas, such as the Grand Valley, was significantly *less* "restricted" than conflict in areas further west that were less intensively cultivated. This is the opposite of what one would expect on the basis of Feil's thesis for the eastern versus western Papua New Guinea highlands. Conversely, relatively "restrained" warfare was prominent among some *non*-core Papua New Guinea highlands groups, including the Siane (Newman 1965:47; Salisbury 1958).

As was the case for insular Melanesia (discussed previously), ritualized battle encounters between sizable political groups can present a stage of balanced opposition that shifts to a rout and dispersal of one group accompanied by high casualties and the demise of parish if not political identity among the vanquished. It is perhaps the size of opposing forces and the periodicity between formalized and unformalized warfare that are greater in some core highlands areas, where groups are larger (Brown and Podolefsky 1976). Likewise, a more elaborate system of exchange and the coordination of larger groups of people by big-men may have created a greater sense of stability and lack of chronic strife in some core highland areas.[68] But this "control" was frequently complemented by warfare that could ultimately make up in virulence what it lacked in regularity. These catastrophic outbursts, of course, were among the first aspects of highland societies to be suppressed by colonial patrol officers and police. In short, available evidence does not

---

67. See Heider 1970, 1979:103–6; Larson 1986: chap. 8; Pospisil 1963a:57, 60; Ploeg 1969: chap. 8.

68. This pattern in core highland areas was noted by early explorers; see Connolly and Anderson 1987.

indicate that killing was less frequent in overall terms in core western highland versus eastern highland areas. However, this violence was often orchestrated within more encompassing political and economic networks, and it sometimes had a more pronounced periodicity.

In several respects, Feil's characterizations for the western Papua New Guinea highlands revisit in a new guise the same problem previously discussed for Wedgwood, Malinowski, and Rivers. These problems include an emphasis on ritual display fighting that leads us to neglect more violent warfare. This illustrates how historical biases may continue in our thinking long after we would appear to have left them behind. Politicoeconomic accounts of cultural development easily shelter long-standing functionalist assumptions, first, that there arises a "need" to mediate conflict, and second, that superordinate political and economic structures develop in satisfaction of this need, for instance, they function to reduce the violence and disruption of warfare. In fact, the reverse argument could equally be made, viz., that superordinate politicoeconomic structures function to disseminate and perpetrate warfare. Indeed, theories of state development based on demographic increase often suggest that the intensification of warfare leads to relations of social subordination and eventually to political stratification (Carneiro 1970).

Big-Men, War, and Exchange

The tendency to assume cultural and psychological transparency in Melanesian warfare—to jump analytically from an assumed human "need" to its violent expression or its necessary control—is also illustrated in explanations that focus on big-men, such as that proposed by Paul Sillitoe (1978). Sillitoe suggests that warfare is caused by big-men who "struggle to maintain their unstable leadership by inducing their fellows to fight wars which will weaken their rivals' communities and so diminish threats to their hegemony" (252). This is the reverse of Feil's reasoning above, in which big-men restrict war rather than exacerbate it. Unfortunately, neither assertion is broadly applicable; the circumstances vary from case to case. Though big-manship has undoubtedly influenced warfare in some highland areas, in others it has acted as a damper or control on those men who are most eager to take revenge. In some cases, leaders are as much prisoner to their group's expectations as they are to personal inclinations.[69] In the New Guinea highlands, it is frequently the "young hotheads" rather than the older and wiser leaders who take the most pressing initiative in warfare.[70] Likewise, it has been frequently recognized that big-men demonstrate their strength by quelling fights as well as by orchestrating hostilities. Andrew Strathern (1971:75–80) documents a strong impetus among Mount Hagen big-men for conciliation and exchange as well as for aggressive action. Gordon and Meggitt (1985:149) comment on the competitive aspects of the Enga Te exchange system in light of the Enga's statement that

> "We make Te first and then we fight." This adage can be inter-preted in two ways: one clan builds up alliances through the Te and then attacks the enemy; or Te transactions inevitably cause bad relations between groups because of inadequate exchanges or defaults that generate excuses for their engaging in warfare. On the surface the Te enables people to establish friendly relations, but in the process it creates potential conflict that lurks beneath the surface of sociality, or actual disputes.

For the Simbu, after mentioning the integrative effects of large-scale ceremonial exchange, Paula Brown (1982a:532) notes,

> But this is only one facet of Simbu society, and a part of the inter-group relations which are included in the larger conflict-integra-tion system. In fact, marital disputes and payments due to affinal relatives are a most important element in the competition and exchange . . . Disputes over payments, which are owed to affines and kin connected by past marriages, are the frequent initiating disputes in fights.

Along with the escalating scope and size of highlands exchanges in the postcolonial era has been a dramatic increase in the amount of material compensation demanded as restitution for homicide; some

---

69. As Kracke (1978) has illustrated for an Amazonian society, the psychocultural dimensions of leadership can also vary significantly from one circumstance or individual to another.

70. E.g., Gordon and Meggitt 1985:150ff.; cf. Meggitt 1977:70–80.

requests are reportedly as high as K100,000 (Gordon 1981:89). In many Papua New Guinea highland areas, escalating homicide compensation demands have become poignant sources of dispute and renewed hostility (Scaglion 1981). Often, large-scale exchange relations now articulate with the patronage and prestige associated with elected political office—along with the potential for payoffs, favoritism, or corruption that such relations entail (e.g., A. J. Strathern 1984, 1993a).

In short, the relationship between leadership and patronage through exchange has intensified in a commoditized, postcolonial era. This continues to be a double-edged sword that can both ameliorate and re-exacerbate collective violence in Melanesia. Regardless of whether the intensification of political economy is seen as increasing or decreasing violence—either precolonially or postcolonially—the cultural motivations and strategies of the actors themselves need to be carefully investigated and assessed rather than assumed or made a reflex of an a priori theoretical paradigm. The kind of postcolonial warfare that is so poignantly depicted by Connolly and Anderson in their film *Black Harvest* (1992) underscores this fact for the contemporary New Guinea highlands.[71] What continues to be lacking is articulation of politicoeconomic models with culturally sensitive understanding of local political strategies and personal aspirations.

Politicoeconomic Intensification and Precolonial New Guinea Highlands Warfare: A Theoretical Evaluation

Perspectives emphasizing political and economic intensification have made several major contributions to the study of Melanesian warfare. First, they introduce a diachronic dimension and view warfare as part of long-term processes of change. Second, they take a wide comparative perspective and consider patterns of developmental divergence or convergence among ethnographic regions. Third, they consider patterns of interrelationship among political, economic, and ecological factors and examine multiple chains of reinforcement rather than adducing single-cause or circular explanations of warfare. In all these respects, perspectives on highlands politicoeconomic intensification

---

71. See Dabrowski 1993 for an extended film review.

are ethnographically and empirically grounded while going beyond major limitations in structural-functional and materialist approaches as previously evaluated.

On the other hand, political and economic perspectives on sociocultural development in highland New Guinea tend to assume a natural condition of unmediated competition that arises as if directly from the environment of human production. This propensity toward unrestrained conflict then generates a "need" for control by higher-order political structures, contracts, and affiliations. Many aspects of Thomas Hobbes's original paradigm—in which violence is deemed natural to humankind—are here recapitulated.[72] In the process, it is easy to assume rather than examine the Hobbesian notion that higher levels of political organization suppress violence rather than perpetuate it. This assumption is undercut by what we know of state-level societies, colonialism, and imperialism more generally.[73] In the process, the rich social reciprocity of Melanesian gift-giving is implicitly reduced to a function of organizational necessity in the amelioration or the pursuit of conflict.[74] Of course, a nuanced conceptualization of "politics" can offer a productive vantage point on the complex developmental relation between warfare and socioeconomic dynamics. It is hence important not to minimize the advances made by increasingly sophisticated treatments of "function" in perspectives based on political economy. The interaction of these factors with cultural dynamics, particularly with respect to male status, prestige, political motivation, and spiritual orientation, remains important and in need of further investigation and analysis. The need for this awareness is thrown into dramatic relief as a less highlands-centric perspective is taken and a fuller range of warfare variants considered from other parts of Melanesia.

Warfare and Culture outside the New Guinea Highlands

Since the late 1950s, studies of Melanesian warfare have focused largely on highlands New Guinea and, with a few exceptions, been particu-

---

72. See Hobbes 1958 [1651].

73. E.g., Giddens 1987; Claustres 1987; Ferguson and Whitehead 1992.

74. For a broader and more ethnographically focused critique, see the compelling arguments of Harrison 1989a, 1993; cf. Sahlins 1972a, 1972b.

larly concerned with the relation of armed conflict to social structure, ecology, and politicoeconomic intensification.[75] A tacit corollary supposition is that highlands warfare tends to be secular in nature, particularly in core highlands areas.[76] Factors of cultural belief have often been unemphasized in the study of core highlands warfare[77]—even though they have been highly important.[78] Conversely, however, consideration of "religious" and "spiritual" factors have been emphasized in the indigenous warfare of *lowland* areas, such as the Sepik and particularly south New Guinea.[79] This is in keeping with Lawrence and Meggitt's (1965) classic assertion that the societies of the New Guinea highlands tend to be more "secular" whereas those of seaboard Melanesia tend to be more "religious." As part of this characterization, the political, economic, and ecological dimensions of lowlands violence have been largely neglected, particularly for south New Guinea.[80] This dovetails with Malinowski's (1941) striking assertion, discussed previously, that head-hunting is not really a kind of "warfare." Much of the primary ethnography of coastal south New Guinea was collected between 1900 and 1935, when earlier influences in the study of Melanesia warfare were paramount. By contrast, it was in the heyday of ecological and social structural approaches in the 1950s and 1960s that warfare in the New Guinea highlands was most intensively studied. Though not denying important genuine differences between New Guinea highlands and lowlands areas,[81] it remains true that accepted contrasts between highlands and lowlands warfare are magnified by the different theoretical proclivities in Melanesian anthropology during the periods when each area was subject to greatest primary study (see this vol., chap. 5).

---

75. A particularly important exception is Harrison 1993; cf. also Roscoe 1997.

76. E.g., Harrison 1989a, b; cf. Lawrence and Meggitt 1965; Malinowski 1941.

77. Contrast Knauft 1993a: chap. 4.

78. See especially Strauss 1990; M. Strathern 1988; Heider 1979; Rappaport 1984; Reay 1987.

79. Concerning the Sepik, see Tuzin 1976; Gewertz 1983; Harrison 1993; Roscoe 1997; Forge 1990. Concerning south coast New Guinea, see Knauft 1993a and specific studies by Landtman 1927; Williams 1924, 1936: chap. 15; Wirz 1933; van Baal 1966: chap. 12; Zegwaard 1959; Boelaars 1981.

80. Contrast Eyde 1967, and, for the Sepik, Roscoe 1997.

81. Lindenbaum 1984; cf. Knauft 1987a.

Witch and Sorcerer Killing Southwest and West of the Papua New Guinea Highlands

Areally intermediate between highland and lowland studies of armed conflict is information concerning witch- and sorcerer-killing in the fringe areas southwest and west of the Papua New Guinea highlands. This work was undertaken particularly from the late 1960s through the 1980s. Of particular present relevance is the Strickland-Bosavi area, bridged in existing work by the Duna and the Hewa of the central range to the Mountain Ok area.[82] Homicide rates in much of this area have been as high as or higher than those associated with "unrestrained" warfare in the highlands. Among Gebusi, at least 32.7 percent of all adult deaths were homicides, the bulk of these being collective killings of suspected sorcerers (Knauft 1985a, 1987b). This rate is exceeded by other groups in the general region; annual homicide rate equivalences increase from at least 683 (per 100,000/annum) among Gebusi to 772 among Hewa and between 815 and 1,832 per year among Etoro.[83] In the Mountain Ok area, warfare accounted for 35 percent of deaths among Baktaman,[84] and warfare and homicide were attributed as the cause of 15 percent of all deaths among Bimin-Kuskusmin.[85] A homicide rate equivalent to 87.5 per 100,000/annum is reported for the Nalumin, the vast bulk of these deaths being witch executions (Bercovitch 1989:158, n. 15). Such figures do not penetrate the diverse internal dynamics of violence in these areas but merely establish its magnitude and empirical range.

In the Strickland-Bosavi area, strongly held beliefs concerning spirituality, sexuality, and bodily depletion informed elaborate public divinations and the lethal scapegoating of sorcery or witchcraft suspects, typically within the local political community and often among kin.[86] Despite the very high rate of homicide among societies such as Etoro and Gebusi, killing was anything but unrestrained; indeed, it was extremely "rule-governed" in following rigorous cultural procedures

---

82. See Knauft 1985a, b, 1987b, 1989b; R. C. Kelly 1993; Schieffelin 1976; Sørum 1980; Steadman 1971, 1975, 1985; Ernst 1984; see Stürzenhofecker 1998; Biersack 1995.

83. Knauft 1985a:376–77; Steadman 1971:215; R. C. Kelly 1993:550.

84. Barth 1971:175; cf. Morren 1984, 1986: chap. 10, concerning warfare among the Miyanmin.

85. Poole 1981b:74 n. 6, cf. Poole 1983.

86. E.g., R. C. Kelly 1976, n.d.; Knauft 1985a, 1989.

for spiritually divining and executing individual sorcery suspects. These killings often generated widespread community support, even among close kin of the victim. This exposes the problematic assumption that "rule-governance" of conflict corresponds with reduction in the degree or intensity of violence. Gebusi violence in particular reveals the corollary problem of assuming that prevailing norms of positive sociality betoken a low rate of violence (see Knauft 1987b).

More generally, the spiritual configurations of sorcery/witchcraft and their corresponding social violence in the Strickland-Bosavi area illustrate that cultural beliefs strongly influence the dynamics and intensities of violence. The "strain" involved in sorcery and witchcraft violence is in significant respects a function of the belief system, which can exacerbate rather than reduce the social structural correlates of violence.[87] Cultural logics interact with politicoeconomic and social structural tendencies in the region, such as relative absence of material compensation payments and emphasis on person-for-person exchange.[88]

Head-hunting and Warfare along the South Coast of New Guinea

Spiritual belief, ritual, and cosmology in Melanesian violence were particularly prominent in warfare that accompanied head-hunting, which has perhaps been most pervasive and best documented along the New Guinea south coast. Head-hunting extended in various permutations for over one thousand miles westward from the Purari[89] and the Kiwai[90] to the Trans-Fly peoples,[91] the famed Marind-anim,[92] the Kolopom,[93] the Jacquai,[94] and the Asmat.[95] Most ethnographic accounts for these groups are atheoretically descriptive, though the connection between cosmological rejuvenation, myth, ritual, and the incorporation

---

87. Knauft 1985a; contrast Marwick 1970.
88. See Knauft 1985b; A. J. Strathern 1982a.
89. Williams 1924: chap. 9; Maher 1961: chap. 2; Holmes 1924: chap. 21.
90. Landtman 1927: chap. 9; Riley 1925: chap. 22.
91. Williams 1936: chap. 15.
92. Van Baal 1966: chap. 12; Wirz 1933; Haddon 1891; van der Kroef 1952; Ernst 1979.
93. Serpenti 1966, 1977.
94. Boelaars 1981.
95. Zegwaard 1959; Eyde 1967.

of life force from enemy heads is clearly evident across the region (see this book, chap. 2, and Knauft 1993a: chaps. 7–8).[96]

This does not mean that ecological potentials and constraints were unimportant in influencing south New Guinea warfare. Along portions of the south New Guinea lowlands, ample food from wild sago and ease of canoe travel facilitated head-hunting expeditions that could cover hundreds of miles.[97] In some cases, human predation was an opportunistic extension of seasonal foraging or pillaging strategies, as among the Bamu and Kikori peoples and possibly among the Marind-anim and the Boazi of the Middle Fly. Major coastal and riverine populations often had good access to (nonhuman) protein resources, tended to be physically larger in body size than their inland counterparts, and often sustained much larger settlement sizes and significantly greater population densities as well. From Marind-anim eastward across the mouths of the Fly, Bamu, and Kikori rivers, coastal populations raided inland "bush" peoples with impunity and often with little fear of retaliation.[98] In terms of resource competition, Eyde (1967) argues that Asmat head-hunting warfare was most intense in those desired habitation zones that had maximal access to both downriver fishing grounds and upriver sago stands.

Crosscutting such ecological conditions, local residential and military organization was importantly mediated by cosmological and religious concerns. The selective descriptive summaries that follow illustrate this, as a point of departure for subsequent theoretical elaboration.

Among Marind-anim, extensive totemic and ritual affiliations provided an elaborate system of dual organization alliance whereby the ten thousand or so Marind were internally peaceful and aided each other in long-distance head-hunting raids outside their territory.[99] In addition to head-hunting, these raids yielded large-scale capture of young women and children, who ended up constituting 8 percent or more of the Marind population (van Baal 1966:29, 32). By killing enemy adults and incorporating their children into their own population,

---

96. Analysis of these relations has lagged, however, and understanding of head-hunting as a cultural form is arguably more developed among southeast Asian specialists than Melanesianists; see McKinley 1976; Needham 1976; Freeman 1979; M. Rosaldo 1977, 1980, 1983; R. Rosaldo 1980; George 1996.

97. Van Baal 1966: chap. 12; Beaver 1920; Busse, pers. comm.

98. Cf. van Baal 1966: chap. 12; Landtman 1917: chap. 13; 1927:9; Beaver 1920.

99. Van Baal 1966:24, chap. 12; Ernst 1979.

Marind were a culturally expanding population despite a deficient internal Marind birth rate. This demographic deficit, in turn, was exacerbated if not caused by ritually enjoined sexual practices in which young Marind women were enjoined for fertility purposes to have sexual intercourse in succession with a substantial number of male partners. This practice, termed *otiv bombari*, was a frequent ordeal that induced vaginal infection and subsequent pelvic inflammatory disease on a scale that rendered a high proportion of Marind women permanently sterile (South Pacific Commission 1955; see Knauft 1993a: chap. 8). Since inability to conceive was itself responded to with intensified coitus in *otiv bombari*—that is, in an attempt to increase fertility—a vicious circle was engaged (van Baal 1966; Ernst 1979). Overall, then, Marind fertility cult practices created a reinforcing cycle of (1) hypersexuality; (2) infertility; (3) heightened emphasis on masculine prowess; (4) intensive head-hunting; (5) child-capture; and (6) intense cult indoctrination to socialize foreign children with Marind beliefs and practices. As part of this cycle, an elaborate system of spiritual affiliations provided Marind the dense crosscutting alliances as well as the cultural logic and psychodynamic motivation for intensive head-hunting beyond their borders.

In contrast to the expanding Marind, the Purari delta or Namau peoples were internally polarized into a small number of large warring villages.[100] Whereas Marind resided in dispersed hamlets strongly connected through ritual and totemic alliance, Purari peoples lived in fortress settlements of up to two thousand persons surrounded by largely uninhabited land.[101] Elaborate dual organization facilitated solidarity within Purari villages but little connection outside of them (excepting individual river clan affiliations; see Weiner 1988b:569f.). Purari head-hunting focused on the taking of life force from other political communities and augmenting the spiritual force of one's own spirit-ancestor embodiments, as previously discussed in chapter 2.

As Maher (1961: chap. 2) notes, the point is not that cosmological beliefs rigidly determined Purari warfare, settlement, and subsistence patterns, but that they exercised an undeniable and distinctive influence upon these relationships.[102] Though cultural differences between

---

100. Williams 1924; Maher 1961, 1967.

101. This land was exploited furtively for rudimentary hidden gardening and for felling sago logs, which were floated back to the village for processing by women.

102. See Forge 1990 for a similar argument concerning warfare among the expansionist Abelam of the Sepik.

groups such as Purari and Marind likely engaged ecological variations, the cultural ecology of cosmological belief is crucial in explaining their divergent systems of sociopolitical organization and development. Such contrasts beg more nuanced understanding of the relation between cultural and spiritual dynamics of warfare vis-à-vis ecological conditions, settlement patterns, and the political economy of "gifts and blows" within and between ethnic groups.[103]

Put more generally, cultural factors exert a qualitative influence on the way the environment is perceived and appropriated and on the way that society is organized, just as ecological and sociodemographic realities present constraints and opportunities that cultural dynamics adjust and respond to. Social and cultural development results from dialectical interconnections between these realms—dialectical in that beliefs and the material world cannot be taken in isolation but are intrinsically interdependent in human action. The nature of this relationship cannot be adduced a priori but needs to be analyzed and then compared ethnographically across a range of cases and regions.

Psychological Dimensions of Melanesian Warfare

Given the differing styles and motivations of Melanesian warfare both within and between regions, it is surprising that the subjective and motivational underpinnings of conflict have not received more widespread scrutiny, at least until recently.[104] Notwithstanding early

---

103. Like south coast New Guinea, warfare in the middle Sepik area of northern New Guinea was frequently associated with headhunting in a lowland rain-forest environment of sago/fish subsistence and, in some cases, elaborate dual organization (e.g., Bateson 1936:137ff.; Harrison 1993:27–28). Here, however, patterns of ethnic differentiation and complementarity created an extensive pattern of areal integration (cf. Schwartz 1963). Dominant riverine groups such as the Iatmul both raided and traded fish with more dispersed "bush" or "mother" groups, which supplied them with sago (see Gewertz 1978, 1983; Bateson 1932, 1936; D'Amato 1979). Patterns of military and ethnic domination that favored waterfront dwellers—and that combined extensive trade with sago dependence on lower-status bush peoples—were common along much of the Sepik, parts of the New Guinea north coast, the Admiralty Islands, and likely in many other regions of insular Melanesia as well, as alluded to many years ago by Rivers (1914: vol. 2: 304–7; see Gewertz 1983; Lutkehaus et al. 1990; Lipset 1985:71–75; Meeker, Barlow, and Lipset 1986:48ff., 55–62; Thurnwald 1916; cf. Bowden 1983:99, 105, 110, 165; Harrison 1982, 1987, 1993; Schwartz 1963).

104. Aggressive male ethos in Melanesia has been considered particularly for the Iatmul by Bateson (1936; cf. D'Amato 1979), for the Avatip by Harrison (1993); for the Gahuku-Gama by Read (1952, 1955, 1959, 1965; see Langness 1974), for the Sambia by Herdt (1981, 1986, 1987a), and more widely in the context of social organization, initia-

acknowledgment of these factors by Read (1954), the dominant tendency has been to follow Langness (1967) and view Melanesian masculinity more as a result than as a cause of warfare. In a much-cited corollary argument, Langness (1974:208) suggests that the functional requisite of warfare in the societies of highland New Guinea demands that men eschew female association and bond with other men. "Given the necessity for strength and cooperation among males, it would be an intolerable situation" if such male bonding did not take place (Langness 1974:208).

> If a man, in the depths of his passion, or even in his everyday routine, came to favor his mother or wife and want to please her more than he wanted to please and help his fellows, the foundation of New Guinea social order would collapse. Men might even refuse to fight if it involved their affines and thus to defend the community. (208)

This perspective easily inverts classic functionalism without transcending it; given an assumed state of male warfare to begin with, heightened masculine aggression—and corollary sexual antagonism against women—become functional requisites of society, viz., so that the "need" for solidary groups of brave male warriors is met.[105] It could be countered, of course, that aggressive Melanesian masculinity has not been portrayed as a function of warfare so much as locked with war in mutual reinforcement. The posing of this relationship as a chicken-and-egg question is ultimately belied, however, by the ultimate reliance on functionalist arguments when coming to final causal or comparative conclusions.[106]

Even aside from ethnographic counterexamples where warfare was endemic but male initiation absent or very benign (such as the Purari, Mae Enga, Dani, and probably Asmat), the question is begged

---

tion, and ritual practices such as homosexuality (e.g., Allen 1967; Herdt 1982, 1984a). An early and influential but problematic characterization of gender and aggression in three Sepik societies was proposed by Mead (1935; contrast critique by Gewertz 1981, 1984).

105. Cf. Allen 1967; see critique by M. Strathern 1988: chap. 3; cf. Ross 1986.

106. E.g., Allen 1967; Langness 1967, 1974. This structural-functionalist legacy is continued in an influential review by Keesing (1982a) of male initiation in Papua New Guinea. Keesing reasons that traumatic male initiation cults have multifaceted dimensions but link ultimately to survival demands posed by endemic warfare and thence to societal needs for rigorous socialization of male warriors.

how cultural and psychological motivations gave rise to such distinctive and widely varying forms of Melanesian warfare to begin with. Why does warfare, as an assumed prime mover, motivate cultural and psychological orientation, rather than the other way around?

Endemic precolonial warfare, particularly in interior New Guinea but in other areas as well, brings to mind a culture of deeply fearful uncertainty and intermittent fright that is only dimly exposed through the lens of sociological and psychological functionalism. One need not be a full-fledged postmodernist to appreciate in work such as Taussig's (1987) the way that violent terror is itself a cultural force with huge impact in social as well as spiritual life.

A tentative step in this direction was arguably attempted in Hallpike's *Bloodshed and Vengeance in the Papuan Mountains* (1977). Having disavowed functionalist explanations of warfare (1973), Hallpike attempts to comprehend the motivational underpinnings of relentless violence among the Tauade. Unfortunately, his interpretation is more reactionary and condemnatory rather than penetrating. Tauade is "a society dominated by pride, bloodshed, and squalor" (1), populated by "savage men in the grip of a collective obsession with blood and death" (253) who "killed, and still do kill for the pleasure of killing" (7). Tauade come across as classic Hobbesians if not late Freudians; their life is not only nasty, brutish, and violently short, but willfully so. Hallpike does give valuable substantive documentation of Tauade political leadership, exchange systems, spiritual and emotional conceptualization, and the history of their pacification. However, the generalizations Hallpike draws from his extensive but superficial accounts of violence echo the nineteenth-century Melanesian trader as much as the twentieth-century ethnographer.

An important and relatively neglected aspect of Melanesian psychologies of violence is the important role played by private fear as the complement to male bravado. The public image of the brave and courageous warrior takes center stage in informant accounts and in most ethnography, viz., the man whose competitive actions speak largely for themselves and certainly louder than his words. To take this masculine ideal as self-evident, however, is to risk collapsing it with our own assumptions about competitive male individualism, thus failing to discern its own distinctive characteristics. This problem is clearly reflected in Marshall Sahlins's (1963:289) influential characterization of the Melanesian big-man:

> The Melanesian big-man seems so thoroughly bourgeois, so remi-
> niscent of the free enterprising rugged individual of our own her-
> itage . . . His every public action is designed to make a competitive
> and invidious comparison with others, to show a standing above
> the masses that is a product of his own personal manufacture.

The ethos portrayed here arguably stems from our own individualistic
and unreciprocating assumptions about manhood rather than the
group-collective assumptions of personhood and reciprocity that have
been pronounced in Melanesia.[107] In Western cultures, emphasis on
individual and heroic male aggression, particularly as a response to
threat or impugnment, was especially strong in the aftermath of World
War II. It was during this same period that ethnographers formed their
lasting impressions of indigenous warfare in interior New Guinea. As a
result, it has been all too easy to leave unexamined the psychology of
masculine aggression in New Guinea warfare by assuming that it is the
same as in our own cultural understanding. The diversity of Melanesian leadership and cultural orientations with respect to violence
underscore the inadequacy of this assumption.

One way to penetrate the psychological black box of male aggression in Melanesia is to consider its alter in uncertainty and fear. Many
accounts of New Guinea warfare, particularly in highland areas, suggest armed conflict was initiated not so much from a positive drive to
seek prestige or reward but from fear of attack—a preemptive raid
being preferable to a defensive response. Indeed, a key obstacle to the
control of highlands warfare has been the difficulty of combating
rumor and suspicion; each side is encouraged to preparedness and
action in the belief that the other side may suddenly attack. Comment-
ing on this pattern, Gordon and Meggitt (1985:147) note "[f]ear is probably a more potent force in shaping human and social destiny than is
bravery or entrepreneurial skill."

Likewise, in many indigenous descriptions of warfare and feuding, the prestige placed upon warfare has an element of post-facto
bravado that is crosscut by private realizations that war is born in
uncertainty and dismal in its results. Langness (1972b:183) notes that
despite the seeming ubiquitousness of Bena Bena violence and its
importance for masculine prestige,

---

107. Contrast Read 1955, 1959; Burridge 1975; M. Strathern 1988; cf. Hau'ofa 1975.

The Bena Bena universally condemn war. It is true that men do recount deeds of bravery and boast of their prowess in battle, but soldiers in many societies do this also, without positively sanctioning warfare.

This distinction is important to move beyond simple assessments that New Guinea warfare is motivated simply by the value of killing for its own sake, viz., the notion that "they fight for fun," as Hallpike and others suggest.[108] Even among the Tauade, admiration of ferocity and courage are complemented by the lack of control that makes these traits "wild" and "bad," whereas "a 'good' man is one who facilitates co-operation by his powers of co-ordination, and who is prepared both to offer and receive compensation in the settlement of disputes" (Hallpike 1977:232). Likewise, Koch (1983:201) notes for the war-ridden Jale,

> While in their songs and boastful speeches the Jale praise their bellicose stance and military feats and extol the pleasures of eating enemies and their pigs, in a more reflective mood several of their best warriors have told me that fighting is a "bad thing."

Tuzin (1982) has found similar gnawing doubts among Ilahita Arapesh during initiations that brutally traumatize junior males. Concerning Ilahita warfare specifically, he states (1976:46):

> Even with superior numbers and the element of surprise, nagging fears assailed them as they waited for their victims to waken. Did they learn of our plans and is it we who are in a trap? If things go wrong can I be sure of escaping through this unfamiliar terrain? Thoughts of death obtruded which were absent in the tumult and bravado of open combat.

Such assessments are only the tip of the iceberg concerning the psychocultural dimensions of collective violence and warfare in Melanesia. Among other caveats, the role of fear and uncertainty may be more applicable in areas where quotidian social conflict escalated easily to violence than in some coastal areas where warfare more often took the form of large-scale but infrequent raids. The masculine ideals

---

108. See similarly Orken 1974; Barnes 1962:9.

of forcefulness and aggressive demeanor are highly valued in many Melanesian societies, and especially in the New Guinea highlands; they are strongly and genuinely motivated and cannot be reduced to mere ideology. Everywhere, however, complementary local notions of shame, fear, and uncertainty combine complexly with emphasis on masculine pride, prowess, and prestige (e.g., Harrison 1990, 1993; Epstein 1984). The perception of intended revenge, victory, and/or spiritual rejuvenation are the positive side of a much more complex psychocultural dynamic that configures the motivations of Melanesian violence and that form the backdrop of continued conflicts in the region today.

Some of the most refined information on ethnopsychology and masculine aggression in Melanesia is found in Gilbert Herdt's extensive ethnographic corpus on the Sambia of the Anga-speaking region, southeast of the Papua New Guinea highlands.[109] Herdt details the idioms of Sambian masculinity, their intricate tie to psychodynamic conflicts and uncertainties in socialization, and the interdigitation of these with ritual initiation, warriorhood, and the configuration of masculine identity more generally. He draws upon structural-functional reasoning—the functional requisites of male socialization in a war-ridden society—but he transcends it both in the cultural nuances of his exposition and the subtle weaving in of alternative types and levels of analysis—the psychodynamics of early socialization, the symbolic and identity transformations of the secret initiation cult, and the uncertainties, fantasies, and predilections of individual men. Finally, Herdt addresses the important and neglected role of sexuality and eroticism in aggression, thus reengaging the study of gender antagonism and male violence at a much deeper level. What Herdt begins to address, and what still needs much greater consideration, is the contemporary relationship between masculine aggression and contemporary gender relations in Melanesia (see this vol., chap. 4).

The larger point is that the cultural and emotional dynamics that have underlain the perceived necessity of violent aggression in Melanesia are highly important; they cannot be taken for granted either as simple valuation of aggressive action and revenge, on the one hand, or as passive psychocultural responses to prior societal, emotional, or

---

109. E.g., Herdt 1981, 1982a, 1982b, 1984b, 1987a, 1987b; Herdt and Stoller 1990; see also the recent film version of "Guardians of the Flutes."

material needs, on the other. The changing configuration of these relationships is of special interest in the postcolonial era, for example, in recent studies of criminal gangs of so-called *raskols*.[110]

Culture, Power, and History

The statements and tactics of participants in Melanesian conflict—their own desires, commitments, and logics of interpretation and action—need to be more deeply penetrated than was often done in functionalist modes of reasoning. In the 1990s, an increasing number of studies have cultivated such awareness through descriptions of discourse and dispute in specific local circumstances.[111] As a complement to this recent work, the larger patterning and structure of sociodemographic, economic, and political opportunities and constraints may be considered, not as separate from subjective orientations, but in relations of reciprocal influence with them. Social action is in many respects a strategic compromise and creative negotiation between cultural dispositions and the constraints and opportunities of sociomaterial conditions. This continues to be the case in the contemporary postcolonial or neocolonial era, as new dimensions of material acquisition and prestige have become increasingly important (see this vol., chaps. 4, 5).

As has often been noted, the analytic notion of "practice" can be helpful in such respects, since it articulates the subjective values and orientations of actors with the pragmatics of sociopolitical constraint and inequality.[112] Such a perspective emphasizes the interface between subjective and politicoeconomic factors. This is particularly appropriate for considering topics such as warfare and violence, which are often concerned with armed assertion or resistance against political and/or ethnic inequity. Beyond social norms, the way that such practices reflect diversity of lived experiences and aspirations is especially important. The interweaving strands that link cultural orientations with sociopolitical and material outcomes can be carefully teased apart and analyzed rather than reducing one to the other or collapsing them by means of simplistic motivational assumptions.

---

110. E.g., A. J. Strathern 1992; Hart Nibbrig 1992; Goddard 1992, 1995; Dinnen 1997.

111. E.g., A. J. Strathern 1993b; Brison 1992; Goldman 1983, 1986, 1993; Merlan and Rumsey 1991; Harrison 1990, 1993.

112. Bourdieu 1977, 1990; Ortner 1984, 1989; Giddens 1979, 1984; see Knauft 1996: chap. 4.

    This form of analysis also encompasses and affords understanding
of historical developments. Indeed, the relationship between orientation and outcome is most richly evident over time. Concerning warfare
in Melanesia, a diachronic perspective becomes all the more crucial as
precolonial patterns of violence are overlain with postcolonial developments. The habitus of tribal conflict is now inflected through new contexts of authority and influence, including the idiosyncrasies and
inequalities of political economy at the regional, state, and international
levels. The public culture of popular perception is also influenced by
widespread new forms of media imagery, technology, and associated
value. In highlands tribal conflicts, for instance, resulting hybridity is
dramatically reflected in the making of homemade guns (A. J. Strathern
1992) and in new fighting shields, which now combine images of clan
solidarity with advertising images of male affiliation associated with
sports teams or bottled beer (see photo 16; O'Hanlon 1995a). The influence of male alcohol consumption is increasingly important to an
understanding of interpersonal violence in the highlands, as emphasized by Wormsley (1987b; more generally, see Marshall 1982).
    Studies of Melanesian conflict in the twenty-first century will need
to move increasingly between fine-grained analysis of local cultural
and sociological processes, on the one hand, and critical analysis of
regional and state-level sociopolitical and economic processes, on the
other.[113] This calls for mediation between larger scale "epochal" and
smaller scale "historical" analyses (more generally, see Donham 1990).
    With respect to such issues, works such as Gordon and Meggitt's
Law and Order in the New Guinea Highlands (1985) are particularly
salient.[114] Gordon and Meggitt analyze the complex political and social
issues that inform modern Enga warfare and attempts to control it.
Among other things, they trace the social and judicial role played by
the colonial kiaps; the reduction of perceived legal constraint in the
highlands following the independence of Papua New Guinea (what
A. J. Strathern [1977] calls the "Administrative Gap"); the political
interests and lack of countermeasures that lead to the resurgence of
warfare; and the opposed interests of the national government and the
highlanders themselves—an opposition that makes the alleviation of

---

    113. Preliminary if somewhat underspecified books on this issue include Fitz-
patrick 1980 and Amarshi, Good, and Mortimer 1979.
    114. See also A. J. Strathern 1984, 1993a, b; Dinnen 1997.

highlands warfare particularly difficult.[115] Similar themes are analyzed in Andrew Strathern's *A Line of Power* (1984). As these works illustrate, the most effective and humane forms of ameliorating violence are likely to be those that draw upon local values and practices of nonviolent sanction and infuse them with legitimate authority without compromising their responsiveness to indigenous conditions and perceptions (see also Dinnen 1997). Recent developments are a reminder that though Melanesian warfare has been a fascinating topic of study, the potentials for reducing contemporary violence should be an important part of our explanatory impetus.

Implications for Future Research

Several implications may be drawn from the present review for future research. First, it is important to consider more seriously and in greater detail the strategies, tactics, goals, and values of actors with respect to armed aggression and collective violence. Indigenous perspectives, articulated through rich case studies, give an effective basis for analyzing local political and economic dynamics that inform collective violence in Melanesia. As well as being relevant to applied concerns, documentation and analysis of indigenous perspectives can articulate with politicoeconomic theory without giving in to simplistic assumptions concerning the ultimate causes of violence.

Second, the division between collective and individual violence needs to be reconceptualized. Increasingly in Melanesia, violence reveals a tension between newer and more individual desires and aspirations, on the one hand, and traditional obligations and affiliations to allies, natal kin, and in cross-gender relationships, on the other. By reconsidering the tension between individual and social concerns, important current problems such as *raskolism* and domestic violence or wife-beating can be articulated with rather than divorced from the study of armed aggression in Melanesia.[116] In the process, the role of

---

115. Gordon and Meggitt's account ends with a reasoned recommendation that social control should be cultivated locally and administered with formal authority through village courts (cf. also Scaglion 1987, 1990). Though village courts carry their own problems and are not a panacea, as Zuckerman (1987) notes for eastern highlands and Wormsley (1987a:72ff.) discusses for Enga, Gordon and Meggitt's general emphasis on local initiative in conflict resolution remains important.

116. For instance, see Goddard 1995; Toft 1990; this volume, chap. 4.

women as targets and sometimes as facilitators of aggression can be much more closely articulated with the study of Melanesian violence than has typically been the case.

Third, it is important to study local conflict and violence in the context of larger structures of political power and attempted control. Increasingly in Melanesia, collective violence is inflected by the assertion of provincial or state or corporate power and local resistance against it. This is not the social control of structural-functionalism, in which order was assumed to be a natural precipitate of political structure (see critique in M. Strathern 1985). Rather, it is a realization of the ways that order and the definition of appropriate social control are themselves contested. As such, local patterns of violence need to be viewed in relation to the assertion of authority at higher political levels, including regional, national, and international corporate contexts.

These relations can have their own predisposing colonial histories. Melanesian interests in and opportunities for collective violence have long been structured by inequality and/or competition at various levels of indigenous political organization, which have differentially subordinated women, children, younger men, adult men, competitive exchange partners, local big-men, and/or alliance leaders. On a larger geographic scale, precolonial warfare was centrally related to areal patterns of military, ethnic, and cultural dominance and/or subordination, as well as regional configurations of exchange, marriage, and leadership rivalry.

During the colonial era, these relations were both encapsulated within and galvanized by coercive force and the threat of such force by patrol officers and administrators. Kiaps and courts became new icons of power, control, and opposition. Now, in the postcolonial era, Melanesian nation-states assume the legacy of this history uneasily as they themselves attempt to solidify or maintain control over disparate provinces and peoples who are frequently restive and occasionally rebellious. Understanding the dynamics and trajectory of these tensions will be increasingly important as Melanesian violence develops in the twenty-first century. These developments become particularly important as various district, provincial, national, and multinational corporate interests are brought into play. In current circumstances it is difficult to understand local patterns of collective violence apart from these relationships.

Fourth and finally, studies of war should find increasing value in

adopting a diachronic perspective. This is not only because the sociopolitical contexts of conflict are developing so rapidly in Melanesia, but
because the wealth of existing ethnography provides an invaluable
baseline from which developmental changes can be understood. In this
respect, a historical perspective can build upon rather than jettison the
classic ethnography on "tribal warfare" in Melanesia.

On a larger temporal scale, it may be noted that conflict, warfare,
and politicodemographic displacement have characterized the spread
of peoples eastward through Melanesia for many millennia (White and
O'Connell 1982). Pressured ultimately from southeast Asia, these
movements have helped inform the great linguistic and cultural diversity of New Guinea and other parts of Melanesia (Wurm 1983).[117]

The contemporary freezing of ethnic and district borders through
nation-state imposition creates friction against the long-standing ferment of indigenous political and demographic movements. Like fault
lines that absorb pressure, fixed boundaries become the focus of local
land and larger regional disputes. In crisis, the tensions indexed and
symbolized at these boundaries send tremors through the political
structure; when they are forcibly altered through warfare, corporate
development projects, or change of political regime, the result may be
tantamount to a sociocultural quake. At the highest level, what is
feared most is tectonic movement that realigns the borders of nation-
states themselves.

Such trends are exemplified by the local, areal, and international
conflicts that have resulted from recent attempts to colonize western
Melanesia from southeast Asia, including Indonesian transmigration
and enculturation of West New Guinea.[118] By virtue of its state-level
political control and military organization, Indonesian encroachment
extends and intensifies the organizational scale of southeast Asian
impingement into Melanesia, pressing politically against the fixed border between Indonesia and Papua New Guinea. Indonesian governance also produces significant counterrepercussions and new forms of
indigenous resistance warfare, such as the OPM freedom fighters and

---

117. A number of ethnographies document local dimensions of this process, for
instance, population movements entailing warfare and displacement in the shifting political geography of precolonial Melanesia; see Roscoe 1989, 1997; Forge 1990; Brown 1972;
Oosterwal 1961:27ff.; 46–59; Larson 1986; Morren 1986: chap. 10; Guiart 1956, 1963a;
Healey 1985; Knauft 1985a: chap. 8; Wagner 1988; Thurnwald 1934.

118. Gietzelt 1988; Rutherford 1996; Monbiot 1989; Lagerberg 1979; Lijphart 1966;
Garnaut and Manning 1974; cf. Hastings 1968, 1982.

the plight of Irian refugees.[119] Such conflicts engage larger tensions between Indonesia and Papua New Guinea across their common border.[120] It is but a crude index of the political and cultural asymmetries that inform this conflict of national interests that the population of Indonesia is well over 200 million persons—the fourth largest nation in the world—as opposed to a population of perhaps four and a half million persons in Papua New Guinea.

As the cultural infrastructure of larger power asymmetries, the politics of ethnic identity are vital to an understanding of local, regional, and national conflicts (see this book, chap. 5). As persuasively suggested by Anderson (1983), nationhood is itself in important respects an imagined identity. In the Melanesian context, the production of modern nation-states has been particularly difficult given the diversity and dispersion if not isolation of local populations (cf. Foster 1995b). Given this, crosscutting influences and affiliations become particularly important. Thus, for instance, it is especially important to the dynamics of conflict and the potentials for collective violence to understand the cultural dynamics of "Indonesianization" in West New Guinea; the tense elaboration of extended ethnic or *wantok* relations across Papua New Guinea; the relation between national control and provincial rebellion in Bougainville; the conflict between nationhood and local *kastom* in Vanuatu and the Solomon Islands; the ethnic schism between Indians and ethnic Fijians, which resulted in a violent coup in Fiji in 1987; and the continuing struggle between Kanaks and the descendants of French colonialism in New Caledonia.[121] In all these cases, local cultural identifications abut tensely and with violent potentials against larger national interests. On the island of Bougainville, such tensions have merged with struggles over large-scale mineral resources and resulted in secessionist warfare. Stalemated by the attempts of the P.N.G. Defense Force to reconquer the island, this conflict has caused a prolonged shutdown of services to the province, prolonging violence, hardship, and misery among the local population.[122]

It is not possible within the scope of the present analysis to give adequate consideration to the articulation of violence with nationalist

119. E.g., Monbiot 1989: chap. 11; Kirsch 1996c.
120. E.g., May 1986; Griffin 1986.
121. See Griffin 1986; A. J. Strathern 1993a; White and Lindstrom 1993; Linnekin and Poyer 1990; Scarr 1988; Lawson 1991; Weitzman 1985; Connell 1987, 1988.
122. See Wesley-Smith 1992; Hyndman 1994.

and micronationalist movements in Bougainville and other parts of Melanesia.[123] In the *longue durée*—patterns of the long term—concern with such developments may benefit from historical and comparative assessment against the rich and extensive but now largely neglected literature on Melanesian cargo cults and resistance movements such as John Frum, Maasina Rule, the Black King Cult, Vailala Madness, Newfela Fashion, and many others.[124]

Looking from the present toward the future, the ferment that links Melanesian cultural and economic aspiration to political resistance increasingly engages local desires and discontents with corporate and national development projects for the extraction of gold, copper, oil and gas, or timber.[125] These nexuses of dispute will certainly be central in the development of Melanesian violence in future decades.

If the course of Melanesian collective violence articulates cultural assumptions, political strategies, and economic interests across local and regional levels, then the study of Melanesian warfare will need increasingly to comprehend these same articulations. That the topic of "warfare" as configured in classic ethnographic parlance may ultimately become an anachronism is less important than that the insights of previous scholarship be both critically and productively employed as part of the larger study of conflict and collective violence, both actual and potential.

Considering the Future from the Past: The Value of Ethnographic Historicism

Given the waning if not the extinction of precolonial warfare in much of Melanesia, it becomes increasingly easy to relegate indigenous warfare to a precolonial period that fades in salience with advancing time. But this would ignore legacies of collective violence both within Melanesian societies and between local populations and colonial or postcolonial powers. To combat this tendency, it is important to critically assess what anthropologists have and have not learned about

---

123. E.g., Hyndman 1987; Beasant 1984; May 1982; Guiart 1983; Connell 1987; Robie 1989.

124. See overviews in Worsley 1968; Knauft 1978; Steinbauer 1979; Bodrogi 1951; and case studies such as Burridge 1960; Lawrence 1964; Schwartz 1962; Kamma 1972; Laracy 1971, 1983; Williams 1923b; cf. Lattas 1992a, 1992b; Wanek 1996.

125. E.g., Hyndman 1994; Filer 1990, 1997; Toft 1997; Bennett 1995; Barlow and Winduo 1997.

Melanesian warfare—where our record of the subject is rich and where
thin, and how the trajectory of our discipline's own theoretical interests
has shaped this corpus of knowledge over more than a century of
study.

To review, warfare was relatively neglected in the early Melanesian ethnography and its violence downplayed in structural-functional
approaches. These biases must be seen, both positively and negatively,
in the historical context of academic concerns during the colonial
period. On the one hand, the portrayal of a well-ordered and functionally controlled primitive society echoed the desires and goals of colonial administration. On the other hand, structural-functional
approaches emphasized the political autonomy of local people and
suggested, at least implicitly, that they functioned quite well without
external governance or interference by colonial authorities.

The explanatory legacy of functional and structural anthropology
has strongly illuminated the connection between Melanesian warfare
and social organizational, ecological, and economic factors. At the same
time, it has also ultimately demonstrated quite strongly that these connections are not ones of simple causality. As such, functional and structural approaches to warfare have been supplemented by perspectives
that emphasize processes of politicoeconomic change and/or intensification. These offer a broader areal and temporal vantage point and
stress how changes relevant to warfare emerge from systemic patterns
of reinforcement among sociomaterial and political conditions.

In hindsight, it can be seen that most existing accounts of warfare
in Melanesia have insufficiently penetrated the indigenous cultural
underpinnings and psychological dynamics of violence. This neglect
becomes all the more important to remedy in a postcolonial era. Most
approaches have been uncritical of their own historical and political
foundations and have often perpetuated assumptions inherited from
previous approaches, for example, an a priori tendency to emphasize
restricted combat and assume a strong relationship between political
organization and social control.

Conceptually, Hobbesian assumptions underlie both the functional analysis of Melanesian warfare as a vehicle for structural or economic control and the ecological analysis of war as a natural expression
of environmental relations. More blatant Hobbesian assumptions, of
course, also informed the earlier nineteenth-century perceptions of
Melanesian savagery. In the earlier Western folk-view, Melanesian sav-

agery cried out for political control by colonial powers, the benevolent Leviathan. In later and more enlightened structural-functionalist views, the inevitability of violent conflict likewise demanded societal control, but this control was self-evident in the rules and regulations of indigenous sociopolitical structure. Native custom became the sociological equivalent of natural law. In ecological functionalism, warfare was a result of inexorable Darwinian or Malthusian competition over biotic and human resources, expressed across a range of environmentally mediated conditions. Both of these latter approaches are easily articulated with a kind of neo-structural-functionalism, in which political units are defined by their effectiveness in internally constraining aggressive competition and orchestrating its expression in forms of conflict among solidary groups—for example, in a highly organized, ritualized, or analogously rule-governed manner.[126] Correspondingly, the organization of warfare derives from the need for structure and order which this competition creates.

As against this, the study of Melanesian violence now focuses increasingly on (1) the motivations and strategies of local actors, (2) larger and more contemporary contexts of politicoeconomic and cultural relationship, (3) temporal change, and (4) the relationship between collective and individual violence, including a greater consideration of gender relations. These emphases broaden our understanding of violence by taking more seriously the motivating power of indigenous cultural and ethnopsychological formulations, on the one hand, and by examining more carefully the articulation between cultural values and politicoeconomic conditions and constraints, both over time and at broader levels of political and economic influence. The relationship among cultural identity, politicoeconomic interest, and the assertion of control through violent conflict can be elucidated by integrating detailed local studies with consideration of larger scale historical, cultural, and politicoeconomic processes. Such work can build upon the ethnographic richness, comparative sweep, and potential for larger theoretical elaboration that the existing literature on Melanesian warfare abundantly affords. Finally, it is important to be mindful of our

---

126. More generally, Marxist, Freudian, and sociobiological perspectives on warfare tend to assume universal causes for violent competition and the need for its control. These are driven, respectively, by the imperatives of political domination, sexual gratification, or biogenetic propagation. In these perspectives, then, warfare emerges from a uniform and underlying competitive drive.

own theoretical and cultural suppositions, their historical roots, and our potential for enlarging them through critical self-awareness. It is important to see armed conflict in Melanesia both as a record of knowledge that reflects the historical and present concerns of those who have studied it, and as a past and present field of experience lived most poignantly by Melanesians themselves.

Chapter 4

Gender and Modernity in Melanesia and Amazonia

Gender relations in Melanesia illustrate the cultural plasticity of relations between men and women. The anthropology of Melanesian gender relations, accordingly, has a long and rich history that echoes this diversity. Ethnographic case studies from individual Melanesian societies have often portrayed gendered beliefs and practices that call into question cross-cultural assumptions about male–female relationships. Even in the 1920s and 1930s, legendary anthropologists such as Bronislaw Malinowski and Margaret Mead used information they had obtained from Melanesian societies to question the universality of the Oedipus complex, on the one hand, and male dominance, on the other.[1] During the 1950s and 1960s, research in highland areas of Melanesia drew on striking new evidence and emphasized the depth of gendered polarity and what has been called "sexual antagonism" in Melanesia.[2] By the 1970s and 1980s, however, important works by authors such as Marilyn Strathern (1972), Annette Weiner (1976), and Rena Lederman (1986) used primary ethnographic data collected from a female perspective to complicate and question models of male-dominated sociopolitical organization that had been prevalent in structural views of kinship and exchange.[3] Over this same period, other authors—both male and female—supplied accounts that further documented the ways and extent to which Melanesian women could also be subordinated to men, sometimes brutally.[4] As these accounts collectively reveal, there is a great deal of cultural variation in gender relations within Melanesia as well as more widely.

---

1. See Malinowski 1927, 1929; Mead 1930, 1935; see also Bateson 1936.

2. See Read 1952, 1954; Berndt 1962; Meggitt 1964; Langness 1967, 1974; cf. Herdt and Poole 1982; see Tuzin 1997.

3. See also Lepowsky 1993; Lutkehaus 1995; Lutkehaus and Roscoe 1995; Errington and Gewertz 1987a.

4. See Josephides 1985; Godelier 1986; A. J. Strathern 1982d; cf. Brown and Buchbinder 1976.

*During the 1980s and 1990s, many previous studies and debates con-
cerning the status of women in Melanesia have been overlain or superseded by
additional concerns. Prominent among these has been the deeper investigation
of how Melanesian gender operates through cultural idioms or cosmologies of
belief. In many cases, more refined perspectives on Melanesian gender have
provided new vantage points for understanding the relationship between social
affiliation, exchange of material items, and the transaction of social services or
bodily substances. Influential in this respect has been Marilyn Strathern's
book* The Gender of the Gift *(1988). Gilbert Herdt's detailed work on ritual
homosexuality and fantasy in Melanesia has additionally undercut a number
of universalizing assumptions about sexual orientations in general and homosexuality in particular.*[5]

*Overall, the diversity of Melanesian gender and sexuality has been
accorded great theoretical importance as well as ethnographic attention by
anthropologists. Happily, this trend is likely to continue into the future.*

*Other dimensions of Melanesian gender and sexuality are also important
and deserve attention. One of these is the way that gender relations are developing in the postcolonial or neocolonial era.*[6] *Since indigenous and introduced
patterns of change are increasingly related, it is important that the distinctiveness of Melanesian gender relations also be seen in the context of broad economic and cultural trajectories. In the present essay, I explore this theme by
combining recent information about Melanesian gender relations with a consideration of larger political economic influences and broadly associated cultural trends. Patterns of change in one world area can sometimes be perceived
more generally when they are compared to those found in another part of the
globe. In the present case, accordingly, Melanesian gender relations are compared to and contrasted with those evident in Amazonia, which is a world area
that exhibits intriguing similarities to and yet significant differences from
Melanesia.*

*Relations between women and men in Melanesia and Amazonia—as in
most other world regions—reflect the impact of modern economic and political
influences. Prominent among these are local desires to be "successful" or
"developed" in acquiring commodities, money, and their associated power or
influence. In the process, local changes often engage more ostensibly "modern"*

---

5. See Herdt 1981, 1982b, 1987a, 1992; Herdt and Stoller 1990.
6. See Jolly 1994; Lutkehaus 1995; Watson 1997; Nihill 1994; Wardlow 1998; Stürzenhofecker 1998.

values; indigenous traditions may be devalued in favor of notions of success and prestige that are seen as more progressive and contemporary. These aspirations often incorporate dimensions of colonial, national, or Christian beliefs or ideologies.

All these developments have a pronounced impact on gender relations. Reciprocally, they are themselves shaped by deeply held views about what activities and aspirations are appropriate for men as opposed to women. The desire to achieve status in a contemporary or modern way often places men and women in relationships that are new and yet informed by long-standing cultural suppositions about what it means to be properly male or female. It has often been noted, more broadly, that local desires to "become more modern" afford new possibilities for personal identification, affiliation, and imagination.[7] Less often appreciated in this literature is how new forms of identity and new values of success are differentially encouraged for men versus women. Attempts to understand large-scale patterns of cultural and socioeconomic change easily relegate gender relations to a peripheral part of the picture.[8] In fact, however, gendered subordination is often maintained and reinforced by the assumption that being "more successful" or "more modern" entails being "more masculine," and vice versa (cf. Boserup 1970).

The present essay evaluates this notion against contemporary patterns of gender and sexuality in Melanesia and Amazonia. In the process, a range of classic literature about gender polarity, antagonism, and domination in these world areas is critically re-evaluated. The larger goal is to assess the gendered dimensions of social and cultural change in contemporary Melanesia and Amazonia.

Over the last four decades, the ethnography of gender in Melanesia and in Amazonia has exhibited a number of common themes. As scholars have noted, both of these world areas have shared significant features pertaining to rain-forest ecology and adaptation, to acephalous sociopolitical organization and exchange, and to elaborate spiritual beliefs, ritual cults, or initiations relating to cosmological life force and

---

7. See Appadurai 1996; Hannerz 1996; cf. also Giddens 1990; Harvey 1990.
8. See authors listed above in note #7; contrast Giddens 1992.

fertility. Cultures in both regions have often foregrounded gendered and sexual polarity or opposition—sometimes associated with aggressive male domination or antagonism against women—as a central dimension of social life and symbolic organization.[9]

In both Melanesia and the Amazon, a number of studies carried out between the 1950s and the 1980s attempted to link opposition between men and women with the structural stresses and effects of collective male bonding, on the one hand, and to a psychology of male insecurity and resentment against women, on the other. Studies from both regions considered the relationship between sexual antagonism, social structure, and psychology.[10] Now, however, these arguments juxtapose uneasily with changing patterns of gender and sexuality in Melanesia and Amazonia. Local notions of manhood and womanhood increasingly engage the tensions created by growing dependence on trade goods, aspirations to economic development, and the intrusion of nationalist economic and political agendas. The intertwining of commodity aspirations with ethnic, racial, and national dimensions of disempowerment is especially important to local constructions of masculine prestige and feminine propriety.

The larger ethnographic and theoretical issue I address is how gendered identities are inflected by local configurations of modernity—what it means for men and for women to be considered successful under contemporary circumstances. These notions draw upon, and often reinforce, long-standing gendered oppositions at the same time

---

9. For instance, Naomi Quinn (1977:215–16) suggests that

> [a] distinctive complex of customs, which has been labeled "sex antagonism," has long been recognized as typical of societies in two widely separated regions of the world—the Brazilian Amazon and the New Guinea Highlands. . . . These customs figure in composite pictures of male supremacy [which include] institutionalized gang rape . . . a concern with female pollution; a preoccupation with male sexual depletion; and elaborate male ceremonial activities, knowledge of which must be kept secret from women. [Elizabeth] Faithorn (1976:87) has summarized ethnographic description of sex antagonism in New Guinea as centering on "the three interrelated themes of sexual segregation, male dominance/female subservience, and male purity/female pollution."

10. E.g., Read 1952; Murphy 1957, 1959, 1960; M. R. Allen 1967; Meggitt 1964; Langness 1967, 1974; see also Herdt and Poole 1982; Keesing 1982a; cf. Chagnon 1983; Divale and Harris 1976.

that they cut across or compromise some of their features. Specific parallels between both world areas are evident in these respects. As will be discussed, however, the major differences in Amazonian and Melanesian gender relations are influenced by (1) a traditional emphasis on bridewealth in much of Melanesia as opposed to emphasis on bride-service in much of Amazonia;[11] (2) the gendered impact of Melanesian politicians as super big-men or great men as opposed to the significance of mestizo patron-client relations for gender relations in Amazonia; and (3) the variable degree to which local gender identities are confronted with national regimes that disparage or attempt to destroy indigenous ways of life.

Classic Views: Male Affiliation and Sexual Antagonism in Melanesia and Amazonia

A number of studies have suggested that sexual antagonism in Melanesia and Amazonia was linked to the structural constraints of collective male bonding and to a psychology of male insecurity and gendered resentment. Much of this view ultimately relied on assumptions about the universality of male aggression and the importance of suppressing discord and promoting affiliation among male groups. The models to which I am referring have suggested that male insecurity is caused in the first instance by warfare or other threats to male corporate identity. To combat this insecurity, the social solidarity and functional integrity of the male group was ostensibly facilitated by men's antagonism toward women and toward enemy groups. Accordingly, a mutually reinforcing relationship has been posited among (1) male bonding; (2) sexual antagonism; and (3) warfare or competitive exchange or alliance. Which of these interrelated features is seen as causal and which is viewed as an effect has depended on the author,

---

11. Bridewealth entails a series of exchanges through which the kin of the groom compensate the kin of the bride for her transfer out of their group and into that of the groom. Brideservice is recompense to the bride's kin by means of labor and services, which are typically performed by the groom for the benefit of his new in-laws. Besides marital exchange through bridewealth or brideservice, direct marital reciprocity or "sister-exchange" marriage—exchanging brides reciprocally between groups—was customary in some parts of both Melanesia and Amazonia. However, this last form of marital exchange is becoming less prominent as outside influence grows and there are greater expectations of receiving cash and commodities in marital transactions.

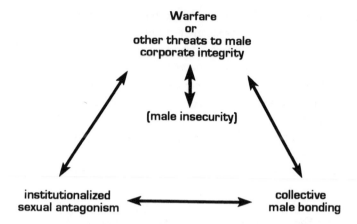

Fig. 6.   Classic connections in Melanesian and Amazonian gender relations

the ethnographic specifics, and the analytic perspective—for instance,
the privileging of psychosexual, social structural, or military imperatives (see fig. 6).

A few permutations of this reasoning may be examined more
closely. Read's (1952) early Durkheimian article on the Nama cult of the
Gahuku Gama in the New Guinea highlands emphasized the structural
significance of male bonding under conditions of masculine competition; it considered sexual antagonism to be functionally related to the
need for male solidarity.[12] Relatedly, Allen (1967) suggested that sexual
antagonism and mandatory male initiation were most developed in
conjunction with patrilocal and patrilineal social organization, which
tended to coalesce male collective interests in opposition to those of
women. Feil (1987: chap. 7) expanded this reasoning and proposed a
suite of features that included (1) intense warfare; (2) a relative paucity
of intergroup exchange; (3) patrilocal social organization; (4) initiation
cults; (5) a high degree of sexual antagonism; and (6) low female status;
he attempted to show that all of these were characteristic of the eastern
highlands of Papua New Guinea and attenuated among the more
developed big-man and elaborate exchange systems of the western
highlands.

Langness (1967), and to some degree Herdt (1987a), also writing

12. See also Read 1954, 1959, 1965.

about New Guinea highland or fringe highland areas, tended to treat warfare as a given to which male-male and male-female relations had to respond. In this view, the collective bonding of male warriors put them in structural opposition to women; sexual antagonism became a functional correlate of the need for male solidarity in warfare. The association of women with outsiders, as stressed by Meggitt (1964), resulted in an identification between women and enemies; men's antagonism was projected onto both. That women in some groups were in-married from the very groups that men fought in warfare ("We marry the people we fight") facilitated the association of women with enemies.

Cross-cultural researchers such as the Whitings (1975) considered the connection between warfare and sex antagonism from the perspective of psychology and child socialization. They suggested that "the widespread belief that contact with women is dangerous or weakening for a warrior before battle . . . may have induced middle level societies who most frequently engaged in war to adopt the rooming apart pattern [for husbands and wives]" (1975:198). Correspondingly, when "the rooming apart pattern was adopted, it had unanticipated consequences of inducing sex identity conflict" (198). This resulted in reduced intimacy and increased aggressiveness among sons, which the authors felt was "adaptive as long as all young men in each generation had to become warriors" (198).

Based on Amazonian data, the assumed functionality of male opposition to women under conditions of warfare received perhaps its most extreme formulation from Divale and Harris (1976) and Chagnon (1988). Following an elaborate train of physiological, social organizational, and demographic reasoning, Divale and Harris suggested that a male supremacist complex—involving patrilocality, polygyny, female infanticide, male fierceness, and female passivity—was adaptive for population control under conditions of intense warfare. Developing a sociobiological interpretation, Chagnon (1988, cf. 1983) reinterpreted his data on Yanomamö violence and kinship and argued that male fierceness and violence could be explained by biogenetic selection. Like its predecessors, this argument contained reductionist assumptions that have been hotly contested on both ethnographic and theoretical grounds.[13]

---

13. See Ramos 1987; Tiffany and Adams 1994; Albert 1985, 1989; Albert and Ramos 1989; Ferguson 1989, 1995; Knauft 1988; Lizot 1985.

Gregor (1979, 1985, 1990), also writing about Amazonia, has emphasized behavioral and psychological means through which sexual competition can be politically defused among men while antagonism is directed against women. Mehinaku men dominate women through what Gregor (1979, 1990) calls the "men's house complex," which excludes women from male secrets and sacrae on the threat of beatings, gang rape, or death. Men also project their sexual desires and anxieties in elaborate dreams and myths. Men have thus used sexual imagery and images of masculine assertiveness to facilitate, rather than compromise, collective male bonding. In contrast to the Yanomamö, male political relations have been surprisingly peaceful and "extramarital affairs seldom provoke serious confrontation" (Gregor 1985:31). Beyond the village, collective notions of male identity informed larger political confederations that facilitated alliances and forestalled intercommunity warfare (Gregor 1994).

The larger relationship between male cohesion, gender antagonism, and psychology was considered under the general umbrella of male power and domination by Langness (1974) in regard to highland New Guinea (cf. chap. 3, this book).[14] Tuzin (1997) has recently provided an extended case study from the Sepik area of New Guinea that considers how the demise of male cults in the postcolonial era produces heightened male insecurity. Discussion of male bonding and sexual antagonism are found more diffusely in a range of Amazonian ethnography.[15] In the Peruvian Amazon, Siskind notes for the Sharanahua that male competition is integral to the structure of village life and that this competition

> is contained by the absolute prohibition of any open competitive behavior between men and finds expression instead in contempt for foreigners and male solidarity in the battle of the sexes. (1973:106)

Writing of Tukanoan symbolism of sexual violence in the northwest Amazon, Jackson suggests,

---

14. Politicoeconomic perspectives on the structure and dynamics of male domination were also developed during the 1980s by Melanesianists such as Godelier (1986), Josephides (1985), A. J. Strathern (1982c), Lederman (1986; cf. also A. B. Weiner 1976; M. Strathern 1972).

15. See T. Turner 1979a, b, Rivière 1984, and Mentore 1987, among others.

Given the ongoing threat to collective male agnatic ability to encompass and subordinate individual men's ties to women, ritual statements about this threat will contain elements emphasizing maleness, fierceness, violence, and assertions of male agnatic solidarity. (1992:14)

Several authors have associated differences in sexual antagonism or gender domination in the northwest Amazon with differences in patrifocal kinship and corresponding patterns of same-sex residence or affiliation.[16]

The most general and influential argument concerning male cohesion, gender antagonism, and psychology for the Amazon was developed by Robert Murphy, beginning in the late 1950s. Murphy (1959:97) suggested that

Institutionalized sex antagonism . . . is not just functional to the sex differentiation of the individual, does not just provide a form of abreaction of primary experiences, but it also maintains the internal solidarity and external boundaries of the sex-ascribed groups through opposition.

In another early article (1957; cf. also 1960), Murphy emphasized the importance of warfare as a means of promoting social cohesion. In a sense, this is the obverse of Langness's later argument for highland New Guinea: namely, that the demands of psychosocial cohesion make warfare a functional necessity.

Critique

There are several criticisms that can be leveled at classic models of sexual antagonism in Melanesia and Amazonia. First, they tend to reify male groups and make male affiliations and identities a product of ostensible group autonomy. As such, the theoretical perspective tends toward static functionalism. Second, the model is reductive and ultimately relies on universal assumptions about men's organizational and psychological or sexual needs. Finally, the associations are patricentric;

---

16. E.g., Langdon 1984; Shapiro 1973, 1982; Ramos 1996; see S. Hugh-Jones 1979; C. Hugh-Jones 1979; Chagnon 1983.

women and their complementary impact on gender relations are neglected or considered epiphenomenal to male status. Features such as male sexual antagonism and male solidarity shortchange the perspective of women; gender becomes determined by relations between men rather than through the co-development of male and female identifications.

From the standpoint of a feminist critique, these perspectives are all open to the charge that they rationalize gender antagonism as a functional necessity. Animosity against women is legitimated as a natural result of cohesion among men. In this respect, they echo rather than question the Hobbesian assumption that social and sexual animosity is a primordial state that needs to be contained by men's moral contracts and collective institutions.[17] The experience of women is often considered residual in these perspectives, despite the rich ethnography of gender relations that has resulted from research in both world areas.[18] Much of this work has revealed how women's practical influence complicates if not counteracts formal structures and ideologies of male gender domination.

Amid accelerating social change and economic intrusion, it is problematic nowadays to assume that social organization (much less gender roles) is a stable feature of analysis. Cultural and politicoeconomic influences combine regional, national, and international influences, as emphasized more generally in Appadurai 1996, Friedman 1994, Hannerz 1992, 1996, and Miller 1994, 1995; see also Harvey 1990; cf. Wolf 1982. However, most of these theories of global cultural change, and its impact in non-Western areas, are mute or minimalist when it comes to issues of gender. Women tend to be left out of the dynamics of late modernity. This belies the key fact that local engagements with and appropriations of what is "modern" tend to be highly different for men as opposed to women (cf. Moore 1994: chap. 3). Indeed, male aspirations to become more "developed" or "successful" are often established through masculine control or constraint of women in these same terms.

17. This line of Hobbesian reasoning has been critiqued and insightfully inverted in the Sepik context of New Guinea by Harrison (1993).

18. E.g., for Melanesia: M. Strathern 1972, 1988; A. B. Weiner 1976; Faithorn 1976; Lederman 1986, 1991; Sexton 1986; Lepowsky 1993; Jolly 1994; Lutkehaus 1995; Lutkehaus and Roscoe 1995; for Amazonia: Bellier 1993; Murphy and Murphy 1974; Siskind 1973; C. Hugh-Jones 1979; Langdon 1984, 1991; Seymour-Smith 1991; Jackson 1992; Kensinger 1995; Ramos 1995, 1996; see also Bamberger 1974.

Given the frequent neglect of gender in general theories of cultural development,[19] it is not hard to see why feminist theories of contemporary gender relations have, particularly in the arts and humanities, emphasized the potential for new and less constrained forms of gendered identity. Many of these more recent theories emphasize the potentials for gendered "resignification" that emerge in a late-modern or postmodern era.[20] These more flexible identities afford women (both straight and lesbian—as well as straight and gay men) the creative possibilities of mix-and-match gender roles. These may take hybrid forms and combine discordant features. This pastiche can both reflect and resist the disparate contexts and disjunctive social affiliations entailed by living in a complex modern world.

From the vantage point of these so-called postmodern or queer perspectives, the classic assumption that gender roles are stable and coherent in regions such as Melanesia is misguided and anachronistic. Assumptions concerning gender coherence may instead reflect assumptions based on our own Western cultural history. In the present case, for instance, the connection ostensibly found during the 1950s and 1960s between male social organization and gender opposition in "tribal societies" might be said to reflect a heightened Western emphasis on institutional male bonding in the wake of World War II. During this period, there was enormous Western concern to maintain and reinforce our own male military and corporate institutions. These emphases were general to our society, and anthropologists were not immune to incorporating their assumptions in their own dispositions and theories of the postwar era.

Even as we acknowledge the impact of Western culture and history upon ethnographic analysis, however, it would be shortsighted to neglect the resonance between classic ethnographic views and the lived experience of gender in Amazonia and Melanesia in previous decades. Classic accounts facilitated the deeper ethnography of gendered beliefs and practices even as they viewed these in a narrow functional way. Robert and Yolanda Murphy (1974; Murphy 1960), among others, emphasized how gendered organization was influenced by historical transformation and external impingement. Criticism of previous stud-

---

19. See Lutz 1995 for a trenchant critique.

20. See, for example, Butler 1990, 1993a; Braidotti 1994; Sedgwick 1993; cf., in anthropology, M. Strathern 1988, 1992; Moore 1994.

ies can draw upon this tradition to propose better models for considering gender under current conditions.

From Warfare and Gifts to Money and Commodities?

Classic analyses and feminist critiques in Melanesia and Amazonia point up a diffuse ethnographic relationship—now exposed and not just legitimated—between male collectivity, group opposition, and sexual antagonism against women by men. Even if this connection is "only an ideology," it has been a powerful ideology within Melanesian and Amazonian cultures themselves, in addition to whatever resonances it has had in the West. But it may now be asked what *contemporary* trajectories inform male affiliation and gendered asymmetry or domination in these world areas? If male identity used to be achieved through warfare, initiation, or men's house activities, is it now ultimately pursued through monetary wealth, commodity transactions, and knowledge of the marketplace? Is there a shift from the phallic fetishism of war clubs, flutes, bullroarers, or masculine gifts and blows to a commodity fetishism of trade goods and money? What is the place of women with respect to current aspirations? Do contemporary changes alter male opposition to women and equalize gender relations, or do they perpetuate previous patterns of domination in new guises?

Of course, it would be a mistake to treat older and newer practices as if they were mutually exclusive. Though customary beliefs and recent developments may be odd bedfellows, they combine and hybridize in fact. Indeed, the "tradition" or "custom" that is reasserted or recreated as locally Melanesian or Amazonian typically reflects the influence—and often the explicitly desired influence—of economic if not cultural "development." Hybrid outcomes are highly evident in both world areas and have been considered in relation to gender in specific cases. Before turning to these, however, it is useful to provide a larger theoretical context.

Modernity and Identity

Gender relations in Melanesia and Amazonia—as in many world regions—are increasingly imbued with local configurations of modernity. As Marshall Berman (1992:33) puts it, modernity emphasizes progress and renewal through identification with the triumphs of Western-style economics, politics, material culture, science, and aesthetics. Relatedly, it is hoped that the free exercise of individual will can improve social life by subordinating custom, superstition, and irrationality (A. Berman 1994:3). In non-Western contexts, the benefits aspired to are often economic development and increased local possession of cash and commodities. Such aspirations are often viewed as departing from a traditional past. The confrontation with modernity thus houses a hierarchy of value—historically bequeathed from colonialism, nationalism, or Christianity—in which local culture is devalued in favor of more "progressive" notions of success and prestige (Friedman 1992:338). These engagements with and appropriations of modernity are psychological and cultural as much as they are economic. Thus, for instance, modernist influences tend to elevate the significance of the individual over and above that of the collective kin group, to disembed social relations from received institutional contexts, and to provide new ways of imagining and constructing identity.[21]

Modernist aspirations are strongly gendered in most world areas; men's and women's engagements with modernity engage differential fantasies and powers (see Moore 1994: chap. 3).[22] In Melanesia and Amazonia, aspirations to be progressive or modern tend to have their deepest gendered connections with men and masculinity. This is especially true of economic activities. Of course, earning cash or goods and participating successfully in an extra-local economy can also be quite important to women in Melanesia and Amazonia (e.g., Sexton 1986). And as social relations are disembedded or recontextualized, they can afford creative new opportunities for women as well as men, as described by Gewertz and Errington (1997:131ff.) in conversations about "the woman who locks up men," or "the woman who triumphs over the big men." But most women are quite constrained in such regards. Masculine success in Amazonia and Melanesia is strongly and "legitimately" associated with wage-earning, the acquisition of commodities, and the control of cash. As Seymour-Smith suggests for the Jivaro of the western Amazon,

---

21. E.g., Appadurai 1990; Giddens 1990:21.

22. See Jolly 1994; C. A. Smith 1995; cf. Stoler 1995. The connection between gender and modernity is now receiving increasing attention in relation to national and ethnic identity, and in the study of women's movements (e.g., B. F. Williams 1996; Alexander and Mohanty 1997; cf. Yanagisako and Delaney 1995).

the introduction of externally manufactured trade goods, of wage labor and the use of money, as well as patron-client relations linking [the] indigenous to . . . [a larger] society, have all been controlled by men. . . . New educational opportunities have been restricted almost entirely to men, as have opportunities to learn the language of the dominant society, to travel to towns and cities and to exercise new roles of leadership and authority which have emerged in the process of social change. (1991:643)

Permutations on this scenario are common in Amazonia and Melanesia. Though women may participate in local trade, church, or educational activities, they are often systematically restricted from wider or more influential participation, both by men and by shared notions of female propriety and domesticity. Longitudinal evidence from both world areas suggests that indigenous axioms of gendered polarity and male domination remain surprisingly robust at the same time that local appropriations of modernity also intensify.[23]

Though modern notions of "success" or "progress" are increasingly important to the construction of gender, they do not thereby replace previous orientations. Commodity possession, individual wealth, and conspicuous display are crosscut by long-standing values that stress generosity in gift-giving and circumspection in personal possession or consumption. This tension is reflected in new beliefs in spiritual malevolence and sorcery.[24] It is thus important to consider aspects of gendered identity that are mutually influential even though they are not consistent. As Moore (1994:55–56) emphasizes, cultures typically do not have a single model of gender but rather *multiple* gender discourses that may conflict (see Knauft 1996: chap. 7). As a result, she suggests, "Anthropology has begun to move away from a simplistic model of a single gender system into which individuals must be socialized" (1994:56).[25] As Stuart Hall (1996:3) puts it, a given form of

---

23. E.g., Lutkehaus 1995; Kensinger 1995.

24. E.g., Zelenietz and Lindenbaum 1981; Taussig 1987.

25. As Moore notes, "Until recently, gender identity was completely unproblematic from an anthropological perspective because it was viewed as a direct consequence of exposure to and compliance with cultural categories." But "if subjectivity is seen as singular, fixed, and coherent, it becomes very difficult to explain how it is that individuals constitute their sense of self—their self-representations as subjects—through several often mutually contradictory subject positions, rather than through one singular subject position" (1994:55).

identity "does *not* signal that stable core of the self, unfolding from beginning to end through all the vicissitudes of history without change." Rather, identities are points of temporary attachment that "suture" an actor contextually to a subject-position—they articulate ego-investments situationally among a variety of subject-positions (6).

This complexity is important: as gendered identities are repositioned vis-à-vis newer ideals, they do not effect a simple transition from indigenous to external orientations, even in the long run. The association of men with modernity is often a fantasy of incorporation.

The changing and conflicted nature of gender identity underscores the tension between received and modern notions of masculinity and femininity. In the present case, this tension can be mediated by critically recontextualizing the early model of Murphy and Steward.[26] Though Murphy and Steward focused on technological and social change, their insights can be articulated with broader contemporary patterns. In their view, trade goods become an integral part of local material technology in decentralized societies; there is an increased reliance on Western commodities. In the process, kin affiliations are increasingly crosscut by commercial relations and impersonal transactions. Within communities, households become more autonomous; collective residence and men's house affiliations decline, and there is an increasing emphasis on the nuclear family as the primary locus of support. Accordingly, valuable goods are shared by men primarily with their wives and direct family members. In the process, men's affiliations with others in the community become more situational, less corporate, and more individualistic.

This model suggests that male status relies increasingly on material acquisition and success in a cash economy (see fig. 7). Correspondingly, the difficulty of satisfying these aspirations poses a threat to emergent notions of masculinity and can fuel new aspects of gender polarity or antagonism toward women. This antagonism is increasingly individual and domestic rather than corporate or collective. Male institutions based on initiation, warriorhood, or men's house obligations decline. In their place, masculine values draw on the prestige associated with individual access to cash, wage labor, and migration to and from towns or cities. Even the promulgation of "custom" in parts

---

26. Murphy and Steward 1956; see R. F. Murphy 1960; Burkhalter and Murphy 1989.

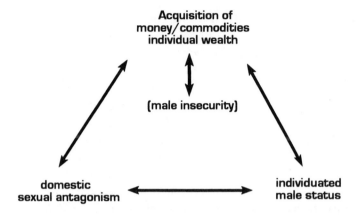

Fig. 7.   Modern connections in Melanesian and Amazonian gender relations

of insular Melanesia, or of "Indianism" in parts of the Amazon, actively appropriates such aspects of a perceived modernity in reconstructions of indigenous identity.[27]

These processes are cultural and psychological as well as economic. Interactions with a wider world—so prominently controlled by men—involve exposure to new languages, forms of education, religious beliefs, political assumptions, and modes of stigma or disparagement. Conversely, local responses are often a complex mix of resistance to and appropriation of these intruding values; the search for material gain is dialectically related to long-standing notions of status and worth. At the center of this process are the potential and the threat posed by new dimensions of female agency (see fig. 8). Extra-local actions and affiliations afford women the possibility of intruding into and competing with if not surpassing men in aspects of market activity, education, and Christian or other nontraditional religious commitments. To these are added potentials for wider female sexual activity. All these initatives can easily be seen as a threat to developing notions of masculine worth under contemporary circumstances. Both directly and indirectly, these can fuel domestic antagonism between men and women.

27. See Keesing and Tonkinson 1982; Jolly and Thomas 1992; White and Lindstrom 1993; M. F. Brown 1993; Conklin and Graham 1995; Conklin 1997; Turner 1992.

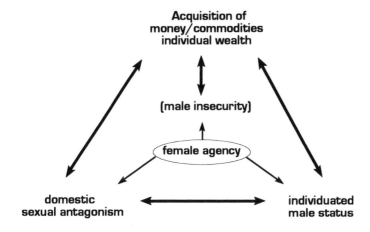

Fig. 8.   Modern connections in Melanesian and Amazonian gendered agency

These tensions are increasingly personal—threats to the individual self. As suggested by Friedman (1992:337), cultural orientations that are indigenous commonly cultivate a sense of authority that extends beyond the individual subject, such as a larger cosmology or social network. By contrast, engagements with modernity foster a more individualistic and self-conscious notion of the self as an autonomous ego. At the same time, the material validation of this individual life-project depends for its success on nonlocal agents and commodities.[28] In both Melanesia and Amazonia, for instance, a young man who wants to marry may be pressured to accumulate a large stock of cash or trade goods through his own effort and to provide wealth to his prospective parents-in-law. This obligation easily competes not only against more extended or collective exchanges, but against men's growing desire to retain possessions or share them primarily with their immediate associates.

Changing Specifics of Gender and Power

Though it is common to adduce political economy as a cause of change in contemporary developments, one can also examine how changes in

28. E.g., Errington and Gewertz 1995, 1996, 1997; Taylor 1981; S. Hugh-Jones 1992.

gendered identifications themselves affect socioeconomic and political conditions. In both the Amazon and Melanesia, indigenous values of masculinity frequently stressed:

1. physical prowess in war or hunting;
2. political success through oratory, alliances, and trade or competitive exchange;
3. knowledge gained through initiation, spiritual experience, and/or secret magical or ritual instruction; and
4. domestic influence extended by successful men through polygyny, clanship, or affinity to adult women, junior men, and in-married or locally resident men as in-laws, refugees, or political dependents.

Increasingly, these dimensions of masculinity now confront values that stress:

1. monetary success and control over disposable wealth;
2. political success through economic patronage and ability to amass or effectively control disposition of money and commodities;
3. knowledge gained through wage-labor or through formal schooling (including knowledge of national languages); and
4. greater but narrower domestic influence within the nuclear family, in selected cases complemented by a leader's patronage or sexual relations outside the community.

There is no rigid division between these scenarios, which are complicated in any event by the great cultural diversity of both world areas. Indigenous Melanesian big-men often controlled followers in significant part through economic patronage (e.g., A. J. Strathern 1971). Amazonian men of status often took many lovers (e.g., Gregor 1985). Warfare and hunting—like spiritual or ritual knowledge—were by no means equally or everywhere important to male status. Likewise in the present, an emphasis on money, wage work, schooling, and nuclear family life are not invariable as aspects of change. These potentials interact with, rather than supplant, preceding masculine values. Yet, there are palpable tensions between customary and contemporary scenarios of male worth.

Repositioned aspects of female identity and resistance are equally subject to change. As women's potential for contact with foreigners or outsiders becomes greater, beliefs about the need for female propriety often elaborate or intensify. Menstrual, ritual, and other forms of female restriction—traditionally enforced by taboos or the threat of gang rape—are often loosened or lessened on the surface. Ritual strictures often attenuate, husbands and wives can live in the same house, and secret male knowledge, cult house residence, or male ritual sacrae diminish in importance. But these changes do not necessarily reduce men's insecurity or their domination over women. While the formal stigmatization of women may decline, it often resurfaces informally in new guises and through alternative forms of domestic expectation and constraint. Masculine control of the cosmos, of fertility, and of spirituality—so important in both world areas[29]—can be increasingly in doubt with the decline of indigenous spirit mediumship, shamanism, ritual cults, and age-grade systems. Correspondingly, the fear of witchcraft or of women's pollution can increase as the ritual means to divine and take formal action against women is lost.[30]

There is often an increased fear of female licentiousness or immorality, especially as women are allowed to trade or travel beyond the confines of the local community.[31] Women's potential for interacting with a larger social universe—going to markets, visiting with relatives in town, attending school, learning a pidgin or national language, or engaging in wage work (not to mention sex-work per se)—can be threatening to emerging but uncertain notions of male status or prestige that are increasingly linked to success in these same contexts. As men's mobility increases, it often becomes particularly important to keep women close to home. And though the rate of polygyny declines and monogamy increases (e.g., Hern 1992), domestic constraints on women—sometimes including restricted neolocal residence in town—can intensify.

Population increase continues unabated in Melanesia and Amazonia; there are more children to care for and more mouths to feed. At the

---

29. E.g., for Amazonia: Reichel-Dolmatoff 1971; S. Hugh-Jones 1979; Maybury-Lewis 1967; for Melanesia: Juillerat 1992; G. Lewis 1980; Allen 1967; Tuzin 1976, 1980; Gell 1975; Godelier 1986; Herdt 1987a.

30. See Zelenietz and Lindenbaum 1981; Stürzenhofecker 1993, 1995; cf. Stephen 1987; R. C. Kelly 1976; Knauft 1985a.

31. E.g., Polier n.d.; Rosi and Zimmer-Tamakoshi 1993; cf. Werner 1984.

same time, increasing numbers of men are away from home for longer periods of time in towns or other commercial centers—working, attempting to find wage work, fraternizing, and spending as well as earning resources.[32] Young men's bonding with other men occurs increasingly in town or urban environments and through consumptive activities such as drinking, partying, or gambling, which require money. For young men in particular, these pose a new collective life of modern male fraternity.

Women's work load is seldom reduced by laborsaving devices. But as women become more desirous of trade goods and more constrained from participating in a wider economy, they often respond by demanding more commodities from men. Conversely, the cultural value afforded women as producers of food, pigs, or woven valuables for gift-exchange can be undercut by the increasing role of male-controlled cash and manufactured goods in ceremonial and life-cycle transactions. The productive and reproductive capacities of women—important in many indigenous cosmologies, as discussed in chapter 2—can decline in symbolic value even as community life becomes increasingly dependent upon women's labor.

This cycle can easily intensify: modernity is masculinized as masculinity is modernized. Rather than being urged to procure more meat, to be better gardeners, or to be more assertive in maintaining honor and avenging insults, men are incited to earn more money for wives and children. Yesterday's commodity luxuries become today's necessities (S. Hugh-Jones 1992). Demands heighten for a better and more consistent supply of store-bought food, clothes, appliances, and the batteries or kerosene needed to run them. Desires mount for expensive goods such as motor-powered boats, trucks, refrigerators, or Western-style houses. Men feel both the need for personal cash and the sting of criticism from family, kin, and relatives for not adequately providing it. The point is not that these demands replace traditional ones, but that they have a double dimension: they link customary expectations up with fantasies of modern identity. This tense articulation becomes a driving force of change in contemporary gender relations.

Male gender identity is thus no longer a local indoctrination organized by the male community, but a struggle to satisfy obligations through a man's individual ability to wrest capital from an external world. This latter pursuit often subjects men to dislocation, disparage-

---

32. E.g., Seymour-Smith 1991; Marksbury 1993.

ment by outsiders, indignity, subordination, and a gnawing sense of personal inadequacy if not failure. Little wonder, then, that men's status insecurity, their aspiration to collective camaraderie, and their antagonism to and subordination of women have not disappeared with the decline of warfare, the demise of the initiation cult, or the disappearance of the men's house.

Melanesia

The dynamics sketched above affect women as much as men. Just as women have long responded to men's domination—through informal influence, complementary avenues of prestige, and collective contexts of opposition or resistance—so, too, they can engage modernity through their own economic initiatives as well as their own demands. In Melanesia, these have included women's economic cooperatives, schooling, and the success of a small but important class of professional women.[33] Rural women still remain the backbone of domestic life and subsistence production. But, as several researchers have suggested, women's long-standing labors and cultural associations may be afforded less prestige nowadays than they were in the past.[34]

Melanesian identities are increasingly informed by Christianity,[35] relations of ethnic or linguistic affiliation (being a *wantok*) in towns or cities,[36] business investment cooperatives,[37] violent gangs of dislocated youths,[38] the increasing importance of educational attainment,[39] millennial aspirations,[40] the formalization of "custom,"[41] and political alliances that resist regional or national government.[42] With few exceptions, these developments tend to be dominated and controlled by

---

33. See Watson 1997; Zimmer-Tamakoshi 1993a, 1995; Rosi and Zimmer-Tamakoshi 1993; Turner 1993; Sexton 1986; Warry 1986; P. Brown 1988.

34. E.g., Lutkehaus 1995; Jolly 1994; cf. A. B. Weiner 1976.

35. E.g., Trompf 1991; Barker 1990; Clark 1989; Tuzin 1989; Robbins 1994, 1995; Robin 1982; Kulick 1990.

36. E.g., Carrier and Carrier 1989; M. Strathern 1975; Battaglia 1986.

37. E.g., Salisbury 1970; Finney 1973; Maher 1961.

38. E.g., Goddard 1992, 1995; Hart Nibbrig 1992; A. J. Strathern 1992, 1993a; Kulick 1991, 1993.

39. E.g., Fife 1995; P. L. Johnson 1993.

40. E.g., Lattas 1991, 1992a; Giay and Godschalk 1993; Rimoldi and Rimoldi 1992; Whitehouse 1995; Roscoe 1988.

41. See Keesing and Tonkinson 1982; Jolly and Thomas 1992; Keesing 1989; White and Lindstrom 1993; Feinberg and Zimmer-Tamakoshi 1995.

42. E.g., Robie 1989; May 1982; Wesley-Smith 1992; Jolly 1994; Keesing 1992; A. J. Strathern 1984; cf. Worsley 1968.

men. Accordingly, the link between masculinity and local appropriations of modernity sows dissonance between natal affiliations and
alternative dimensions of identity.[43] Indigenous languages are overlaid
and in some cases relinquished amid the spreading lingua franca of
Melanesian pidgin.[44] This process of creolization continues even as
women in rural areas may be disparaged or considered suspect if they
become fluent in this language.[45] Kinship obligations compete with the
drive for individual wealth and prestige, and marriage intertwines
with "business" through the inflation of bridewealth payments and
compensation demands.[46] In the process, men's access to and rights
over women appear more commoditized.[47] Likewise, in reasserting
local custom, the politics of male control over women emerge at the
core of postcolonial identity.[48]

Cash crops such as coffee increase women's labor. While some of
the resulting cash may be garnered temporarily by women,[49] it is often
appropriated by men—not infrequently leading to an increase of
female resentment and gender antagonism.[50]

These tensions all have poignant sexual and gendered dimensions.
Under intense pressures for cash and goods, masculine identities are
stressed and threatened. Men may delay marriage and extend their
absence from the village in hopes of amassing brideprice. Women are
constrained by norms of propriety from fuller participation in the cash
economy, yet are subject to the backlash of masculine insecurities. For
men, these disappointments can fuel longer periods of travel or residence away from home, increased opportunities for serial sexual relationships (and their various complications), the lure of participating in
theft or other criminal activities, and the struggle to secure or maintain
wage-employment or advanced schooling.[51] Men can easily feel caught

---

43. E.g., Connell and Lea 1994; MacLean 1994; see also Errington and Gewertz 1995;
Gewertz and Errington 1991; Battaglia 1986; M. Strathern 1975; Ryan 1989; Rodman 1992.
44. E.g., Kulick 1992.
45. E.g., Jolly 1994:89.
46. E.g., Marksbury 1993; Scaglion 1981; see also Errington and Gewertz 1995, 1996;
Battaglia 1995; MacLean 1994.
47. E.g., Jolly 1994:139.
48. Jolly 1994; cf. Jolly and Thomas 1992; see also Keesing 1989, 1992; Keesing and
Tonkinson 1982; Grijp and Meijl 1993; Jolly 1994; Foster 1995a, b.
49. E.g., Sexton 1986; Warry 1986.
50. E.g., A. J. Strathern 1979b, 1982c; Wardlow 1992; cf. Meggitt 1989.
51. See Fife 1995; Goddard 1995; Nihill 1994; Marksbury 1993; Jenkins 1994; Johnson
1993.

between the values and expectations of two worlds, unable to master either, and denigrated by women in the process.[52] Against this, men's shared experience of transient life or work in town provides new forms of collective male bonding that can oppose them to women while affirming new types of exclusive male understandings and economic opportunities.

Discrimination against and victimization of women can persist or increase in tandem with men's frustration and transient male bonding (e.g., Zimmer-Tamakoshi 1993a, b). Though good data are sparse, several researchers have suggested that the incidence of domestic antagonism against women may have increased during the postcolonial era.[53] According to one account, the killing of wives by husbands accounted for one-third of *all* homicides in Papua New Guinea over one eighteen-month period.[54]

In many parts of Melanesia, indigenous beliefs concerning sexuality abut newer practices that commoditize sex and enforce a moral divide between marriage and prostitution. The absence of husbands and the delay of bridewealth raise the threat that women may use sexual favors to redirect wealth to themselves. It is evident from several parts of New Guinea that exchange of sex for cash or gifts is increasingly common in towns and cities—and increasingly represents, for men and women alike, a degrading marker of female status.[55] Correspondingly, women of traditional virtue or Christian propriety are increasingly judged not just against standards of female pollution but against those of being a loose woman or prostitute.[56] For men, however, transient sexual relations with women that entail little by way of enduring social obligation may be pursued as a form of ostensibly modern masculinity (e.g., Wardlow 1998). Michael Nihill (1994:48) suggests that "gender and sexuality are key domains in which the changes wrought by capitalism, Christianity, and the state in colonial and postcolonial settings are manifested in rural Highland Papua New Guinea societies."

Status distinctions based on postcolonial notions of ethnicity, race,

---

52. This passage is paraphrased from Feinberg 1995:95.

53. Zimmer-Tamakoshi 1993a, b; Counts 1990; Toft 1990; Jolly n.d.

54. Morley 1994:31, after Kivung, Lee, and Warakai 1985:79–80.

55. E.g., Hammar 1992, 1995, 1996; Clark 1997; Clark and Hughes 1995; Jenkins 1994.

56. Zimmer-Tamakoshi 1993a, b; Polier n.d.

religion, and class easily compound those based on gender and sexuality to overdetermine the "immorality" of women's participation in a larger social world. Women can be tainted with the diffuse aura of being sexually "loose" insofar as they are seen as geographically mobile, educated, fluent in pidgin, un-Christian, greedy for money, or uncaring of kin—irrespective of their sexual relationships per se. Particularly in the village, any of these attributes may be seen to imply sex-for-cash relationships on the part of women. The point is not that Melanesian women engage increasingly in extramarital liaisons, but that women can be stigmatized by values that build upon previous beliefs concerning female pollution, depletion, or witchcraft and impute the misuse of female sexuality. These orientations inform current standards of gendered status and disparagement that are often adopted by women as well as men. Accordingly, there is no simple "transition" from an indigenous set of values to a Western one. Rather, there is an articulation between indigenous and contemporary notions of power and stigma.

Amazonia

In Amazonia as in Melanesia, masculinity and male agency are increasingly associated with trade goods and money. These changes pose a particular challenge to social relations insofar as the political economy of kinship revolved around male brideservice in much of Amazonia.[57] In many Amazonian societies, commodity acquisition and an increase of material possessiveness have dovetailed with increasing nuclear family autonomy and reduced commitments to collateral kin. Older men now have less control over the resources of sons-in-law; they cannot command younger men's cash as they were once able to control their labor. It is particularly noteworthy that

> a man's control over his son-in-law is mediated through the authority he has over his daughter. . . . It is the subordination of women, above all younger women, that allows a man a degree of control over his sons-in-law; in other words it permits an extension of the control over women to control over men. (Rivière 1984:91, 93)

---

57. See Turner 1979a; Kensinger 1984. This generalization is less applicable to the northwest Amazon.

The increased autonomy of younger men reinforces and reflects both the declining control over young wives by fathers-in-law and the increasingly direct control over these women by young men as heads of nuclear families. These arrangements include an increase of neolocal residence at the expense of uxorilocality—the setting up of a new independent household instead of residing with a wife's parents (Murphy and Steward 1956). As Crocker notes for the Bororo,

> [i]n modern times, the husband, as a son-in-law, is becoming freed from the ancient social pressures (kindred and elders) that forced him to stay with his wife's family for the sake of the children. (1984:68)

Insofar as cash and commodities become increasingly important to male prestige, the labor of women—so intensive in manioc production—declines in relative terms as the basis of hospitality. The valorization of male wealth also has pronounced effects on corporate organization. Maybury-Lewis (1987:456) notes for the Xerente that by 1963 the age-set system was "moribund." When he returned again in 1984, he found that

> only older Xerente remember how their society should properly be organized according to their ancient traditions. Younger Xerente have a keen sense that their traditional culture is disappearing, but only a hazy idea of how it used to be. Young adult men do not know their clan affiliations, for they are less interested in Xerente politics than they are in Brazilian affairs. (1987:456)[58]

An insightful account of changing sexual dynamics has been supplied by Siskind (1973) for the Sharanahua of eastern Peru. While parts of indigenous Amazonia had raucous festivals based on the consumption of cassava beer—especially by men—these take on new dimensions through the binge-drinking of alcohol (for Melanesia, see Marshall 1982). Drunk by midday on the rotgut *cashasa* of traders, "young men show off their Spanish and imitate Peruvian bravado, speaking aggressively about honor" (Siskind 1973:127). Taunts between men

---

58. Dimensions of dual organization continued to persist among the Xerente, but such binary organization has become attenuated and has virtually disappeared among some other Amazonian groups (for instance, see Townsley 1987).

concerning lack of control over wealth or women can easily provoke fights between men or give rise to wife-beating. Siskind (1973:180) comments that "a few women at Marcos have sexual relations with a trader in exchange for trade goods such as cloth, hair dressing, or kerosene." As a result, these women can be chastised into tears of rage for immoral behavior. By contrast, indigenous gender antagonism is described as a

> battle between equals, with little compassion, perhaps, but no contempt, and sexual relations are not viewed as a loss to the women's side. The Peruvian making a sexual conquest reduces the woman to the commodity he has given in exchange. He is the winner and she, the trophy. (Siskind 1973:180)

An analogous process has occurred along the south coast of New Guinea in the transition from extramarital sexual relations that were customary during fertility rituals to contemporary patterns of abusive prostitution and sex-work among groups such as the Bamu and the Kiwai.[59]

In both world areas, female sexuality is increasingly treated—especially outside of marriage—as a kind of commodity. There is an increasing moral divide between men, who are empowered by extramarital exploits, and women, who are stigmatized by them. This presents a marked contrast to patterns of discreet and socially accepted extramarital liaisons among many indigenous Amazonian societies.[60] A number of these, including the Sharanahua, accepted adulterous relations in which women granted sexual favors in exchange for gifts of meat (Siskind 1973). Among the Cashinahua, men publicly acknowledged in cases of adulterous dispute that "a woman has a right to [have an extramarital affair] if her husband does not provide sufficient meat" (Kensinger 1995:188). As in Melanesia, however, the commoditization of gender relations increases moral stigma when sexual favors are granted in reciprocity for trade goods, especially with outsiders.

The stigma of prostitution has implications not only for women who expand upon customary sexual license, but for the bulk of rural women who do not; they may be suspected of impropriety by suspicious husbands. Masculine insecurity can be exacerbated by a growing

---

59. E.g., Hammar 1995, 1996; cf. Knauft 1993a: chaps. 2, 8.
60. E.g., Gregor 1985; W. Crocker 1974; Holmberg 1969:165.

sense of male honor based on sexual control coupled with men's absences from wives as they leave to acquire money or goods. New circumscriptions of sexual propriety for women, and greater sexual opportunities for men, twist received gender beliefs and practices into an escalating double standard that valorizes male sexual conquest and stigmatizes women for being adventurous. William Crocker (1974: 192–93) summarizes the situation among the Canela as follows:

> Especially since the mid-fifties, therefore, with their giving up of their negative attitudes toward the local Brazilian way of life, feelings that extramarital practices may actually be uncivilized and wicked have been changing many aspects of the Canela traditions. . . . Sexual jealousy is not suppressed as effectively as it used to be so that angry young husbands with new ideas about marital rights, unfaithful wives, and prostitutes can cause a considerable amount of inter-family trouble and serious intra-tribal bad feeling. . . . It is most likely that as a result of the changes in the attitude toward extramarital sexual practices, the nuclear husband-wife family unit will be increasingly emphasized at the expense of the activities of the joking relative group and the secondary affinal family relationships.

Missionary and other religious initiatives have often preached Christian morality at the same time that they introduced trade goods and fueled hopes of economic development (e.g., Taylor 1981). At the same time, these linked developments promote an ethic of discipline, individualism, and male labor associated with the acquisition of trade goods and with commercial development more generally (cf., historically, Weber 1958).

Though they sometimes promote female participation in local church activity, these developments often constrain women's wider initiatives while reinforcing pressures on men. If male prestige places more emphasis on economic success and control of female sexuality than previously, the onus on men in lowland Amazonia to "come up with the goods" can be strong indeed. This is an extension, and also a transformation, of indigenous patterns common in many parts of the Amazon (notably excepting the northwest) in which a young man as son-in-law was largely responsible, through hunting and trading, for the extradomestic subsistence and economy of the extended household. The connection between increased reliance on trade goods, male prestige, and men's control of wives is effectively described by Christopher Crocker for the Bororo of the southern Amazon; his description is worth quoting at length.

> Wives owe their husbands sexual fidelity, and husbands their wives gifts of both practical and non-utilitarian value. The Bororo quite explicitly equate this reciprocity, saying that all female sexual favors should be "paid for". . . and that there should be some rough equivalence between frequency and length of sexual services and their material rewards. One of the most pernicious effects of the Brazilian presence has been to change the character of these gifts and to inflate the amounts demanded by wives. Bororo women, especially younger ones, now consider themselves to have rights to a certain standard of living, defined in terms of a sufficiency of metal pots, kettles, buckets, and other utensils (scissors and machetes), and of textiles such as blankets, dresses, and mosquito nets. At the same time, they are covetous of prestige goods: perfumes, beads, jewelry, sunshades, ribbons, and the like. The only way Bororo men can gain these items is through wage work for Brazilians, which pays very badly indeed, and for the most onerous kind of labor. Even though the manufactured items are not individually very expensive, even the minor ones require a great amount of paid work. A large cooking pot, for example, can only be purchased with over a month of wages. At the same time, men desire to buy guns, cartridges, fishing nets, and fishhooks, which are likewise grossly inflated in relation to income. And, of course, the husband's parents and unmarried sisters are entitled to their share of what little he can purchase. Many conjugal battles arise over the conflicts of interests engendered by these expectations, and divorce is often their only resolution. (1985:111–12)

What one finds, in short, is an intensifying cycle of (1) inflated economic aspirations that men attempt individually to fulfill, (2) male–female resentment, (3) increasing male emphasis on controlling women sexually and domestically, and (4) increased domestic strife. Bouts of male alcohol consumption can reinforce and galvanize this cycle, as they do in Melanesia, since drinking dissipates economic assets and can increase male shame at the same time that it increases women's resentment and material demands. This dynamic can easily aggravate spousal antagonism and wife-beating. That customary institutions of corporate kin authority and mediation are often attenuated or absent can exacerbate this process. Correspondingly, the demise of traditional men's group, ritual, or initiation groups reduces obligations to collateral kin and co-residents. Gender relations change accordingly, not as a replacement of traditionally gendered expectations and activities but as an elaboration upon newly intensified spousal and domestic relations.

Insofar as men feel constrained to work with and for outsiders, their sense of dignity and integrity can be harshly compromised. As Maybury-Lewis notes for the Xerente of the southeastern Amazon:

> It was no longer stray backwoodsmen the Xavante had to deal with, but cattle ranchers, mining companies, and land speculators who came in private airplanes and were backed up by their private armies of hired gunmen. Brazil's surviving Indians . . . were harried, killed or driven off their lands. (1992:29)

In the Peruvian Amazon, Kensinger notes that traders

> operated in terms of a hierarchical system and considered themselves to be morally, economically, and socially superior to the Cashinahua. They gave orders and expected to be obeyed, reacting angrily when their wishes went unheeded. (1995:262)

Cashinahua were highly ambivalent toward traders, considering them a source of valued goods but also of "sickness, confusion, discord, and despair" (1995:262).

Ethnocide and encroachment by outsiders has a direct impact on local constructions of masculinity across a wide range of Amazonian peoples, including in Ecuador, Peru, Colombia, Guyana, Venezuela, and Bolivia as well as Brazil.[61] In the context of increasing economic "development" through gold mining, road-building, and timber extraction, Amazonian masculinity is caught in a vice between the economic benefit that can temporarily accrue from assisting these intru-

---

61. E.g., Campbell 1995; Brown and Fernandez 1991; Brown 1993; Whitten 1976, 1981; Taussig 1987.

sions and the strong desire to maintain indigenous traditions and lands against settlers, squatters, and national initiatives. This tension is reflected in patterns of local leadership; economic accommodations are both embraced and criticized (e.g., McCallum 1990). The sense of ethnic divide between "Indians" and "nationals" gradually becomes a more complex relationship of syncretism and hybridity.[62] As noted by Michael Brown (1993:312), "The headman who possesses undisputed knowledge of his own culture is pushed aside by the chameleon-like leader who can successfully walk in two worlds." Emergent forms of masculine leadership in Amazonia thus "illustrate a key feature of modernity: the disembedding of social systems" (1993:312).

Contrasts and Complications

Local inflections of modernity—both cultural and politicoeconomic— engage indigenous notions of male prestige, female propriety, and sexual identity in both Amazonia and Melanesia. Customary parallels between these two regions continue in new guises; male status is decorporatized and linked increasingly to the cash economy, while women's extradomestic activity is constrained, threatening to men, and polarized against male status.

These rough parallels are also crosscut by significant differences. Whereas marriage in much of highland and insular Melanesia was transacted through bridewealth,[63] marriages in Amazonian societies were often transacted through male brideservice—labor and meat contributed by a young man to his parents-in-law.[64] As Shapiro noted in a review of Amazonian marriage practices,

> [b]rideservice, rather that bridewealth, is the general practice in the region, which accords with the processual nature of marriage. While relations of affinity are accompanied by relations of exchange, it is not generally exchange that serves to legitimate the marriage. (1984:27)

Though the contrast between bridewealth and brideservice can be overdrawn (see critique by Kelly 1993), it has significant implications

---

62. E.g., Gow 1991; Whitten 1981, 1985; Chibnik 1994; cf. Wagley 1953.

63. E.g., Glasse and Meggitt 1969; cf. Marksbury 1993.

64. See Turner 1979a, b; Kensinger 1984; Rivière 1984; cf. more generally Collier and Rosaldo 1981; Collier 1988.

for the way that commodity pressures articulate with gender relations in the two regions. In both Amazonia and Melanesia, there is increased emphasis on the nuclear family as the domestic unit. In the Amazon, however, inability to satisfy the demands of in-laws and spouses for trade goods places newly established marriages at risk. In highland and insular areas of Melanesia, by contrast, the inflation of bridewealth makes marriage more difficult to legitimately establish in the first place.

Despite these differences, both world areas now see increasing cultural emphasis on brideprice—a substantial payment of goods and cash at the onset of marriage. An effective brideprice payment tends to abrogate the necessity of subsequent affinal exchanges, brideservice, or the direct reciprocity of sister-exchange marriage. In lieu of these, a large payment legitimates the marriage and effectively compensates the bride's parents for their loss. In addition to marking a relatively complete transfer of women's labor, reproductive, and sexual capacities to their husbands, these transactions also reduce the cultural and cosmological value of women's work and fertility, which were important in indigenous cycles of social exchange and cosmic rejuvenation.[65] As stated by one Melanesian woman from Vanuatu, "Brideprice makes me feel like a speed boat or a truck for sale" (Jolly 1997:129). As such, "it makes her family greedy for a high price, her affines angry if she doesn't give them a baby boy, and her husband believe that she must always obey him" (130).

Of course, material payments surrounding marriage combine with rather than supplant preexisting orientations.[66] As S. Hugh-Jones (1992:52) suggests more generally for the northwest Amazon, it is important to combat "the tendency to overemphasize the disjunction between the economies of Indians and Whites." As commodity relations become more important to marriage, conjugal expectations and obligations tend to increase, at the same time that other kinship and exchange commitments within the community may decline in significance. Expectations of marital satisfaction escalate and are easily fueled by modern notions that link romantic courtship with utopian images of enduring love (e.g., Zimmer-Tamakoshi 1995). The influences of the mass media both disseminate and inflate these images. But such expectations easily lead to a sense of marital despair or betrayal as they go

---

65. See, for Melanesia: Weiner 1976; Lepowsky 1993; M. Strathern 1972; Lutkehaus 1995; for Amazonia: C. Hugh-Jones 1979; Murphy and Murphy 1974; Bamberger 1974.
66. See Nihill 1996; Dean 1995, 1998; Knauft 1998.

unfulfilled in fact. These patterns readily link back to the problems of economic insufficiency and sexual jealousy discussed previously. As a result, domestic circumscription of women, and fears of wives' infidelity, can intensify at the same time that men feel unable to "come up with the goods" to support family expectations and their own sense of identity.

Participation in the extra-local economy is increasingly crucial to masculinity in both world areas but has distinctive features in each. In much of Melanesia, towns and cities are populated mostly by other indigenous peoples rather than by foreigners or colonial descendants.[67] In Papua New Guinea, up to one-quarter of the population is now estimated to reside in cities or towns.[68] As opposed to polarization between foreignness in town and indigenousness in the village, an escalating circulation of men and masculine imagery facilitates the elaboration of wider male ethnic identity in Melanesia. This is often reflected in extra-local identifications among men who consider themselves *wantok;* that is, those who speak the same language and treat each other as extended kin or comrades.

Though colonial control was historically pivotal in Melanesia, the Amazon has a much longer and more devastating history of ethnocide, displacement of indigenous peoples, and land alienation. As Jonathan Hill (1996) has suggested, Indian identity is in many ways intrinsically related to external encroachment. These historical patterns have had a powerful influence upon contemporary politics and leadership. Amazonia harbors a long tradition of patron-client relations and Indian indebtedness to mestizos or non-Indians. As a consequence, Indian aspirations to large-scale or extra-local leadership are particularly conflicted and compromised.[69] In Melanesia, by contrast, the colonial and postcolonial period has seen a marked expansion of indigenous "great man" or "big-men" leadership. Effective local leaders compete for larger spheres of power and influence; though fraught with competition, leadership has the potential to escalate into the "super big-manship" associated with the prerogatives of provincial authority, parliamentary office, and control of national funds.[70] Some have described

---

67. New Caledonia and Irian Jaya are exceptions in this regard, and Fiji is an intermediate case.

68. See Cole 1993; cf. critique by Hayes 1995; see also Coiffier 1992.

69. See Brown 1993; Campbell 1995; McCallum 1990; Conklin and Graham 1995.

70. See A. J. Strathern 1984, 1993a; Errington and Gewertz 1995: chap. 5; contrast Godelier and M. Strathern 1991.

this as a new "super-tribe" of rich Melanesian leaders who have emerged from different areas and coalesced as a power elite in major towns and cities.[71] This contrast reflects an overarching *patronage* system of *interethnic subordination* and *economic dependency* in Amazonia as opposed to a *wantok* system of *expanded ethnic affiliation, competitive aggrandizement,* and *regional or national political aspiration* in significant parts of postcolonial Melanesia. In Amazonia, Indianism is constructed in essential contrast to national identity. In this sense, it is more akin to the assertion of custom (*kastom*) as local resistance to national unity, as has occurred in parts of insular Melanesia,[72] than to the political aspirations of large indigenous ethnic groups in countries such as Papua New Guinea.

These differences reflect the fact that the descendants and agents of colonial intervention have more direct control over land and political authority in Amazonia than they do in Melanesian nation-states such as Papua New Guinea, Vanuatu, and the Solomon Islands. (However, the eastern and western extremities of Melanesia—Irian Jaya and New Caledonia—are more similar to the Amazon in these respects.)[73] A growing pattern in all these areas, however, is the expropriation of native lands for large-scale logging or mining operations. Such intrusions are now a major threat throughout Melanesia[74] as well as continuing a long and devastating history of deforestation and displacement in the Amazon. As if ripe for ominous trends, countries such as Papua New Guinea still have well over 90 percent of their land locally owned and used for subsistence, often by holders susceptible to financial inducements and pressure from logging or mining negotiators. By contrast, indigenous groups in the Amazon—in Brazil, Guyana, Ecuador,

---

71. See Wanek 1996:305ff.

72. E.g., Jolly 1994; Keesing 1992.

73. West New Guineans have become a disparaged racial minority within the large Indonesian state (e.g., Gietzelt 1988; Monbiot 1989; Garnaut and Manning 1974; May 1986; Osborne 1985). The indigenous inhabitants of New Caledonia have had a particularly pernicious colonial history and are still subjects of France (Connell 1987; see Guiart 1983; Weitzman 1985). In postcolonial Fiji, racial and political contestation, including between indigenous peoples and the resident Indian population, has been especially complex (Emberson 1993; Howard 1991; Lawson 1991; Kaplan 1995; J. D. Kelly 1991; Lal 1990a, b; Ravuvu 1991). Even within Papua New Guinea, the colonization of constituent areas by the postcolonial state is exemplified by the subjugation of Bougainville by the P.N.G. government and its defense force (May and Spriggs 1991; Liria 1993; Wesley-Smith 1992). Tensions between local custom and the symbolic capital of national or regional identification are now evident in many parts of Melanesia (e.g., Errington and Gewertz 1995, 1996; Foster 1995a, b; Jolly 1994; Keesing 1989, 1992).

74. See Filer 1997; Barlow and Winduo 1997.

Peru, Venezuela, Colombia, and Bolivia—have endured a more catastrophic history of encroachment and have both opposed and accom-
modated foreign intrusion and economic exploitation.[75] In Brazil, 45
percent of the land belongs to one percent of the population, and land
possession can still be established by occupation and use: land occupied and used for ten years becomes the property of the person living
on it (Schemo 1996). Encroachment on Amazonian land and resources
seems relentless.[76] In eastern Ecuador, Whitten (1976:28; see 1985) provides a detailed example how rain forest Quichua attempt to "maintain
ethnic integrity, expand their culture, increase their population, and at
the same time find a new position in a disappearing frontier." Campbell (1995) has described analogous processes in a Brazilian context. In
Amazonia, gendered tensions are sometimes coupled with the potential and the threat of mixed-race sexual unions (cf. Nugent 1997). One
recalls the drunken male retort described by Siskind (1973:127) among
the Sharanahua: "If anyone calls me a *caboclo* [a half-caste], I'll kill him."
In both world regions, the difficulty of establishing male prestige
through personal wealth, control of female labor, or the control of
junior clansmen or in-laws places a special burden on the domestic services and sexual propriety of wives.

Preliminary Conclusions

In Melanesia and Amazonia, male prestige is increasingly dependent
on the acquisition of cash and commodities; conversely, it is less
directly dependent on the efficacy of local corporate or collective male
activities. The survival of communities is at least as dependent upon
women as it was in the past, but relative to men's economic pursuits,
women's labor and fertility are often afforded less value and prestige
than they previously were. Culturally as well as economically, female
propriety is associated with constraint and conservatism. Correspondingly, male status remains culturally and morally dependent—in some
ways more so than previously—on constraining female sexuality and
limiting women's wider cultural and economic relationships. Male
insecurity, opposition to women, and the desire for male collectivity
have been reinstated in new guises at the same time that they have dis-

75. E.g., Galvão 1979; M. F. Brown 1993; Brown and Fernandez 1991; Whitten 1981;
Skar and Salomon 1987; Hill 1988; cf. Wagley 1953.
76. See Browder and Godfrey 1997; Pace 1997; Chibnik 1994; Schemo 1998.

engaged from customary institutions such as the male cult, the men's house, or the warrior society. These changes are linked to widespread patterns of individuation and to the importance of masculine success in the pursuit of economic gain. At the same time, male social life involves an increasing proportion of transient and nontraditional affiliations, including work groups and male comradeship through leisure activities such as drinking or gambling, which require money.

More generally, gendered identification in Melanesia and Amazonia melds customary gender hegemonies with local appropriations of idioms and objects of modernity. This process echoes a prominent if not general trend that Henrietta Moore (1994:61) also finds in Western advertising: "it continually reinscribes dominant categories and discourses through reference to a fixed relationship of difference, while appearing to embody challenge, resistance, and change." Moore may go too far in stating that "hegemonic masculinity is now global," but she is certainly correct that "it has found resonances with a number of local or indigenous masculinities" (1994:63). Exactly how this process articulates specific local patterns of kinship, religion, exchange, ethnic competition, or racial subordination remains an important question for further investigation.

Global Contexts

The masculinization of commodity acquisition and wage-labor is a common and important pattern among decentralized or "fourth world" peoples. However, the pattern of change evident in Melanesia and Amazonia is by no means universal. Among some indigenous peoples, social disruption is so great and dependency relations upon a highly developed state apparatus are so strong that masculine initiatives are more thoroughly undercut, demoralized, and precluded. Disempowerment of masculine initiative can in these cases occur in tandem with escalating self-destructive and disruptive behavior by men, including the escalation of alcoholism, violence, and social apathy to epidemic proportions. Under these conditions, somewhat ironically, men are so disempowered that there may appear to be a relative increase of the importance of local women in local political as well as economic affairs. This result can be seen in some native North American and aboriginal Australian groups (e.g., Povinelli 1991).

On the other hand, the feminization of labor, in which young women in particular are seen as a cheap and obedient labor pool, is widespread in countries where export industries are an important area of economic growth (Standing 1989). In this case, light manufacturing and service industries are perceived as well-fitted to the ostensible "nimble fingers" and social docility that are often attributed to young adult women. The reliance on women's labor in these regards is prominent in a number of urban and peri-urban areas of Latin America and in East and Southeast Asia.[77]

By contrast, in Melanesia and the Amazon, as well as many parts of Africa, economic development is still focused largely on extractive industries such as mining and logging; it does not include the proliferation of light manufacturing. Accordingly, the little work available for the local population in these areas, such as hard physical labor, is typically considered "manly." Elite work, on the other hand, requires technical expertise or advanced education that is usually associated with upper-class men or with expatriates.[78]

In this respect, Melanesia and Amazonia may be on the initial downslope of what Cagatay and Ozler (1995) characterize as a "feminization U" (cf. Boserup 1970). In this model, the ratio of women to men in wage labor initially declines, as men are favored during incipient processes of capital development. However, this trend can level out and even reverse itself with the later development of export manufacturing and/or service industries in which more women may be hired.

There is no guarantee, of course, that such industries will develop in Melanesia and Amazonia; many parts of the world have proven refractory to the development of light export manufacturing and service industries. And even under these potential later developments, there is no necessary tendency for women's status in domestic or political relations to improve when they become wage-earners. In some circumstances, indeed, the exploitation of women can increase; wages paid to women can be appropriated by husbands or male kin at the same time that women's domestic obligations remain unabated, and women's employment may be threatening to men.[79] This is a pattern widely reported in both Latin America and East and Southeast Asia.

---

77. E.g., Zavella 1987; Tiano 1994; Ong 1987; Ong and Nonini 1997; Bonacich 1994.

78. Under these less economically developed conditions, educated women are often found in professions such as nursing or teaching.

79. E.g., Bonacich 1994; Tiano 1994; Ong 1987.

Many women pursue such employment as an avenue to economic benefit and at least a small degree of gendered autonomy.

To refine such large-scale generalizations, the economic and political consideration of gender needs to combine deeper understanding of local gender orientations, on the one hand, and larger and longer histories of politics and economy, on the other. If the self-conscious "modernization" of culture relates dialectically to the enculturation of modernity, so, too, the ostensible modernization of gender relates to the fact that regional and local permutations of modernity are fundamentally gendered.

Final Caveats

This chapter has considered general changes in gender relations and cultural economy in Melanesia and Amazonia. These broad outlines may also be compared and contrasted to the relation between modernity and gender in other world areas. But the present generalizations are also ripe for more nuanced evaluation and refinement through a new generation of research in more specific Melanesian and Amazonian contexts. Beyond regional generalities, local orientations reflect a complex combination of receptivity to and resistance against cultural and economic "modernization." The hybrid melding of local beliefs with transnational influences—which is so dramatically evident in the millenarian movements of both regions—is richly creative.[80] Local views of "economic success" and "progress" intertwine with longstanding patterns of women's influence or resistance against men's prerogatives and assertions. These countermovements can take on distinctive postcolonial dimensions, including, in parts of both Melanesia and Amazonia, women's action in promoting Christianized beliefs, practices, and moral initiatives that may underscore women's propriety and their economic or social "advancement."[81] Participation in nongovernmental organizations (NGOs), including projects that support local education or health initiatives, can also be significant for women. If gendered identifications combine competing and conflicting orienta-

---

80. E.g., Hill 1988; Brown and Fernandez 1991; Lattas 1992c; Worsley 1968; Lawrence 1964; Burridge 1960.

81. For striking Melanesian examples, see Errington and Gewertz 1997; Tuzin 1997; contrast Minnegal and Dwyer 1997.

tions, it is intrinsically difficult to generalize about them without also encouraging more refined case studies that may crosscut and complement such generalizations.

Examining gender through the lenses of modernity—that is, through the local perceptions and appropriations of an assumedly "modern" or "progressive" way of life—begs the reactions, creativities, and resistances of daily life. The present chapter has sketched a few articulations between customary orientations and the gendered appropriation of modernity in Melanesia and Amazonia. Amid such patterns of regional change, the investigation of both larger interregional comparisons and smaller and more local exceptions and countermovements will be valuable in a new generation of productive research.

Chapter 5

Post-Melanesian Studies?
A Contemporary Look
at the Anthropology
of Melanesia

Melanesia has often been considered a special or even privileged region for ethnographic research and anthropological theory. At the same time, the region has often been perceived—particularly by those who are not specialists—as a "stone age land" or a "land that time forgot." In one of the very few news stories about Melanesia to be aired on the U.S. national evening television news, New Guinea was recently described as "a land apart, cut off from the modern world by geography and time."[1] In contrast to such images, Melanesia today is confronted with the challenges and tensions experienced by many if not most third world areas: ethnically diverse peoples aggregated uneasily into postcolonial nations or neocolonial provinces; expropriation of resources by multinational corporations; the promises and many problems of development projects; difficulties associated with urbanization, class stratification, corruption, and unemployment; and the threat of social disruption. Underlying many of these tensions is an imbalance between strong desires for economic development and the relative lack of infrastructure, per capita capital investment, and training or advanced education for local people.

Of course, local identifications and rivalries that used to be considered "indigenous" or "tribal" continue to be enormously important in contemporary Melanesia. But they do so through contemporary concerns. This is also the case in large parts of Africa, Asia, Latin America, and elsewhere. In these respects, the problems of anachronistic perception concerning Melanesia highlight biases common to the perception of politically and economically marginal areas of the world more generally. This perception belies the fact that Melanesia is undergoing remarkable developments that offer enormous opportunities

---

1. *ABC Nightly News*, May 26, 1997.

for understanding the relationship between cultural diversity and contemporary change.

The present chapter documents the relation between Melanesian studies and the history of anthropology, and it analyzes the relationship of this world area to current trends in the discipline. A strong heritage of ethnographic detail and analytic sophistication make Melanesian studies an important counterbalance to the thinness or flights of fancy that can accompany current approaches associated with international studies, on the one hand, and cultural studies or experimental ethnography, on the other (see Ortner 1995; Knauft 1996). However, the cultural richness of Melanesian anthropology has its own historical bias of emphasizing the traditional and locally specific side of Melanesian beliefs and practices rather than larger dimensions of contemporary change. This received tendency makes it particularly important for the anthropology of Melanesia to further open itself to new sets of intellectual and cross-disciplinary influence, at the same time that it maintains rather than relinquishes its commitment to ethnographic rigor.

Melanesian studies now address contemporary circumstances that transcend village boundaries and engage features of nationalism, mass media, regional political economy, education, Christianity, crime and social control, militarism, sexually transmitted diseases, urbanization, corruption, large-scale mining and logging projects, environmental degradation, and other factors. These developments are inflected by a strong Melanesian desire for the cash and commodities associated with economic development. Research on these and other issues documents the key articulation between received cultural orientations and trajectories of socioeconomic and cultural change.

Melanesia remains especially distinctive in its degree of cultural diversity, the richness of its ethnographic record, and the speed of colonial and postcolonial developments. These afford special opportunity for understanding the growing self-consciousness of culture and politics among Melanesians today. Correspondingly in theoretical terms, Melanesian studies now provide a special vantage point on the challenges, potentials, and pitfalls of late modern sociocultural anthropology.

For much of anthropology's professional history, Melanesia has been a special if not privileged ethnographic region. Distant from European metropoles and one of the last areas of the colonial world to be explored or pacified, Melanesia (and New Guinea in particular) became a region where belated colonial intrusion dovetailed with the persistence of indigenous customs considered authentic and often exotic. Given current sensibilities in cultural anthropology, however, Melanesian research is grappling with new ways to draw upon the traditionalist accounts that have been among the region's strongest attractions to anthropologists, while also surpassing their limitations. This tension informs at least three major challenges that Melanesian studies now confront: (1) the rise of cultural studies and of globalization as alternative discourses of cultural representation and analysis; (2) changing notions of space, place, and region in anthropological perception; and (3) the growing tensions between political representation, Western social science, and indigenous scholarship. The present essay analyzes the relationship of Melanesian anthropology to these trends and contextualizes the region's significance vis-à-vis historical and contemporary directions in sociocultural anthropology. The account proceeds by way of an internal dialogue between complementary points of view. These viewpoints are, at turns, both appreciative and critical of historical precedents in Melanesian studies and, reciprocally, of broader trends in current anthropology. The larger goal is to identify ways in which these tensions are being productively mediated in Melanesian studies and to show how contemporary trends can be drawn on yet more productively in the future.

Received Trajectories

As Arjun Appadurai (1986, 1988) has suggested, the concepts, approaches, and authors most associated with a world area tell us much about its place in academic perception.[2] Within its privileged topic of tribal ethnography, Melanesian studies has been at the forefront of many if not most of the major theoretical developments in modernist anthropology. It is worth recalling, if only briefly and metonymically, the prominent place of Melanesian ethnography in anthropology's history.

Following upon the milestone Cambridge Expedition to the Torres

---

2. See also Fardon 1990; Manganaro 1990; cf. Said 1978; Guha 1988a; Mudimbe 1994.

Strait in 1898, Melanesia was considered by influential anthropologists such as A. C. Haddon to be a pivotal region for analyzing the distribution and diffusion of primitive customs.[3] This interest was prominent in Victorian anthropology and paved the way for a closer examination of the relationship between various social and cultural traits (see Stocking 1995). In subsequent decades, Melanesian research continued to be at the root of many approaches that have been particularly influential in anthropology. The structural study of kinship and social organization was grounded in the first instance in W. H. R. Rivers's fieldwork and analysis of information from insular Melanesia during the 1910s.[4] Modern techniques of ethnographic fieldwork, including participant-observation and linguistic competence in the local vernacular, were galvanized by Bronislaw Malinowski's research among the Trobriand Islanders.[5] The theoretical perspective developed by Malinowski during the 1920s, which stressed the rational function of indigenous customs and institutions, was also influential and important for anthropology.[6] The mid-1920s saw Marcel Mauss's (1967 [1925]) seminal analysis of Melanesian gift exchange; this exposed the relation between social and material transaction and provided the foundation for modern exchange theory and the transactional analysis of cultural processes. During the late 1920s, the 1930s, and early 1940s, the anthropological study of emotion, personhood, and socialization was developed through the key Melanesian research of scholars such as Margaret Mead (e.g., 1930, 1935), Gregory Bateson (e.g., 1936), and Maurice Leenhardt (e.g., 1979 [1947]).

During the mid–twentieth century, African ethnography became preeminent for the development of British structural-functionalism, while the Amazon became the ethnological focus of Lévi-Straussian structuralism. However, Melanesian research was pivotal for the evaluation, critique, and further development of these approaches, particularly with respect to political organization, kinship, subsistence, and gender.[7] In addition, critical perspectives on culture change and so-

---

3. See Urry 1993; Quiggin 1942; see Haddon 1901–35, 1920; Seligmann 1910; Lewis 1932.

4. E.g., Rivers 1914, 1924.

5. E.g., Malinowski 1922, 1935.

6. E.g., Malinowski 1926, 1927, 1929, 1948.

7. E.g., Meggitt 1965a, 1977; A. J. Strathern 1971, 1972; M. Strathern 1972; R. C. Kelly 1977; Rubel and Rosman 1978; Godelier 1977; Brown and Buchbinder 1976.

called cargo cults were developed in the early Marxist analyses of Peter Worsley and Jean Guiart, among others.[8]

During the late 1960s, cultural materialism and ecological anthropology were importantly shaped and defined through the Melanesian research of Roy Rappaport (1968), Andrew Vayda (1976), and others.[9] During the late 1960s, 1970s, and early 1980s, Melanesian research provided signal contributions to symbolic anthropology and the study of metaphor and meaning, as developed by Roy Wagner[10] and Edward Schieffelin,[11] and in Alfred Gell's (1975) structuralist analysis of Umeda ritual. The ethnographic rigor of Marxist anthropology was developed through the Melanesianist work of Maurice Godelier,[12] while the sociology of knowledge transmission was theoretically developed in the Melanesian ethnography of Fredrik Barth (1975, 1987). Overlapping with this work, and extending from the 1970s and through much of the 1980s, patterns of gendered exchange and/or sexuality in Melanesia became central for the analysis of these issues more generally in anthropology—as evident in influential ethnographies by Marilyn Strathern, Annette Weiner, Deborah Gewertz, Rena Lederman, Shirley Lindenbaum, Lorraine Sexton, Gilbert Herdt, and, more recently, Gillian Gillison, Maria Lepowsky, Margaret Jolly, Nancy Lutkehaus, James Weiner, Pascale Bonnemère, Donald Tuzin, David Lipset, and Gabriele Stürzenhofecker, among others.[13] Influenced by Roger Keesing and others more recently—including Robert Foster (1995a), Deborah Gewertz and Frederick Errington (1991; Errington and Gewertz 1995) James Carrier (1992a), Geoffrey White (1991), Lamont Lindstrom (1990, 1993), and Nicholas Thomas (1991, 1994)—concern with culture change, including the self-conscious elaboration of culture as contemporary Melanesian

---

8. Worsley 1968 [1957]; Guiart 1956; Guiart and Worsley 1958; see also Harrisson 1937; Keesing and Corris 1980; cf. Burridge 1960; Lawrence 1964; Schwartz 1963.

9. Rappaport 1968, 1984; cf. Brookfield and Brown 1963; Salisbury 1962.

10. E.g., Wagner 1967, 1972, 1975, 1978.

11. See Schieffelin 1976, 1980, 1985; Schieffelin and Crittenden 1991.

12. See Godelier 1982, 1986; Godelier and Strathern 1991; Josephides 1985; A. J. Strathern 1982d; see also Worsley 1968.

13. See M. Strathern 1972, 1988; Weiner 1976, 1992; Errington and Gewertz 1987a; Lederman 1986; Lindenbaum 1979; Sexton 1986; Herdt 1981, 1984a, 1987a; Herdt and Stoller 1990; Gillison 1993; Lepowsky 1993; Jolly 1994; Lutkehaus 1995; J. F. Weiner 1995; Bonnemère 1996; Tuzin 1997; Stürzenhofecker 1998.

"custom" (*kastom*), has also been developed in a number of important recent volumes.[14]

Numerous other authors and works could also be mentioned. That these citings are selective—the tip of the iceberg—is itself the point: Even a cursory list of icons and paragons illustrates how Melanesian studies has spearheaded or facilitated many of the key developments in sociocultural anthropology over much of the last century.

The larger point is that there are important relationships between geographical areas and anthropology's theories. And if the world map of our interests is intellectual as well as geographic, this affords a distinctive and important angle of perception on our discipline's past and on its present trajectories (see Appadurai 1988; Fardon 1990). Correspondingly, other world areas outside Melanesia have their own historical ties with various approaches in social and cultural anthropology. The ethnography of Native North America was seminal for Boasian particularism and linguistic anthropology; Africa, with respect to British structural-functionalism and then with structural Marxism; the Amazon, with Lévi-Straussian structuralism; South India, with Dumontian hierarchy and more recently with subaltern or postcolonial studies; Southeast Asia, with the aesthetics of Geertzian thick description; Latin America with the political economy of land and labor; Polynesia, with Sahlinsian structural history; and so on.[15] But even vis-à-vis larger and much more populous areas, Melanesian studies has had a distinctive impact, decade after decade, in defining, shaping, and refining a diverse *range* of theoretical developments that have been key for anthropology. In this regard, Melanesia has been fundamental for anthropology and has helped galvanize many of the field's theoretical initiatives. For the period of a century—from the 1880s to the 1980s—Melanesia has been a special place of anthropological discovery. Reciprocally, anthropology has had a special penchant for rediscovering itself in Melanesia.

In more recent years, the relationship between anthropology as a discipline and Melanesia as an ethnographic area has been changing,

---

14. See Keesing and Tonkinson 1982; Keesing and Corris 1980; Keesing 1989, 1992; White and Lindstrom 1993; Otto and Thomas 1997; Grijp and van Meijl 1993; Feinberg and Zimmer-Tamakoshi 1995.

15. Concerning labels, approaches, and ethnographic areas see Appadurai 1988; Manganaro 1990; Fardon 1990.

along with increasing interest in globalization, on the one side, and criticisms of traditionalist anthropology, on the other. Part of Melanesia's historical impact in anthropology stems from long-standing interest in the region as a kind of "natural laboratory" for tribal variation. With one-quarter of the world's languages and associated cultures, Melanesia—and New Guinea in particular—has been used as an anthropological testing ground for examining cultural diversity and the correlates and possible causes of variation in subsistence adaptation, sociopolitical organization and development, warfare, exchange, ritual and religion, gendered relationships, and sexual orientation. That this research often considered Melanesia as a "pre-state" world area dovetailed with anthropology's classical interests in earlier phases of human cultural evolution and with customs presumed to be relatively uninfluenced by state societies and imperial economies. As Melanesia's contemporary circumstances and their connection with international influences is appreciated, however, these assumptions seem increasingly untenable.

Recent Critiques

As we approach the twenty-first century, it can be argued that *no* world area can be afforded the intrinsic interest or significance that it may have been accorded by Western scholars during previous decades of high modernity. Area studies have come under attack from many quarters. These include the intellectual view that the interconnections between regions should be emphasized rather than their distinctiveness (Appadurai 1996; contrast Trouillot 1997). Another argument—particularly pronounced in political science, economics, and sociology—is that area studies are at the same time theoretically bland and not sufficiently accommodating to contemporary business and political interests.[16]

Amid globalization, the reified places and labels of the ethnographic world areas are increasingly effaced by the diasporas, interconnections, and modernities that simultaneously link and blur them. Focus on ethnographic world areas is also compromised by deconstructive analyses, which consider regions to be a function of the labels and the categories of knowledge that are projected onto them. In anthropology, ethnographic regions operate increasingly "under era-

---

16. Shea 1997; Bates 1996, 1997; contrast Johnson 1997; Karp 1997; Haugerud 1997.

sure." The configuration of ethnographic regions provides a convenient target for criticism, even as these continue to operate as a subcurrent of unexamined assumption in many accounts and analyses.

These trends have particular significance for Melanesia, which has had such special regional importance in anthropology. Some suggest that there is now declining scholarly research and graduate interest in Melanesia relative to several other world areas. Others suggest that it is increasingly difficult or dangerous to conduct fieldwork in parts of Melanesia.[17] Though this is true of selected cities and areas, fieldwork is equally if not more insecure in many world areas outside Melanesia. But new ethnography is often privileged for parts of the world that are seen as economically burgeoning or politically prominent on the global stage, particularly if it focuses on contexts that are transnational or "complex." But even in terms of international investment development, it may be noted that Papua New Guinea recorded one of the highest GDP growth rates in the world in selected years of the early 1990s, due to profits from petroleum and mining ventures.[18] Various parts of Melanesia contain enormous gold and copper reserves, and interior New Guinea may in future years become the largest supplier of natural gas in the southern hemisphere. The region also has the ominous possibility of witnessing massive clear-cut logging of some of the

---

17. Core highland areas of New Guinea, and major cities such as Port Moresby, can be physically dangerous for Western researchers due to vandalism, burglary or theft, assault, rape, and continuing intertribal violence (e.g., Goddard 1995; Hart Nibbrig 1992; A. J. Strathern 1993a; cf. Kulick 1991). The increasing use of guns is particularly worrisome (A. J. Strathern 1992). However, perceptions should not be overgeneralized, and important long-term field research continues to be completed. This includes new types and venues of investigation. For instance, Adam Reed (1997; pers. comm.) has quite successfully completed innovative recent fieldwork among inmates of Bomana prison in Port Moresby. West New Guinea (Irian Jaya) has been largely closed to Western anthropologists since it became part of Indonesia in 1963, though several researchers have recently completed concentrated field research in parts of this region (e.g., Rupert Stasch, pers. comm.; Danilyn Rutherford, pers. comm.). Depending on timing, location, and bureaucratic uncertainty, some anthropologists have reported difficulty obtaining research visas for ethnographic fieldwork in the Solomon Islands and in a very few parts of Papua New Guinea.

18. Papua New Guinea is calculated to have had a GDP increase of 9.5% in 1991, 11.8% in 1992, and 16.6% in 1993 (AUSAID 1996:113). Of course, GDP increase from windfall profits in mining and oil export does not translate equally into per capita earnings increases or infrastructural development in the country as a whole. What it does reflect is a relative change in the internationally recognized significance of Papua New Guinea as an exporter of exploitable natural resources, and in profits that may accrue to an emergent class of elite Melanesian professionals and politicians.

world's largest remaining rain forests. To these challenges have been added the widespread food shortages and famines associated with the El Niño drought that struck New Guinea and other parts of Melanesia in 1997. This crisis, in turn, has generated initiatives to support food relief by a range of nations. Regardless of whether one finds current changes to be "development" or not, they certainly indicate an increasingly complex and international impact on the circumstances and directions of change in Melanesia.

In contrast to such developments is the lingering perception of Melanesia as the locus of exotic or primitive cultures. This assumption has sometimes dovetailed with the suspicion that anthropology's interest in Melanesia is mutually exclusive toward issues of social change, wider political economy, and the challenges of complexity in late modernity. This is not the case: far from it. Yet, older perceptions of Melanesia as a classic anthropological "place" persist. These now beg more refined evaluation against the historical trajectory and actual current developments in Melanesian anthropology. Beyond generalizations, we need to be more subtle in understanding the relative value and purpose of received anthropological perspectives in specific ethnographic areas. At larger analytic issue is the relationship between anthropology's history and its present, and the changing status of "ethnographic world areas" more generally.

Tribal Concerns

One can both appreciate and admit that Melanesian studies have had a long and rich history of tribal ethnography.[19] This ethnographic record has been rigorous and often marvelously theorized, but it also frequently assumed the autonomy of indigenous customs—their relative isolation from external influences. The question thus becomes how Melanesian ethnography can be vigorously continued while assumptions of local autonomy are increasingly transcended. In larger terms, this is an issue that anthropological fieldwork faces generally in the future of the discipline.

In historic and geographic terms, Melanesian anthropology has frequently been influenced by—and has made much of its symbolic capital on—its search for the remote, the authentic, and the exotic.

---

19. *Tribal* here refers to a type of ethnography as well as to a type of society.

Though admitting significant exceptions,[20] Melanesianists have often bypassed more contacted or "acculturated" peoples in order to study groups at the outer margins of colonial contact. This motivation is reflected in the changing regions of Melanesia that have been targeted for research during the last hundred years. In the 1890s and 1910s, the survey ethnology of A. C. Haddon, C. G. Seligmann, W. H. R. Rivers, A. B. Lewis, and others directed itself to salvage for science the vanishing customs and beliefs of seaboard Melanesia—to reach and record them before they were "bastardized" by traders or transformed by missionaries. That commercial trade was often encouraged by Melanesians themselves was typically ignored or criticized by anthropologists as a focus of academic research.[21] Long-term professional fieldwork was pursued particularly in backwater areas of insular Melanesia during the 1910s and 1920s, including by figures such as Richard Thurnwald, Reo Fortune, Bernard Deacon, John Layard, Felix Speiser, Albert Lewis, Margaret Mead, and Gregory Bateson, in addition to Malinowski.[22] This trend continued in later decades with Ian Hogbin's and then Roger Keesing's important work in the Solomon Islands, Jean Guiart's research on Vanuatu, Douglas Oliver's work in Bougainville, and Theodore Schwartz's studies of Manus, among many others.[23] For remote areas of the south coast of New Guinea, one finds a large ethnographic corpus from major figures such as F. E. Williams, Gunnar Landtman, Laurent Serpenti, Robert Maher, Paul Wirz, J. H. M. C. Boelaars, Jan van Baal, and Jan Verschueren.[24] Most of this work was conceived as emanating from the peripheries if not beyond the pale of effective colonial influence.

After pushing inland and into remaining insular nooks, Melanesian research exploded into the interior of New Guinea, ethnography's "last great unknown," following World War II. The discovery of over a

---

20. E.g., Hogbin 1951; Belshaw 1957, 1964; Mead 1956; Maher 1961, Worsley 1968; M. Strathern 1975.

21. See critiques by Thomas 1991; Carrier 1992a.

22. See Thurnwald 1916, 1965; Fortune 1932, 1935; Deacon 1934; Layard 1942; Speiser 1991; Lewis 1932; Mead 1930, 1935, 1938–49; Bateson 1936.

23. See Hogbin 1964, cf. 1970; Guiart 1956, 1963a; Harrisson 1937; Oliver 1955; Schwartz 1962, 1963; Keesing and Corris 1980, 1982b, 1992. A number of these authors became interested in issues of historical development and colonial inequality, though their ethnographic focus was often on remote and relatively isolated communities.

24. See Landtman 1917, 1927; Wirz 1922–25, 1928; Williams 1930, 1936, 1940; Serpenti 1977; Maher 1961; Boelaars 1981; Zegwaard and Boelaars 1955; van Baal 1966, 1982.

million New Guinea highlanders—whose existence had been largely unknown by Westerners prior to 1930—afforded a particular opportunity for anthropologists.[25] Not only were the peoples of highland New Guinea unacculturated and "pristine," but the details of their subsistence, economy, politics, and religion provided a trove of information for a generation of dedicated young anthropologists armed with a refined sense of ethnographic data collection and theoretical acumen. Highland customs pertaining to conflict and warfare, initiation, and gender relations often seemed especially violent or brutal to observers at the same time that they articulated with elaborate practices of social exchange and beautiful body decoration. This was particularly fascinating to Western sensibilities. For a number of reasons, then, the highlands of New Guinea became a hotbed for the intensive and sophisticated tribal ethnography.

The publication of this research, accordingly, was both rich and richly rewarded; it fueled a cascade of important monographs and subsequent academic careers. This growing corpus coincided with florescence of anthropology faculty employment during the late 1960s and 1970s, especially in the United States.[26] Melanesianist research was hence solidified as important if not pivotal for the growth of anthropology during its high water mark of modernist scholarship.

The first wave of work from the New Guinea highlands and adjacent areas—from the late 1950s to the early 1970s—included major published monographs by:[27]

Ronald Berndt (on the Fore)
Ernest Brandewie (on the Mbowamb)
Paula Brown (on the Chimbu (Simbu))

25. See bibliography in Hays 1976; see Hays 1992; Connolly and Anderson 1987; cf. Ploeg 1997.

26. Melanesianist research was also particularly important in Australian anthropology (along with the ethnography of aboriginal Australian societies). In England during this period, economic problems led to academic retrenchment; many prominent British anthropologists—including Melanesianists—moved to the United States during the 1970s and 1980s.

27. See Meggitt 1965a, 1977; A. J. Strathern 1971, 1972; M. Strathern 1972; Brandewie 1981 [cf. Strauss 1990; Vicedom and Tischner 1943–48]; Reay 1959; Read 1965; Brookfield and Brown 1963; Brown 1972; Berndt 1962; Glasse 1968; Newman 1965; Ploeg 1969; Pospisil 1958, 1963a; Heider 1970; Wagner 1967, 1972, 1978; Watson 1964, 1983; see more generally P. Brown 1978; Hays 1976, 1992; Feil 1987; Lemonnier 1990.

Robert Glasse (on the Huli)
Karl Heider (on the Dani)
Mervyn Meggitt (on the Mae Enga)
Phillip Newman (on the Gururumba)
Anton Ploeg (on the Wanggulam)
Leopold Pospisil (on the Kapauku)
Kenneth Read (on the Gahuku-Gama)
Marie Reay (on the Kuma)
Andrew Strathern (on the Melpa)
Marilyn Strathern (on the Melpa)
James Watson (on the Tairora)

(see Terence Hays 1976; 1992)

All of these persons became permanent faculty members at major universities or colleges.

The association in this list between ethnographer name, published monograph, and tribal name is an important aspect of professional as well as ethnographic sociology. The archetypical progression here has been: individual anthropologist → single isolated people → published monograph → permanent academic career. One aspect was the common sense that the surest route to a regular university position was the publication of one's ethnographic monograph by a major university press. Reciprocally, there was a career association between professional ethnographer and the tribal name given to the group of people for which the monograph claimed coverage. With only a few exceptions, the preceding list reflects a separation of "tribes" and their association with individual professional identities. As such, myriad New Guinea highland areas and overlapping groups have been monographically divided into assumedly autonomous tribes and corresponding professional careers (contrast Hays 1993).[28] In the majority of cases, ethnographic research was undertaken primarily by one anthropologist (or a team of husband

28. This is graphically represented in ethnographic atlases of Melanesia. The *Atlas of World Cultures* for instance, depicts 257 numbers on the map of New Guinea (Price 1989:76–77). Each of these numbers is taken to indicate a separate individual tribe and is indexically keyed from the map to one published monograph (or two, maximum) on this group by the principal ethnographer(s). A more sophisticated and descriptive atlas has been compiled on the basis of ethnographer contributions for individual Oceanian societies by Hays (1991).

and wife) in one or a few closely related communities. The population of this locale was then taken as representative of a larger group
that comprised thousands or even tens of thousands of people. Just
as the community and given tribal name became iconic of a wider
ethnographic conglomeration, so, too, the persona of the anthropologist who had published major works about these people stood as
their professional icon in academic perception. In this system of
knowledge, much less prestige was afforded to the restudy of an
existing group or to a network of research that transected groups
across space. Rather, the eminence of individual groups was associated primarily with the eminence of individual anthropologists. This
process was congealed as academic claims were solidified through
published monographs and major journal articles.

The point, of course, is *not* that "tribes" or careers or areas *were* in
fact discrete, but rather, that they tended to appear so in the way classic
ethnography was configured and transmitted as a system of professional knowledge and prestige (cf. Bourdieu 1988).

During the late 1960s, the 1970s, and 1980s, these trends diffused in
fieldwork location as well as in academic influence. During this period,
core areas of the New Guinea highlands were progressively seen as
more influenced by outside impact and decreasingly "pristine." There
was a growing perception that the core highlands had already been
studied, even though there was little information published about
many topics and about many constituent subgroups. Accordingly, new
waves of ethnographers pushed into more remote and less contacted
"fringe highland" areas of interior New Guinea.[29] This attention resulted in a fresh outpouring of new primary ethnography, including
over a score of monographs and associated faculty careers concerning
hitherto seemingly undocumented areas. Many of these new groups
were also elevated quickly onto the world map of ethnographic awareness, even though—in contrast to many of the core highland peoples
studied earlier—their populations were often surprisingly small.
Beginning with the early influential work of figures such as Roy Rappaport (1968) and Roy Wagner (1967), research in the fringe and

---

29. A few smaller groups from the "fringe highlands" were also studied in the 1950s
or 1960s; the point is not that all the groups from this area were studied at a later time, but
that there was an overall shift of primary ethnography to fringe highlands areas during
the late 1960s and 1970s.

peripheral highland areas of interior New Guinea burgeoned during the mid-1970s through 1980s. This impetus resulted in major published monographs (through 1990) by persons such as[30]

    Fredrik Barth (on the Baktaman)
    Ralph Bulmer (on the Kalam)
    Peter Dwyer (on the "Etolo")
    Daryl Feil (on the Tombema Enga)
    Steven Feld (on the Kaluli)
    Stephen Frankel (on the Huli)
    Alfred Gell (on the Umeda)
    Maurice Godelier (on the Baruya)
    Laurence Goldman (on the Huli)
    Christopher Hallpike (on the Tuade)
    Christopher Healey (on the Maring)
    Gilbert Herdt (on the Sambia)
    Lisette Josephides (on the Kewa)
    Bernard Juillerat (on the Yafar)
    Raymond Kelly (on the Etoro)
    Bruce Knauft (on the Gebusi)
    Rena Lederman (on the Mendi)
    John Le Roy (on the Kewa)
    Shirley Lindenbaum (on the Fore)
    Edward LiPuma (on the Maring)
    Anna Meigs (on the Hua)
    Jadran Mimica (on the Iqwaye)
    George Morren (on the Miyanmin)
    Roy Rappaport (on the Maring)
    Bambi Schieffelin (on the Kaluli)
    Edward Schieffelin (on the Kaluli)
    R. Daniel Shaw (on the Samo)
    Paul Sillitoe (on the Wola)

---

30. Other areas of New Guinea are considered further below. For authors presently mentioned, see Rappaport 1968; Wagner 1967, 1972, 1978; E. Schieffelin 1976; B. Schieffelin 1990; Feld 1982; R. C. Kelly 1977, 1993; Knauft 1985a; Dwyer 1989; Shaw 1990; Koch 1974; Gell 1975; Juillerat 1986; Lindenbaum 1979; LiPuma 1988; Healey 1985, 1990; Meigs 1984; Weiner 1988a, 1993, 1995; Le Roy 1985a, b; Josephides 1985; Sillitoe 1979; Herdt 1981, 1987a; Godelier 1986; Mimica 1988; Barth 1975; Morren 1986; Feil 1984; Goldman 1983, 1993; Frankel 1986; Hallpike 1977; Majnep and Bulmer 1977; Gillison 1993; Stürzenhofecker 1998; Bonnemère 1996.

Roy Wagner (on the Daribi)
James Weiner (on the Foi)

and, then, more recently, monographs from:

Pascale Bonnemère (on the Ankave)
Gillian Gillison (on the Gimi)
Gabriele Stürzenhofecker (on the Duna)

Almost all of these persons have obtained permanent or tenure-track positions in major universities, colleges, or institutional programs. As in the previous list, other names and groups could be added (or subtracted), depending in part on the definition of what constitutes the "fringe highlands" of New Guinea and what constitutes a major "published monograph."[31] During this period, indeed, monographs become more diverse in treatment and topical specialization; by the 1990s, what constituted a "monograph" at all became increasingly uncertain. It may also be noted that the above list contains an increased number of "duplications"; it is more common to have multiple monograph authors per named ethnic group.

My own primary fieldwork among the 450 Gebusi in a remote part of interior Papua New Guinea in 1980–82 fits firmly within this "tribalist" mold. And it should be acknowledged that this fieldwork has subsequently influenced my view of Melanesia and of the prominence of interior New Guinea. But the broader point is that this same emphasis has been prominent in the allocation of symbolic capital, ethnographic attention, and academic success within and beyond Melanesia until relatively recently: my perception is part of a system that has its larger facticity as a regime of knowledge. When I began to plan my first fieldwork, almost twenty years ago, the search for a remote tribe was quite literal. My adviser and I picked for my research a blank spot on the ethnographic map, in the remote Tomu River area of P.N.G.'s extensive

---

31. Cf. Hays 1993. I underscore that it is *not* my intention to exclude or devalue the important work of many other professional anthropologists of the 1970s and 1980s who worked in fringe and core highland areas of New Guinea, not to mention in *other* areas of Melanesia, whose names do not appear on the preceding lists. And my apologies to any persons I may have missed, including those foreign language scholars whose works I have not been able to appreciate! My purpose is simply to illustrate and give evidence for the dominant professional model of symbolic capital through monographic tribal association in interior New Guinea during the period in question.

Western Province. During the first weeks of fieldwork, my wife and I searched for the people—termed the "Kramo" in some patrol reports—who were thought to inhabit this area. At the end of an expeditionary trek, however, we found that the area in question *was*, in fact, virtually uninhabited. I thus had the dubious distinction of having been funded to study a tribe that was, in important respects, a figment of ethnographic imagination.[32]

The continuing search for the remote and the tribal was one of the reasons that the far reaches of Melanesia have been so important on the world ethnographic map—and one of the reasons why the resulting ethnography has been so rich and influential among scholars and students who have not worked in this region. The fruits of this search, however, have declined in recent years. Despite this, even in 1996, Western mass media continue to be lured by the possibility of so-called lost or uncontacted tribes in remote areas of interior New Guinea (see Kirsch 1997b; ASAONET 1996).

To the sizable list of researchers and publications concerned with highland and adjacent areas of interior New Guinea can be added those pertaining to other areas of Melanesia. In recent decades, research has been particularly abundant in Sepik regions of northern New Guinea and in insular parts of the Massim and adjacent areas off the eastern coast of New Guinea.[33] These areas have provided an important ethnographic complement—as well as a key analytic and theoretical counterbalance—to work in highland and fringe highland New Guinea. In

---

32. As far as I could ascertain, the thin and scattered population of the Tomu River had moved to a crocodile skin trading post along the Wawoi River. I ended up settling among the nearby Gebusi—who seemed quite remote enough—and studied their practices of spirit mediumship, sorcery divination, violence, and homosexuality (Knauft 1985a, b, 1986, 1987a, b, c, 1989, cf. 1993a). For my purposes at the time, this choice was more than appropriate; indeed, the strong continuation of such practices into the 1980s was more remarkable than I then realized, even for interior New Guinea. I do not regret my initial decision; it fit well with the state of the discipline and my own motivations at the time. And research of this kind was championed by dedicated and humane intellectuals with keen minds. I was especially fortunate to have had an extremely astute and conscientious adviser, Raymond C. Kelly. The Gebusi, moreover, were a wonderful people to work among.

33. See, for Massim and adjacent areas: Young 1971, 1983a; A. B. Weiner 1976, 1987; Leach and Leach 1983; Munn 1986; Battaglia 1990; Damon and Wagner 1989; Clay 1986; Damon 1990; Wagner 1986; Foster 1995a; Whitehouse 1995; Maschio 1994; and Lepowsky 1993; cf. also Kahn 1986; for Sepik/north coast New Guinea: Hogbin 1970, 1978; Tuzin 1976, 1980, 1997; Gell 1975; Juillerat 1986; Harrison 1990, 1993; Lewis 1975, 1980; Gewertz 1983; Gewertz and Errington 1991; Errington and Gewertz 1987a; Brison 1992; Gesch 1985; Lutkehaus 1995; Lipset 1997; Lutkehaus et al. 1990. A significant number of non-English volumes are also available.

addition, of course, there has been a wide variety of research in other areas of Melanesia, as will be discussed further. Taken as a whole, Melanesianists have been a remarkably large and productive professional cadre in anthropology during the 1970s and 1980s, particularly given the small population and geographic size of Melanesia relative to other world areas.

Over most of the last century, until relatively recently, field research in more heavily contacted or "acculturated" areas of Melanesia has not been a high priority. But now, interest in culture change—and in the longer colonial histories of insular and eastern areas of Melanesia—emerges at the cutting edge of Melanesianists' theoretical articulations concerning history, memory, public culture, and political economy. Before turning to this work, however, it is important to look at the other side of the coin and acknowledge the contribution made by tribal ethnography in Melanesian anthropology, including in terms of its own "past present" (cf. Stocking 1989, 1992).

Beyond Primitive Polarities in Ethnographic Critique

It would be disingenuous to take past developments out of context and judge them synchronically against the presumed superiority of new sensibilities. It can easily be argued that there has been an unprecedented degree of cultural diversity in interior New Guinea and related parts of Melanesia, and that Melanesian ethnographers have often maintained humane personal commitments and high professional standards in the face of daunting conditions. In addition, cultural orientations in large parts of Melanesia *have* for much of the present century been less massively transformed than those in many other world regions. This has presented a unique opportunity for professional study and for human understanding. Viewed in retrospect, Melanesian studies has been extremely important to our appreciation of human diversity and the remarkable possibilities of cultural variety.

It is important to find productive ways to juxtapose anthropology's traditionalist and current sensibilities; it would be unfortunate to view these as mutually exclusive. Indeed, we can use the strengths of one to inform the other. The goal is not to polarize the so-called indigenous against the so-called postcolonial, nor to cultivate antagonism between objectivist and reflexive or deconstructive moments of analysis. Rather, our purpose is to see how ethnographic history can be critically employed to deepen our current understanding of both Melanesia as a cultural region and the tensions and challenges of anthropology as a developing field of study. For instance, the objectivist assumptions of traditional Melanesian ethnography can be limiting or anachronistic, but they have had the benefit of maximizing ethnographic rigor and documentary detail.[34] Almost all of the authors and monographs previously mentioned are significant if not exemplary in this respect. By contrast, many of the more provocative and reflexive or experimental perspectives that have emerged in cultural anthropology over the last fifteen years seem remarkably superficial—at the same time that they can be provocative and stimulating as we give much greater attention to contemporary developments (see Knauft 1996).

The crossroads that now confronts Melanesian anthropology is thrown into relief by the knowledge and power that the idea of "Stone Age peoples" has held in anthropology's deeper imagination. Today, it is at once too easy and not easy enough to exorcize "the primitive" from our thinking. There have been numerous critiques of anthropology's past tendency to assert the existence of primitive tribes while assuming the role of the enlightened scholar as superior subject. Many of these critiques have brought fresh critical awareness to understanding our intellectual history.[35] But by the late 1990s, such critiques now risk reinscribing a kind of simplistic Othering *within* anthropology at the same time that such Othering is deplored in relation to our subjects of study. Ethnographic accounts that aspire to be rigorous, systematic, and objectively descriptive can be criticized as out-of-date or insufficiently self-critical. The epithet of being "primitive" has been removed from disfavored tribes but can be reapplied to disfavored approaches within anthropology itself.

This is not to say that critiques of traditionalism in anthropology are unwarranted; in many cases they have been vital to rejuvenate our field. But the relentless critique of objectivist assumptions, as in some versions of cultural studies, easily neglects a penetrating assessment of what actually *was* or *is* going on among the people in question. The critique may serve, unwittingly, to immunize the critic from having to reveal his or her own claims to intellectual or moral superiority.[36] The

34. For work published during the 1990s, see, for example Harrison 1990; Healey 1990; Brison 1992; Stephen 1994; Merlan and Rumsey 1991; Goldman 1993; Lipset 1997; Bonnemère 1996.

35. See Kuklick 1991; Kuper 1988 (cf. also 1983); Pagden 1986; Hodgen 1964; Trouillot 1991; Clifford 1988.

36. For a more extended discussion of these issues in regard to cultural studies, postcolonial studies, and postmodernism, see Knauft 1996: chap. 3.

trumpeting of new approaches that pretend to be beyond or outside a longer academic tradition risk reinscribing rather than transcending their own academic history. Rather than doing the scholarly trench work of documenting and appreciating others' realities, it is typically easier to criticize those who *have* attempted such comprehension. "Deconstruction" not only critiques; it can preclude attempts at better reconstruction. To debunk classic ethnography perpetuates rather than attenuates a sense of moral distance and superiority by the new author over his or her predecessors. In terms of knowledge and power, then, the moral distance implied by assertions of "the primitive Other" can come back to haunt the late modern or postmodern critic of anthropology through the very process by which he or she purports to expunge them.

In its own time, the notion of the primitive had some inflections that housed a then-progressivist edge. For leftist anthropologist Stanley Diamond (1974), the "search for the primitive" was anthropology's ultimate critique of the emotional, political, and technological barrenness of the modern world. In this perspective, communicating with primitive peoples—and with the primitive within ourselves—signaled a radical rejection of Civilization as the yardstick of humanity. In some selected respects, such an argument could be continued today—even as we hasten to move past the last vestiges of antinomy between the "primitive" or "undeveloped" and the "complex," "modern," or "advanced." Many of our most contemporary cultural theories reduce "peripheral peoples" to one or another dimension of late modern influence or capitalization—global modernity, postcoloniality, or subaltern diaspora. Civilization as a yardstick has given way to the fragmentation of late modern identity and tokenization of culture as benchmarks for an alienated humanity. In the process, what is subjectively meaningful and culturally distinctive about life in different parts of the world is in danger, through unwitting new reductionisms, of being effaced.

Rather than aggrandizing the present by excoriating our academic ancestors, it is more productive to cultivate a dialogue that combines critique with appreciative mediation of past and present authorships. The attempt to annihilate or negate the seemingly primitive in our prior perspectives often reinscribes the absolute differences it would seek to eradicate. The rigorous understanding of our intellectual past and of cultural differences are intricately linked. In the present chapter, I am attemping to pursue this project as an ongoing dialogue—with some moments that are critical and others that are appreciative. This is preferable to imagining and then attempting to obliterate the specter of the savage Other within anthropology's collective self.

Institutional Support for Area Studies?

On a practical level, anthropological research is made possible by money as well as by intellectual sensibilities, professional commitments, and personal dedication. In this respect, it has often been an uphill battle to gain institutional support for Melanesian studies. This may seem paradoxical given the success of Melanesian anthropologists as individual faculty. But the success of the anthropologist as lone hero often comes at the expense of wider institutionalization. As is also true for other parts of the insular Pacific, Melanesian research training and scholarship has seldom received dependable support through area studies programs or agencies. In the continental United States, there have been almost no institutional programs for Pacific Studies, much less "Melanesian Studies." As opposed to the common development of area studies programs at major universities for "Latin American Studies," "Middle Eastern Studies," "African Studies," "East Asian Studies," "East European Studies," "South Asian Studies," "American Studies," and so on, the insular Pacific has rarely been considered a region of economic or political significance, high culture, or great religion that might merit areal programs or support.

Exceptions to this generalization exist in the Pacific Islands themselves, including the Centre for Pacific Studies at the University of the South Pacific in Suva, Fiji. At Honolulu, Hawaii, there is the Center for Pacific Islands Studies and the East–West Center—though the latter has now sadly been shorn of much of its funding. Other exceptions, worldwide, include a French CNRS center for Oceanian Studies in Marseilles and an Irian Jayan Studies program at the University of Leiden in the Netherlands. But in the large cadre of American academia, the institutional neglect of the Pacific Islands and Melanesia in particular stands in stark contrast to other area study programs and to the historical importance of Melanesianists within anthropology.[37]

---

37. It is perhaps in part because of this lack of institutional centralization that scholars of Melanesia have found so much benefit in international on-line bulletin boards, such as ASAONET (listserve of the Association for Social Anthropology in Oceania) and ESOf-l (listserve of the European Society of Oceanists).

Correspondingly, there are few funding agencies or private foundations that focus on Pacific Island language training or research. For instance, the various areal divisions of the U.S. Social Science Research Council have typically not accepted funding applications for research in the insular Pacific (unless as construed as part of Southeast Asia). Indeed, one of the classic mandates in training American graduate students for research in Melanesia was that their research proposals should be held to the highest analytic and theoretical standards since they would *not* qualify for institutional or financial support from area studies programs; they had to vie for funding based on their contribution to general knowledge in competition against proposals for study in all other world areas. The professional success of Melanesianists was thus consistent with heroic notions of fieldwork in remote locations and the perception that their research was singularly brilliant as well as physically demanding.[38]

This special status of Melanesian anthropology dovetailed with the reciprocal tendency for scholarly work in Melanesia to be archetypally associated with *anthropology* as opposed to other disciplines. This contrasts to the prominence of social scientists and humanists from other fields in the Western scholarship of Asia, Latin America, Africa, and Eastern Europe. Institutionally, the tendency to associate "Melanesia" as a world area with "anthropology" as a discipline has meant that cross-disciplinary interest has—with some exceptions, notably in Oceania itself—been less directed to Melanesia than to other world areas. For a number of reasons, then, there has been less impetus for "Melanesian studies" to become interdisciplinary than is the case for many other regions of the world.[39]

More recently, the institutional problems faced by Melanesian studies are also felt by other area studies programs and centers. Area studies now compete with interdisciplinary programs and agendas that crosscut and compromise the configuration of discrete culture areas. Growing emphasis on international studies is often in direct

---

38. This is in no way to suggest that such fieldwork was less than difficult nor that its intellectual contributions have been overrated. It is rather to suggest that these features were recognized and valued in Melanesian research to a degree that was not always accorded research in other world areas.

39. This generalization is most applicable to American colleges and universities. As implicit previously, there is somewhat more institutional support in Europe and Oceania for research in specific parts of Melanesia that were a colony of the country in question, e.g., of France, the Netherlands, Germany, or Australia.

financial competition with funding for area studies programs; the latter
are being questioned and diminished in many colleges and universities. Recently, the U.S. Social Science Research Council has reconfigured and made vestigial its commitment to area studies. In Australia,
programs and projects that do not directly bear upon the economic and
political development of the Pacific Rim are at risk of losing institutional support.

As discussed by Rafael (1994), the notion that world areas were
coherent cultural and strategic units was a Western view of the
post–World War II era that seeped into anthropology during a period
of high modernity. In the 1990s, however, it is harder to justify the
coherence of culture areas, much less to vouchsafe their remote corners
for study by anthropology. It is thus unlikely that a groundswell of
institutional support will emerge from Western universities for world
regions such as Melanesia.

If Melanesia's associations with the remote, the primitive, and the
exotic were its frequent attraction to anthropologists, these now
become the region's academic liabilities. Despite the changing realities
of the region itself, Melanesia's place on the world ethnographic map
remains uncomfortably close to what Rolph Trouillot (1991) calls the
savage slot. This is particularly the case for non-Melanesianists or
anthropologists who hear about big-men, tribal warfare, or ritual
homosexuality in Anthropology 101. This is certainly not a valid characterization of Melanesia; rather, it is a pedagogical and larger Western
perception of the region, and New Guinea in particular. It is against this
perception that neither the trope nor the place of Melanesia occupies
the privilege that it did during the theoretical and ethnographic past of
academic anthropology. This is due to changes in Melanesia itself and
to the contours of a late modern world, but it is also due to the changing contexts of anthropology's own values and labels; all of these are
increasingly complex and increasingly postcolonial. Melanesianists
have sometimes cultivated and gotten intellectual capital from tribal
images, but they are now at pains to reject them.

Before such polarization is engaged, however, a broader perspective may be encouraged. As Foster (1995a) has emphasized, the opposition between traditional and new Melanesian anthropology is ultimately a false one. Indeed, a tradition of rich and detailed ethnography
makes contemporary Melanesian anthropology particularly ripe for
contributing to the most recent and timely debates in anthropology. As

discussed later, this trend has been especially evident for research conducted in insular eastern Melanesia. The extension of these intellectual trends across Melanesia as a whole is now particularly important, not only for Melanesian studies, but for anthropology. The theoretical and antitheoretical developments now inflecting cultural anthropology need to be more rigorously engaged with traditions of detailed and rigorous ethnographic scholarship.

Beyond Local Boundaries: Tracing Networks in Late Modernity

Anthropology's regions are increasingly caught up in global influences and are increasingly theorized as such. Far beyond the unilineal conceptualization of capital intrusion or "modernization," networks of economic and symbolic influence proliferate, crosscut, and complicate each other across the disparate spaces and places of late modernity. The privileged areas of research in late modern cultural anthropology, accordingly, are the nodes or paths that articulate among local, regional, and trans-areal strands of identification and representation.[40] Amid flexible streams of signification, interconnections cross boundaries and throw assumptions of local autonomy into question. In the process, the search for pristine or authentic groups not only becomes difficult, it seems misguided as a kind of endeavor. Likewise, on a regional scale it becomes more difficult to attribute particular characteristics or tie special analytic insights to specific cultural areas; there is declining symbolic capital in emphasizing the particularity of almost any world area for its own sake. The articulation of culture, power, and history—much less the emphasis on border crossings in cultural studies—compromise local autonomy and geographic integrity.[41] The intellectual value of delimiting any culture area becomes a matter of contention. These patterns are general, but they have a distinctive impact on research in world regions such as Melanesia that enjoyed an especially prominent place in anthropology's modernist past.

David Harvey (1990) links the fragmentation of contemporary identities to the time-space compression of postmodernity. In anthro-

---

40. E.g., Marcus 1995; cf. M. Strathern 1996.

41. See Dirks, Eley, and Ortner 1994; Grossberg, Nelson, and Treichler 1992; During 1993; cf. monographs such as Fischer and Abedi 1990; Lavie 1990; Tsing 1993; Steedly 1993; Taussig 1987.

pological theory, correspondingly, ethnoscapes and imaginaries abound, space has new meaning, rhizomatic connections proliferate, the local connects to the global, and late modern hegemonies entail new hybrid forms of resistance.[42] Influences from cultural studies,[43] postcolonial and subaltern studies,[44] post-Marxism,[45] postmodernism,[46] postmodern feminism and queer theory,[47] black cultural studies,[48] and experimentalism in ethnographic writing/representation[49] are all now relevant to cultural anthropology—even as they are often difficult to work through or to apply ethnographically. Culture is now best seen as a contested representation rather than as a discrete or autonomous system.

The underside of this timely concern with the global, the hybrid or diasporic, and the late modern or postcolonial is that it underemphasizes and sometimes totally misses the tenacity and richness of received cultural orientations. These persist even as they twist and redefine amid forces of change. Global theorizations of late modernity and critical perspectives on representation—as in cultural studies—can push us importantly to think in larger and more contemporary terms. But as I have discussed elsewhere, many of these perspectives are woefully unrefined when it comes to documenting the details of lived experience

42. See Appadurai 1996; Hannerz 1996; Friedman 1994; Gupta and Ferguson 1992, 1997; Lash and Friedman 1992; cf. Wolf 1982, 1988; see also Taussig 1987, 1992, 1993; Marcus and Myers 1995; Comaroff and Comaroff 1992, 1993; Yanagisako and Delaney 1995; Ginsburg and Rapp 1995. World systems theory articulations include Schneider and Rapp 1995; Wolf 1982; Wallerstein 1979, 1980, 1989, 1991; and Worsley 1984.

43. E.g., Hall 1986a–c; Grossberg, Nelson, and Treichler 1992; During 1993; Rosaldo 1989, 1994; cf. critique by Harris 1992.

44. E.g., Ashcroft, Griffiths, and Tifflin 1989, 1995; Williams and Chrisman 1994; Bhabha 1990, 1994; Guha 1988a, b, 1989; Fanon 1968, 1991; cf. critiques by Dirlik 1994; Chakrabarty 1992; and Jacoby 1995.

45. E.g., Taussig 1987, 1992; Donham 1990; Comaroff 1985, Comaroff and Comaroff 1992, 1993; cf. Gramsci 1971; Laclau and Mouffe 1985.

46. E.g., Lyotard 1984; Jameson 1991; Harvey 1990; Baudrillard 1988; cf. Foucault 1984.

47. See Butler 1990, 1993a, b; Sedgwick 1990; Nicholson 1990; Benhabib 1992; Benhabib et al. 1995; M. Strathern 1988; Braidotti 1994; Haraway 1990; Fuss 1989; Halperin 1995; Abelove, Barale, and Halperin 1993; see critiques in Bordo 1992; Mohanty 1991; Mohr 1992.

48. E.g., West 1989, 1993a, b; hooks 1981, 1990, 1992; Gilroy 1987, 1993; Collins 1990; Wallace 1990; Dyson 1993; Mercer 1994; Carby 1987.

49. E.g., Clifford and Marcus 1986; Clifford 1988; Marcus and Fischer 1986; Marcus and Myers 1995; Fischer and Abedi 1990; Taussig 1987; Pratt 1992; Manganaro 1990; Behar and Gordon 1995.

(Knauft 1996). Contemporary cultural theory and antitheory tend to be both rarefied and clever; they are empirically underspecified at the same time that they are creative and provocative in assessing patterns of change and finding critical new vantage points for examining them. Many newer theoretical influences derive ultimately from humanities fields and the study of texts. As such, they can be critically perceptive in their understanding of representation and the powers of signification. But they are often very weak in understanding, much less documenting, the activities, beliefs, and expressions of people in lived time. The latest theoretical pushes in cultural anthropology are often deficient in comprehending social and historical context as well. In all these respects, the documentation and analysis of action and experience are shortchanged. This is just what ethnographers of Melanesia have *not* neglected. Substantive ethnography is all the more important as a counterbalance to the impressionistic insights but poor empiricism of fields such as cultural studies and postcolonial studies.

Part of anthropology's current tension between ethnographic substance and critical provocation is due to generational time. Those proponents of new academic trends who have already crossed into the world of tenure are less likely to be ethnographically substantive in their future work than are a new generation of fieldworkers. A recommitment to rigorous ethnography has the potential to winnow the insights and provocations of resituated perspectives and critical theories. It is here that Melanesian research has special potential. The tradition of rich and detailed ethnography in Melanesia makes its scholarship ripe for further development in light of the most important recent debates in anthropology.

High Modern versus Late Modern: Recent Articulations in Melanesian Anthropology

Twenty-five years ago, it was often held heuristically that linguistic or political units were relatively self-contained in many areas of Melanesia. In the context of the 1990s, such a notion seems almost absurd. The region has long since entered a world of village-town hybrids, evangelical transformations, postcolonial politics, the continuing if continually compromised pursuit of economic development, and movements that are both attracted to and resistant of national or multinational corporate agendas. Even as it is easy to overweight the force of these developments in many rural areas, it is also true that their impact, even if indirect, is increasingly prominent. Even in the absence of much direct outside contact, members of one of the ethnic groups near the Gebusi—whom I studied and described as in *Good Company* (1985a; cf. Wilson 1963)—are now more accurately described as "Waiting for Company": they wait in fervent wishfulness for large-scale corporate intervention to take their land's resources and make them rich (Dwyer and Minnegal 1998).

Classic Melanesian monographs were typically grounded in village-based ethnography. Assuming the homogeneity if not autonomy of indigenous local culture, they often focused on kinship or descent, leadership structure, ritual organization, or on topics such as subsistence intensity, sexual antagonism or pollution, socioeconomic exchange, or symbolism. The resulting documentation has been justifiably renowned and provides perhaps the richest corpora of ethnography from any world area. But this tradition now reinvents itself as it accommodates new developments. The sites of Melanesian experience now include the school, the church, the courts, the disco or cinema, the store, and relatives or *wantoks* in towns or urban centers, the mines, the parliament, and the multinational corporations seeking huge logging or mineral rights—as well as those who experience such developments only sporadically or indirectly.

Complemented importantly by Pacific scholars interested in history, political science, and sociology, Melanesian anthropology now embraces a host of topics that combine "traditional" concerns with deep postcolonial tensions concerning access to national resources and development, fundamentalist Christianity, law and order, and the mediation of ethnic and economic identity.[50] Personal and collective identity is increasingly forged in creative tension across local, regional, and urban networks of affiliation even as natal identifications remain primary.[51] Caught between demands from relatives and increasing reliance on personal cash, incipient cleavages of class overlay those of kinship connection.[52] Even and indeed especially in reasserting local

50. E.g., Errington and Gewertz 1995, 1996; Gewertz and Errington 1991; Barlow and Winduo 1997; Filer 1997; Otto and Thomas 1997; Smith 1994; Barker 1990; Trompf 1991; Foster 1995a, b; Strathern 1984; Gordon and Meggitt 1985; Scaglion 1981; Robbins 1994, 1997; see Ogan 1996b.

51. E.g., Connell and Lea 1994; Battaglia 1985.

52. E.g., Errington and Gewertz 1995, 1997; Carrier and Carrier 1989; Wanek 1996.

custom (*kastom*), status conflicts of a postcolonial nature emerge at the core of politics and representation.[53]

It is not possible here to analyze individual topics in detail, but all these developments rebound in complex relation to the attempts of Melanesia's states to create national identities in the face of social and political fragmentation.[54] Media, art, tourism, and language combine the local and the national if not the global.[55] Tensions between different venues of value and power easily engage problems as diverse as town and urban migration, vandalism, robbery, sexual abuse, a skyrocketing incidence of STDs, ecocide and land alienation by multinational mining and logging corporations, local warfare, rebellions against regional or national governments, and political turmoil and corruption.

Equally important and often less emphasized are the ways that indigenous people assert meaning, dignity, and resilience if not resistance amid these new contexts and influences. Even as land is now threatened by logging and mining schemes, countries such as Papua New Guinea, Vanuatu, and the Solomon Islands still have the vast bulk of their land locally owned and used for subsistence. That most Melanesians still spend most time cultivating their gardens entails not just continuity but recontexted significance from a global perspective in which land ownership by indigenous peoples is often so tenuous (Bodley 1982, 1988). This larger pattern accentuates the special threat posed by land alienation through the dramatic expansion of logging, mining, petroleum, and natural gas projects in Melanesia.[56] The key resource of locally owned land is no longer vouchsafed but has become a commodity of enormous postcolonial contestation.[57] The intensifying pressure from large Southeast Asian corporations for clear-cut logging in the Solomon Islands, Vanuatu, and New Guinea greatly expands the

---

53. See Feinberg and Zimmer-Tamakoshi 1995; White and Lindstrom 1993; Jolly and Thomas 1992; Jolly 1994; Keesing 1989, 1992; Keesing and Tonkinson 1982; van der Grijp and van Meijl 1993; G. M. White 1991.

54. See Foster 1995b; Errington and Gewertz 1996; Otto and Thomas 1997; Rutherford 1996.

55. See Foster 1996/97; Sullivan 1993; Wardlow 1996; Kulick and Willson 1994; Kulick 1990, 1992; Feld 1995.

56. E.g., about logging: Filer 1997; Barlow and Winduo 1997; Bennett 1994; Wood 1996; Schieffelin 1995; about mining and petroleum: Hyndman 1994; Banks and Ballard 1997; Burt 1996; Toft 1997; Kirsch 1993; Polier 1994; Knauft 1993b; cf. Stürzenhofecker 1994; Weiner 1994.

57. E.g., Toft 1997; Banks and Ballard 1997; Filer 1990; Kirsch 1996a, 1997a; see Multinational Monitor 1996; Kennedy 1996; Imhof 1996; Pacific Islands Monthly 1994.

threat of land alienation beyond more restricted mining and drilling sites.[58]

It is increasingly important to understand the continuities as well as the disjunctions brought by contemporary change. Migration, transformation, and cultural elaboration are indigenous in Melanesia and have been documented as such from early to late in the present century (e.g., from Seligmann [1910] to Strathern and Stürzenhofecker [1994]). Over this period, indigenous practices and beliefs have continued with surprising robustness. More than a simple retention or transformation of custom, traditions are actively recreated while they are reproduced—as importantly shown in recent monographs by Jolly (1994), Lutkehaus (1995), Foster (1995b), Stürzenhofecker (1998), and Lipset (1997) that relate history, gender, and custom in diverse areas of Melanesia. Even as they endure, customs are internalized in the face of changing circumstances and take on new significance (see Biersack 1995). Conversely, certain practices may disappear only to reappear later in altered form or with newly creative agency—as illustrated in O'Hanlon's (1995a) description of the modernized design motifs and meanings now associated with highlands fighting shields (see photo 16). Even the most geographically grounded beliefs assert themselves in new forms of expression or influence that are both similar to and different from their antecedents.[59]

In the face of new and intruding forms of change, it is all the more important to realize how selectively and creatively outside influences are appropriated by local people. Often, new images, values, or goods are used to reassert and redefine "the customary" and the local. While the relation between the global and the local is a key point of anthropological interest, the specific ways that local senses of space and place have or have not in fact been transformed deserve much greater attention.[60] Though the configuration of locality can be partly discerned through a consideration of public culture, mass media, and official discourse, the way less empowered people configure their locality in specific communities and informal contexts begs more understanding. In Melanesia, the link between social space and environmental place is particularly rich and important, and especially well documented in

---

58. See Filer 1997; Barlow and Winduo 1997; Bennett 1995.

59. E.g., Clark 1993; Stürzenhofecker 1994; Weiner 1994; Robbins 1995; Goldman and Ballard 1998.

60. See Feld and Basso 1996; cf. Gupta and Ferguson 1992, 1997.

both classical and recent works.[61] These associations, including their spiritual entailments and mythical tracks, are integrally tied to collective affiliation. These dynamic linkages between identity, place, and space elaborate creatively as local peoples contemplate changes in their landscape, the significance of towns and other sites of power, and the possibility of economic development through mining or logging projects.[62] Such projects negotiate land identifications, compensation payments, and adjustment to the cultural and environmental disruptions that engagements with modernity invariably bring.

New configurations of local identity and "custom" emerge in Melanesia through the aspirations for and complications of modernity. In the process, identity is often self-consciously asserted in opposition—to traditional enemies, to women, or to urban or national or corporate institutions—at the same time that it selectively embraces more "modern" notions of distinction and success. A growing sensitivity to identities that are at once indigenous and postcolonial allows Melanesianists to bridge classic ethnographic concerns with those that are more contemporary. At broader levels of analysis, this affords greater purchase on local issues of place, space, and identity in relation to larger politicoeconomic and cultural processes.[63] Amid the tensions and problems of postcolonial and neocolonial circumstances, the practical ways that Melanesians articulate long-standing orientations with new pressures and desires is a growing source of anthropological understanding.

Decentering and Recentering Field Research: Theoretical Dimensions

Marcus (1995) has argued that translocal identities call for new strategies of ethnography that do not presume a stable research location or community of study. This multisited emphasis can be importantly creative and even pivotal for comprehending the complexities of contemporary life in Melanesia. But newer research strategies still need to

---

61. E.g., Schieffelin 1976; Rappaport 1968; LiPuma 1988; Wagner 1967, 1972; A. J. Strathern 1971; M. Strathern 1972; Battaglia 1990; Weiner 1988a.

62. E.g., Goldman and Ballard 1998; Kirsch 1996a, 1997a; Stürzenhofecker 1994; Wardlow 1997.

63. See Errington and Gewertz 1995, 1996; Foster 1995a; White 1991; Jolly 1994; Smith 1994; Stürzenhofecker 1998; Weiner 1994; Robbins 1994; Brison 1994; Leavitt 1994; White and Lindstrom 1993; Feinberg and Zimmer-Tamakoshi 1995.

yield detailed documentation of social and cultural circumstances.[64] We still need ethnography of concrete experience. How do different fields of prestige get constituted and juxtapose against each other in individual lives? What types of meaning and dignity form amid long-standing and emergent inequalities? Which competing forms of post-colonial practice are most deeply motivating and which are most consciously strategized about? How are traditional forms of gender, age, and ethnic domination reproduced even as they are greatly transformed and in some cases subverted? These questions may be productively engaged by working in multiple sites and tracking people, images, things, or meanings across a semiotic or imaginary landscape. But ethnographic rigor should not be sacrificed to superficial renderings or a thin understanding of traveling cultures (e.g., Clifford 1992, 1997).

Though critical interest in representation has galvanized anthropologists' understanding of late modern diversity, the latest theoretical fashions have too often either collapsed these differences into a singular and undifferentiated Space—the abstract space of late modernity—or legislated all spaces, deconstructively, to a reflex of our own representation.[65] Alternatively, when practices are viewed in actual spatial locations and not just as microcosms of a theoretical world, the specific features that inflect the relationship between power and culture come into clearer view. To be ethnographic is not to ignore inequality but to underscore its operation and its representation.

In the postcolonial present, we may not be able to assume the coherence of "cultures" or "systems" or "structures," much less "hegemonies" or "ethnoscapes." But the notion of individual and collective practices continues to be helpful.[66] We can study the contours of practical experience whereby individuals construct alternative goals and identities. We can study how they employ limited resources to negotiate competing sources of symbolic capital. The abstract space of postmodernism or the textualized space that continues to haunt cultural

64. It can be argued, of course, that the contributions of cultural studies and critical theory are not *intended* to be ethnographic and should not be judged by these empiricist standards. In order for these perspectives to be useful in cultural *anthropology*, however, they need to inform rigorous documentation of social action and belief.

65. See Miller 1995; Hannerz 1996; Keith and Pile 1993; Appadurai 1996; Bird et al. 1993; Featherstone 1991; Featherstone, Lash, and Robertson 1995; Lash and Friedman 1992; Lash and Urry 1987, 1994; Soja 1989.

66. See Knauft 1996: chap. 4; cf. Ortner 1984; Bourdieu 1977, 1990.

studies can be effectively concretized by looking at the construction of identity and domination in the concrete practices of individuals as they trace over time and place. That these practices mediate between conflicting identities and aspirations injects a dynamism that practice theories originally lacked. This mediation makes processes of concrete choice and change intrinsic rather than residual to practice. It opens up rather than closes a rich and emergent understanding of agency. And it grounds these processes in actors' social experience, as opposed to the abstract individuals of grand theory or the fragmentary signs of postmodern pastiche.

Practices also emerge on a larger scale of time and place. Positing regional or national or transnational contours may be a separatist reification, as Bourdieu (1991:223) suggests. And the guises of late modernity may make the world seem increasingly postnational (Appadurai 1996). But the political assertion of boundaries remains key to both identity and conflict. Indeed, the defense of borders and of a shared history can be intensified by the very perception of their permeability. This is painfully evident in the realpolitik of power and culture that continues to assert and context national or ethnic identities as geographic territories. Territorial aspirations of nation-states, like those of ethnic groups of "tribes," have not been undercut so much as reasserted in the face of crosscurrents that threaten them. This is amply evident not only in the dramatic catastrophes that have plagued Bosnia, Rwanda, Iraq, or Cambodia but on a smaller scale in the Indonesianization of West New Guinea,[67] the postcolonial politics of ethnic and class domination in Fiji,[68] the continuing colonial dispossession of the indigenous peoples of New Caledonia,[69] and Papua New Guinea's disastrous military attempt to repossess its rebellious province of Bougainville.[70] And on the local level, as most Melanesians avidly attest, the boundaries of land and territory matter if anything more than ever under neocolonial or postcolonial conditions. Accordingly, the connections between local places and larger spaces are now as ripe for ethnographic documentation and critical reappraisal as they

---

67. E.g., Gietzelt 1988; Monbiot 1989; May 1986; Osborne 1985; Giay and Godschalk 1993; Rutherford 1996.

68. E.g., Lawson 1991; Lal 1990a, b; Howard 1991; see in Hooper et al. 1987.

69. E.g., Connell 1987, 1988; Guiart 1983; Weitzman 1985.

70. E.g., Sandline 1997; Murdoch 1997a, b; Wesley-Smith 1992; May and Spriggs 1991; cf. May 1993; Liria 1993.

ever were when uncharted tribal groups and boundaries were subject to earlier versions of Melanesian anthropology (see Foster 1995b).

The fluid potentials of contemporary identity require ethnographic grounding and geographic mapping in light of historical trends. Changes need to be documented in social and political as well as in imaginary terms, and in ways that include rather than neglect the legacy of indigenous cultural commitments. If the analysis of these changing affiliations is more complex than it was for people once thought to be without history, they remain as important on the sociological ground as they are in the airwaves of affiliation. Melanesian anthropology is becoming particularly attuned to these concerns.[71]

Subjectivities in Melanesian Postcolonies/Neocolonies

In late colonial or postcolonial circumstances, regimes of knowledge tend to compete and combine. In social terms, subjectivity and agency become especially complex. As Mbembe and Roitman (1995) have elaborated in an African context, and as Fanon (1991) foreshadowed, postcolonial crisis is integrally bound with crises of subjectivity. In many parts of Melanesia, for instance, the tension between giving and keeping has been an intrinsic if sometimes underappreciated dimension of traditional exchange and affiliation.[72] These tensions are accentuated with the advent of a cash economy, wage labor, commodity possession, and the attractions of theft. Under these conditions, collectively constituted notions of subjectivity and identity—what Marilyn Strathern (1988) called the Melanesian "dividual"—become especially problematic for the very reason that they are deeply internalized and refractory to extinction. Demands for reciprocity and contribution in collective exchange or remittances now compete against the personal value placed on commodity ownership, the raising of one's own bridewealth, or the importance of capital accumulation.[73] The tension between exchange and retention or dissipation—as between village and town or between haves and have-nots—inflects the continuing deep relation-

---

71. E.g., Errington and Gewertz 1995; White 1991; Foster 1995a, b; Stürzenhofecker 1998; Jolly 1994; Lutkehaus 1995.

72. E.g., Bercovitch 1994; Weiner 1992.

73. E.g., Marksbury 1993; Carrier and Carrier 1989.

ship between sorcery and social change in Melanesia.[74] The workings of kinship—long celebrated and now neglected as a topic of anthropological study[75]—become particularly important as the expanding idioms of ethnic and linguistic affiliation—being a *wantok*—engage the potentials and problems of social affiliation in towns or cities. These tensions have poignant implications for sexuality and gender, as discussed previously in chapter 4.

The difficulties of postcolonial subjectivity are well known, along with the excesses if not banality of patriarchal power that they articulate with. As Mbembe (1992) notes, again in an African context, these easily dovetail with the proliferation of violence once Westerners have left. Though refractory to good documentation, this has occurred to some degree in selected parts of Melanesia, including through the Indonesianization of West New Guinea and the violent opposition between Papua New Guinea state and rebel forces on Bougainville.[76] Though also present in police force abuses, such coercion is less pronounced in the Solomon Islands, Vanuatu, and the mainland of Papua New Guinea, where authority structures have stayed relatively decentralized and where the colonial encounter was relatively nonviolent and nonalienating of land, at least when viewed on a comparative global scale. But if an African-style banality of power is not imminent, huge and increasing problems of political corruption, ecocide, insurrection, guns, drugs, lawlessness, gendered abuse, and STDs do raise the possibility of an ultimate slide down some parallel path, particularly in cities and other areas of high population density, such as the highlands of Papua New Guinea.[77] As Andrew Strathern (1993a:56) has pointed out, "violence is becoming more and more an *expected* part of political activity the more complex and sophisticated in other respects the political process becomes."

If this is one potential side of the story, however, it is not the only

74. E.g., Lattas 1993; Zelenietz and Lindenbaum 1981; Stephen 1987; cf. Burridge 1969.

75. See in general Peletz 1995.

76. E.g., for West New Guinea: Gietzelt 1988; Monbiot 1989; Osborne 1985; May 1986; for Bougainville: Wesley-Smith 1992; May and Spriggs 1991; Hyndman 1994; see Ogan 1991, 1996a.

77. Sobering reviews of the social and political problems facing Papua New Guinea have recently been authored by Jorgensen (1995), Wesley-Smith (1995), and A. J. Strathern (1992, 1993a; cf. 1984); see also Hart Nibbrig (1992), Goddard (1995), and Dinnen (1997).

one. Melanesian cultures have survived and thrived in the face of collective violence for many centuries prior to colonial intervention. And current problems run up against the bulk of common people, who maintain creative resilience and social commitments in everyday practices. Notwithstanding difficulties, Melanesian peoples remain creative and dynamic, including in the towns and urban centers that are still so understudied. As Africanist Kwame Appiah (1991:356) suggests, resilience persists in even the most dire circumstances:

> Despite the overwhelming reality of economic decline; despite unimaginable poverty; despite wars, malnutrition, disease, and political instability, African cultural productivity grows apace: popular literatures, oral narrative and poetry, dance, drama, music, and visual art all thrive. The contemporary cultural production of many African societies, and the many traditions whose evidences so vigorously remain, is an antidote to the dark vision of the postcolonial novelist.

The workings of knowledge and desire in the context of social power lead us back to rather than away from agency and practice. Here again, ethnographic portrayal of lived experience is crucial. Even as we dispense with grander narratives of practice as totalizing theory (Bourdieu 1977, 1990), the smaller practices of concrete actors persist with creative vengeance. Powers and resistances that tend to be taken for granted in the West can be productively defamiliarized by considering Melanesian agents and objects of desire.

Larger Parameters of Political Economy

Melanesian studies has a particular opportunity—and challenge—to put postcolonial or subaltern affiliations in the context of larger political and economic influences. The varieties of colonialism in Melanesia combined an especially thick color bar between whites and blacks with a relative paucity of both land alienation and economic development, at least when compared to many other world areas. In many areas, this pattern of intrusion articulated with distinctively Melanesian notions of social equivalence and materiality to spawn what were called cargo cults—social movements of Melanesian economic aspiration that combined religious supplication of Western goods or money with political change and, sometimes, opposition to and resistance against Western-ers.[78]

These remarkable developments and their continuing incarnations are difficult to adequately understand in terms that are either indigenous to Melanesia or externally caused. As Ranajit Guha (1989) cogently reminds us, colonial intrusion that largely bypasses the social and cultural infrastructure of indigenous belief and practice is not really an introduced "hegemony" so much as colonial dominance ultimately backed up by the threat of coercive force. Though this view is too simple for Melanesia—the cultural and social import of Christianity, business, and colonial government have been immense—it remains true that Western influences have often been appropriated by Melanesians on their own terms and played out through their own initiatives. So, too, it is harder to explain the present problems of Melanesian states by invoking the ghost of colonial exploitation than has often been attempted, sometimes all too easily, for other world areas.

Despite detailed studies of its indigenous culture areas, New Guinea is only beginning to generate a powerful corpus of critical scholarship from either a historicized politicoeconomic or a more broadly theorized postcolonial perspective.[79] Though cultural and social change are being actively studied and documented by Melanesianist anthropologists on a local level, larger trajectories of political economy and postcolonial cultural development, especially in New Guinea, are yet to be critically engaged with many postcolonial concerns now emerging strongly from African, South and Southeast Asian, Mideastern, and Latin American studies.

The relatively sparse politicoeconomic analysis of east and west New Guinea is complemented, however, by a greater range of relevant

---

78. See Worsley 1968; Lawrence 1964; Burridge 1960; Schwartz 1963; Knauft 1978. Recent studies of millenarian movements in Melanesia include Rimoldi and Rimoldi 1992; Whitehouse 1995; Wanek 1996; and Lattas (e.g., 1991, 1992a, b, 1993); see critique of "cargo cult" as an analytic category by McDowell (1988), Lattas (1992b), and Lindstrom (1993). The important linkage between utopian or millenarian aspirations and micronationalist movements, as presaged by Worsley (1968), has yet to be effectively retheorized for postcolonial Melanesia in general; cf. May (1982), Robie (1989a), and recent historical contributions by J. D. Kelly (1991), Kaplan (1995), and an edited collection by Lattas (1992c).

79. Available works for western Melanesia include Nelson 1976, 1982; Connolly and Anderson 1987; Brookfield 1972; Fitzpatrick 1980; Amarshi, Good, and Mortimer 1979; Garnaut and Manning 1974; see a more analytic overview by Griffin, Nelson, and Firth 1979; cf. Worsley 1968; see Wanek 1996.

work (particularly from a historical perspective) for eastern insular Melanesia.[80] Interest in the relationship between culture, politics, and colonial history was presaged by critical studies of "cargo cults" and was subsequently elaborated in several important works by Roger Keesing during the 1980s and early 1990s.[81] Ethnographic and theoretical studies of the culture–history interface in insular Melanesia have since proliferated during the 1990s.[82]

Some of these works smudge if not efface the boundary between Melanesia and Polynesia to the east. Indeed, larger parameters of political economy and culture reopen questions about the status of "Melanesia" itself as a geographic or cultural region (see Thomas 1989). As discussed above, regional and global interconnections render the conceptual integrity of any culture area problematic in late modern anthropology. This critique acquires special relevance for Melanesia— literally, the "black islands"—as classically contrasted to "chiefly" cultures in Polynesia, "stately" traditions in southeast Asia, and "hunter-gatherers" in Australia. More narrowly, the metonymic tendency in high modernist anthropology was to consider New Guinea, and interior New Guinea in particular, as the most archetypal or quintessentially Melanesian part of Melanesia—the most unknown, the most unacculturated, the most violent and exotic (perhaps even the darkest), and, reciprocally, the most attractive for anthropology. This area's tribal tradition in anthropology has made it more difficult for the region—and New Guinea in particular—to be effectively evaluated from a critically theorized political and cultural point of view (except, perhaps, concerning developments that were primarily *pre*-colonial).[83]

My own portrayals here have not been immune from the metonymic elevation of interior New Guinea to the status of being "archetypally Melanesian." Eastern and insular Melanesia, especially Fiji and New Caledonia, have been relatively neglected in my account.

---

80. E.g., Connell 1987; Guiart 1983; Weitzman 1985; Bennett 1987; Emberson-Bain 1993; Thomas 1991, 1994; Kaplan 1995; J. D. Kelly 1991; Wanek 1996; cf. also Worsley 1968.

81. E.g., Keesing 1982b, 1983, 1989, 1992; Keesing and Corris 1980; Keesing and Tonkinson 1982. These may be compared (and contrasted) to preceding works in an earlier generation by Felix Keesing (e.g., 1941, 1945; cf. Stanner 1953).

82. E.g., Thomas 1991, 1994; Otto and Thomas 1997; White 1991; Lindstrom and White 1990; Carrier 1992a; Foster 1995a; Wanek 1996; cf., for interior New Guinea, works such as Connolly and Anderson 1987; O'Hanlon 1993; P. Brown 1995.

83. E.g., Feil 1987; A. J. Strathern 1982d; Godelier 1986.

And with a few exceptions, most of the luminaries mentioned at the outset of this chapter as icons of Melanesianist scholarship worked in what is now Papua New Guinea. But this, too, has been changing. If the longer contact history and syncretic developments of insular and eastern Melanesia rendered it relatively less exotic for high modernist anthropology, these very features now recommend it on a number of budding theoretical fronts in a late modern era. Indeed, trenchant reappraisals of Melanesian economics, history, and voicing now seem if anything most powerfully developed for insular areas of Melanesia to the east of the New Guinea mainland, as amply illustrated in a spate of important recent volumes by Nicholas Thomas, Margaret Jolly, Geoffrey White, Lamont Lindstrom, James Carrier, Robert Foster, John Kelly, Martha Kaplan, and Andrew Lattas, among others.[84]

Melanesia is increasingly considered not only as an entity but also as a conduit that articulates with the rest of the insular Pacific, Southeast and East Asia, and Australia. The increasing importance of multinational development projects in Melanesia, including the operations of Southeast Asian logging firms as well as oil and mineral conglomerates, underscores this articulation in New Guinea as well as in insular Melanesia. The analysis of local and historical identities that is evident in much of the scholarship just referred to is quickly coming to terms with these larger and ever more powerful dynamics.

Large-Scale Power in Contemporary Melanesia

In a postcolonial era, local disputes, ethnic rivalries, antinational or anticorporate rebellions, and international conflicts all tunnel through Melanesia. At the present moment—early 1998—the anticipated new "century of the Asian Pacific" is mired in monetary and economic crisis among the countries of the western Pacific Rim. Regardless of how this crisis is mediated, size and population greatly favor the growing economic and political impact of East and Southeast Asia in Melanesia, including the growing geopolitical power of nation-states such as China, Indonesia, and Malaysia. So, too, on a smaller scale *within* Melanesia, the economic and political clout of Papua New Guinea is much greater than that of countries such as the Solomon Islands or

---

84. See Thomas 1989, 1991, 1994, 1997; Otto and Thomas 1997; Jolly 1994; Jolly and MacIntyre 1989; White 1991; White and Lindstrom 1993; Lindstrom 1990, 1993; Carrier 1992a; Carrier and Carrier 1989, 1991; Foster 1995a, b; J. D. Kelly 1991; Kaplan 1995.

Vanuatu. Against these patterns, the contemporary culture economy of Asian geopolitical influence in Melanesia is just beginning to be seriously considered by anthropologists (e.g., Wood 1995; Rutherford 1997). Amid if not in conjunction with these influences, political tensions and economic aspirations that burgeon to new heights in Melanesia are likely to inform a great deal of the organized and less organized violence in the years ahead. Against regional and national hegemonies, anthropologists' voices are particularly important; we maintain a distinctive scholarly and human perspective on local concerns in Melanesia, and on the larger tectonics that induce inequity and influence how this inequality is known about and perceived by the rest of the world.

The spiraling collusion between national governments and multinational corporations in logging, drilling, and mining ventures in Melanesia is particular cause for concern. Since the nineteenth century, appropriations of timber and ore were a fulcrum point of colonial exploitation across Melanesia, from New Caledonia and Fiji to Vanuatu, the Solomon Islands, and New Guinea.[85] The search for gold caused significant waves of intrusion into Melanesia over the decades, including the prospecting expeditions that eventually led to the Western discovery of the New Guinea Highlands.[86] Nickel mining has been a dominant factor in the development of New Caledonia since the 1870s (e.g., Connell 1987). The enormous Panguna copper mine on Bougainville, which opened in 1969, provided up to one-fourth of the gross domestic product for the entire country of Papua New Guinea until it was seized by local rebels in 1989.[87] But even as Panguna has been closed, a whole series of major gold and/or copper mines have been brought on line or projected in New Guinea and adjacent areas, and some are now also being developed in the Solomon Islands. A highly profitable 159-mile oil pipeline from the interior of Papua New Guinea to the south coast was constructed in the early 1990s by Chevron (Knauft 1993b). Additional petroleum strikes have followed, and now there are major plans to build gas pipelines across major tracts of rain forest from interior areas to both the north and the south coast of Papua New Guinea. West New Guinea—the Indonesian province of Irian Jaya—now harbors the largest gold mine in the world, and the Indonesian government hopes to move forward with a massive hydro-

85. E.g., Shineberg 1967; Bennett 1987; Connell 1987.
86. See Nelson 1976; Connolly and Anderson 1987.
87. See Wesley-Smith 1992; May and Spriggs 1991; Hyndman 1994.

electric development project and resettlement scheme along the Mamberano River to the north (Chidley 1998). Viewed in politicoeconomic perspective, state dependence on large-scale mineral or petroleum resource extraction easily creates a "boom and bust" cycle that increases national dependency on multinational corporate contracts, facilitates corruption while escalating nonproductive state expenditures, and is highly destabilizing to civic and political development, especially when prices fall or as windfall profits later subside into "bust" conditions. On a global scale, this is what political economist Terry Karl (1997) analyzes as the "Paradox of Plenty" that afflicts third world countries that are rich in natural resources such as petroleum reserves.

Large-scale development projects in Melanesia are almost invariably beset by land alienation and/or compensation disputes as well as environmental problems; these frequently leave landowners angry and restive if not rebellious.[88] In the Western Province of Papua New Guinea, ecological and social problems have been seething as a result of the huge Ok Tedi gold and copper mine.[89] In addition to major disputes over land compensation, lack of employment, and social disruption, the heavy metals and other sediment from the Ok Tedi and Porgera mines have ravaged downstream environments along the massive Fly and Strickland River systems.[90]

In Bougainville, at the eastern end of Papua New Guinea, festering local opposition to compensation arrangements led to armed revolt and indefinite shutdown of the Panguna mine.[91] It also triggered a violent toppling of the Bougainville provincial government and a period of effective secession by the island province from the Papua New Guinea state (Robie 1989b). In response, the P.N.G. government attempted to crush rebel leaders by invading the province with its army; when this was unsuccessful, the state withdrew and blockaded the island.[92] Cut off from external contact or support, Bougainville's infrastructure collapsed, food sources became scarce, and essential services ceased. Caught in the middle, the local populace has suffered

88. See Filer 1990, 1997; Toft 1997.

89. See Hyndman 1994; Kirsch 1993, 1997a.

90. E.g., Kirsch 1996a, 1997a, 1997c; Banks and Ballard 1997; P. Shearman, pers. comm.

91. Concerning the initial events of the Bougainville rebellion, see Hiambohn 1989; Bromby 1990.

92. See Senge 1990a, b; Liria 1993.

major hardships; it was reported that up to 12,000 people may have died between 1990 and 1997.[93] In 1997, the prime minister of Papua New Guinea, Sir Julius Chan, attempted to hire a South African mercenary organization to route out and kill the members of the Bougainville Republican Army (BRA) with sophisticated military weaponry, and to retake the Panguna mine.[94] When the secret arrangement was preemptively revealed, leaders of the P.N.G. Defense Force protested and the country lapsed into governmental chaos until Chan agreed to resign.

Across Papua New Guinea's western border, in Irian Jaya, it is hard to ignore the alliance between the Indonesian state and the Fortune 500 company of Freeport-McMoRan, Inc. The well-documented result of this collusion has been the ecocide of major river systems and a reinforcement of the forceful suppression of indigenous peoples by the Indonesian government. Tactics have included intimidation, beatings, occasional burning of villages, relocation of villagers, and sporadic killing of opponents.[95] The financial stakes are enormous: an estimated $50 billion from the world's largest gold and third largest copper mine.[96] In 1995, Freeport took out full-page ads in the *New York Times* to defend itself and chide its opponents: anthropological critics were castigated for wanting "to create a human zoo in Irian Jaya" (Burnett 1995). The actions of Freeport were subsequently defended against so-called environmental imperialism in an editorial that appeared in the guise of a feature news article in *Forbes Magazine* (McMenamin 1996).

Another major corporate challenge for Melanesia is large-scale logging projects, which are pursued by Southeast Asian timber conglomerates such as Rimbunan Hijau. The clear-cutting of timber is being expanded at an alarming rate across large stretches of rain forest in Papua New Guinea and the Solomon Islands.[97] Though this process has temporarily slackened due to financial crisis in southeast Asia, it is likely to re-intensify in future years. Logging firms wield considerable clout at the national and provincial level, and they have the financial resources to pay off politicians and local leaders in legal and illegal ways. As a result, they frequently get lenient contract provisions that minimize their environmental and compensatory obligations or allow them to neglect those that are technically in place.

---

93. Murdoch 1997b; Sasako 1991; see Wesley-Smith 1992; May and Spriggs 1991.
94. Sandline 1997; Murdoch 1997a, b.
95. E.g., Press 1995; Burnett 1995; Australian Council 1995; *Pembaruan Daily* 1998.
96. See Bryce 1995; Shari, McWilliams, and Crock 1995.
97. E.g., Bennett 1995; Filer 1997; Barlow and Winduo 1997; Wood 1996.

At the same time, many if not most of these developments are invited and welcomed by local people, at least initially, when the shortcomings and unintended consequences of large-scale development are on the other side of a seemingly wealthy and rosy horizon. The desire for cash and commodities—underscored by a local sense of being impoverished and left behind by the allure of modernity—seems to grow relentlessly in Melanesia. This impetus is unlikely to be undercut and may be intensified by the severe shortage of edible food in large parts of western Melanesia due to the El Niño–induced drought of 1997 (see Allen and Bourke 1997a, b).

Tracking the fields of power, politics, and inequity that galvanize Melanesia now leads to the boardroom as well as to the men's house or its postcolonial equivalent (cf. Rival 1997). Issues of representation and perception are not just ephemeral or abstract; they are integral to understanding the dynamics of action and power. If it is now an anachronism to assume a synchronic equivalence of comparative facts, comparison needs increasingly to consider the political vantage points that inflect different accounts. In the present case, the way that coercive influence and resistant response have played off the political imagination of savagery, paradise, pacification, neocolonialism, nationalism, environmentalism, and economic development by multinational corporations is crucial to understanding the ethnographic past in relation to contemporary developments.[98] In the final analysis, it is important to make sure that this awareness encourages rather than inhibits our ability to be more vigorous and more diverse in our ethnography, more critical in our analyses, and broader in our theorizations.

Auspices of Authorship

The relation between Melanesian anthropology and late modernity raises a further key issue: the role of power and authorship in the formation of knowledge. Issues of power and representation have been less engaged in Melanesian anthropology than in the anthropology of many other world areas. Part of this hesitation stems from Melanesianists' salutary desire to maintain the highest criteria of ethnographic rigor against the looser empirical standards sometimes associated with postcolonial critiques, cultural studies, and experimental ethnogra-

---

98. See Fry (1997) concerning the current eclipsing of "exotic" with "doomsday" images of the South Pacific in the Western imaginary.

phy.[99] The underlying threat posed by such approaches is self-indulgent cleverness, superficiality, and prosaic narcissism.[100]

There seems no reason on the face of it, however, that critically viewing the lens of authorship and representation cannot facilitate a richer rather than a more impoverished view of other peoples—as O'Hanlon (1993) nicely illustrates in his account of material culture, collecting, and representation in the contemporary New Guinea highlands. These possibilities can be broadened in both ethnographic and theoretical terms. Reflexive engagements can, if taken in reasonable doses, promote rather than compromise the ethnography of practices across spaces in areas such as Melanesia. Now more than a century old, Melanesian ethnography and the history of Melanesian engagement with outsiders have their own trajectories of representation that form part of our critical self-consciousness. The reevaluation of our own representations can provide a better understanding of Melanesian realities and not just a mirror for our own reflection; perspectival relativity can fuel rather than compromise our ability to work through representations and make our analysis more refined rather than simply more rarefied.

Historically, the many decades of scholarly observation in Melanesia encode major shifts of signification, projection, and authorship. Though certainly reflecting change in Melanesia itself, these perspectival shifts also mark changes—and continuities—of Western interests and projections. In a postcolonial era, changing practices and perspectives of authorship need to be considered in specific relation to Melanesian practices as objects of knowledge. As discussed in chapter 3, for instance, the representation of "warfares" in association with particular historical periods and particular areas within Melanesia is partly a function of intellectual history, including the shifting interests of Western interpretive lenses and the different kinds of alterity that have been acceptable or desirable to project onto Melanesians, for example, savage warfare, cathartic warfare, ecologically adaptive warfare, the warfare of Western pacification, the resurgence of tribal fighting, disruptive raskolism, postcolonial rebellion, and so on. What we know as the

---

99. See Williams and Chrisman 1994; Grossberg, Nelson, and Treichler 1992; Clifford and Marcus 1986; and Marcus and Myers 1995.

100. See critiques by Sangren (1988), Polier and Roseberry (1989), and Birth (1990), among others.

"history" of violence and warfare in Melanesia is configured through the sedimentation of these lenses of Western concern. Even a preliminary history of collective violence in Melanesia reveals major shifts of authorial as well as ethnographic difference. A similar argument could be made about both venerable and more recent topics of anthropological interest in Melanesia, including "sexual customs," "material artifacts," "taboos," "competitive exchange," "lineage structure," "male initiation," "big-man political organization," "ritual adaptation," "man-land intensification," "sexual antagonism," "ritualized homosexuality," "gender relations," and "*kastom*" as opposed to the "customs" of earlier ethnography. Each of these concepts and topics evokes a particular style and period of analysis in Melanesian anthropology.

Being reflexive about scholarly interests in Melanesia now also means considering authorship in relation to contemporary social problems and cultural and political contestations. In the postcolonial present, Melanesians are quite capable of speaking for themselves. The current state of the professional literature soberly reminds us of the thickness of the line that continues to separate interpretations by Western academics from those by Melanesians.[101] Here one must respond to Spivak's (1994:75) general assertion that, "it is impossible for contemporary [Western] intellectuals to imagine the kind of Power and Desire that would inhabit the unnamed subject of the Other of Europe." But aside from Spivak's rhetoric, we are not limited to a Western imagination, nor even her own. Indigenous voices do speak. In Melanesia, this includes important creative writing and novels by indigenous authors (see bibliography compiled by Elliston [1997]), as well as a robust tradition of Melanesian journalism and debate.

For a number of important historical reasons, however, Melanesia—and New Guinea in particular—has not developed a kind of indigenous critical scholarship and associated scholarly literature akin to those that have emerged from, say, subaltern India, Africa, or Latin or Native America. Those Melanesian authors who *have* developed critical perspectives, such as Warilea Iamo (1992), John Waiko (1992), and Bernard Narokobi (1980, 1983)—and compare works by Epeli Hau'ofa (1975, 1983) and Gullahorn-Holecek (1983)—have not always been con-

---

101. It was startling to realize that in my own comparative book on south coast New Guinea (Knauft 1993a), only two New Guinean authors—Billai Laba (1975a, b) and Abraham Kuruwaip (1984)—were referenced out of 404 persons cited.

sidered as frequently or seriously by Western scholars as they might (see Morauta 1979).[102]

By contrast, African studies, South Asian studies, and Latin American studies, among others, have been strongly impacted by indigenous interpretations and critiques. More broadly, these critical reflections have had a major impact on theories of culture and history. But postcolonial critiques have exerted a minimal impact upon Melanesian anthropology. Despite a few significant exceptions, this contrasts to a more developed tradition of critical scholarly authorship in other parts of the insular Pacific, including the work of Pacific Islanders such as Tjibaou (1978), Walker (1990), Meleisea (1987), Emberson-Bain (1994), Ravuvu (1991), Trask (1991), and Hau'ofa (1994a, b), among many others.[103]

It is important to note and to encourage those special indigenous institutions within Melanesia that *do* foster an interchange between local, national, and international scholarship. These include especially the Institute for Pacific Studies at the University of the South Pacific, in Suva, Fiji, and Papua New Guinea's National Research Institute, which combines the previous Institute for Papua New Guinea Studies and IASER (the Institute for Applied Social and Economic Research). New Caledonia under the Matignon Accords is finally now investing in a new cultural complex that should support indigenous education and research in Kanak culture.

Though creative writing and other forms of fiction have flourished in Melanesia, as they have in other parts of the Pacific, the relative dearth of indigenous social science and anthropology in particular is both significant and predisposed (contrast Hau'ofa 1975, 1983). Especially in western Melanesia, these antecedents include a relatively short duration of intensive colonial contact and a paucity of colonial infrastructure; the strength of the colonial racial bar against the academic training of indigenous peoples; relative lack of more recent opportunity for higher education; and the postcolonial siphoning of some Melanesians who do have university education into the lucrative possibilities of corporate contracts and business consultantships. Many bud-

---

102. Early scholarly publications by Papua New Guineans include Sarei 1974; Simet 1976, 1977; Enos 1972; Hau'ofa 1975, 1983; and Kituai 1974.

103. Concerning the intellectual stakes entailed for Pacific Studies generally, see especially Chappell 1995; Howe, Kiste, and Lal 1992; and Linnekin 1992; cf. Obeyesekere 1992; Sahlins 1995.

ding Melanesian intellectuals have been either absorbed into or stigmatized by the so-called super-tribe of power elite professionals who have
disproportionate personal access to the riches and profits generated by
the region's natural resources.[104] Speaking of the insular Pacific more
broadly, Epeli Hau'ofa (1987:1) suggests that

> there already exists in our part of the world a single regional econ-
> omy upon which has emerged a South Pacific Society, the privi-
> leged groups of which share a single dominant culture with
> increasingly marginalised local sub-cultures shared by the poorer
> classes.

Melanesian voices—constituting such a large portion of the
world's languages—are anything but monolithic. To encourage indigenous authorship is not to say that indigenous voices are in harmony,
nor that one should agree with any given expression. Literacy is itself
selective, and it can be elitist among Melanesians as well as among academics. There can be major differences between elite indigenous views
and the perspectives of those who are less educated or less economically advantaged. These latter persons are much less apt to write or
publish. It would hence be shortsighted to replace older essen-
tialisms—in which natives are objects rather than subjects of authorship—with new ones that pose indigenous authors as invariably
authentic and Western ones as artificial. It is important to avoid the
"romance of victimization," which presumes that entities deriving
from Western intrusion or influence are invariably oppressive to local
peoples. This is certainly not the general view held by many Melanesians, including on matters of Western political and religious influence
as well as those of economic development. As noted by Chappell
(1995:309) in the context of Pacific historiography, the status of "victim"
carries disempowering connotations of passivity, helplessness, and
vulnerability, notwithstanding its rhetorical appeal.[105] This is just the
opposite of the grass roots agency and self-definition favored by Pacific
Island authors such as Hau'ofa (1994a).

One of the productive ways that Melanesian anthropologists can
engage these issues—and have done so, especially in eastern Melane-

---

104. See, for example, Wanek 1996: chap. 16 and pp. 305ff.
105. See also especially Thomas 1994.

sia—is by considering the politics of tradition and *kastom*.[106] As Errington and Gewertz (1997:129) suggest, there is a remarkable intensity to the way contemporary Melanesians engage the politics of self and group construction. The way that local configurations of tradition are asserted amid regional or corporate or national agendas entails not just political or symbolic dynamics but the politics of representation itself. The anthropologist as observer/writer/activist/interpreter is likewise engaged in representations that have political implications and repercussions. Rather than lamenting or trying to escape from this reality, anthropologists of Melanesia have the potential to more actively analyze the relationship between symbolic and politicoeconomic capital as it negotiates across a range of local, regional, national, and academic discourses. Such analysis need not devolve into a thin portrayal of surface images or superficial traveling cultures. Rather, we need to dig beneath the surface of representations and plumb countercurrents that inform the desires, morals, and actions of Melanesians in their daily lives. That our own suppositions as Western anthropologists often assume an appreciation of cultural diversity and a critique of inequality can sharpen rather than blunt our values and ethics amid these tensions (Knauft 1996: chap. 2).

These commitments require more objectivity, not less. And they entail a refusal to project "good guy" or "bad guy" status based simply on a person's local or government or corporate affiliation, much less their skin color. Even as our interests are importantly directed to inequality, it is patently evident that inequities of gender, ethnicity, class, nationality, and age crosscut one another, as illustrated in chapter 4 above. Moreover, resistance against one axis of disempowerment or disparagement often reinforces rather than alleviates others. Asserting ethnic pride through *kastom* can subordinate youths or women; national empowerment can trample local rights to land or resources; the individual's drive to escape poverty can compromise equality between *wantoks;* and the destabilization of state power can disenfranchise some groups while empowering others.

Grappling with such complexities requires a careful analysis of alternative opinions and perspectives as contexted by the documentation of empirical conditions. This means cultivating rather than sup-

---

106. See Feinberg and Zimmer-Tamakoshi 1995; White and Lindstrom 1993; Jolly and Thomas 1992.

pressing a diversity of Melanesian voices even as they may be housed within a Western-edited, Western-authored, or cowritten text.[107] So, too, the traditional strengths of Melanesian ethnography in presenting the village-based perspective of less educated or less influential Melanesians need to be maintained. Greater emphasis is still needed on the portrayal of women's perspectives, people of different ages, and those with both more and less exposure to urban life, employment, education, and wealth. Along this continuum, the line between indigenous and Western voicing can be creatively dialogic rather than polarized between "insiders" and "outsiders."[108]

Alongside issues of history and power, then, those of authorship and dialogue engage the potentials as well as the limitations of Melanesian anthropology. As we expand our purview in future years, it will be increasingly important to look both sympathetically and critically at the full diversity of Melanesian medias of representation—including art, film, song, printed text, and public culture.[109] A critical understanding of Melanesian expressions in print and in public culture can enable rather than impede this finer empiricism. It is not necessary to pit scholarly portrayal and analysis of Melanesian realities against the encouragement of Melanesian voices or the analysis of our own representations. These can be mutually facilitating.

Conclusion

A late modern anthropology should have vested interest in finding ethnographic value and importance in each and every part of the inhabited world. In an era of globalization and hybrid complexity, however, the perception of tribal history in Melanesia makes it important to reassert the contemporary significance of this region in ethnographic and theoretical terms. As Anna Tsing (1993, 1994) has pointed out more generally, the dynamics of culture change are also pronounced in the marginality of seemingly out-of-the-way places. By contrast, the relegation of local dynamics to postmodern fragmentation or,

---

107. See Majnep and Bulmer 1977; Kyakas and Wiessner 1992; A.J. Strathern 1979c, 1993b; White 1991; cf. also Lindstrom and White 1990; Jenkins 1994.

108. See more generally Narayin 1993; Abu-Lughod 1991; T. Turner 1993; Rosaldo 1994. These issues are discussed more generally in Knauft (1996: chap. 9).

109. E.g., Stella 1994; Sullivan 1993; Foster 1995b, 1996/97; Wardlow 1996; Feld 1995; Gewertz and Errington 1996.

at another extreme, to a world system of late modern capitalism, is ultimately dehumanizing of anthropology's subjects. To critically engage
the abstract potentials of these perspectives necessitates an ethnography of diverse places that documents what local people actually do,
what they believe, and what they want. In Melanesia, rich ethnography
allows for a much more nuanced history than is possible in many world
areas concerning the background and trajectories of social and cultural
change. Melanesian ways of life mediate tensions between gift and
commodity, cult and church, indigenous leadership and electoral politics, subsistence production and economic development, and clan connections and class relations. Because the social baseline against which
these mediations occurs is so richly documented in Melanesia, understanding the causes and consequences of change becomes all the more
feasible and compelling.

That a reflexively critical and an objectivist view are now both necessary in Melanesian anthropology can make it (like the present
account) appear ambivalent. The problem is not ambivalence, however. Indeed, it would be more problematic to refuse to wrestle concretely with both sides of a relationship that is inherently ambivalent,
that is, between Melanesia as a region of study and anthropology as a
contemporary academic discipline. In this regard, a dialogue of critical
complementarity is better than polarizing alternatives that actually
inhere in each other or embracing a one-sided view. The anthropological enterprise is often if not intrinsically ambivalent, and it can seem
increasingly so in contemporary circumstances. But this tension has
less frequently been seen as a signal and productive *strength* in anthropology, as opposed to being a disciplinary weakness. A scholarly and
personal commitment to a human enterprise in which easy answers are
problematic and deeper questions make for better results is one of the
things that makes anthropology—and the anthropology of Melanesia
in particular—especially important in a late modern world. We steer
more carefully and productively in our endeavors by acknowledging
the problems posed by conservative traditionalism, on the one hand,
and the excesses of the newfangled and the ideologies associated with
postcoloniality, on the other.

Particularly for students, it may be useful for me to end by summarizing
some of the things that make Melanesia especially significant for contemporary anthropology. First, Melanesia's incredible cultural diver-

sity—for which it is justifiably famous—becomes all the more significant for a field that is dedicated to exploring contemporary notions of
difference.[110] If one is interested in the mixing and blending of identities,
or in culture as a dialogue or tension between different voices, a world
area that has so many of the world's languages and associated cultures
is of particular interest and importance. That current developments in
Melanesia unfold as transformations upon remarkable indigenous orientations, and amid spiraling fields of contemporary power, makes
them particularly rich and worthy of understanding.

Second, the era of colonial influence has been relatively recent and
compressed in much of Melanesia, at least when compared to most
areas of North and South America, Asia, Africa, and many other parts
of Oceania. This means that the temporal compressions of late modernity—including the tension between indigenous dispositions and
newer institutions, social networks, and technologies—are particularly
striking and momentous in Melanesia. As Gewertz and Errington
(1997:127) suggest, many parts of Melanesia are now "where the global
intersects the local in axiomatically condensed form." Accordingly, the
twisting paths of Melanesian cultural and political change are especially ripe for documentation and theoretical analysis.

Third, Melanesian practices and beliefs have often been detailed at
an early period in the colonial era, and much more consistently so than
in many world areas. In the present, this record provides a unique lens
of cultural history through which current developments can be viewed.
This affords us special understanding about the cultural roots of social
developments and how these have emerged over time. An especially
rich understanding of sociocultural change and transformation is thus
possible.

Fourth, the representation of Melanesia as an area, and of Melanesians as people, has a distinctive place in the history of anthropology.
On the one hand, these representations have often been at the forefront
of anthropology's modernist contributions. On the other, they have
often relegated Melanesians to a tribal slot and considered them more as
objects than as subjects. In a late modern era, the fullness of this history
exposes key issues for rigorous analysis and careful reflection. That
Melanesians are self-consciously drawing upon representations of tradition in their own negotiations with regional, national, and corporate

---

110. I thank Michael O'Hanlon for raising this point.

interests makes the effective use of Melanesianists' ethnographic record all the more relevant and important for contemporary assessment. In the process, Melanesian studies can yield key insights about the course of anthropology's past and expose fresh directions for its future.

In the same way that Melanesia has moved from a colonial to a postcolonial or neocolonial era, the field of Melanesian studies has now turned from high modern to a late-modern or postcolonial anthropology. In neither case, however, has this transition meant giving up the strengths of the past. In Melanesian studies, the transition is toward what Robert Foster (1995a) calls "New Melanesian Anthropology." We are indeed moving beyond "Melanesia" and "Melanesian studies" as they have been classically configured. But the challenges of this transition are paralleled by its prospects and its potential. As an ethnographic world area, Melanesia has a particularly rich ethnographic tradition. This tradition is especially important given the tendency toward ethnographic superficiality in what are otherwise some of the most important new theoretical developments in cultural anthropology. The long-standing concerns of Melanesian studies remain important but expand fundamentally to engage social, cultural, and theoretical changes. Insofar as our ethnographic inquiries engage the practices, beliefs, and voices of Melanesians themselves, Melanesian studies have a promising future.

References

Abel, Charles W.

1902   *Savage Life in New Guinea.* London: London Missionary Society.

Abelove, Henry, Michele A. Barale, and David M. Halperin, eds.

1993   *The Lesbian and Gay Studies Reader.* New York: Routledge.

Abu-Lughod, Lila

1991   Writing Against Culture. In *Recapturing Anthropology: Working in the Present,* ed. Richard G. Fox, 137–62. Santa Fe, NM: School of American Research Press.

Agyei, William K. A.

1988   *Fertility and Family Planning in the Third World: A Case Study of Papua New Guinea.* London: Croom Helm.

Albert, Bruce

1985   *Temps du Sang, Temps des Cendres: Representations de la Maladie, Système Rituel et Espace Politique chez les Yanomami du Sud-est (Amazonie Bresilienne).* Doctoral diss., Université de Paris X (Nanterre).

1989   Yanomamo "Violence": Inclusive Fitness or Ethnographers Representation? *Current Anthropology* 30:637–40.

Albert, Bruce, and Alcida R. Ramos

1989   Yanomamo Indians and Anthropological Ethics. *Science* 244:632.

Alcoff, Linda, and Elizabeth Potter, eds.

1993   *Feminist Epistemologies.* New York: Routledge.

Aldrich, Robert

1990   *The French Presence in the South Pacific, 1842–1940.* Honolulu: University of Hawaii Press.

Alexander, M. Jacqui, and Chandra T. Mohanty, eds.

1997   *Feminist Genealogies, Colonial Legacies, Democratic Futures.* New York: Routledge.

Allen, Bryant J., and R. Michael Bourke

1997a   Report of an Assessment of the Impacts of Frost and Drought in Papua New Guinea. Australian Agency for International Development, Oct.

1997b   Report of an Assessment of the Impacts of Frost and Drought in Papua New Guinea—Phase 2. Australian Agency for International Development, Dec.

Allen, Michael R.

1967   *Male Cults and Secret Initiations in Melanesia.* Melbourne: Melbourne University Press.

1984   Elders, Chiefs, and Big-Men: Authority Legitimation and Political Evolution in Melanesia. *American Ethnologist* 11:20–40.

Allen, Michael R., ed.

1981   *Vanuatu: Politics, Economics, and Ritual in Island Melanesia.* New York: Academic Press.

Amarshi, Azeem, Kenneth Good, and Rex Mortimer
  1979   *Development and Dependency: The Political Economy of Papua New Guinea.* Melbourne: Oxford University Press.
Anderson, Benedict
  1983   *Imagined Communities: Reflections on the Origin and Spread of Nationalism.* London: Verso.
Appadurai, Arjun
  1986   Theory in Anthropology: Center and Periphery. *Comparative Studies in Society and History* 28:356–61.
  1988   Introduction: Place and Voice in Anthropological Theory. *Cultural Anthropology* 3:16–20.
  1990   Disjuncture and Difference in the Global Cultural Economy. *Public Culture* 2:1–24.
  1991   Global Ethnoscapes: Notes and Queries for a Transnational Anthropology. In *Recapturing Anthropology: Working in the Present,* ed. Richard G. Fox, 191–210. Santa Fe, NM: School of American Research Press.
  1993   Patriotism and Its Futures. *Public Culture* 5:411–29.
  1996   *Modernity at Large: Cultural Dimensions of Globalization.* Minneapolis: University of Minnesota Press.
Appiah, Kwame Anthony
  1991   Is the Post- in Postmodernism the Post- in Postcolonial? *Critical Inquiry* 17:336–57.
  1992   *In My Father's House: Africa in the Philosophy of Culture.* New York: Oxford University Press.
Armstrong, Nancy, and Leonard Tennenhouse, eds.
  1989   *The Violence of Representation: Literature and the History of Violence.* London: Routledge.
ASAONET
  1996   Postings on "Lost Tribes," Apr.–May on <asaonet@listserv.uic.edu>.
Ashcroft, Bill, Gareth Griffiths, and Helen Tiffin
  1989   *The Empire Writes Back: Theory and Practice in Post-Colonial Literatures.* London: Routledge.
Ashcroft, Bill, Gareth Griffiths, and Helen Tiffin, eds.
  1995   *The Post-Colonial Studies Reader.* New York: Routledge.
Aufenanger, H.
  1959   The War-magic Houses in the Wahgi Valley and Adjacent Areas (New Guinea). *Anthropos* 54:1–26.
AUSAID
  1996   *The Economy of PNG: 1996 Report.* Australian Agency for International Development (AUSAID), International Development Issues No. 46. Canberra.
Australian Council for Overseas Aid
  1995   Trouble at Freeport. Report of April 5. Canberra.
Baden-Powell, B. F. S.
  1892   *In Savage Isles and Settled Lands.* London: Richard Bentley and Son.
Bamberger, Joan
  1974   The Myth of Matriarchy: Why Men Rule in a Primitive Society. In *Woman, Culture, and Society,* ed. Michelle Z. Rosaldo and Louise Lamphere, 263–80. Stanford: Stanford University Press.
Banks, Glenn, and Chris Ballard, eds.
  1997   *The Ok Tedi Settlement: Issues, Outcomes, and Implications.* Canberra: Australian National University Press.

Barker, John
    1990   *Christianity in Oceania: Ethnographic Perspectives.* Lanham, MD: University Press of America.
Barlow, Kathleen, and Steven Winduo, eds.
    1997   *Logging the Southwest Pacific: Perspectives from Papua New Guinea, Solomon Islands, and Vanuatu. The Contemporary Pacific,* vol. 19, no. 1 (special issue).
Barnes, J. A.
    1962   African Models in the New Guinea Highlands. *Man* 62:5–9.
    1967   Agnation among the Enga: A Review Article. *Oceania* 38:33–43.
Barth, Fredrik
    1971   Tribes and Intertribal Relations in the Fly Headwaters. *Oceania* 41:171–91.
    1975   *Ritual and Knowledge among the Baktaman of New Guinea.* New Haven: Yale University Press.
    1987   *Cosmologies in the Making: A Generative Approach to Cultural Variation in Inner New Guinea.* Cambridge: Cambridge University Press.
Bates, Robert H.
    1996   Letter from the President: Area Studies and the Discipline. *APSA-CP: Newsletter of the APSA Organized Section on Comparative Politics* 7 (1): 1–2.
    1997   Area Studies and the Discipline: A Useful Controversy? *PS: Political Science and Politics* (June): 166–69.
Bateson, Gregory
    1932   Social Structure of the Iatmul People of the Sepik River. *Oceania* 2:245–90, 401–51.
    1936   *Naven: A Survey of the Problems Suggested by a Composite Picture of a Culture of a New Guinea Tribe Drawn from Three Points of View.* Cambridge: Cambridge University Press. [2d ed. Stanford, CA: Stanford University Press, 1958.]
    1972   *Steps to an Ecology of Mind.* New York: Ballantine.
    1979   *Mind and Nature: A Necessary Unity.* New York: Bantam.
Battaglia, Debbora
    1985   "We Feed Our Father": Paternal Nurture among the Sabarl of Papua New Guinea. *American Ethnologist* 12:427–41.
    1986   Bringing Home to Moresby: Urban Gardening and Ethnic Pride among Trobriand Islanders in the National Capital. Special Publication 11. Port Moresby: Institute of Applied Social and Economic Research.
    1990   *On the Bones of the Serpent: Person, Memory, and Mortality in Sabarl Island Society.* Chicago: University of Chicago Press.
    1995   On Practical Nostalgia: Self-Prospecting among Urban Trobrianders. In *Rhetorics of Self-Making,* ed. Debbora Battaglia, 77–96. Berkeley: University of California Press.
Baudrillard, Jean
    1988   *Jean Baudrillard: Selected Writings,* ed. Mark Poster. Stanford: Stanford University Press.
Beaglehole, J. C.
    1968   *The Exploration of the Pacific.* 3d ed. Stanford: Stanford University Press.
Beasant, John
    1984   *The Santo Rebellion: An Imperial Reckoning.* Honolulu/Richmond, Australia: University of Hawaii Press/Heinemann.
Beaver, Wilfred N.
    1920   *Unexplored New Guinea.* London: Seeley, Service.
Behar, Ruth, and Deborah A. Gordon, eds.
    1995   *Women Writing Culture.* Berkeley: University of California Press.

Bell, F. L. S.
  1934a Warfare among the Tanga. *Oceania* 5:253–80.
  1934b Organized Violence in a Primitive Community. *Mankind* 2:186–87.
Bellier, Irène
  1993 Réflexions sur la Question du Genre dans les Sociétés Amazoniennes. *L'Homme* 33:517–26.
Belshaw, Cyril S.
  1957 *The Great Village: The Economic and Social Welfare of Hanuabada, an Urban Community in Papua.* London: Routledge and Kegan Paul.
  1964 *Under the Ivi Tree: Society and Economic Growth in Rural Fiji.* Berkeley: University of California Press.
Benedict, Ruth
  1934 *Patterns of Culture.* Boston: Houghton Mifflin.
Benhabib, Seyla
  1992 *Situating the Self: Gender, Community and Postmodernism in Contemporary Ethics.* New York: Routledge.
Benhabib, Seyla, Judith Butler, Drucilla Cornell, and Nancy Fraser
  1995 *Feminist Contentions: A Philosophical Exchange.* New York: Routledge.
Bennett, Judith A.
  1987 *Wealth of the Solomons: A History of a Pacific Archipelago, 1800–1978.* Honolulu: University of Hawaii Press.
  1995 Forestry, Public Land, and the Colonial Legacy in Solomon Islands. *The Contemporary Pacific* 7:243–75.
Bercovitch, Eytan
  1989 Mortal Insights: Victim and Witch in the Nalumin Imagination. In *The Religious Imagination in New Guinea,* ed. Gilbert H. Herdt and Michele Stephen, 122–59. New Brunswick, NJ: Rutgers University Press.
  1994 The Agent in the Gift: Hidden Exchange in Inner New Guinea. *Cultural Anthropology* 9:498–536.
Bergmann, Frithjof
  1975 On the Inadequacies of Functionalism. *Michigan Discussions in Anthropology* 1:2–23.
Berman, Art
  1994 *Preface to Modernism.* Urbana: University of Illinois Press.
Berman, Marshall
  1992 Why Modernism Still Matters. In *Modernity and Identity,* ed. Scott Lash and Jonathan Friedman, 33–58. Oxford: Blackwell.
Berndt, Ronald M.
  1962 *Excess and Restraint: Social Control among a New Guinea Mountain People.* Chicago: University of Chicago Press.
  1964 Warfare in the New Guinea Highlands. In *New Guinea: The Central Highlands,* ed. James B. Watson. Special publication, *American Anthropologist* 66 (4), pt. 2:183–203.
  1971 Political Structure in the Eastern Central Highlands of New Guinea. In *Politics in New Guinea,* ed. Ronald M. Berndt and Peter Lawrence, 381–423. Nedlands: University of Western Australia Press.
Bernheimer, Richard
  1952 *Wild Men in the Middle Ages.* Cambridge: Harvard University Press.
Bhabha, Homi K.
  1994 *The Location of Culture.* London: Routledge.

Bhabha, Homi K., ed.
    1990   *Nation and Narration*. London: Routledge.
Biersack, Aletta
    1982   Ginger Gardens for the Ginger Woman: Rites and Passages in a Melanesian Society. *Man* 17:239–58.
Biersack, Aletta, ed.
    1995   *Papuan Borderlands: Huli, Duna, and Ipili Perspectives on the Papua New Guinea Highlands*. Ann Arbor: University of Michigan Press.
Bird, John, Bary Curtis, Tim Putnam, George Robertson, and Lisa Tickner
    1993   *Mapping the Futures: Local Cultures, Global Change*. London: Routledge.
Birth, Kevin K.
    1990   Reading and the Righting of Writing Ethnographies. *American Ethnologist* 17: 549–57.
Bitterli, Urs
    1989   *Cultures in Conflict: Encounters Between European and Non-European Cultures, 1492–1800*, trans. Ritchie Robertson. Stanford: Stanford University Press.
Black, Donald
    1976   *The Behavior of Law*. New York: Academic.
    1983   Crime as Social Control. *American Sociological Review* 48:34–45.
Blackwood, Beatrice
    1935   *Both Sides of Buka Passage: An Ethnographic Study of Social, Sexual, and Economic Questions in the North-Western Solomon Islands*. Oxford: Clarendon.
Bodley, John H.
    1982   *Victims of Progress*. 2d ed. Mountain View, CA: Mayfield.
    1988   *Tribal Peoples and Development Issues: A Global Overview*. Mountain View, CA: Mayfield.
Bodrogi, Tibor
    1951   Colonization and Religious Movements in Melanesia. *Acta Ethnografica Academiae Hungaricae* 2:259–92.
Boelaars, J. H. M. C.
    1981   *Head-hunters about Themselves: An Ethnographic Report from Irian Jaya, Indonesia*. Verhandelingen van het kononklijk, Instituut voor Taal-, Land-, en Volkenkunde 92. The Hague: Martinus Nijhoff.
Bonacich, Edna, ed.
    1994   *Global Production: The Apparel Industry in the Pacific Rim*. Philadelphia: Temple University Press.
Bone, Robert C.
    1964   The International Status of West New Guinea until 1884. *Journal of Southeast Asian Studies* 7:102–18.
Bonnemère, Pascale
    1996   *Le Pandanus Rouge: Corps, différence des sexes et parenté chez les Ankave-Anga*. Paris: CNRS/Maison des Sciences de l'Homme.
Bordo, Susan
    1992   Postmodern Subjects, Postmodern Bodies. *Feminist Studies* 18:159–75.
    1993   *Unbearable Weight: Feminism, Western Culture, and the Body*. Berkeley: University of California Press.
Borofsky, Robert and Alan Howard
    1989   The Early Contact Period. In *Developments in Polynesian Ethnology*, ed. Alan Howard and Robert Borofsky, 241–75. Honolulu: University of Hawaii Press.

Boserup, Ester
  1970   *Women's Role in Economic Development.* London: Allen and Unwin.
Bourdieu, Pierre
  1977   *Outline of a Theory of Practice.* Cambridge: Cambridge University Press.
  1988   *Homo Academicus.* Stanford: Stanford University Press.
  1990   *The Logic of Practice.* Stanford: Stanford University Press.
  1991   *Language and Symbolic Power: The Economy of Linguistic Exchange,* ed. John B. Thompson. Cambridge: Harvard University Press.
Bowden, Ross
  1983   *Yena: Art and Ceremony in a Sepik Society.* Oxford: Pitt Rivers Museum.
Braidotti, Rosi
  1994   *Nomadic Subjects: Embodiment and Sexual Difference in Contemporary Feminist Theory.* New York: Columbia University Press.
Brandewie, Ernest
  1981   *Contrast and Context in New Guinea Culture: The Case of the Mbowamb of the Central Highlands.* Studia Instituti Anthropos, vol. 39. St. Augustin, West Germany: Anthropos.
Brison, Karen J.
  1992   *Just Talk: Gossip, Meetings, and Power in a Papua New Guinea Village.* Berkeley: University of California Press.
  1994   New Visions of Person and Community in an East Sepik Village. Paper presented at the Annual Meetings of the American Anthropological Association, Atlanta, GA.
  1995   Changing Constructions of Masculinity in a Sepik Society. *Ethnology* 34:155–75.
Bromby, Robin.
  1990   The Bougainville Horror: Mine Shutdown, Etc., Sends the PNG Economy Crashing. *Pacific Islands Monthly* (February): 23–25.
Bromilow, William Edward
  1929   *Twenty Years among Primitive Papuans.* London: Epworth Press. Reprint, New York: AMS Press, 1977.
Brookfield, Harold C.
  1972   *Colonialism, Development and Independence.* Cambridge: Cambridge University Press.
Brookfield, Harold C., and Paula Brown
  1963   *Struggle for Land: Agriculture and Group Territories among the Chimbu of the New Guinea Highlands.* Melbourne: Oxford University Press.
Brookfield, Harold C., with Doreen Hart
  1971   *Melanesia: A Geographical Interpretation of an Island World.* London: Methuen.
Browder, John O., and Brian J. Godfrey
  1997   *Rainforest Cities: Urbanization, Development, and Globalization of the Brazilian Amazon.* New York: Columbia University Press.
Brown, D. J. J.
  1979   The Structuring of Polopa Feasting and Warfare. *Man* 14:712–32.
  1988   Unity in Opposition in the New Guinea Highlands. *Social Analysis* 23:89–105.
Brown, George
  1910   *Melanesians and Polynesians: Their Life-Histories Described and Compared.* London: Macmillan. Reprint, New York: Benjamin Blom, 1972.
Brown, Michael F.
  1986   Power, Gender, and the Social Meaning of Aguaruna Suicide. *Man* 21:311–28.

1993   Facing the State, Facing the World: Amazonia's Native Leaders and the New Politics of Identity. *L'Homme* 33:307–26.

Brown, Michael F., and Eduardo Fernandez
1991   *War of Shadows: The Struggle for Utopia in the Peruvian Amazon.* Berkeley: University of California Press.

Brown, Paula
1964   Enemies and Affines. *Ethnology* 3:335–56.
1971   The Chimbu Political System. In *Politics in New Guinea*, ed. Ronald M. Berndt and Peter Lawrence, 207–23. Nedlands: University of Western Australia Press.
1972   *The Chimbu: A Study of Change in the New Guinea Highlands.* Cambridge, MA: Schenkman.
1978   *Highland Peoples of New Guinea.* Cambridge: Cambridge University Press.
1982a   Conflict in the New Guinea Highlands. *Journal of Conflict Resolution* 26 (3): 525–46.
1982b   Chimbu Disorder: Tribal Fighting in Newly Independent Papua New Guinea. *Pacific Viewpoint* 22:1–21.
1986   Simbu Aggression and the Drive to Win. *Anthropological Quarterly* 59 (4): 165–70.
1988   Gender and Social Change: New Forms of Independence for Simbu Women. *Oceania* 59:123–42.
1995   *Beyond a Mountain Valley: The Simbu of Papua New Guinea.* Honolulu: University of Hawaii Press.

Brown, Paula, and Georgeda Buchbinder, eds.
1976   *Man and Woman in the New Guinea Highlands.* Washington, DC: American Anthropological Association.

Brown, Paula, and Aaron Podolefsky
1976   Population Density, Agricultural Intensity, Land Tenure, and Group Size in the New Guinea Highlands. *Ethnology* 15:211–38.

Brown, Paula, and Donald F. Tuzin, eds.
1983   *The Ethnography of Cannibalism.* Washington, DC: Society for Psychological Anthropology.

Bryce, Robert
1995   Aid Canceled for Gold Project in Indonesia. *The New York Times,* Nov. 2. (International Business Section.)

Buchbinder, Georgeda, and Roy A. Rappaport
1976   Fertility and Death among the Maring. In *Man and Woman in the New Guinea Highlands,* ed. Paula Brown and Georgeda Buchbinder, 13–35. Washington, DC: American Anthropological Association (Special Publication no. 8).

Burkhalter, S. Brian, and Robert F. Murphy
1989   Tappers and Sappers: Rubber, Gold, and Money among the Mundurucu. *American Ethnologist* 16:100–116.

Burnett, John
1995   Radio Report. Morning Edition, National Public Radio. Broadcast on Dec. 14.

Burridge, Kenelm O. L.
1969   *Mambu: A Melanesian Millennium.* London: Methuen.
1969   *Tango Traditions: A Study of the Way of Life, Mythology, and Developing Experience of a New Guinea People.* Oxford: Clarendon.
1975   The Melanesian Manager. In *Studies in Social Anthropology: Essays in Memory of E. E. Evans-Pritchard,* ed. John H. Beattie and R. Godfrey Lienhardt, 86–104. Oxford: Oxford University Press.

Burt, B., ed.
  1996   *Environment and Development in the Pacific.* Canberra: Australian National University Press.
Burton-Bradley, B. G.
  1974   The Psychological Dimension. In *Problem of Choice: Land in Papua New Guinea's Future,* ed. Peter G. Sack, 32–39. Canberra: Australian National University Press.
Butler, Judith
  1990   *Gender Trouble: Feminism and the Subversion of Identity.* New York: Routledge.
  1993a *Bodies that Matter: On the Discursive Limits of "Sex."* New York: Routledge.
  1993b Critically Queer. *GLQ: A Journal of Lesbian and Gay Studies* 1:17–32.
Cagatay, Nilufer, and Sule Ozler
  1995   Feminization of the Labor Force: The Effects of Long-Term Development and Structural Adjustment. *World Development* 23 (11): 1883–94.
Caley-Webster, H.
  1898   *Through New Guinea and the Cannibal Countries.* London: T. Fisher Unwin.
Campbell, Alan T.
  1995   *Getting to Know Wai Wai: An Amazonian Ethnography.* London: Routledge.
Cantrell, Eileen M.
  1998   Woman the Sexual, A Question of When: A Study of Gebusi Adolescence. In *Adolescence in the Pacific Island Societies,* ed. Gilbert H. Herdt and Stephen C. Leavitt, 92–120. Pittsburgh: University of Pittsburgh Press.
Carby, Hazel V.
  1987   *Reconstructing Womanhood: The Emergence of the Afro-American Woman Novelist.* New York: Oxford University Press.
Carneiro, Robert
  1970   A Theory of the Origin of the State. *Science* 169:733–38.
Carrier, Achsah H., and James G. Carrier
  1991   *Structure and Process in a Melanesian Society: Ponam's Progress in the Twentieth Century.* Chur, Switzerland: Harwood.
Carrier, James G.
  1992b The Gift in Theory and Practice in Melanesia: A Note on the Centrality of Gift Exchange. *Ethnology* 31:185–93.
  1995   *Gifts and Commodities: Exchange and Western Capitalism.* London: Routledge.
Carrier, James G., ed.
  1992a *History and Tradition in Melanesian Anthropology.* Berkeley: University of California Press.
Carrier, James G., and Achsah H. Carrier
  1989   *Wage, Trade, and Exchange in Melanesia: A Manus Society in the Modern State.* Berkeley: University of California Press.
Chagnon, Napoleon
  1983   *Yanomamo: The Fierce People.* 3d ed. New York: Holt, Rinehart, and Winston.
  1988   Life Histories, Blood Revenge, and Warfare in a Tribal Population. *Science* 239:985–92.
Chakrabarty, Dipesh
  1992   The Death of History? Historical Consciousness and the Culture of Late Capitalism. *Public Culture* 4:47–65.
Chalmers, James
  1887   *Pioneering in New Guinea.* London: Religious Tract Society.
Chappell, David A.
  1995   Active Agents versus Passive Victims: Decolonized Historiography or Problematic Paradigm? *The Contemporary Pacific* 7:303–26.

Chauvet, S.
   1930   Les Arts Indigènes en Nouvelle Guinée. Paris.
Cheyne, Andrew
   1971   The Trading Voyages of Andrew Cheyne [1841–44], ed. Dorothy Shineberg. Hon-
          olulu: University of Hawaii Press.
Chibnik, Michael
   1994   Risky Rivers: The Economics and Politics of Floodplain Farming in Amazonia. Tucson:
          University of Arizona Press.
Chidley, Liz
   1998   Foreign Investors Back Mamberamo River Megaproject. Media Indonesia. Biak,
          Feb. 2; <dtecampaign.gn.apc.org>.
Chowning, Ann
   1977   An Introduction to the Peoples and Cultures of Melanesia. 2d ed. Menlo Park, CA:
          Cummings.
   1979   Leadership in Melanesia. Journal of Pacific History 14:66–84.
Chowning, Ann, and Ward H. Goodenough
   1971   Lakalai Political Organization. In Politics in New Guinea, ed. Ronald M. Berndt
          and Peter Lawrence, 113–75. Nedlands: University of Western Australia Press.
Clark, Jeffrey
   1989   God, Ghosts, and People: Christianity and Social Organization among Takuru
          Wiru. In Family and Gender in the Pacific: Domestic Contradictions and the Colonial
          Impact, ed. Margaret Jolly and Martha MacIntyre, 170–92. Cambridge: Cam-
          bridge University Press.
   1993   Gold, Sex, and Pollution: Male Illness and Mythology at Mt. Kare. American
          Anthropologist 20:742–57.
   1997   State of Desire: Transformations in Huli Sexuality. In Sites of Desire, Economies of
          Pleasure: Sexualities in Asia and the Pacific, ed. Lenore Manderson and Margaret
          Jolly, 191–211. Chicago: University of Chicago Press.
   n.d.   Desire in the Time of AIDS: Huli Sexuality and the State. (ms.)
Clark, Jeffrey, and Jenny Hughes
   1995   A History of Sexuality and Gender in Tari. In Papuan Borderlands: Huli, Duna,
          and Ipili Perspectives on the Papua New Guinea Highlands, ed. Aletta Biersack,
          315–40. Ann Arbor: University of Michigan Press.
Claustres, Pierre
   1987   Society Against the State: Essays in Political Anthropology. New York: Zone Books.
Clay, Brenda Johnson
   1977   Pinikindu: Maternal Nurture, Paternal Substance. Chicago: University of Chicago
          Press.
   1986   Mandak Realities: Person and Power in Central New Ireland. New Brunswick, NJ:
          Rutgers University Press.
Clifford, James
   1988   The Predicament of Culture: Twentieth-Century Ethnography, Literature, and Art.
          Cambridge, MA: Harvard University Press.
   1992   Traveling Cultures. In Cultural Studies, ed. Lawrence Grossberg, Cary Nelson,
          and Paula A. Treichler. New York: Routledge.
   1994   Diasporas. Cultural Anthropology 9:302–38.
   1997   Routes: Travel and Translation in the Late Twentieth Century. Cambridge: Harvard
          University Press.
Clifford, James, and George E. Marcus, eds.
   1986   Writing Culture: The Poetics and Politics of Ethnography. Berkeley: University of
          California Press.

Clunie, Fergus
  1977   *Fijian Weapons and Warfare.* Bulletin of the Fiji Museum, no. 2. Suva: Fiji Museum.
Codrington, R. H.
  1890   On Poisoned Arrows in Melanesia. *Journal of the Royal Anthropological Society* 19:215–19.
  1891   *The Melanesians: Studies in Their Anthropology and Folklore.* Oxford: Clarendon Press. Reprint, New York: Dover, 1972.
Coiffier, Christian
  1992   From Exploitation of the Forest to Urban Dependence in Papua New Guinea. *TDSR (Traditional Dwellings and Settlements Review)* 3 (2): 49–58.
Cole, Rodney V., ed.
  1993   *Pacific 2010: Challenging the Future.* National Centre for Development Studies, Pacific Policy Paper no. 9. Fyshwick, Australia: National Capital Printing.
Collier, Jane
  1988   *Marriage and Inequality in Classless Societies.* Stanford: Stanford University Press.
Collier, Jane, and Michelle Z. Rosaldo
  1981   Politics and Gender in Simple Societies. In *Sexual Meanings: The Cultural Construction of Gender and Sexuality,* ed. Sherry B. Ortner and Harriet Whitehead, 275–329. New York: Cambridge University Press.
Collins, Patricia Hill
  1990   *Black Feminist Thought: Knowledge, Consciousness, and the Politics of Empowerment.* Boston: Unwin Hyman.
Colson, Elizabeth
  1989   Overview (of a career). *Annual Review of Anthropology* 18:1–16.
Comaroff, Jean
  1985   *Body of Power, Spirit of Resistance: The Culture and History of a South African People.* Chicago: University of Chicago Press.
Comaroff, Jean, and John Comaroff, eds.
  1993   *Modernity and its Malcontents: Ritual and Power in Postcolonial Africa.* Chicago: University of Chicago Press.
Comaroff, John, and Jean Comaroff
  1992   *Ethnography and the Historical Imagination.* Boulder: Westview Press.
Comrie, P.
  1877   Anthropological Notes on New Guinea. *Journal of the Anthropological Institute of Great Britain and Ireland* 6:102–13.
Conklin, Beth A.
  1997   Body Paint, Feathers, and VCRs: Aesthetics and Authenticity in Amazonian Activism. *American Ethnologist* 24:711–37.
Conklin, Beth A., and Laura R. Graham
  1995   The Shifting Middle Ground: Amazonian Indians and Eco-Politics. *American Anthropologist* 97:695–710.
Connell, John
  1987   *New Caledonia or Kanaky? The Political History of a French Colony.* Canberra: Australian National University (Pacific Research Monograph no. 16).
  1988   New Caledonia: The Matignon Accord and the Colonial Future. Research Institute for Asia and the Pacific Occasional Paper no. 5. Sydney, Australia: University of Sydney.
Connell, John, and John Lea
  1994   Cities of Parts, Cities Apart? Changing Places in Modern Melanesia. *The Contemporary Pacific* 6:267–309.

Connolly, Bob, and Robin Anderson
    1987   *First Contact.* New York: Viking.
    1992   *Black Harvest.* Film. Sydney: Arundel Productions.
Cooper, Matthew
    1983   On the Beginnings of Colonialism in Melanesia. In *The Pacification of Melanesia,*
            ed. Margaret Rodman and Matthew Cooper, 25–41. ASAO Monograph no. 7.
            New York: University Press of America.
Corris, Peter
    1968   "Blackbirding" in New Guinea Waters. *Journal of Pacific History* 3:85–105.
    1970   Pacific Island Labour Migrants in Queensland. *Journal of Pacific History* 5:43–64.
    1973   *Passage, Port, and Plantation: A History of Solomon Islands Labour Migration
            1870–1914.* Carlton, Australia: Melbourne University Press.
Counts, Dorothy, ed.
    1990   *Domestic Violence in Oceania. Pacific Studies,* vol. 13, no. 3 (special issue).
Counts, Dorothy, and David Counts
    1983   Father's Water Equals Mother's Milk: The Conception of Parentage in Kaliai,
            West New Britain. *Mankind* 14:46–56.
Crocker, Jon Christopher
    1984   Canela Marriage: Factors in Change. In *Marriage Practices in Lowland South Amer-
            ica,* ed. Kenneth M. Kensinger, 63–98. Illinois Studies in Anthropology no. 14.
            Urbana: University of Illinois Press.
    1985   *Vital Souls: Bororo Cosmology, Natural Symbolism, and Shamanism.* Tucson: Uni-
            versity of Arizona Press.
Crocker, William H.
    1974   Extramarital Sexual Practices of the Ramkokamekra-Canela Indians: An Analy-
            sis of Socio-Cultural Factors. In *Native South Americans: Ethnology of the Least
            Known Continent,* ed. Patricia J. Lyon, 184–94. Boston: Little, Brown.
Dabrowski, Wojciech
    1993   *"Black Harvest."* Film review. *Oceania* 64:79–84.
D'Amato, John
    1979   The Wind and the Amber: Notes on Headhunting and the Interpretation of
            Accounts. *Journal of Anthropological Research* 35 (1): 61–84.
Damon, Frederick H.
    1990   *From Muyuw to the Trobriands: Transformations along the Northern Side of the Kula
            Ring.* Tucson: University of Arizona Press.
Damon, Frederick H., and Roy Wagner, eds.
    1989   *Death Rituals and Life in the Societies of the Kula Ring.* DeKalb: Northern Illinois
            University Press.
Danks, B.
    1887   On the Shell Money of New Britain. *Journal of the Royal Anthropological Institute.*
            17:305–17.
    1892   On Burial Customs of New Britain. *Journal of the Royal Anthropological Institute.*
            21:348–56.
de Certeau, Michel
    1984   *The Practice of Everyday Life.* Berkeley: University of California Press.
Deacon, A. Bernard
    1934   *Malekula: A Vanishing People in the New Hebrides,* ed. Camille Wedgwood. Lon-
            don: Routledge.
Dean, Bartholomew
    1995   Forbidden Fruit: Infidelity, Affinity, and Brideservice among the Urarina of
            Peruvian Amazonia. *Journal of the Royal Anthropological Institute* 1:87–110.

1998   Brideprice in Amazonia? *Journal of the Royal Anthropological Institute.* 4:345–46.
Deleuze, Gilles, and Félix Guattari
1987   *A Thousand Plateaus: Capitalism and Schizophrenia.* Minneapolis: University of Minnesota Press.
Diamond, Stanley
1974   *In Search of the Primitive: A Critique of Civilization.* New Brunswick, NJ: Transaction Books.
Dinnen, Sinclair
1997   Challenges of Order in a Weak State: Crime, Violence, and Control in Papua New Guinea. Ph.D. thesis, The Australian National University, Canberra.
Dirks, Nicholas, Geoff Eley, and Sherry B. Ortner, eds.
1994   *Culture/Power/History.* Princeton: Princeton University Press.
Dirlik, Arif
1994   The Postcolonial Aura: Third World Criticism in the Age of Global Capitalism. *Critical Inquiry* 20:328–56.
Divale, William T., and Marvin Harris
1976   Population, Warfare, and the Male Supremacist Complex. *American Anthropologist* 78:521–38.
Docker, Edward W.
1970   *The Blackbirders: The Recruiting of South Seas Labour for Queensland, 1863–1907.* Sydney: Angus and Robertson.
Donham, Donald L.
1990   *History, Power, Ideology: Central Issues in Marxism and Anthropology.* Cambridge: Cambridge University Press.
Douglas, Brownwen
1979   Rank, Power, Authority: A Reassessment of Traditional Leadership in South Pacific Societies. *Journal of Pacific History* 14:2–27.
1992   Doing Ethnographic History: The Case of Fighting in New Caledonia. In *History and Tradition in Melanesian Anthropology,* ed. James G. Carrier, 86–115. Berkeley: University of California Press.
Drost, E.
1938   *Forced Labor in the South Pacific, 1850–1914.* Iowa City: Iowa State University Press.
Dunbabin, Thomas
1935   *Slavers of the South Seas.* Sydney: Angus and Robertson.
During, Simon
1993   *The Cultural Studies Reader.* London: Routledge.
Dwyer, Peter D.
1982   Prey Switching: A Case Study from New Guinea. *Journal of Animal Ecology* 51:529–42.
1983   Etolo Hunting Performance and Energetics. *Human Ecology* 11:141–71.
1985a   Choice and Constraint in a Papua New Guinean Food Quest. *Human Ecology* 13:49–70.
1985b   A Hunt in New Guinea: Some Difficulties for Optimal Foraging Theory. *Man* 20:245–53.
1985c   The Contributions of Non-Domesticated Animals to the Diet of Etolo, Southern Highlands Province, Papua New Guinea. *Ecology of Food and Nutrition* 17:101–15.
1989   *The Pigs That Ate the Garden: A Human Ecology from Papua New Guinea.* Ann Arbor: University of Michigan Press.

Dwyer, Peter D., and Monica Minnegal
1998 Waiting for Company: Ethos and Environment among Kubo of Papua New Guinea. *Journal of the Royal Anthropological Institute* 4:23–42.

Dyson, Michael E.
1993 *Reflecting Black: African-American Cultural Criticism.* Minneapolis: University of Minnesota Press.

Edge-Partington, J.
1902 Stone-headed Clubs from the Outer Coast of British New Guinea. *Man* 2:58–59, article no. 44.
1906 Decorated Shields from the Solomon Islands. *Man* 6:129–30, article no. 86.

Elkin, A. P.
1956 Camilla Hildegarde Wedgwood: 1901–1955. *Oceania* 26:174–80.

Elliston, Deborah A.
1997 Occasionally Annotated Bibliography of Pacific Islander Novels. Posted on the ASAONET <asaonet@listserv.uic.edu>, June 2, 1997.

Emberson-Bain, Atu
1993 *Labour and Gold in Fiji.* Cambridge: Cambridge University Press.

Enos, Apisai
1972 Niugini Literature. In *Teaching Literature in Papua New Guinea,* ed. E. Brash and M. Breicus, 43–48. Port Moresby: University of Papua New Guinea.

Epstein, A. L.
1984 *The Experience of Shame in Melanesia.* RAI Occasional Paper no. 40. London: Royal Anthropological Institute.

Epstein, T. Scarlett
1968 *Capitalism, Primitive and Modern: Some Aspects of Tolai Economic Growth.* Manchester: Manchester University Press.

Ernst, Thomas M.
1979 Myth, Ritual and Population among the Marind-Anim. *Social Analysis* 1:32–53.
1984 Onabasulu Local Organisation. Ph.D. diss., Department of Anthropology, University of Michigan, Ann Arbor.
1991 Onabasulu Male Homosexuality: Cosmology, Affect, and Prescribed Male Homosexual Activity among the Onabasulu of the Great Papuan Plateau. *Oceania* 62:1–11.

Errington, Frederick K.
1974 *Karavar: Masks and Power in a Melanesian Ritual.* Ithaca, NY: Cornell University Press.

Errington, Frederick K., and Deborah Gewertz
1987a *Cultural Alternatives and a Feminist Anthropology: An Analysis of Culturally Constructed Gender Interests in Papua New Guinea.* Cambridge: Cambridge University Press.
1987b Of Unfinished Dialogues and Paper Pigs. *American Ethnologist* 14:367–76.
1995 *Articulating Change in the "Last Unknown."* Boulder, CO: Westview.
1996 The Individuation of Tradition in a Papua New Guinea Modernity. *American Anthropologist* 98:114–26.
1997 The Wewak Rotary Club: The Middle Class in Melanesia. *Journal of the Royal Anthropological Institute* 3:333–53.

Eyde, David
1967 Cultural Correlates of Warfare among the Asmat of Southwest New Guinea. Ph.D. diss., Yale University.

Faithorn, Elizabeth
    1976   Women as Persons: Aspects of Female Life and Male–Female Relations among
        the Kafe. In *Man and Woman in the New Guinea Highlands,* ed. P. Brown and G.
        Buchbinder, 86–95. Washington, DC: American Anthropological Association
        (Special Publication no. 8).

Fanon, Frantz
    1968   *The Wretched of the Earth.* Harmondsworth, UK: Penguin.
    1991   *Black Skin, White Masks.* New York: Weidenfeld.

Fardon, Richard, ed.
    1990   *Localizing Strategies: Regional Traditions of Ethnographic Writing.* Washington, DC:
        Smithsonian Institution Press.

Featherstone, Mike
    1991   *Consumer Culture and Postmodernism.* London: Sage.

Featherstone, Mike, Scott Lash, and Roland Robertson, eds.
    1995   *Global Modernities.* London: Sage.

Feher, Michel, Ramona Nadaff, and Nadia Tazi, eds.
    1989   *Fragments for a History of the Human Body.* 3 vols. New York: Urzone.

Feil, Daryl K.
    1978   Women and Men in the Enga *Tee. American Ethnologist* 5:263–79.
    1984   *Ways of Exchange: The Enga Tee of Papua New Guinea.* St. Lucia, Australia: Uni-
        versity of Queensland Press.
    1986   A Social Anthropologist's View of Papua New Guinea Highlands Prehistory.
        American Anthropologist 88:623–36.
    1987   *The Evolution of Highland Papua New Guinea Societies.* Cambridge: Cambridge
        University Press.
    1995   The Evolution of Highland Papua New Guinea Societies: A Reappraisal. *Bijdra-*
        gen tot de Taal-, Land- en Volkenkunde 151:23–43.

Feinberg, Richard
    1995   Introduction: Politics of Culture in the Pacific Islands. *Ethnology* 34:91–98.

Feinberg, Richard, and Laura Zimmer-Tamakoshi, eds.
    1995   *The Politics of Culture in the Pacific Islands. Ethnology* 34 (3), special issue.

Feld, Steven
    1982   *Sound and Sentiment: Birds, Weeping, Poetics, and Song in Kaluli Expression.*
        Philadelphia: University of Pennsylvania Press.
    1995   From Schizophonia to Schismogenesis: The Discourses and Practices of World
        Music and World Beat. In *The Traffic in Culture: Refiguring Art and Anthropology,*
        ed. George E. Marcus and Fred R. Myers, 196–226. Berkeley: University of Cali-
        fornia Press.

Feld, Steven, and Keith H. Basso, eds.
    1996   *Senses of Place.* Santa Fe, NM: School of American Research Press.

Fenbury, David
    1968   Those Mokolkos! New Britain's Bloody Axemen. *New Guinea (and Australia, the*
        Pacific and South-East Asia), vol. 3, no. 2 (June–July): 33–50.

Ferguson, R. Brian
    1989   Do Yanomamo Killers Have More Kids? *American Ethnologist* 16:564–65.
    1995   *Yanomami Warfare: A Political History.* Santa Fe, NM: School of American
        Research Press.

Ferguson, R. Brian, with Leslie E. Farragher
    1988   *The Anthropology of War: A Bibliography.* Occasional Papers of the Harry Frank
        Guggenheim Foundation, no. 1. New York: H. F. Guggenheim Foundation.

Ferguson, R. Brian, and Neil L. Whitehead, eds.
  1992   *War in the Tribal Zone: Expanding States and Indigenous Warfare.* Santa Fe, NM: School of American Research Press.
Fife, Wayne
  1995   Models for Masculinity in Colonial and Postcolonial Papua New Guinea. *The Contemporary Pacific* 7:277–302.
Filer, Colin
  1990   The Bougainville Rebellion, the Mining Industry, and the Process of Social Disintegration in Papua New Guinea. *Canberra Anthropology* 13 (1): 1–39.
Filer, Colin, ed.
  1997   *The Political Economy of Forest Management in Papua New Guinea.* National Research Institute of Papua New Guinea, Monograph no. 32. Port Moresby: National Research Institute; London: IIED <iieduk@gn.apc.org>.
Finegan, Edward, and Niko Besnier
  1989   *Language: Its Structure and Use.* San Diego: Harcourt Brace Jovanovich.
Finney, Ben
  1973   *Big Men and Business: Entrepreneurship and Economic Growth in the New Guinea Highlands.* Honolulu: University of Hawaii Press.
Firth, Raymond
  1936   *Art and Life in New Guinea.* London: Studio.
  1951   *Elements of Social Organization.* London: Watts.
Firth, Stewart
  1982   The Germans in New Guinea. In *Melanesia: Beyond Diversity,* vol. 2, ed. R. J. May and Hank Nelson, 151–56. Canberra: Australian National University.
  1983   *New Guinea Under the Germans.* Carlton, Australia: Melbourne University Press.
Fischer, Michael M. J., and Mehdi Abedi
  1990   *Debating Muslims: Cultural Dialogues in Postmodernity and Tradition.* Madison: University of Wisconsin Press.
Fison, Lorimer
  1871   The Murder of Bishop Patteson. *Sydney Morning Herald,* Nov. 18, 1871.
  1872–73   The South Seas Labour Traffic. *Daily Telegraph.* (Series of nine articles from December 21, 1972 to March 15, 1873, under the *nom de plume* "Outis".)
  1907   *Tales from Old Fiji.* London: Alexander Moring.
Fitzpatrick, Peter
  1980   *Law and State in Papua New Guinea.* London: Academic Press.
Forge, Anthony
  1966   Art and Environment in the Sepik. *Proceedings of the Royal Anthropological Institute, 1965,* 23–31.
  1970   Prestige, Influence and Sorcery: A New Guinea Example. In *Witchcraft Confessions and Accusations,* ed. Mary Douglas, 257–75. London: Tavistock.
  1972   The Golden Fleece. *Man* 7:527–40.
  1990   The Power of Culture and the Culture of Power. In *Sepik Heritage: Tradition and Change in Papua New Guinea,* ed. Nancy Lutkehaus et al., 160–70. Durham, NC: Carolina Academic Press.
Fortune, Reo F.
  1932   *Sorcerers of Dobu: The Social Anthropology of the Dobu Islanders.* London: E. P. Dutton.
  1935   *Manus Religion.* Philadelphia: American Philosophical Society.
  1939   Arapesh Warfare. *American Anthropologist* 41:22–41.

1947a The Rules of Relationship Behavior in One Variety of Primitive Warfare. *Man* 47:108–10.

1947b Law and Force in Papuan Societies. *American Anthropologist* 49:244–59.

1960 New Guinea Warfare: Correction of a Mistake Previously Published. *Man* 60:108.

Foster, Robert J.

1991 Making National Cultures in the Global Ecumene. *Annual Reviews in Anthropology* 20:235–60.

1995a *Social Reproduction and History in Melanesia: Mortuary Ritual, Gift Exchange, and Custom in the Tanga Islands.* Cambridge: Cambridge University Press.

1996/97 Commercial Mass Media in Papua New Guinea: Notes on Agency, Bodies, and Commodity Consumption. *Visual Anthropology Review* 12 (2): 1–17.

Foster, Robert J., ed.

1995b *Nation Making: Emergent Identities in Postcolonial Melanesia.* Ann Arbor: University of Michigan Press.

Foucault, Michel

1980 *The History of Sexuality, Volume 1: An Introduction.* New York: Vintage.

1984 *The Foucault Reader,* ed. Paul Rabinow. New York: Pantheon.

1985 *The Use of Pleasure* (vol. 2 of *The History of Sexuality*). New York: Vintage.

1986 *The Care of the Self* (vol. 3 of *The History of Sexuality*). New York: Vintage.

Fox, Charles Elliot

1925 *The Threshold of the Pacific: An Account of the Social Organization, Magic, and Religion of the People of San Cristoval in the Solomon Islands.* With a preface by G. Elliott Smith. New York: A. A. Knopf.

Fox, Richard G., ed.

1991 *Recapturing Anthropology: Working in the Present.* Santa Fe, NM: School of American Research Press.

Frankel, Stephen

1986 *The Huli Response to Illness.* Cambridge: Cambridge University Press.

Freeman, Derek

1979 Severed Heads that Germinate. In *Fantasy and Symbol,* ed. R. Hook, 233–46. London: Academic.

Friedman, John B.

1981 *The Monstrous Races in Medieval Art and Thought.* Cambridge: Harvard University Press.

Friedman, Jonathan

1974 Marxism, Structuralism and Vulgar Materialism. *Man* 9:444–69.

1992 Narcissism, Roots, and Postmodernity: The Constitution of Selfhood in Global Crisis. In *Modernity and Identity,* ed. Scott Lash and Jonathan Friedman, 331–66. Oxford: Blackwell.

1994 *Cultural Identity and Global Process.* Thousand Oaks, CA: Sage.

Fry, Greg

1997 Framing the Islands: Knowledge and Power in Changing Australian Images of "the South Pacific." *Contemporary Pacific* 9:305–44.

Fuss, Diana

1989 *Essentially Speaking: Feminism, Nature, and Difference.* New York: Routledge.

Galvão, Eduardo

1979 The Encounter of Tribal and National Societies in the Brazilian Amazon. In *Brazil: Anthropological Perspectives: Essays in Honor of Charles Wagley,* ed. Maxine L. Margolis and William E. Carter, 25–38. New York: Columbia University Press.

Garnaut, Ross, and Chris Manning
    1974   *Irian Jaya: The Transformation of a Melanesian Economy.* Canberra: Australian National University Press.
Gell, Alfred
    1975   *Metamorphosis of the Cassowaries: Umeda Society, Language and Ritual.* London: Athlone.
George, Kenneth M.
    1996   *Showing Signs of Violence: The Cultural Politics of a Twentieth-Century Headhunting Ritual.* Berkeley: University of California Press.
Gesch, Patrick F.
    1985   *Initiative and Initiation: A Cargo Cult-Type Movement in the Sepik Against its Background in a Traditional Village Religion.* St. Augustin, West Germany: Anthropos.
Gewertz, Deborah
    1978   The Myth of the Blood-Men: An Explanation of Chambri Warfare. *Journal of Anthropological Research* 34 (4): 577–88.
    1981   An Historical Reconstruction of Female Dominance among the Chambri of Papua New Guinea. *American Ethnologist* 8:94–106.
    1983   *Sepik River Societies: A Historical Ethnography of the Chambri and their Neighbors.* New Haven: Yale University Press.
    1984   The Tchambuli View of Persons: A Critique of Individualism in the Works of Mead and Chodorow. *American Anthropologist* 86:615–29.
Gewertz, Deborah, and Frederick Errington
    1991   *Twisted Histories, Altered Contexts: Representing the Chambri in a World System.* New York: Cambridge University Press.
    1994   What Cambri Desire: Some Ethnographic Reflections about Contemporary Papua New Guineans. Paper presented at the Annual Meetings of the American Anthropological Association, Atlanta, GA.
    1996   On PepsiCo and Piety in a Papua New Guinea "Modernity." *American Ethnologist* 23:476–93.
    1997   Why We Return to Papua New Guinea. *Anthropological Quarterly* 70:127–35.
Giay, Benny, and Jan. A. Godschalk
    1993   Cargoism in Irian Jaya Today. *Oceania* 63:330–44.
Giddens, Anthony
    1979   *Central Problems in Social Theory: Action, Structure and Contradiction.* London: Macmillan.
    1984   *The Constitution of Society: Outline of the Theory of Structuration.* Berkeley: University of California Press.
    1987   *The Nation-State and Violence.* Berkeley: University of California Press.
    1990   *The Consequences of Modernity.* Stanford: Stanford University Press.
    1992   *The Transformation of Intimacy: Sexuality, Love, and Eroticism in Modern Societies.* Stanford: Stanford University Press.
Gietzelt, Dale
    1988   The Indonesianization of West Papua. *Oceania* 59:201–21.
Gilles, William E.
    1968   *A Cruize in a Queensland Labour Vessel to the South Seas,* ed. Deryk Scarr. Canberra: Australian National University Press.
Gillison, Gillian
    1980   Images of Nature in Gimi Thought. In *Nature, Culture and Gender,* Carol MacCormack and Marilyn Strathern, eds., 143–73. Cambridge: Cambridge University Press.

1983   Cannibalism among Women in the Eastern Highlands of Papua New Guinea. In *The Ethnography of Cannibalism*, ed. Paula Brown and Donald F. Tuzin, 33–50. Washington, DC: Society for Psychological Anthropology.

1987   Incest and the Atom of Kinship: The Role of the Mother's Brother in a New Guinea Highlands Society. *Ethos* 15:166–202.

1993   *Between Culture and Fantasy: A New Guinea Highlands Mythology.* Chicago: University of Chicago Press.

Gilroy, Paul

1987   *There Ain't No Black in the Union Jack: The Cultural Politics of Race and Nation.* London: Hutchinson.

1993   *The Black Atlantic: Modernity and Double Consciousness.* Cambridge: Harvard University Press.

Ginsburg, Faye D., and Rayna Rapp, eds.

1995   *Conceiving the New World Order: The Global Politics of Reproduction.* Berkeley: University of California Press.

Glasse, Robert M.

1959   Revenge and Redress among the Huli. *Mankind* 5 (7): 273–89.

1968   *Huli of Papua: A Cognatic Descent System.* (Cahiers de l'Homme, Nouvelle Série 8.) Paris: Mouton.

Glasse, Robert M., and Mervyn J. Meggitt, eds.

1969   *Pigs, Pearlshells, and Women: Marriage in New Guinea Highland Societies.* Englewood Cliffs, NJ: Prentice-Hall.

Glick, Leonard B.

1973   Sorcery and Witchcraft. In *Anthropology in Papua New Guinea*, ed. H. Ian Hogbin. Melbourne: Melbourne University Press.

Goddard, Michael

1992   Big-Men, Thief: The Social Organization of Gangs in Port Moresby. *Canberra Anthropology* 154:20–34.

1995   The Rascal Road: Crime, Prestige, and Development in Papua New Guinea. *The Contemporary Pacific* 7:55–80.

Godelier, Maurice

1982   Social Hierarchies among the Baruya of New Guinea. In *Inequality in New Guinea Highlands Societies*, ed. Andrew J. Strathern, 3–34. Cambridge: Cambridge University Press.

1986   *The Making of Great Men: Male Domination and Power among the New Guinea Baruya.* Cambridge: Cambridge University Press.

Godelier, Maurice, ed.

1977   *Perspectives in Marxist Anthropology.* Cambridge: Cambridge University Press.

Godelier, Maurice, and Marilyn Strathern, eds.

1991   *Big Men and Great Men: Personifications of Power in Melanesia.* Cambridge: Cambridge University Press.

Goldman, Laurence

1983   *Talk Never Dies: The Language of Huli Disputes.* London: Tavistock.

1986   The Presentational Style of Women in Huli Disputes. *Papers in New Guinea Linguistics*, no. 24, 213–89. *Pacific Linguistics*, A-70.

1993   *The Culture of Coincidence: Accident and Absolute Liability in Huli.* Oxford: Oxford University Press.

Goldman, Laurence R., and Chris Ballard, eds.

1998   *Fluid Ontologies: Myth, Ritual, and Philosophy in the Highlands of Papua New Guinea.* Westport, CT and London: Bergin and Garvey.

Golson, Jack
  1982 The Ipomoean Revolution Revisited: Society and the Sweet Potato in the Upper Wahgi Valley. In *Inequality in New Guinea Highlands Societies*, ed. Andrew J. Strathern, 109–36. Cambridge: Cambridge University Press.
Goodale, Jane C.
  1980 Gender, Sexuality and Marriage: A Kaulong Model of Nature and Culture. In *Nature, Culture and Gender*, ed. Carol MacCormack and Marilyn Strathern, 119–43. New York: Cambridge University Press.
  1985 Pig's Teeth and Skull Cycles: Both Sides of the Face of Humanity. *American Ethnologist* 12:228–44.
  1995 *To Sing with Pigs Is Human: The Concept of Person in Papua New Guinea.* Seattle: University of Washington Press.
Goodenough, Ward
  1971 The Pageant of Death in Nakanai. In *Melanesia: Readings on a Culture Area*, ed. L. L. Langness and John C. Weschler, 279–92. Scranton: Chandler.
Gordon, Robert
  1981 Some Notes towards Understanding the Dynamics of Blood Money. In *Homicide Compensation in Papua New Guinea: Problems and Prospects*, ed. Richard Scaglion, 88–102. Port Moresby: Law Reform Commission/Office of Information.
  1983 The Decline of the Kiapdom and the Resurgence of "Tribal Fighting" in Enga. *Oceania* 53 (3): 205–23.
Gordon, Robert, and Mervyn J. Meggitt
  1985 *Law and Order in the New Guinea Highlands.* Hanover: University Press of New England.
Gow, Peter
  1991 *Of Mixed Blood: Kinship and History in Peruvian Amazonia.* Oxford: Clarendon.
Gramsci, Antonio
  1971 *Selections from the Prison Notebooks of Antonio Gramsci*, ed. Quintin Hoare and Geoffrey Nowell Smith. London: Lawrence and Wishart.
Gregor, Thomas
  1979 Secrets, Exclusion, and the Dramatization of Men's Roles. In *Brazil: Anthropological Perspectives*, ed. Maxine L. Margolis and William E. Carter, 250–69. New York: Columbia University Press.
  1985 *Anxious Pleasures: The Sexual Lives of an Amazonian People.* Chicago: University of Chicago Press.
  1990 Male Dominance and Sexual Coercion. In *Cultural Psychology: Essays on Comparative Human Development*, ed. James W. Stigler, Richard A. Shweder, and Gilbert Herdt, 477–95. Cambridge: Cambridge University Press.
  1994 Symbols and Rituals of Peace in Brazil's Upper Xingu. In *The Anthropology of Peace and Nonviolence*, ed. Leslie E. Sponsel and Thomas Gregor, 241–57. Boulder, CO: Lynne Rienner.
Gregory, Christopher A.
  1982 *Gifts and Commodities.* London: Academic.
Greub, Suzanne, ed.
  1985 *Authority and Ornament: Art of the Sepik River, Papua New Guinea.* Basel, Switzerland: Tribal Art Centre/Meier+Cie AG Schaffhausen.
Griffin, James
  1986 Cautious Deeds and Wicked Fairies: A Decade of Independence in Papua New Guinea. *Journal of Pacific History* 21:183–201.

1987   Current Developments in the Pacific: The Papua New Guinea Elections of 1987. *Journal of Pacific History* 23:106–16.

Griffin, James, Hank Nelson, and Steward Firth
    1979   *Papua New Guinea: A Political History.* Richmond, Victoria: Heinemann Educational Australia.

Grossberg, Lawrence, Cary Nelson, and Paula A. Treichler, eds.
    1992   *Cultural Studies.* New York: Routledge.

Groves, William C.
    1935   Tabar To-day: A Study of a Melanesian Community in Contact with Alien Non-Primitive Cultural Influences. *Oceania* 5:224–40, 346–60.
    1936   Secret Beliefs and Practices in New Ireland. *Oceania* 7:220–45.

Guha, Ranajit
    1988a   On Some Aspects of Historiography of Colonial India. In *Selected Subaltern Studies,* ed. Ranajit Guha and Gayatri C. Spivak, 37–44. New York: Oxford University Press.
    1988b   The Prose of Counter-Insurgency. In *Selected Subaltern Studies,* ed. Ranajit Guha and Gayatri C. Spivak, 45–86. New York: Oxford University Press.
    1989   Dominance without Hegemony and Its Historiography. *Subaltern Studies,* vol. 6, ed. Ranajit Guha, 210–309. Delhi: Oxford University Press.

Guiart, Jean
    1956   *Un Siècle et Demi de Contacts Culturels à Tanna, Nouvelles-Hébredies.* Paris: Musée de l'Homme.
    1963a   *La Structure de la Chefferie en Mélanésie du Sud.* (Travaux et Mémoires de l'Institut d'Ethnologie, 66.) Paris: Université de Paris.
    1963b   *The Arts of the South Pacific,* trans. Anthony Christie. London: Thames and Hudson.
    1966   *Mythologie du Masque en Nouvelle-Calédonie.* Paris: Musée de l'Homme.
    1983   *La Terre est le sang des morts: La Confrontation entre blancs et noirs dans le pacifique sud français.* Paris: Editions Anthropos.

Guiart, Jean, and Peter Worsley
    1958   La reparition des movements millénaristes en Mélanésie. *Archives de Sociologie des Religions* 3:38–47.

Gullahorn-Holocek, Barbara
    1983   *Anthropology on Trial.* Film. Boston: WGBH-TV.

Gupta, Akhil, and James Ferguson
    1992   Beyond "Culture": Space, Identity, and the Politics of Difference. *Cultural Anthropology* 7:6–23.

Gupta, Akhil, and James Ferguson, eds.
    1997   *Anthropological Locations: Boundaries and Grounds of a Field Science.* Berkeley: University of California Press.

Haddon, Alfred C.
    1891   The Tugeri Head-hunters of New Guinea. *Internationales Archiv für Ethnographie* 4:177–81.
    1897   The Saving of Vanishing Knowledge. *Nature* 55:305–6.
    1901   *Headhunters, Black, White, and Brown.* London: Methuen.
    1908   Quarrels and Warfare. *Reports of the Cambridge Anthropological Expedition to Torres Strait* 6:189–91, ed. A. C. Haddon. Cambridge: Cambridge University Press.
    1910   A Classification of the Stone Clubs of British New Guinea. *Journal of the Royal Anthropological Society* 30:221–50.
    1912   Weapons and Objects Employed in Warfare. *Reports of the Cambridge Anthropological Expedition to Torres Strait* 4:172–204, ed. A. C. Haddon. Cambridge: Cambridge University Press.

1920   The Migrations of Cultures in British New Guinea. *Journal of the Royal Anthropo-
        logical Institute of Great Britain and Ireland* 50:234–80.

1923   Stuffed Human Heads from New Guinea. *Man* 23:36–39. Article no. 20.

Haddon, Alfred C., ed.

1901–35 *Reports of the Cambridge Anthropological Expedition to Torres Strait.* Cambridge:
        Cambridge University Press.

Haddon, A. C., and A. Wilken

1904   Warfare. *Reports of the Cambridge Anthropological Expedition to Torres Strait*
        5:298–307, ed. A. C. Haddon. Cambridge: Cambridge University Press.

Hale, Charles R.

1994   *Resistance and Contradiction: Miskitu Indians and the Nicaraguan State, 1894–1987.*
        Stanford: Stanford University Press.

Hall, Stuart

1986a   Gramsci's Relevance for the Study of Race and Ethnicity. *Journal of Communica-
        tion Inquiry* 10:5–27.

1986b   The Problem of Ideology—Marxism without Guarantees. *Journal of Communica-
        tion Inquiry* 10:28–44.

1986c   On Postmodernism and Articulation: An Interview with Stuart Hall. *Journal of
        Communication Inquiry* 10:45–60.

1996   Introduction: Who Needs Identity? In *Questions of Cultural Identity*, ed. Stuart
        Hall and Paul Du Gay, 1–17. London: Sage.

Hall, Stuart, and Paul Du Gay, eds.

1996   *Questions of Cultural Identity.* London: Sage.

Hallpike, Christopher R.

1973   Functionalist Interpretations of Primitive Warfare. *Man* 8:451–73.

1974   Aristotelian and Heraclitean Societies. *Ethos* 2:69–76.

1975   Two Types of Reciprocity. *Comparative Studies in Society and History* 17:113–19.

1977   *Bloodshed and Vengeance in the Papuan Mountains: The Generation of Conflict in
        Tuade Society.* Oxford: Clarendon Press.

Halperin, David M.

1995   *Saint Foucault: Towards a Gay Hagiography.* New York: Oxford.

Hammar, Lawrence

1992   Sexual Transactions on Daru, with Some Observations on the Ethnographic
        Enterprise. *Research in Melanesia* 16:21–54.

1995   Crisis in the South Fly: The Problem with Sex and the Sex Industry on Daru
        Island, Western Province, Papua New Guinea. Ph.D. thesis, Department of
        Anthropology, Graduate Center, City University of New York.

1996   Bad Canoes and *Bafalo:* The Political Economy of Sex on Daru Island, Western
        Province, Papua New Guinea. *Genders* 23:212–47.

Hannerz, Ulf

1990   Cosmopolitans and Locals in World Culture. *Theory, Culture and Society*
        7:237–52.

1992   The Global Ecumene as a Network of Networks. In *Conceptualizing Society*, ed.
        Adam Kuper. New York: Routledge.

1996   *Transnational Connections: Culture, People, Places.* New York: Routledge

Haraway, Donna

1990   *Simians, Cyborgs, and Women: The Reinvention of Nature.* London: Free Associa-
        tion Books.

Harris, David

1992   *From Class Struggle to the Politics of Pleasure: The Effects of Gramscianism on Cul-
        tural Studies.* London: Routledge.

Harrison, Simon J.
　1982　Yams and the Symbolic Representation of Time in a Sepik River Village. *Oceania* 53:141–62.
　1987　Cultural Efflorescence and Political Evolution on the Sepik River. *American Ethnologist* 14:491–507.
　1989a　The Symbolic Construction of Aggression and War in a Sepik River Society. *Man* 24:583–99.
　1989b　Magical and Material Polities in Melanesia. *Man* 24:1–20.
　1990　*Stealing People's Names: History and Politics in a Sepik River Cosmology.* Cambridge: Cambridge University Press.
　1993　*The Mask of War: Violence, Ritual, and the Self in Melanesia.* Manchester: Manchester University Press.
Harrisson, Tom H.
　1937　*Savage Civilisation.* London: Gollancz.
Hart Nibbrig, Nand E.
　1992　Rascals in Paradise: Urban Gangs in Papua New Guinea. *Pacific Studies* 15: 115–34.
Harvey, David
　1989　*The Condition of Postmodernity: An Enquiry into the Origins of Culture Change.* Cambridge: Blackwell.
Hastings, Peter
　1968　West Irian—1969: The End of the Line? *New Guinea (and Australia, the Pacific and South-East Asia)* Sept.–Oct.: 12–16.
　1982　Double Dutch and Indons. In *Melanesia: Beyond Diversity*, vol. 1, ed. R. J. May and Hank Nelson, 157–61. Canberra: Australian National University Press.
Haugerud, Angelique, ed.
　1997　*The Future of Regional Studies.* Special issue of *Africa Today* 44 (2).
Hau'ofa, Epeli
　1975　Anthropology and Pacific Islanders. *Oceania* 45:283–89.
　1983　*Mekeo: Inequality and Ambivalence in a Village Society.* Canberra: Australian National University Press.
　1987　The New South Pacific Society: Integration and Independence. In *Class and Culture in the South Pacific*, ed. Antony Hooper, Steve Britton, Ron Crocombe, Judith Huntsman, and Cluny Macpherson, 1–12. Suva, Fiji: Centre for Pacific Studies at the University of Auckland, and Institute of Pacific Studies at the University of the South Pacific.
　1994a　Our Sea of Islands. *The Contemporary Pacific* 6:148–61.
　1994b　Thy Kingdom Come: The Democratization of Aristocratic Tonga. *The Contemporary Pacific* 6:414–28.
Hayano, David
　1974　Marriage, Alliance, and Warfare: A View from the New Guinea Highlands. *American Ethnologist* 1:281–93.
Hayes, Geoffrey
　1995　Review of Rodney V. Cole, ed., *Pacific 2010. The Contemporary Pacific* 7:191–94.
Hays, Terence E.
　1976　*Anthropology in the New Guinea Highlands: An Annotated Bibliography.* New York: Garland.
　1993　"The New Guinea Highlands": Region, Culture Area, or Fuzzy Set? *Current Anthropology* 34:141–64.
Hays, Terence E., ed.
　1991　*Encyclopedia of World Cultures, Volume II: Oceania.* Boston: G. K. Hall.

1992   *Ethnographic Presents: Pioneering Anthropologists in the Papua New Guinea Highlands.* Berkeley: University of California Press.

Hayward, Douglas
1997   *Vernacular Christianity among the Mulia Dani.* Lanham, MD: University Press of America.

Healey, Christopher J.
1978   The Adaptive Significance of Systems of Ceremonial Exchange and Trade in the New Guinea Highlands. *Mankind* 11:198–207.
1985   *Pioneers of the Mountain Forest: Settlement and Land Redistribution among the Kundagai Maring of the Papua New Guinea Highlands.* Oceania Monograph no. 29. Sydney: Oceania Publications.
1990   *Maring Hunters and Traders: Production and Exchange in the Papua New Guinea Highlands.* Berkeley: University of California Press.

Heider, Karl G.
1970   *The Dugam Dani: A Papuan Culture in the Highlands of West New Guinea.* Chicago: Aldine. Viking Fund Publications in Anthropology, no. 49. New York: Wenner-Gren Foundation.
1979   *Grand Valley Dani: Peaceful Warriors.* New York: Holt, Rinehart, and Winston.

Herdt, Gilbert H.
1981   *Guardians of the Flutes: Idioms of Masculinity.* New York: McGraw-Hill.
1982a   Sambia Nosebleeding Rites and Male Proximity to Women. *Ethos* 10:189–231.
1982b   Fetish and Fantasy in Sambia Initiation. In *Rituals of Manhood: Male Initiation in Papua New Guinea,* ed. Gilbert H. Herdt, 44–99. Berkeley: University of California Press.
1984b   Semen Transactions in Sambia Culture. In *Ritualized Homosexuality in Melanesia,* ed. Gilbert H. Herdt, 167–210. Berkeley: University of California Press.
1986   Aspects of Socialization for Aggression in Sambia Ritual and Warfare. *Anthropological Quarterly* 59: 160–65.
1987a   *The Sambia: Ritual and Gender in New Guinea.* New York: Holt, Rinehart, and Winston.
1987b   The Accountability of Sambia Initiates. In *Anthropology in the High Valleys: Essays on the New Guinea Highlands in Honor of Kenneth E. Read,* ed. L. L. Langness and Terence E. Hays, 237–81. Novato, CA: Chandler and Sharp.

Herdt, Gilbert H., ed.
1982c   *Rituals of Manhood: Male Initiation in Papua New Guinea.* Berkeley: University of California Press.
1984a   *Ritualized Homosexuality in Melanesia.* Berkeley: University of California Press.
1992   *Ritualized Homosexuality in Melanesia,* rev. ed. Berkeley: University of California Press.

Herdt, Gilbert H., and Fitz J. P. Poole
1982   "Sexual Antagonism": The History of a Concept in New Guinea Anthropology. In *Sexual Antagonism, Gender, and Social Change in Papua New Guinea,* ed. Fitz J. P. Poole and Gilbert H. Herdt. *Social Analysis,* no. 12. Adelaide.

Herdt, Gilbert H., and Robert J. Stoller
1990   *Intimate Communications: Erotics and the Study of Culture.* New York: Columbia University Press.

Hern, Warren M.
1992   Shipobo Polygyny and Patrilocality. *American Ethnologist* 19:501–22.

Hill, Jonathan D., ed.
1988   *Rethinking History and Myth: Indigenous South American Perspectives on the Past.* Urbana: University of Illinois Press.

1996   *History, Power, and Identity: Ethnogenesis in the Americas After 1492.* Iowa City: University of Iowa Press.

Hobbes, Thomas
1958   *Leviathan, Parts I and II.* Indianapolis: Bobbs-Merrill. Original, 1651.

Hocart, A. M.
1931   Warfare in Eddystone of the Solomon Islands. *Journal of the Royal Anthropological Society* 61:301–24.

Hodgen, Margaret T.
1964   *Early Anthropology in the Sixteenth and Seventeenth Centuries.* Philadelphia: University of Pennsylvania Press.

Hogbin, Herbert Ian
1934   Culture Change in the Solomon Islands: Report of Field Work in Guadalcanal and Malaita. *Oceania* 4:233–67.
1951   *Transformation Scene: The Changing Culture of a New Guinea Village.* London: Routledge and Kegan Paul.
1964   *A Guadalcanal Society: The Kaoka Speakers.* New York: Holt, Rinehart, and Winston.
1970   *The Island of Menstruating Men: Religion in Wogeo, New Guinea.* Scranton, PA: Chandler Publishing.
1978   *The Leaders and the Led: Social Control in Wogeo, New Guinea.* Carlton: Melbourne University Press.

Holmberg, Allan R.
1969   *Nomads of the Long Bow: The Siriono of Eastern Bolivia.* New York: Doubleday.

Holmes, J. H.
1924   *In Primitive New Guinea.* New York: G. P. Putnam's Sons. Reprint, New York: AMS Press, 1978.

hooks, bell
1981   *Ain't I a Woman: Black Women and Feminism.* Boston: South End Press.
1990   *Yearning: Race, Gender, and Cultural Politics.* Boston: South End Press.
1992   *Black Looks: Race and Representation.* Boston: South End Press.

Hooper, Antony, Steve Britton, Ron Crocombe, Judith Huntsman, and Cluny Macpherson, eds.
1987   *Class and Culture in the South Pacific.* Suva, Fiji: Centre for Pacific Studies at the University of Auckland, and Institute of Pacific Studies at the University of the South Pacific.

Hopkins, A. I.
1928   *In the Isles of King Solomon: Twenty-Five Years among the Primitive Solomon Islanders.* London: Seeley, Service.

Howard, Michael C.
1991   *Fiji: Race and Politics in an Island State.* Vancouver: University of British Columbia Press.

Howe, Kerry R.
1974   Firearms and Indigenous Warfare: A Case Study. *Journal of Pacific History* 9:21–38.

Howe, Kerry R., Robert C. Kiste, and Brij V. Lal, eds.
1994   *Tides of History: The Pacific Islands in the Twentieth Century.* Honolulu: University of Hawaii Press.

Hugel, Anatole
1906   Decorated Shields from the Solomon Islands. *Man* 6:33. Article no. 21.
1908   Decorated Maces from the Solomon Islands. *Man* 33–34. Article no. 16.

Hugh-Jones, Christine
   1979   *From the Milk River: Spatial and Temporal Processes in Northwest Amazonia.* Cambridge: Cambridge University Press.
Hugh-Jones, Stephen
   1979   *The Palm and the Pleiades: Initiation and Cosmology in Northwest Amazonia.* Cambridge: Cambridge University Press.
   1992   Yesterday's Luxuries, Tomorrow's Necessities: Business and Barter in Northwest Amazonia. In *Barter, Exchange, and Value: An Anthropological Perspective*, ed. Caroline Humphrey and Stephen Hugh-Jones, 42–74. Cambridge: Cambridge University Press.
Humphreys, Clarence Blake
   1926   *The Southern New Hebrides: An Ethnological Record.* Cambridge: Cambridge University Press. Reprint, New York: AMS Press, 1978.
Hyndman, David C.
   1987   Mining, Modernization, and Movements of Social Protest in Papua New Guinea. *Social Analysis* 21:20–38.
   1994   *Ancestral Rain Forests and the Mountain of Gold: Indigenous Peoples and Mining in New Guinea.* Boulder, CO: Westview Press.
Iamo, Warilea
   1992   The Stigma of New Guinea: Reflections on Anthropology and Anthropologists. In *Confronting the Margaret Mead Legacy: Scholarship, Empire, and the South Pacific*, ed. Lenora Foerstel and Angela Gilliam, 75–99. Philadelphia: Temple University Press.
Imhof, Aviva
   1996   The Big, Ugly Australian Goes to Ok Tedi. *Multinational Monitor* 17 (3): 15–18.
Inglis, John, ed.
   1872   *The Slave Trade in the New Hebrides.* Edinburgh: Edmonson and Douglas.
Ivens, Walter G.
   1927   *Melanesians of the Southeast Solomon Islands.* London: Kegan Paul, Trench, Trubner.
   1930   *The Island Builders of the Pacific.* London: Seeley, Service.
Jack-Hinton, Colin
   1969   *The Search for the Islands of Solomon.* Oxford: Clarendon Press.
Jackson, Jean E.
   1992   The Meaning and Message of Symbolic Sexual Violence in Tukanoan Ritual. *Anthropological Quarterly* 65:1–18.
Jacoby, Russell
   1995   Marginal Returns: The Trouble with Post-Colonial Theory. *Lingua Franca* (Sept.–Oct.): 30–37.
Jameson, Frederic
   1991   *Postmodernism, Or, the Cultural Logic of Late Capitalism.* Durham, NC: Duke University Press.
Jenkins, Carol
   1994   *National Study of Sexual and Reproductive Knowledge and Behavior in Papua New Guinea.* Papua New Guinea Institute of Medical Research Monograph 10. Goroka, PNG.
Jenness, Diamond, and Rev. A. Ballantyne
   1920   *The Northern d'Entrecasteaux.* Oxford: Clarendon Press. Reprint, New York: Johnson Reprint Corp., 1970.

Johnson, Chalmers
  1997 Preconception vs. Observation, or the Contributions of Rational Choice Theory
        and Area Studies to Contemporary Political Science. *PS: Political Science and Pol-
        itics* (June): 170–74.
Johnson, Patricia L.
  1993 Education and the "New" Inequality in Papua New Guinea. *Anthropology and
        Education Quarterly* 24:183–204.
Jolly, Margaret
  1994 *Women of the Place: Kastom, Colonialism, and Gender in Vanuatu.* Chur, Switzer-
        land: Harwood Academic.
  1997 Women-nation-state in Vanuatu: Women as Signs and Subjects in the Dis-
        courses of Kastom, Modernity, and Christianity. In *Narratives of Nationhood in the
        Pacific Islands,* ed. Ton Otto and Nicholas Thomas, 119–14. Newark : Gordon and
        Breach.
  n.d.   Domestic Violence in Vanuatu: A View from Australia (ms.).
Jolly, Margaret, and Martha MacIntyre, eds.
  1989 *Family and Gender in the Pacific: Domestic Contradictions and the Colonial Impact.*
        Cambridge: Cambridge University Press.
Jolly, Margaret, and Nicholas Thomas, eds.
  1992 *The Politics of Tradition. Oceania* 62 (4): 241–354.
Jorgensen, Dan
  1983a The Facts of Life, Papua New Guinea Style. *Mankind* 14:1–12.
  1983b Mirroring Nature? Men's and Women's Models of Conception in Telefolmin.
        Mankind 14:57–65.
  1995 [Overview of recent developments in Papua New Guinea.] *Northeast Wantok
        System Newsletter (N.E.W.S.),* Namba 22, parts 1–6. Internet: <dwj@julian.
        uwo.ca>.
Josephides, Lisette
  1983 Equal But Different? The Ontology of Gender Among Kewa. *Oceania*
        53:291–307.
  1985 *The Production of Inequality: Gender and Exchange among the Kewa.* New York:
        Tavistock.
Juillerat, Bernard
  1986 *Les Enfants du Sang: Société, Reproduction, et Imaginaire en Nouvelle-Guinée.* Paris:
        Maison des Sciences de l'Homme.
Juillerat, Berhard, ed.
  1992 *Shooting the Sun: Ritual and Meaning in West Sepik.* Washington, DC: Smithsonian
        Institution Press.
Kaberry, Phyllis M.
  1971 Political Organization among the Northern Abelam. In *Politics in New Guinea,*
        ed. Ronald M. Berndt and Peter Lawrence, 35–73. Nedlands: University of West-
        ern Australia Press.
Kahn, Miriam
  1986 *Always Hungry, Never Greedy: Food and the Expression of Gender in a Melanesian
        Society.* Cambridge: Cambridge University Press.
Kamma, Freerk C.
  1972 *Koreri Messianic Movements in the Biak-Numfor Culture Area,* trans. M. J. van de
        Vathorst-Smit. Koninklijk Institut voor Taal-, Land-, en Volkenkunde. The
        Hague: Martinus Nijhoff.

Kaplan, Martha
    1995   *Neither Cargo Nor Cult: Ritual Politics and the Colonial Imagination in Fiji.* Durham,
           NC: Duke University Press.
Karl, Terry Lynn
    1997   *The Paradox of Plenty: Oil Booms and Petro-States.* Berkeley: University of Califor-
           nia Press.
Karp, Ivan
    1997   Does Theory Travel? Area Studies and Cultural Studies. *Africa Today* 44:281–96.
Keesing, Felix M.
    1941   *The South Seas in the Modern World.* New York: John Day.
    1945   *Native Peoples of the Pacific World.* New York: Macmillan.
Keesing, Roger M.
    1982a Introduction. In *Rituals of Manhood: Male Initiation in Papua New Guinea,* ed.
           Gilbert H. Herdt, 1–43. Berkeley: University of California Press.
    1982b *Kwaio Religion: The Living and the Dead in a Solomon Island Society.* New York:
           Columbia University Press.
    1983   *Elota's Story: The Life and Times of a Solomon Islands Big Man.* New York: Holt,
           Rinehart, and Winston.
    1985a Kwaio Women Speak: The Micropolitics of Autobiography in a Solomon Island
           Society. *American Anthropologist* 87:27–39.
    1985b Killers, Big Men, and Priests on Malaita: Reflections on a Melanesian Troika Sys-
           tem. *Ethnology* 24:237–52.
    1989   Creating the Past: Custom and Identity in the Contemporary Pacific. *Contempo-
           rary Pacific* 1:19–42.
    1992   *Custom and Confrontation: The Kwaio Struggle for Cultural Autonomy.* Chicago:
           University of Chicago Press.
Keesing, Roger M., and Peter Corris
    1980   *Lightning Meets the West Wind: The Malaita Massacre.* New York: Oxford Univer-
           sity Press.
Keesing, Robert M., and Robert Tonkinson, eds.
    1982   *Reinventing Traditional Culture: The Politics of Kastom in Island Melanesia.* Special
           issue, *Mankind* 13:297–399.
Keith, Michael, and Steve Pile, eds.
    1993   *Place and the Politics of Identity.* London: Routledge.
Kelly, John D.
    1991   *A Politics of Virtue: Hinduism, Sexuality, and Countercolonial Discourse in Fiji.*
           Chicago: University of Chicago Press.
Kelly, Raymond C.
    1968   Demographic Pressure and Descent Group Structure in the New Guinea High-
           lands. *Oceania* 39:36–63.
    1976   Witchcraft and Sexual Relations: An Exploration in the Social and Semantic
           Implications of the Structure of Belief. In *Man and Woman in the New Guinea
           Highlands,* ed. Paula Brown and Georgeda Buchbinder, 36–53. Washington, DC:
           American Anthropological Association (Special Publication no. 8).
    1977   *Etoro Social Structure: A Study in Structural Contradiction.* Ann Arbor: University
           of Michigan Press.
    1985   *The Nuer Conquest: A Case Study in the Structure of Non-equilibrium Systems.* Ann
           Arbor: University of Michigan Press.
    1988   Etoro Suidology: A Reassessment of the Pig's Role in the Prehistory and Com-
           parative Ethnology of New Guinea. In *Mountain Papuans: Historical and Compar-*

ative Perspectives from New Guinea Fringe Highlands Societies, ed. James F. Weiner, 111–86. Ann Arbor: University of Michigan Press.

1993   *Constructing Inequality: The Fabrication of a Hierarchy of Virtue among the Etoro.* Ann Arbor: University of Michigan Press.

Kennedy, Danny

1996   Drilling Papua New Guinea: Chevron Comes to Lake Kutubu. *Multinational Monitor* 17 (3): 10–14.

Kensinger, Kenneth M.

1995   *How Real People Ought to Live: The Cashinahua of Eastern Peru.* Prospect Heights, IL: Waveland.

1996   Hierarchy vs. Equality in Cashinahua Gender Relations. Paper presented at the Wenner-Gren Symposium "Amazonia and Melanesia: Gender and Anthropological Comparison." Mijas, Spain.

Kensinger, Kenneth M., ed.

1984   *Marriage Practices in Lowland South America.* Illinois Studies in Anthropology no. 14. Urbana: University of Illinois Press.

Kirk, Malcom, with Andrew J. Strathern

1981   *Man as Art: New Guinea.* New York: Viking.

Kirsch, Stuart

1993   Resisting the Mine: Pollution as Environmental "Sorcery." Paper presented at the annual meetings of the American Anthropological Association. Washington, DC.

1996a   Return to Ok Tedi. *Meanjin* (Dec.): 657–66.

1996b   Anthropologists and Global Alliances. *Anthropology Today* 12 (4): 14–15.

1996c   Refugees and Representation: Politics, Critical Discourse, and Ethnography Along the New Guinea Border. In *Mainstream(s) and Margins: Cultural Politics in the 90s*, ed. Michael Morgan and Susan Leggett, 222–36. Westport, CT: Greenwood.

1997a   Indigenous Response to Environmental Impact along the Ok Tedi. *Compensation and Resource Development*, ed. Susan Toft. Papua New Guinea Law Reform Commission Monograph No. 6.

1997b   Lost Tribes: Indigenous People and the Social Imaginary. *Anthropological Quarterly* 70:58–67.

1997c   Is Ok Tedi a Precedent? Implications of the Settlement. In *The Ok Tedi Settlement: Issues, Outcomes, and Implications*, ed. Glenn Banks and Chris Ballard. Resource Management in Asia-Pacific and National Centre for Development Studies, Pacific Policy Paper 25, 118–40. Canberra.

Kituai, August

1974   Historical Narratives of the Bundi People. *Oral History* 2 (8): 8–16.

Kivung, Peri, Wendy Lee, and Vincent Warakai, eds.

1985   Women and Crime: Women and Violence. In *From Rhetoric to Reality? Papua New Guineas Eight Point Plan and National Goals After a Decade*, ed. Peter King, Wendy Lee, and Vincent Warakai, 74–80. Papers from the Fifteenth Waigani Seminar. Port Moresby: University of Papua New Guinea.

Knauft, Bruce M.

1978   Cargo Cults and Relational Separation. *Behavior Science Research* 13: 185–240.

1985a   *Good Company and Violence: Sorcery and Social Action in a Lowland New Guinea Society.* Berkeley: University of California Press.

1985b Ritual Form and Permutation in New Guinea: Implications of Symbolic Process for Sociopolitical Evolution. *American Ethnologist* 12:321–40.

1986 Text and Social Practice: Narrative 'Longing' and Bisexuality among the Gebusi of New Guinea. *Ethos* 14:252–81.

1987a Homosexuality in Melanesia. *Journal of Psychoanalytic Anthropology* 10:155–91.

1987b Reconsidering Violence in Simple Human Societies: Homicide among the Gebusi of New Guinea. *Current Anthropology* 28:457–500.

1987c Managing Sex and Anger: Tobacco and Kava Use among the Gebusi of Papua New Guinea. In *Drugs in Western Pacific Societies: Relations of Substance*, ed. Lamont Lindstrom, 73–98. Lanham, MD: University Press of America.

1988 Reply (to further CA Commentary on "Reconsidering Violence in Simple Societies"). *Current Anthropology* 29:629–33.

1989 Imagery, Pronouncement, and the Aesthetics of Reception in Gebusi Spirit Mediumship. In *The Religious Imagination in New Guinea*, ed. Gilbert H. Herdt and Michele Stephen, 67–98. New Brunswick, NJ: Rutgers University Press.

1993a *South Coast New Guinea Cultures: History, Comparison, Dialectic*. Cambridge: Cambridge University Press.

1993b Like Money You See in a Dream: Petroleum and Patrols in South New Guinea. *Oceania* 64:187–90.

1994 Foucault Meets South New Guinea: Knowledge, Power, Sexuality. *Ethos* 22:391–438.

1995 Beyond Classic Scribes and Others' Dia-tribes: Ethnography and History along the New Guinea South Coast. *Pacific Studies* 18:176–91.

1996 *Genealogies for the Present in Cultural Anthropology*. New York: Routledge.

1997 Theoretical Currents in Late Modern Cultural Anthropology: Toward a Conversation. *Cultural Dynamics* 9:277–300.

1998 Reply to Dean's "Brideprice in Amazonia?" *Journal of the Royal Anthropological Institute* 4:346–47.

Knibbs, S. G. C.
1929 *The Savage Solomons as They Were and Are*. Philadelphia: J. B. Lippincott.

Koch, Klaus-Friedrich
1974 *War and Peace in Jalemo: The Management of Conflict in Highland New Guinea*. Cambridge: Harvard University Press.

1978 Pigs and Politics in the New Guinea Highlands: Conflict Escalation among the Jale. In *The Disputing Process: Law in Ten Societies*, ed. Laura Nader and H. Todd, 41–58. New York: Columbia University Press.

1983 Epilogue—Pacification: Perspectives from Conflict Theory. In *The Pacification of Melanesia*, ed. Margaret Rodman and Matthew Cooper, 199–207. Lanham, NJ: University Press of America.

Konner, Melvin J.
1981 Evolution of Human Behavior Development. In *Handbook of Cross-Cultural Human Development*, ed. Ruth H. Munroe, Robert L. Munroe, and Beatrice B. Whiting, 3–52. New York: Garland STPM Press.

Konrad, Gunter, Ursula Konrad, and Tobias Schneebaum
1981 *Asmat: Life with the Ancestors*. Glasshutten, West Germany: Friedhelm Bruckner.

Kracke, Waud H.
1978 *Force and Persuasion: Leadership in an Amazonian Society*. Chicago: University of Chicago Press.

Kramer, Augustin F.
1925 *Die Malanggane von Tombara*. Munich: G. Muller.

Küchler, Suzanne
  1997   Sacrificial Economy and Its Objects: Rethinking Colonial Collecting in Oceania. *Journal of Material Culture* 2:39–60.
Kuklick, Henrika
  1991   *The Savage Within: The Social History of British Anthropology, 1885–1945*. Cambridge: Cambridge University Press.
Kulick, Don
  1990   Christianity, Cargo, and Ideas of Self: Patterns of Literacy in a Papua New Guinea Village. *Man* 25:286–304.
  1991   Letter to *Anthropology Today* 7:43–44.
  1992   *Language Shift and Cultural Reproduction: Socialization, Self, and Syncretism in a Papua New Guinean Village*. Cambridge: Cambridge University Press.
  1993   Heroes from Hell: Representations of "Rascals" in Papua New Guinea Village. *Anthropology Today* 9:9–14.
Kulick, Don, and Margaret Willson
  1994   Rambo's Wife Saves the Day: Subjugating the Gaze and Subverting the Narrative in a Papua New Guinean Swamp. *Visual Anthropology Review* 10:1–13.
Kuper, Adam
  1988   *Anthropology and Anthropologists: The Modern British School*. London: Routledge and Kegan Paul.
Kuruwaip, Abraham
  1984   The Asmat Bis Pole: Its Background and Meaning. In *An Asmat Sketch Book no. 4*, ed. Frank Trenkenschuh, 11–30. Hastings, NE: Crosier Missions.
Kyakas, Alome, and Polly Wiessner
  1992   *From Inside the Women's House: Enga Women's Lives and Traditions*. Buranda, Queensland: Robert Brown.
Laba, Billai
  1975a Waidoro—A Papuan Village in an Era of Change. Part One: The Village and its Neighbours. *South Pacific Bulletin (Official Journal of the South Pacific Commission)* 25 (3): 31–37.
  1975b Waidoro—A Papuan Village in an Era of Change. Part Two: The Village Today. *South Pacific Bulletin (Official Journal of the South Pacific Commission)* 25 (4): 15–23.
Laclau, Ernesto, and Chantal Mouffe
  1985   *Hegemony and Socialist Strategy: Towards a Radical Democratic Politics*. London: Verso.
Lagerberg, Kees
  1979   *West Irian and Jakarta Imperialism*. New York: St. Martin's Press.
Lal, Brij V.
  1990b *Fiji Coups in Paradise: Race, Politics, and Military Intervention*. London: Zed Books.
Lal, Brij V., ed.
  1990a *As the Dust Settles: Impact and Implications of the Fiji Coups*. Special Issue, *Contemporary Pacific* 2:1–146.
  1992   *Pacific Islands History: Journeys and Transformations*. Canberra: Australian National University Press.
Landtman, Gunnar
  1917   *The Folk-Tales of the Kiwai Papuans*. (Acta Societatis Scientiarum Fennicae, vol. 47.) Helsinki: Finnish Society of Literature.
  1927   *The Kiwai Papuans of British New Guinea*. London: Macmillan.
Langdon, E. Jean
  1982   Ideology in the Northwest Amazon: Cosmology, Ritual, and Daily Life. *Reviews in Anthropology* 9:349–59.

1984   Sex and Power in Siona Society. In *Marriage Practices in Lowland South America*, ed. Kenneth M. Kensinger, 16–23. Illinois Studies in Anthropology no. 14. Urbana: University of Illinois Press.

1991   When the Tapir is an Anaconda: Women and Power among the Siona. *Latin American Indian Literatures Journal* 7 (1): 7–19.

Langlas, Charles M., and James F. Weiner

1988   Big-Men, Population Growth, and Longhouse Fission among the Foi, 1965–79. In *Mountain Papuans: Historical and Comparative Perspectives from New Guinea Fringe Highlands Societies*, 73–110. Ann Arbor: University of Michigan Press.

Langmore, Diane

1974   *Tamate—A King: James Chalmers in New Guinea, 1877–1901*. Melbourne: Melbourne University Press.

1989   *Missionary Lives: Papua, 1874–1914*. Honolulu: University of Hawaii Press.

Langness, L. L.

1967   Sexual Antagonism in the New Guinea Highlands: A Bena Bena Example. *Oceania* 37:161–77.

1972a   Political Organization. *Encyclopaedia of Papua New Guinea*, ed. Peter Sack, 922–35. Melbourne: Melbourne University Press.

1972b   Violence in the New Guinea Highlands. In *Collective Violence*, ed. James F. Short and Marvin E. Wolfgang, 171–85. Chicago: Aldine.

1974   Ritual Power and Male Domination in the New Guinea Highlands. *Ethos* 2:189–212.

Laracy, Hugh

1971   Marching Rule and the Missions. *Journal of Pacific History* 6:96–114.

Laracy, Hugh, ed.

1983   *Pacific Protest: The Maasina Rule Movement, Solomon Islands, 1944–1952*. Suva, Fiji: Institute of Pacific Studies.

Larmour, Peter

1992   The Politics of Race and Ethnicity: Theoretical Perspectives on Papua New Guinea. *Pacific Studies* 15:87–108.

Larson, Gordon F.

1986   The Structure and Demography of the Cycle of Warfare among the Ilaga Dani of Irian Jaya. Ph.D. diss., Department of Anthropology, University of Michigan, Ann Arbor.

Lash, Scott, and Jonathan Friedman, eds.

1992   *Modernity and Identity*. Oxford: Blackwell.

Lash, Scott, and John Urry

1987   *The End of Organised Capitalism*. Oxford: Basil Blackwell.

1994   *Economies of Signs and Space*. London: Sage.

Latham, Linda

1974   Revolt Reexamined in the 1878 Insurrection in New Caledonia. *Journal of Pacific History* 10:48–63.

Latham, Robert

1859   *Descriptive Ethnology*. 2 vols. London.

Lattas, Andrew

1991   Sexuality and Cargo Cults: The Politics of Gender and Procreation in West New Britain. *Cultural Anthropology* 6:230–56.

1992a   The Double Skinned Self: Personhood, Redemption and Cargo Cults in West New Britain. *Oceania* 63:27–54.

1992b Introduction: Hysteria, Anthropological Discourse and the Concept of the Unconscious: Cargo Cults and the Scientification of Race and Colonial Power. *Oceania* 63:27–54.

1993   Sorcery and Colonisation: Illness, Dreams and Death as Political Languages in West New Britain. *Man* 28:51–77.

Lattas, Andrew, ed.

1992c   *Alienating Mirrors: Christianity, Cargo Cults and Colonialism in Melanesia. Oceania* 63 (1): 1–93.

Lavie, Smadar

1990   *The Poetics of Military Occupation: Mzeina Allegories of Bedouin Identity Under Israeli and Egyptian Rule.* Berkeley: University of California Press.

Lawrence, Peter

1964   *Road Belong Cargo: A Study of Cargo Cults in the Southern Madang District, New Guinea.* New York: Humanities Press.

Lawrence, Peter, and Mervyn J. Meggitt

1965   Introduction. In *Gods, Ghosts and Men in Melanesia,* ed. Peter Lawrence and Mervyn J. Meggitt, 1–26. Melbourne: Oxford University Press.

Lawson, Stephanie

1991   *The Failure of Democratic Politics in Fiji.* Oxford: Clarendon.

Layard, John

1942   *Stone Men of Malekula.* London: Chatto and Windus.

Leach, Jerry, and Edmund R. Leach, eds.

1983   *The Kula: New Perspectives on Massim Exchange.* Cambridge: Cambridge University Press.

Leavitt, Stephen C.

1991   Sexual Ideology and Experience in a Papua New Guinea Society. *Social Science and Medicine* 33:897–907.

1994   Doing Cargo Dreams: The Rhetoric of Cargo Wishes in Bumbita Arapesh Dream Reports. Paper presented at the Annual Meetings of the American Anthropological Association; Atlanta, GA.

1995   Political Domination and the Absent Oppressor: Images of Europeans in Bumbita Arapesh Narratives. *Ethnology* 34:177–89.

Lederman, Rena

1986   *What Gifts Engender: Social Relations and Politics in Mendi, Highland Papua New Guinea.* Cambridge: Cambridge University Press.

1991   Who Speaks Here? Formality and the Politics of Gender in Mendi, Highland Papua New Guinea. In *Dangerous Words: Language and Politics in the Pacific,* ed. Donald Brenneis and Fred R. Myers, 85–107. Prospect Heights, IL: Waveland.

Leenhardt, Maurice

1930   *Notes d'ethnologie néo-calédonienne.* Paris: L'Institut d'Ethnologie, Université de Paris.

1979   *Do Kamo: La Personne et le Myth dans le Monde Melanésian,* trans. Basia Miller Gulati. Chicago: University of Chicago Press. Original ed., 1947, Paris: Gallimard.

Le Hunte, George

1901   Despatches from His Excellency the Lieutenant Governor of British New Guinea. *Man* 1:45–47. Article no. 36.

Lemonnier, Pierre

1990   *Guerres et Festins: Paix, échanges et competition dans les highlands de Nouvelle-Guinée.* Paris: Maison de l'homme.

Lepowsky, Maria
1993 *Fruit of the Motherland: Gender in an Egalitarian Society*. New York: Columbia University Press.
LeRoy, John
1985a *Kewa Tales*. Vancouver: University of British Columbia Press.
1985b *Fabricated World: An Interpretation of Kewa Tales*. Vancouver: University of British Columbia Press.
Lévi-Strauss, Claude
1964–71 *Mythologiques I–IV*. Paris: Plon.
Lewis, Albert B.
1945 *Ethnology of Melanesia*. Chicago: Field Museum of Natural History. [1932.]
Lewis, Gilbert
1975 *Knowledge of Illness in a Sepik Society*. London: Althone.
1980 *Day of Shining Red: An Essay on Understanding Ritual*. New York: Cambridge University Press.
Lewis-Harris, Jacquelyn
1996 *Art of the Papuan Gulf*. The Bulletin of the Saint Louis Art Museum, vol. 22, no. 1. St. Louis: St. Louis Art Museum.
Lijphart, Arend
1966 *The Trauma of Decolonization: The Dutch and West New Guinea*. New Haven: Yale University Press.
Lindenbaum, Shirley
1979 *Kuru Sorcery: Disease and Danger in the New Guinea Highlands*. Palo Alto, CA: Mayfield.
1984 Variations on a Sociosexual Theme in Melanesia. In *Ritualized Homosexuality in Melanesia*, ed. Gilbert H. Herdt, 337–61. Berkeley: University of California Press.
1987 The Mystification of Female Labors. In *Gender and Kinship: Essays Toward a Unified Analysis*, ed. Jane F. Collier and Sylvia J. Yanagisako, 221–43. Stanford, CA: Stanford University Press.
Lindstrom, Lamont
1984 Doctor, Lawyer, Wise Man, Priest: Big-Men and Knowledge in Melanesia. *Man* 19:291–309.
1990 *Knowledge and Power in a South Pacific Society*. Washington, DC: Smithsonian Institution Press.
1993 *Cargo Cult: Strange Stories of Desire from Melanesia and Beyond*. Honolulu: University of Hawaii Press.
Lindstrom, Lamont, and Geoffrey White
1990 *Island Encounters: Black and White Memories of the Pacific War*. Washington, DC: Smithsonian Institution Press.
Linnekin, Jocelyn
1992 On the Theory and Politics of Cultural Construction in the Pacific. *Oceania* 62:249–63.
Linnekin, Jocelyn, and Lin Poyer, eds.
1990 *Cultural Identity and Ethnicity in the Pacific*. Honolulu: University of Hawaii Press.
Lipset, David M.
1985 Seafaring Sepiks: Warfare, Prestige, and Change in Murik Trade. *Research in Economic Anthropology* 7:67–94.
1997 *Mangrove Man: Dialogics of Culture in the Sepik Estuary*. Cambridge: Cambridge University Press.

LiPuma, Edward
  1988   *The Gift of Kinship: Structure and Practice in Maring Social Organization.* Cambridge: Cambridge University Press.
Liria, Yauka Aluambo
  1993   *Bougainville Campaign Diary.* Melbourne: Indra Publishing.
Lizot, Jacques
  1985   *Tales of the Yanomami: Daily Life in the Venezuelan Forest.* Cambridge: Cambridge University Press.
Lomnitz-Adler, Claudio
  1992   *Exits from the Labyrinth: Culture and Ideology in the Mexican National Space.* Berkeley: University of California Press.
Lowman-Vayda, Cherry
  1971   Maring Big Men. In *Politics in New Guinea,* ed. Ronald M. Berndt and Peter Lawrence, 317–61. Nedlands: University of Western Australia Press.
Lutkehaus, Nancy
  1984   Wargames: The Ritualization of Violence and Competition in Manam Culture. Paper presented at the Annual Meetings of the American Anthropological Association. Denver, Colorado.
  1995   *Zaria's Fire: Engendered Moments in Manam Ethnography.* Durham, NC: Carolina Academic Press.
Lutkehaus, Nancy, Christian Kaufmann, William E. Mitchell, Douglas Newton, Lita Osmundsen, and Neinhard Schuster, eds.
  1990   *Sepik Heritage: Tradition and Change in Papua New Guinea.* Durham, NC: Carolina Academic Press.
Lutkehaus, Nancy C., and Paul B. Roscoe, eds.
  1995   *Gender Rituals: Female Initiation in Melanesia.* New York: Routledge.
Lutz, Catherine
  1995   The Gender of Theory. In *Women Writing Culture,* ed. Ruth Behar and Deborah A. Gordon, 249–66. Berkeley: University of California Press.
Lyotard, Jean-François
  1984   *The Postmodern Condition: A Report on Knowledge,* trans. Geoff Bennington and Brian Massumi. Minneapolis: University of Minnesota Press. [Original, 1979.]
Maaka, Roger C. A.
  1994   The New Tribe: Conflicts and Continuities in the Social Organization of Urban Maori. *The Contemporary Pacific* 6:311–36.
Macdonald, D.
  1878   *The Labour Traffic versus Christianity in the South Sea Islands.* Melbourne: Hutchinson.
MacGregor, William Sir
  1893   Despatches Reporting Expedition Undertaken with Object of Meeting Tugeri Invaders. *Annual Report of British New Guinea, 1891–92,* appendixes K and L, 49–53. Brisbane: Government Printer.
  1897a *British New Guinea: Country and People.* London: John Murray.
  1897b Expeditions Undertaken to Repel Tugeri Invaders. *Annual Report of British New Guinea, 1895–96.* Section 26, 30–31. London: Government Printer.
MacIntyre, Martha
  1983   Warfare and the Changing Context of "Kune" (Kula) on Tubetube (Southern Massim). *Journal of Pacific History* 18 (1): 11–34.
MacLean, Neil
  1994   Freedom or Autonomy?: A Modern Melanesian Dilemma. *Man* 29:667–88.

Maher, Robert F.

1961 *The New Men of Papua: A Study in Culture Change.* Madison: University of Wisconsin Press.

1967 From Cannibal Raid to Copra Kompani: Changing Patterns of Koriki Politics. *Ethnology* 6:309–31.

Majnep, I. S., and Ralph Bulmer

1977 *Mnmon yad Kalam Kakt: Birds of My Kalam Country.* Auckland: Auckland University Press.

Malinowski, Bronislaw

1916 Baloma: The Spirits of the Dead in the Trobriand Islands. *Journal of the Royal Institute,* vol. 45. Reprinted in B. Malinowski, *Magic, Science, and Religion.* Garden City: Doubleday Anchor Books, 1954.

1920 War and Weapons among the Natives of the Trobriand Islands. *Man* 20:10–12.

1922 *Argonauts of the Western Pacific. An Account of the Native Enterprise and Adventure in the Archipelagoes of Melanesian New Guinea.* New York: Dutton.

1926 *Crime and Custom in Savage Society.* London: Routledge and Kegan Paul.

1927 *The Father in Primitive Psychology.* New York: W. W. Norton.

1929 *The Sexual Lives of Savages in North-Western Melanesia.* London: Routledge and Sons.

1935 *Coral Gardens and Their Magic* (2 vols.). London: Allen and Unwin.

1941 An Anthropological Analysis of War. *American Journal of Sociology* 46:521–50.

1948 *Magic, Science, and Religion and Other Essays.* Glencoe, IL: Free Press.

Malkki, Liisa H.

1995 *Purity and Exile: Violence, Memory, and National Cosmology among Hutu Refugees in Tanzania.* Chicago: University of Chicago Press.

Manganaro, Marc, ed.

1990 *Modernist Anthropology: From Field Work to Text.* Princeton, NJ: Princeton University Press.

Marcus, George E.

1995 Ethnography of/in the World System: The Emergence of Multi-Sited Ethnography. *Annual Review of Anthropology* 24:95–117.

Marcus, George E., and Michael M. J. Fischer

1986 *Anthropology as Cultural Critique: An Experimental Moment in the Human Sciences.* Chicago: University of Chicago Press.

Marcus, George E., and Fred R. Myers, eds.

1995 *The Traffic in Culture: Refiguring Art and Anthropology.* Berkeley: University of California Press.

Markham, Albert H.

1873 *The Cruize of the "Rosario" amongst the New Hebrides and Santa Cruz Islands, Exposing the Recent Atrocities with the Kidnaping of Natives of the South Seas.* 2d ed. London: S. Low, Marston, Low and Searle, Dawsons, Folkstone.

Marksbury, Richard A., ed.

1993 *The Business of Marriage: Transformations in Oceanic Matrimony.* Pittsburgh: University of Pittsburgh Press.

Marshall, Mac

1982 *Through a Glass Darkly: Beer and Modernization in Papua New Guinea.* Boroko, Papua New Guinea: Institute of Applied and Economic Research.

Martin, Emily

1994 *Flexible Bodies: Tracking Immunity in American Culture.* Boston: Beacon.

Marwick, Max G.

1970   Sorcery as a Social Strain Gauge. In *Witchcraft and Sorcery: Selected Readings,* ed.
Max G. Marwick, 280–95. Harmondsworth: Penguin.

Marx, Karl

1964   *Economic and Philosophic Manuscripts.* New York: International. [Originally written 1844.]

1974   *The Eighteenth Brumaire of Louis Bonaparte.* New York: Random House. [Origi-
nally written 1852.]

Marx, Karl, and Frederick Engels

1970   *The German Ideology.* New York: International. [Original ed., 1846.]

Maschio, Thomas

1994   *To Remember the Faces of the Dead: The Plenitude of Memory in Southwestern New
Britain.* Madison: University of Wisconsin Press.

Mauss, Marcel

1967   *The Gift.* New York: W. W. Norton. [Original ed., 1925.]

May, R. J., ed.

1982   *Micronationalist Movements in Papua New Guinea.* Canberra: Australian National
University.

1986   *Between Two Nations: The Indonesia–Papua New Guinea Border and West Papua
Nationalism.* Bathurst, N.S.W., Australia: Robert Brown.

1993   *The Changing Role of the Military in Papua New Guinea.* Canberra: Australian
National University Press.

May, R. J., and Matthew Spriggs, eds.

1991   *The Bougainville Crisis.* Bathurst, N.S.W., Australia: Crawford House Press.

Maybury-Lewis, David

1967   *Akwe-Shavante Society.* Oxford: Clarendon.

1987   Time and Social Theory: Reconsiderations from Central Brazil. In *Natives and
Neighbors in South America: Anthropological Essays,* ed. Harald O. Skar and Frank
Salomon, 443–69. Goteberg, Sweden: Ethnographic Museum. (Ethnological
Studies no. 38.)

1992   *Millennium: Tribal Wisdom and the Modern World.* New York: Viking.

Mayo, John

1973   A Punitive Expedition in British New Guinea, 1886. *Journal of Pacific History*
8:89–99.

Mbembe, Achille

1992   The Banality of Power and the Aesthetics of Vulgarity in the Postcolony. *Public
Culture* 4:1–31.

Mbembe, Achille, and Janet Roitman

1995   Figures of the Subject in Times of Crisis. *Public Culture* 7:323–52.

McArthur, Margaret

1974   Pigs for the Ancestors: A Review Article. *Oceania* 45 (2): 87–123.

McCallum, Cecilia

1990   Language, Kinship and Politics in Amazonia. *Man* 25:412–33.

McDowell, Nancy

1988   A Note on Cargo Cults and Cultural Constructions of Change. *Pacific Studies*
11:121–34.

McFarlane, Samuel

1873   *The Story of the Lifu Mission.* London: J. Nisbet.

McKinley, Robert

1976   Human and Proud of It! A Structural Treatment of Headhunting Rites and the
Social Definition of Enemies. In *Studies in Borneo Societies: Social Process and*

Anthropological Explanation, ed. G. N. Appell. Special Report no. 12, Center for Southeast Asian Studies, Northern Illinois University.

McMenamin, Brigid
  1996   Environmental Imperialism. *Forbes Magazine,* May 20, 124–36.

Mead, Margaret
  1930   *Growing Up in New Guinea.* New York: Blue Ribbon.
  1935   *Sex and Temperament in Three Primitive Societies.* New York: Morrow.
  1938–49   *The Mountain Arapesh* (in 5 installments). *The American Museum of Natural History* 36 (3): 139–349; 37 (3): 319–451; 40 (3): 163–232; 40 (4): 233–419; 41 (3): 289–390.
  1956   *New Lives for Old: Cultural Transformation, Manus, 1928–1953.* New York: William Morrow.

Meeker, Michael E., Kathleen Barlow, and David M. Lipset
  1986   Culture, Exchange, and Gender: Lessons from the Murik. *Cultural Anthropology* 1:6–73.

Meggitt, Mervyn J.
  1964   Male–Female Relationships in the Highlands of Australian New Guinea. In *New Guinea: The Central Highlands.* Special publication, ed. James B. Watson. *American Anthropologist* 66 (4), pt. 2:204–24.
  1965a   *The Lineage System of the Mae-Enga of New Guinea.* Edinburgh: Oliver and Boyd.
  1965b   (Religion of) The Mae-Enga of the Western Highlands. In *Gods, Ghosts and Men in Melanesia: Some Religions of Australian New Guinea and the New Hebrides,* ed. Peter Lawrence and Mervyn Meggitt, 105–31. Melbourne: Oxford University Press.
  1971   The Pattern of Leadership among the Mae-Enga of New Guinea. In *Politics in New Guinea,* ed. Ronald M. Berndt and Peter Lawrence, 191–206. Nedlands: University of Western Australian Press.
  1974   "Pigs Are Our Hearts!": The *Te* Exchange Cycle among the Mae Enga of New Guinea. *Oceania* 44:165–203.
  1975   From Tribesmen to Peasants: The Case of the Mae Enga of New Guinea. In *Anthropology in Oceania,* ed. L. R. Hiatt and C. Jayawardena, 191–209. Sydney: Angus and Robertson.
  1977   *Blood is Their Argument: Warfare among the Mae Enga Tribesmen of the New Guinea Highlands.* Palo Alto, CA: Mayfield.
  1989   Women in Contemporary Enga Society, Papua New Guinea. In *Family and Gender in the Pacific: Domestic Contradictions and the Colonial Impact,* ed. Margaret Jolly and Martha MacIntyre, 135–55. Cambridge: Cambridge University Press.

Meigs, Anna S.
  1976   Male Pregnancy and the Reduction of Sexual Opposition in a New Guinea Highlands Society. *Ethnology* 15:393–407.
  1984   *Food, Sex, and Pollution: A New Guinea Religion.* New Brunswick: Rutgers University Press.
  1987   Semen, Spittle, Blood, and Sweat: A New Guinea Theory of Nutrition. In *Anthropology in the High Valleys: Essays on the New Guinea Highlands in Honor of Kenneth E. Read,* ed. L. L. Langness and Terence E. Hays, 27–43. Novata, CA: Chandler and Sharp Publishers.

Meleisea, Malama
  1987   Ideology in Pacific Studies: A Personal View. In *Class and Culture in the South Pacific,* ed. Antony Hooper, 140–52. Suva: Institute for Pacific Studies, University of the South Pacific.

Mentore, George P.
  1987 Waiwai Women: The Basis of Wealth and Power. *Man* 22:511–27.
Mercer, Kobena
  1994 *Welcome to the Jungle: New Positions in Black Cultural Studies.* New York: Rout-
        ledge.
Merlan, Francesca, and Alan Rumsey
  1991 *Ku Waru: Language and Segmentary Politics in the Western Nebilyer Valley, Papua
        New Guinea.* Cambridge: Cambridge University Press.
Meyer, A. B., and R. Parkinson
  1895 *Schnitzerein und Masken vom Bismark Archipelago und Neu Guinea.* Koningliches
        Ethnographiches Museum in Dresen, Pub. 10. Dresden.
Miedema, Jelle
  1988a War and Exchange: The Bird's Head of Irian Jaya in a Historical and Structural
        Comparative Perspective. Paper presented at the meetings of the Association
        for Social Anthropology in Oceania, San Antonio, Texas.
  1988b Anthropology, Demography and History: Shortage of Women, Intertribal Mar-
        riage Relations and Slave Trading in the Bird's Head of New Guinea. *Bijdragen
        tot de Taal-, Land-, en Volkenkunde* 144:494–509.
Miklouho-Maclay, Nikolai
  1874 On the Political and Social Position of the Papuans of the Papua Kowiai Coast
        on the Southwestern Shore of New Guinea. In *Travels to New Guinea: Diaries, Let-
        ters, Documents,* ed. D. Tumarkin, trans. S. Mikhailov, 439–44. Moscow, USSR:
        Progress Publishers, 1982.
  1881 Notes *In Re* Kidnaping and Slavery in the Western Pacific. In *Travels to New
        Guinea: Diaries, Letters, Documents,* ed. D. Tumarkin, trans. S. Mikhailov, 461–71.
        Moscow, USSR: Progress Publishers, 1982.
Miller, Daniel
  1994 *Modernity, An Ethnographic Approach: Dualism and Mass Consumption in Trinidad.*
        Oxford: Berg.
Miller, Daniel, ed.
  1995 *Worlds Apart: Modernity through the Prism of the Local.* London: Routledge.
Mimica, Jadran
  1988 *Intimations of Infinity: The Mythopoeia of the Iqwaye Counting System and Number.*
        Oxford: Berg.
Minnegal, Monica, and Peter D. Dwyer
  1997 Women, Pigs, God, and Evolution: Social and Economic Change among Kubo
        People of Papua New Guinea. *Oceania* 68:47–60.
Modjeska, Nicholas
  1982 Production and Inequality: Perspectives from Central New Guinea. In *Inequality
        in New Guinea Highlands Societies,* ed. Andrew J. Strathern, 50–108. Cambridge:
        Cambridge University Press.
Mohanty, Chandra T., ed.
  1991 *Third World Women and the Politics of Feminism.* Bloomington: Indiana University
        Press.
Mohr, Richard D.
  1992 *Gay Ideas: Outing and Other Controversies.* Boston: Beacon.
Monbiot, George
  1989 *Poisoned Arrows: An Investigative Journey through Indonesia.* London: Michael
        Joseph.

Moore, Henrietta L.
 1994 *A Passion for Difference; Essays in Anthropology and Gender.* Bloomington: Indiana University Press.

Morauta, Louise
 1979 Indigenous Anthropology in Papua New Guinea. *Current Anthropology* 20:561–76.

Moresby, John, Cpt.
 1876 *Discoveries and Surveys in New Guinea and the D'Entrecasteaux Islands.* London: John Murray.

Morley, Rebecca
 1994 Wife-Beating and Modernization: The Case of Papua New Guinea. *Journal of Comparative Family Studies* 25:25–52.

Morren, George
 1984 Warfare in the Highland Fringe of New Guinea: The Case of the Mountain Ok. In *Warfare, Culture, and Environment,* ed. R. Brian Ferguson, 169–207. Orlando, FL: Academic Press.
 1986 *The Miyanmin: Human Ecology of a Papua New Guinea Society.* UMI Studies in Cultural Anthropology, no. 9. Ann Arbor: UMI Press.

Moseley, H. N.
 1877 On the Inhabitants of the Admiralty Islands &c. *Journal of the Anthropological Institute of Great Britain and Ireland* 6:379–420.

Mosko, Mark
 1983 Conception, De-Conception and Social Structure in Bush Mekeo Culture. *Mankind* 14:24–32.

Mudimbe, V. Y.
 1994 *The Idea of Africa.* Bloomington: Indiana University Press; London: James Curry.

Multinational Monitor
 1996 Defending Papua New Guinea: An Interview with Brian Brunton. *Multinational Monitor* 17 (3): 19–21.

Munn, Nancy D.
 1986 *The Fame of Gawa: A Symbolic Study of Value Transformation in a Massim (Papua New Guinea) Society.* New York: Cambridge University Press.

Murdoch, Lindsay
 1997a Chan Quits: "I Hear the Call." *Asia Online,* March 27. <http://www.theage.com/au/special/asiaonline>.
 1997b PNG Support for [Bougainville] Peace Strategy. *Asia Online,* June 11. <http://www.theage.com/au/special/asiaonline/aust.htm>.

Murphy, Robert F.
 1957 Intergroup Hostility and Social Cohesion. *American Anthropologist* 59:1018–35.
 1959 Social Structure and Sex Antagonism. *Southwestern Journal of Anthropology* 15:89–98.
 1960 *Headhunters' Heritage: Social and Economic Change among the Mundurucu Indians.* Berkeley: University of California Press.

Murphy, Robert F., and Julian H. Steward
 1956 Tappers and Trappers: Parallel Process in Acculturation. *Economic Development and Cultural Change* 4:335–55.

Murphy, Yolanda, and Robert F. Murphy
 1974 *Women of the Forest.* New York: Columbia University Press.

Murray, J. Hubert P.

    1912   *Papua or British New Guinea.* London: T. Fisher Unwin.

Nachman, Steven R.

    1982   Anti-humor: Why the Grand Sorcerer Wags His Penis. *Ethos* 10:117–35.

Narayan, Kirin

    1993   How Native is a "Native" Anthropologist? *American Anthropologist* 95:671–86.

Narokobi, Bernard

    1980   *The Melanesian Way.* Port Moresby: Institute of Papua New Guinea Studies.

    1983   *Life and Leadership in Melanesia.* Port Moresby: University of Papua New Guinea.

Needham, Rodney

    1976   Skulls and Causality. *Man* 11:80–99.

Nelson, Hank

    1976   *Black, White and Gold: Goldmining in Papua New Guinea, 1878–1930.* Canberra: Australian National University Press.

    1982   *Taim Bilong Masta: The Australian Involvement with Papua New Guinea.* Sydney: Australian Broadcasting Commission.

Nevermann, H.

    1933   *Masken und Gehiembinder in Melanesien.* Berlin.

Newman, Philip

    1965   *Knowing the Gururumba.* New York: Holt, Rinehart, and Winston.

Newman, Philip L., and David J. Boyd

    1982   The Making of Men: Ritual and Meaning in Awa Male Initiation. In *Rituals of Manhood: Male Initiation in Papua New Guinea,* ed. Gilbert H. Herdt, 239–86. Berkeley: University of California Press.

Newton, Janice

    1983   Orokaiva Warfare and Production. *Journal of the Polynesian Society* 92:487–507.

Nicholson, Linda J., ed.

    1990   *Feminism/Postmodernism.* New York: Routledge.

Nihill, Michael

    1994   New Women and Wild Men: "Development," Changing Sexual Practice, and Gender in Highland Papua New Guinea. *Cambridge Anthropology* 17:48–72.

    1996   Beyond Bodies: Aspects of the Politicisation of Exchange in the South-West Highlands of Papua New Guinea. *Oceania* 67:107–26.

Nugent, Stephen

    1997   The Coordinates of Identity in Amazonia: At Play in the Fields of Culture. *Critique of Anthropology* 7:33–51.

Obeyesekere, Gananath

    1992   *The Apotheosis of Captain Cook: European Mythmaking in the Pacific.* Princeton: Princeton University Press.

Ogan, Eugene

    1991   Cultural Background to the Bougainville Crisis. *Journal de la Société des Océanistes* 92–93, no. 1–2:61–67.

    1996a Copra Came Before Copper: The Nasioi of Bougainville and Plantation Colonialism, 1902–1964. *Pacific Studies* 19:31–51.

    1996b The (Re)Making of Modern New Guinea. *Reviews in Anthropology* 25:95–106.

O'Hanlon, Michael

    1989   *Reading the Skin: Adornment, Display, and Society among the Wahgi.* London: British Museum.

    1992   "Unstable" Images and Second Skins: Artefacts, Exegesis and Assessments in the New Guinea Highlands. *Man* 27:587–608.

1993   *Paradise: Portraying the New Guinea Highlands.* London: British Museum Press.
1995a Modernity and the "Graphicalization" of Meaning: New Guinea Highland Shield Design in Historical Perspective. *Journal of the Royal Anthropological Institute* (incorporating *Man*) 1:469–93.
1995b Wysiswyg: What You See is *Sometimes* What You Get: And Some Further Thoughts on the Skin, the Body, and Decoration in Melanesia. *JASO* (Journal of the Anthropological Society of Oxford) 26 (2): 155–62.

Oliver, Douglas L.
1955   *A Solomon Island Society: Kinship and Leadership among the Siuai of Bougainville.* Cambridge: Harvard University Press. Reprint, Boston: Beacon Press, 1967.
1971   Southern Bougainville. In *Politics in New Guinea,* ed. Ronald M. Berndt and Peter Lawrence, 276–97. Nedlands: University of Western Australia Press.
1989   *Oceania: The Native Cultures of Australia and the Pacific Islands,* 2 vols. Honolulu: University of Hawaii Press.

Ong, Aihwa
1987   *Spirits of Resistance and Capitalist Discipline: Factory Women in Malaysia.* Albany: State University of New York Press.

Ong, Aihwa, and Donald M. Nonini, eds.
1997   *Ungrounded Empires: The Cultural Politics of Modern Chinese Transnationalism.* New York: Routledge.

Oosterwal, Gottfried
1961   *People of the Tor: A Cultural-Anthropological Study on the Tribes of the Tor Territory (Northern Netherlands New-Guinea).* Assen: Van Gorcum.

Orken, M. B.
1974   They Fight for Fun. In *Problem of Choice: Land in Papua New Guinea's Future,* ed. Peter G. Sack, 141–50. Canberra: Australian National University Press.

Ortner, Sherry B.
1984   Theory in Anthropology Since the Sixties. *Comparative Studies in Society and Culture* 26:126–66.
1989   *High Religion: A Cultural and Political History of Sherpa Buddhism.* Princeton: Princeton University Press.
1990   Gender Hegemonies. *Cultural Critique* 14:35–80.
1995   Resistance and the Problem of Ethnographic Refusal. *Comparative Studies in Society and History* 37:173–93.

Osborne, Robin
1985   *Indonesia's Secret War: The Guerilla Struggle in Irian Jaya.* Sydney: Allen and Unwin.

Otterbein, Keith F.
1968   Internal War: A Cross-Cultural Study. *American Anthropologist* 70:277–89.

Otterbein, Keith F., and Charlotte S. Otterbein
1965   An Eye for an Eye, A Tooth for a Tooth: A Cross-Cultural Study of Feuding. *American Anthropologist* 67:1470–82.

Otto, Ton, and Nicholas Thomas, eds.
1997   *Narratives of Nation in the South Pacific.* Amsterdam: Harwood Academic Publishers.

Pace, Richard B.
1997   *The Struggle for "Amazon Town": Gurupá Revisited.* Boulder, CO: Lynne Rienner.

Pacific Islands Monthly
1994   The Tree Trap: Solomon Islands Caught up in Vicious Logging Circle. March.

Pagden, Anthony
    1986   *The Fall of Natural Man: The American Indian and the Origins of Comparative Eth-
           nology.* Cambridge: Cambridge University Press.
Palmer, George
    1871   *Kidnaping in the South Seas: Being a Narrative of a Three Month's Cruise of H. M.
           Ship "Rosario."* Edinburgh.
Parkinson, R.
    1907   *Dreissig Jahre in der Sudsee.* Stuttgart, Germany: Strecker und Schroder.
Paton, John G.
    1907   *John G. Paton, Missionary to the New Hebrides: An Autobiography.* Chicago: Flem-
           ing H. Revell.
    1927   *The Story of John G. Paton's Thirty Years with South Sea Cannibals,* ed. James Paton
           and A. K. Langridge. London.
Paton, Rank H. L.
    1913   *Slavery under the British Flag.* Melbourne: Brown Prior.
Patterson, Mary
    1974   Sorcery and Witchcraft in Melanesia. *Oceania* 45:132–60, 212–34.
Peletz, Michael G.
    1995   Kinship Studies in Late Twentieth-Century Anthropology. *Annual Reviews of
           Anthropology* 24:343–72.
Pembaruan Daily
    1998   Mimika Local Government and Freeport Will Resettle 2,100 Individuals from
           the Amungme, Damal, and Dani Tribes. *Suara Pembaruan Daily,* Feb. 2. Posted in
           translation   at   <http://www.suarapembaruan.com/News/1998/02/020298/
           Kesra/ks02/ks02 .html>.
Peoples, James
    1982   Individual or Group Advantage? A Reinterpretation of the Maring Ritual Cycle.
           Current Anthropology 23:291–310.
Ploeg, Anton
    1969   *Government in Wanggulam.* Verhandelingen Van Het Koninklijk Instituut voor
           Taal-, Land-, en Volkenkunde 57. The Hague.
    1988   Legacies of an Unknown Past. *Bijdragen Tot de Taal-, Land- en Volkenkunde*
           144:510–22.
    1997   Observations on the Value of Early Ethnographic Reports: Paul Wirz's Research
           in the Toli Valley, Irian Jaya, in 1921. *Zeitschrift für Ethnologie* 122:209–28.
Podolefsky, Aaron
    1984   Contemporary Warfare in the New Guinea Highlands. *Ethnology* 23:73–87.
    1990   Mediator Roles in Simbu Conflict Management. *Ethnology* 29:67–81.
Polier, Nicole
    1994   A View from the "Cyanide Room": Politics and Culture in a Mining Township
           in Papua New Guinea. *Identities* 1:63–84.
    n.d.   Stella's Story: Colonialism, Christianity, and Conflict in the Life of a Papua New
           Guinea Migrant Woman. (ms.)
Polier, Nicole, and William Roseberry
    1989   Tristes Tropes: Postmodern Anthropologists Encounter the Other and Discover
           Themselves. *Economy and Society* 18:245–64.
Poole, Fitz J. P.
    1981a Transforming 'Natural' Woman: Female Ritual Leaders and Gender Ideology
           among Bimin-Kuskusmin. In *Sexual Meanings,* ed. Sherry B. Ortner and Harriet
           Whitehead, 116–65. Cambridge: Cambridge University Press.

1981b *Tamam:* Ideological and Sociological Configurations of 'Witchcraft' among the Bimin-Kuskusmin. In *Sorcery and Social Change in Melanesia,* ed. Marty Zelenietz and Shirley Lindenbaum, 58–76. *Social Analysis,* special issue no. 8. Adelaide, Australia.

1982a The Ritual Forging of Identity: Aspects of Person and Self in Bimin-Kuskusmin Male Initiation. In *Rituals of Manhood,* ed. Gilbert H. Herdt, 99–154. Berkeley: University of California Press.

1982b Couvade and Clinic in a New Guinea Society: Birth Among the Bimin-Kuskusmin. In *The Use and Abuse of Medicine,* ed. Marten W. deVries, Robert L. Berg, and Mac Lipkin Jr., 54–95. New York: Praeger Scientific.

1983 Cannibals, Tricksters, and Witches: Anthropophagic Images among Bimin-Kuskusmin. In *The Ethnography of Cannibalism,* ed. Paula Brown and Donald Tuzin, 6–33. Washington, DC: Special Publication of the Society for Psychological Anthropology.

1984 Cultural Images of Women as Mother: Motherhood among the Bimin-Kuskusmin of Papua New Guinea. In *Gender and Social Life,* ed. Anna Yeatman. *Social Analysis* 5:73–93.

1985 Coming into Social Being: Cultural Images of Infants in Bimin-Kuskusmin Folk Psychology. In *Person, Self, and Experience: Exploring Pacific Ethnopsychologies,* ed. Geoffrey M. White and John Kirkpatrick, 183–242. Berkeley: University of California Press.

1986 The Erosion of a Sacred Landscape: European Exploration and Cultural Ecology among the Bimin-Kuskusmin of Papua New Guinea. In *Mountain People,* ed. Michael Tobias, 169–82. Norman: University of Oklahoma Press.

1987a Ritual Rank, the Self, and Ancestral Power: Liturgy and Substance in a Papua New Guinea Society. In *Drugs in Western Pacific Societies: Relations of Substance,* ed. Lamont Lindstrom, 149–96. Lanham, MD: University Press of America.

1987b Morality, Personhood, Tricksters, and Youths: Some Narrative Images of Ethics among Bimin-Kuskusmin. In *Anthropology in the High Valleys: Essays on the New Guinea Highlands in Honor of Kenneth E. Read,* ed. L. L. Langness and Terence E. Hays, 283–366. Novato, CA: Chandler and Sharp.

1987c Personal Experience and Cultural Representation in Children's "Personal Symbols" among Bimin-Kuskusmin. *Ethos* 15:104–35.

Poole, Fitz J. P., and Gilbert H. Herdt, eds.

1982 *Sexual Antagonism, Gender, and Social Change in Papua New Guinea. Social Analysis,* special issue no. 12. Adelaide.

Pospisil, Leopold

1958 *Kapauku Papuans and Their Law.* New Haven: Yale University Publications in Anthropology, no. 54.

1963a *The Kapauku Papuans of West New Guinea.* New York: Holt, Rinehart, and Winston.

1963b *Kapauku Papuan Economy.* Yale University Publications in Anthropology, no. 67. New Haven: Yale University Press

Povinelli, Elizabeth A.

1991 Organizing Women: Rhetoric, Economy, and Politics in Process among Australian Aborigines. In *Gender at the Crossroads of Knowledge: Feminist Anthropology in the Postmodern Era,* ed. Micaela di Leonardo, 235–54. Berkeley: University of California Press.

1993 *Labor's Lot: The Power, History, and Culture of Aboriginal Action.* Chicago: University of Chicago Press.

Powdermaker, Hortense
   1931   Mortuary Rites in New Ireland. *Oceania* 2:26–43.
   1979   *Life in Lesu: The Study of a Melanesian Society in New Ireland*. New York: AMS Press. Original ed., London: Williams and Norgate, 1933.
Powell, Wilfred
   1883   *Wanderings in a Wild Country: Or, Three Years amongst the Cannibals of New Britain*. London: Sampson Low, Marston, Searle, and Rivington.
Prakash, Gyan, ed.
   1995   *After Colonialism: Imperial Histories and Postcolonial Displacements*. Princeton, NJ: Princeton University Press.
Pratt, Mary L.
   1992   *Imperial Eyes: Travel Writing and Transculturation*. New York: Routledge.
Press, Eyal
   1995   Freeport: Corporate Predator. *The Nation*, July 31, 125–30.
Price, David H.
   1989   *Atlas of World Cultures: A Geographical Guide to Ethnographic Literature*. Newbury Park, CA: Sage.
Priday, H. E. L.
   1944   *Cannibal Island: The Turbulent Story of New Caledonia's Cannibal Coasts*. Wellington, New Zealand: A. H. and A. W. Reed.
Pritchard, James C.
   1836–47 *Researches into the Physical History of Mankind*. 3d ed. 5 vols. London.
Quiggin, A. Hingston
   1942   *Haddon the Head Hunter: A Short Sketch of the Life of A. C. Haddon*. Cambridge: Cambridge University Press.
Quinn, Naomi
   1977   Anthropological Studies on Women's Status. *Annual Review of Anthropology* 6:181–225.
Radcliffe-Brown, A. R.
   1922   *The Andaman Islanders*. Cambridge: Cambridge University Press.
   1948   *A Natural Science of Society*. New York: Free Press.
   1952   *Structure and Function in Primitive Society*. London: Oxford University Press.
Rafael, Vincente L.
   1994   The Cultures of Area Studies in the United States. *Social Text* 41:91–111.
Ramos, Alcida R.
   1987   Reflecting on the Yanomami: Ethnographic Images and the Pursuit of the Exotic. *Cultural Anthropology* 2:284–304.
   1995   *Sanuma Memories: Yanomami Ethnography in Times of Crisis*. Madison: University of Wisconsin Press.
   1996   Yanomami and Gender: Toward a Sanuma Theory of Knowledge. Paper presented at the Wenner-Gren Symposium "Amazonia and Melanesia: Gender and Anthropological Comparison." Mijas, Spain.
Rannie, Douglas
   1912   *My Adventures among South Sea Cannibals: An Account of the Experiences and Adventures of a Government Official among the Natives of Oceania*. London: Seeley, Service.
Rappaport, Roy A.
   1968   *Pigs for the Ancestors: Ritual in the Ecology of a New Guinea People*. New Haven, CT: Yale University Press.

1984   *Pigs for the Ancestors: Ritual in the Ecology of a New Guinea People.* 2d, enlarged edition. New Haven: Yale University Press.

1993   The Anthropology of Trouble. *American Anthropologist* 95:295–303.

Ravuvu, Asesela

1991   *The Facade of Democracy: Fijian Struggles for Political Control, 1830–1987.* Suva, Fiji: Institute for Pacific Studies, University of the South Pacific.

Read, Kenneth E.

1952   Nama Cult of the Central Highlands, New Guinea. *Oceania* 23:1–25.

1954   Cultures of the Central Highlands, New Guinea. *Southwestern Journal of Anthropology* 10:1–43.

1955   Morality and the Concept of the Person. *Oceania* 25:233–82.

1959   Leadership and Consensus in a New Guinea Society. *Man* 61:425–36.

1965   *The High Valley.* New York: Scribner's.

Reay, Marie O.

1959   *The Kuma: Freedom and Conformity in the New Guinea Highlands.* Melbourne: Melbourne University Press.

1982   Lawlessness in the Papua New Guinea Highlands. In *Melanesia: Beyond Diversity,* vol. 2, ed. R. J. May and H. Nelson, 623–38. Canberra: Australian National University Press.

1987   The Magico-Religious Foundations of New Guinea Highlands Warfare. In *Sorcerer and Witch in Melanesia,* ed. Michele Stephen, 83–120. New Brunswick, NJ: Rutgers University Press.

Redlich, Edwin

1876   Galewo Strait and Salwatti Islands [off Vokelkop Peninsula]. In *Discoveries and Surveys in New Guinea and the D'Entrecasteaux Islands,* by John Moresby, 318–21. London: John Murray.

Reed, Adam

1997   Friendship: The Possibility of New Social Forms in a Papua New Guinea Prison. Paper presented at the meetings of the American Anthropological Association. Washington, DC.

Reed, Stephen W.

1943   *The Making of Modern New Guinea, with Special Reference to Culture Contact in the Mandated Territory.* Philadelphia: American Philosophical Society.

Reichel-Dolmatoff, Gerard

1971   *Amazonian Cosmos: Sexual and Religious Symbolism of the Tukano Indians.* Chicago: University of Chicago Press.

Renselaar, H. C., and R. L. Mellema

1956   *Asmat Zuidwest Nieuw Guinea.* Koninkluk Instituut voor de Tropen: Afdeling Culturele en Physische Anthropologie no. 55. Amsterdam: N. V. Drukkerij Sigfried.

Riley, E. Baxter

1923   Dorro Head-hunters. *Man* 23:33–35. Article no. 18.

1925   *Among Papuan Headhunters.* Philadelphia: J. P. Lippincott. Reprinted, New York: AMS Press, 1982.

Rimoldi, Max, and Eleanor Rimoldi

1992   *Hahalis and the Labour of Love: A Social Movement on Buka Island.* Oxford: Berg.

Rival, Laura

1997   Oil and Sustainable Development in the Latin American Humid Tropics. *Anthropology Today* 13 (6): 1–3.

Rivers, W. H. R.
1914   *The History of Melanesian Society,* 2 vols. Cambridge: Cambridge University Press.
1924   *Social Organization.* New York: Knopf.
Rivers, W. H. R., ed.
1922   *Essays on the Depopulation of Melanesia.* Cambridge: Cambridge University Press.
Rivière, Peter
1980   Dialectical Societies. *Man* 15:533–40.
1984   *Individual and Society in Guiana: A Comparative Study of Amerindian Social Organization.* Cambridge: Cambridge University Press.
Robbins, Joel
1994   Christianity and Desire among the Urapmin of Papua New Guinea. Paper presented at the Annual Meetings of the American Anthropological Association, Atlanta, GA.
1995   Dispossessing the Spirits: Christian Transformations of Desire and Ecology among the Urapmin of Papua New Guinea. *Ethnology* 34:211–24.
1997   "When Do You Think the World Will End?": Globalization, Apocalypticism, and the Moral Perils of Fieldwork in "Last New Guinea." *Anthropology and Humanism* 22 (1): 6–30. (Special issue, *Fieldwork Revisited: Changing Contexts of Ethnographic Practice in the Era of Globalization,* ed. Joel Robbins and Sandra Bamford.). Arlington, VA: American Anthropological Association.
Robie, David
1989a *Blood on their Banner: Nationalist Struggles in the South Pacific.* London: Zed Books.
1989b Bougainville One Year Later. *Pacific Islands Monthly* (November): 10–18.
Robin, Robert W.
1982   Revival Movements in the Southern Highlands Province of Papua New Guinea. *Oceania* 52:320–43.
Rockefeller, Michael C., and Adrian A. Gerbrands
1967   *The Asmat of New Guinea: The Journal of Michael Clark Rockefeller.* New York: Museum of Primitive Art.
Rodman, Margaret
1992   Empowering Place: Multilocality and Multivocality. *American Anthropologist* 94:640–56.
Rodman, Margaret, and Matthew Cooper, eds.
1983   *The Pacification of Melanesia.* ASAO Monograph No. 7. Lanham, NJ: University Press of America.
Roheim, Geza
1946   Yaboaine, A War God of Normanby Island. *Oceania* 16:210–33, 319–36.
Romilly, Hugh Hastings
1886   *The Western Pacific and New Guinea: Notes on the Natives, Christian and Cannibal, with Some Account of the Labour Trade.* 2d ed. London: John Murray.
Rosaldo, Michelle
1977   Correspondence, "Skulls and Causality." *Man* 12:168–70.
1980   *Knowledge and Passion.* Cambridge: Cambridge University Press.
1983   The Shame of Headhunters and the Autonomy of Self. *Ethos* 11: 135–51.
Rosaldo, Renato
1980   *Ilongot Headhunting, 1883–1974.* Stanford: Stanford University Press.
1989   *Culture and Truth: The Remaking of Social Analysis.* Boston: Beacon.
1994   Whose Cultural Studies? *American Anthropologist* 96:524–29.

Roscoe, Paul B.
  1988   The Far Side of Hurun: The Management of Melanesian Millenarian Move-
         ments. *American Ethnologist* 15:515–29.
  1989   The Flight from the Fen: The Prehistoric Migrations of the Boiken of the East
         Sepik Province, Papua New Guinea. *Oceania* 60:139–54.
  1997   War and Society in Sepik New Guinea. *Journal of the Royal Anthropological Society*
         2:645–66.
Roscoe, Paul B., and R. B. Graber, eds.
  1988   *Circumscription and the Evolution of Society*. (*American Behavioral Scientist* 31, no.
         4). Newbury Park, CA: Sage.
Rosi, Pamela, and Laura Zimmer-Tamakoshi
  1993   Love and Marriage among the Educated Elite in Port Moresby. In *The Business of
         Marriage: Transformations in Oceanic Matrimony*, ed. Richard A. Marksbury,
         175–204. Pittsburgh: University of Pittsburgh Press.
Ross, Marc
  1986   The Limits to Social Structure: Social Structural and Psychocultural Explana-
         tions for Political Conflict and Violence. *Anthropological Quarterly* 88:843–58.
Rouse, Roger
  1991   Mexican Migration and the Space of Postmodernism. *Diaspora* 1:8–23.
Rubel, Paula G., and Abraham Rosman
  1978   *Your Own Pigs You May Not Eat: A Comparative Study of New Guinea Societies*.
         Chicago: University of Chicago Press.
Rutherford, Danilyn
  1996   Of Birds and Gifts: Reviving Tradition on an Indonesian Frontier. *Cultural
         Anthropology* 11:577–616.
  1997   Raiding the Market: Money and Violence in Biak, Irian Jaya, Indonesia. Paper
         presented at the Annual Meetings of the American Anthropological Associa-
         tion, Washington, DC.
Ryan, D'Arcy
  1959   Clan Formation in the Mendi Valley. *Oceania* 29:257–89.
Ryan, Dawn
  1989   Home Ties in Town: Toaripi in Port Moresby. *Canberra Anthropology* 12:19–27.
Sahlins, Marshall D.
  1963   Poor Man, Rich Man, Big-Man, Chief: Political Types in Melanesia and Polyne-
         sia. *Comparative Studies in Society and History* 5:285–303.
  1972a The Spirit of the Gift. In *Stone Age Economics*, by M. D. Sahlins, 149–83. Chicago:
         Aldine.
  1972b On the Sociology of Primitive Exchange. In *Stone Age Economics*, by M. D.
         Sahlins, 175–285. Chicago: Aldine.
  1983   Raw Women, Cooked Men, and Other "Great Things" of the Fiji Islands. In *The
         Ethnography of Cannibalism*, ed. Paula Brown and Donald F. Tuzin, 72–93. Wash-
         ington, DC: Society for Psychological Anthropology.
  1990   The Return of the Event, Again; With Reflections on the Beginnings of the Great
         Fijian War of 1843 to 1855 between the Kingdoms of Bau and Rewa. In *Clio in
         Oceania: Toward a Historical Anthropology*, ed. Aletta Biersack, 37–99. Washing-
         ton, DC: Smithsonian Institution Press.
  1995   *How Natives Think: About Captain Cook, For Example*. Chicago: University of
         Chicago Press.
Said, Edward
  1978   *Orientalism*. New York: Pantheon.

Salisbury, Richard
    1958   Political Organization in Siane Society. Unpublished ms. Cited in Langness
           1972a.
    1962   *From Stone to Steel: Economic Consequences of a Technological Change in New
           Guinea.* Melbourne: Melbourne University Press.
    1964   Despotism and Australian Administration in the New Guinea Highlands. In
           New Guinea: The Central Highlands, ed. James B. Watson. *American Anthropologist*
           66 (pt. 4): 225–39.
    1966   Politics and Shell-Money Finance in New Britain. In *Political Anthropology,* ed.
           M. Schwartz and A. Tuden. Chicago: Aldine.
    1970   *Vunamami.* Berkeley: University of California Press.
Sandline
    1997   The Sandline Document. *Asia Online,* Mar. 21. <http://www.theage.com.
           au/special/asiaonline/sandline.htm>.
Sangren, Steven P.
    1988   Rhetoric and the Authority of Ethnography: "Postmodernism" and the Social
           Reproduction of Texts. *Current Anthropology* 29:405–35.
Sarei, A. H.
    1974   Traditional Marriage and the Impact of Christianity on the Solos of Buka Island.
           New Guinea Research Bulletin, no. 57.
Sasako, Alfred
    1991   Inside Bougainville: There is No Turning Back, Says Francis Ona, as Supplies
           Run Out and Doctors Watch Women and Children Die. *Pacific Islands Monthly*
           (February): 19–21.
Scaglion, Richard
    1990   Legal Adaptation in a Papua New Guinea Village Court. *Ethnology* 29:17–33.
Scaglion, Richard, ed.
    1981   *Homicide Compensation in Papua New Guinea.* Law Reform Commission of Papua
           New Guinea, Monograph 1. Port Moresby: Office of Information.
    1987   *Customary Law and Legal Development in Papua New Guinea.* Special issue. *Journal
           of Anthropology* 6 (1–2).
Scarr, Deryck
    1967   Recruits and Recruiters: A Portrait of the Pacific Islands Labour Trade. *Journal of
           Pacific History* 2:5–24.
    1988   *Fiji, The Politics of Illusion: The Military Coups in Fiji.* Kensington: New South
           Wales University Press.
Scheffler, Harold W.
    1964a The Genesis and Repression of Conflict on Choiseul Island. *American Anthropol-
           ogist* 66 (4), part 1: 789–804.
    1964b The Social Consequences of Peace on Choiseul Island. *Ethnology* 3:398–403.
    1965   *Choiseul Island Social Structure.* Berkeley: University of California Press.
    1966   Ancestor Worship in Anthropology: Or, Observations on Descent and Descent
           Groups. *Current Anthropology* 7:541–51.
    1985   Filiation and Affiliation. *Man* 20:1–21.
Schemo, Diana J.
    1996   Violence Grows in Brazilian Land Battle. *New York Times,* Apr. 21, International
           Section.
    1998   Brazil Says Recent Burning of Amazon Is Worst Ever. *The New York Times* (on-
           line), Jan. 27.

Schieffelin, Bambi B.

1990   *The Give and Take of Everyday Life: Language Socialization of Kaluli Children.* New York: Cambridge University Press.

Schieffelin, Edward L.

1976   *The Sorrow of the Lonely and the Burning of the Dancers.* New York: St. Martin's.

1979   Mediators as Metaphors: Moving a Man to Tears in Papua New Guinea. In *The Imagination of Reality: Essays in Southeast Asian Coherence Systems,* ed. Alton L. Becker and Aram A. Yengoyan, 127–44. Norwood, NJ: Ablex.

1980   Reciprocity and the Construction of Reality. *Man* 15:502–17.

1982   The *Bau A* Ceremonial Hunting Lodge: An Alternative to Initiation. In *Rituals of Manhood: Male Initiation in Papua New Guinea,* ed. Gilbert H. Herdt, 155–201. Berkeley: University of California Press.

1983   Anger and Shame in the Tropical Forest: On Affect as a Cultural System in Papua New Guinea. *Ethos* 11:181–91.

1985   Performance and the Cultural Construction of Reality. *American Ethnologist* 12:707–24.

1995   Attitudes Toward Logging on the "Great Papuan Plateau." ASAONET Bulletin Board <asaonet@listserv.uic.edu>. Sept. 13.

Schieffelin, Edward L., and Robert Crittenden, eds.

1991   *Like People You See in a Dream: First Contact in Six Papuan Societies.* Stanford: Stanford University Press.

Schiltz, Marc

1987   War, Peace, and the Exercise of Power: Perspectives on Society, Gender, and the State in the New Guinea Highlands. *Social Analysis* 21:3–19.

Schneebaum, Tobias

1985   *Asmat Images: From the Collection of the Asmat Museum of Culture and Progress.* Minneapolis: Crosier Mission.

1988   *Where the Spirits Dwell: An Odyssey in the New Guinea Jungle.* New York: Grove Press.

Schneider, Jane, and Rayna Rapp, eds.

1995   *Articulating Hidden Histories: Exploring the Influence of Eric R. Wolf.* Berkeley: University of California Press.

Schwartz, Theodore

1962   *The Paliau Movement in the Admiralty Islands, 1946–1954.* Anthropological Papers of the American Museum of Natural History 49, pt. 2. New York.

1963   Systems of Areal Integration: Some Considerations Based on the Admiralty Islands of Northern Melanesia. *Anthropological Forum* 1:56–97.

1975   Cultural Totemism: Ethnic Identity, Primitive and Modern. In *Ethnic Identity: Cultural Continuities and Change,* ed. George DeVos and Lola Romanucci-Ross, 106–31. Palo Alto, CA: Mayfield.

Schwimmer, Eric

1973   *Exchange in the Social Structure of the Orokaiva.* New York: St. Martin's Press.

1979   Reciprocity and Structure: A Semiotic Analysis of Some Orokaiva Exchange Data. *Man* 14:271–85.

1983   La Guerre Aux Femmes (Nouvelle-Guinée): Propos et Discussions. *Anthropologie et Sociétés* 7:187–92.

Sedgwick, Eve K.

1990   *Epistemology of the Closet.* Berkeley: University of California Press.

1993   *Tendencies.* Durham, NC: Duke University Press.

Seligman[n], C. G.
  1910   *The Melanesians of British New Guinea.* Cambridge: Cambridge University Press.
Senge, Frank
  1990a   Papua New Guinea: Counting the Losses in a State of War. *Pacific Islands Monthly* (February): 12–13.
  1990b   Bougainville: The Crisis Deepens. *Pacific Islands Monthly* (June): 17–18.
Serpenti, Laurent M.
  1966   Headhunting and Magic on Kolepom. *Tropical Man* 1:116–39.
  1977   *Cultivators in the Swamps.* 2d ed. Assen, The Netherlands: Van Gorcum. 1st ed., 1965.
Sexton, Lorraine
  1986   *Mothers of Money, Daughters of Coffee: The Wok Meri Movement.* Ann Arbor, MI: UMI Research Press.
Seymour-Smith, Charlotte
  1991   Women Have No Affines and Men No Kin: The Politics of the Jivaroan Gender Relation. *Man* 26:629–49.
Shapiro, Judith
  1973   Male Bonds and Female Bonds. Paper presented at the 72d Annual Meetings of the American Anthropological Association, New Orleans.
  1982   Male Solidarity, Gender Display, and Patrilineality: Some South American Examples. Ms.
  1984   Marriage Rules, Marriage Exchange, and the Definition of Marriage in Lowland South American Societies. In *Marriage Practices in Lowland South America,* ed. Kenneth M. Kensinger, 1–30. Illinois Studies in Anthropology no. 14. Urbana: University of Illinois Press.
Shari, Michael, Gary McWilliams, and Stan Crock
  1995   Gold Rush in New Guinea. *Business Week,* Nov. 20, 66, 68.
Shaw, R. Daniel
  1990   *Kandila: Samo Ceremonial and Interpersonal Relationships.* Ann Arbor: University of Michigan Press.
Shea, Christopher
  1997   Political Scientists Clash Over Value of Area Studies: Theorists Say That a Focus on Individual Regions Leads to Work That Is Mushy. *Chronicle of Higher Education,* Jan. 10, A13–14.
Shineberg, Dorothy
  1967   *They Came for Sandalwood.* Melbourne: Melbourne University Press.
  1971   Guns and Men in Melanesia. *Journal of Pacific History* 6:61–82.
Shlomowitz, Ralph
  1987   Mortality and the Pacific Island Labour Trade. *Journal of Pacific History* 22:34–55.
  1988   Mortality and Indentured Labour in Papua (1885–1941) and New Guinea (1920–1941). *Journal of Pacific History* 23:70–79.
Sillitoe, Paul
  1977   Land Shortage and War in New Guinea. *Ethnology* 16:71–81.
  1978   Big Men and the War in New Guinea. *Man* 13:252–71.
  1979   *Give and Take: Exchange in Wola Society.* New York: St. Martin's Press.
  1985   Divide and No One Rules: The Implications of Sexual Divisions of Labour in the New Guinea Highlands. *Man* 20:494–522.
  1987   Wola Sorcery Divination. In *Sorcerer and Witch in Melanesia,* ed. Michele Stephen, 121–46. New Brunswick, NJ: Rutgers University Press.

Simet, Jacob
    1976   The Future of the Tubuan Society. Institute of Papua New Guinea Studies Dis-
           cussion Paper 24.
    1977   How Not to Do Research. Institute of Papua New Guinea Studies Discussion
           Paper 28.
Siskind, Janet
    1973   To Hunt in the Morning. New York: Oxford University Press.
Skar, Harald O., and Frank Salomon, eds.
    1987   Natives and Neighbors in South America: Anthropological Essays. Goteberg, Swe-
           den: Ethnographic Museum. (Ethnological Studies no. 38.)
Smith, Carol A.
    1995   Race-Class-Gender Ideology in Guatemala: Modern and Anti-Modern Forms.
           Comparative Studies in Society and History 37:723–49.
Smith, Michael French
    1994   Hard Times on Kairiru Island: Poverty, Development, and Morality in a Papua New
           Guinea Village. Honolulu: University of Hawaii Press.
Soja, Edward
    1989   Postmodern Geographies. London: Verso.
Sørum, Arve
    1980   In Search of the Lost Soul: Bedamini Spirit Seances and Curing Rites. Oceania
           50:273–96.
    1982   The Seeds of Power: Patterns of Bedamini Male Initiation. Social Analysis
           10:42–62.
South Pacific Commission (Population Study S-18 Project)
    1955   Rapport van het Bevolkingsonderzoek onder de Marind-anim van Nederlands
           Zuid Nieuw Guinea. Unpublished manuscript.
Speiser, Felix
    1991   Ethnology of Vanuatu: An Early Twentieth-Century Study. Bathurst, Australia:
           Crawford House Press.
Spencer, Herbert
    1873–81   Descriptive Sociology; Or, Groups of Sociological Facts, Classified and Arranged. 8
              vols. London.
Spencer, Michael, Alan Ward, and John Connell, eds.
    1988   New Caledonia: Essays in Nationalism and Dependency. St. Lucia, Queensland: Uni-
           versity of Queensland Press.
Spivak, Gayatri C.
    1994   Can the Subaltern Speak? In Colonial Discourse and Post-Colonial Theory: A Reader,
           ed. Patrick Williams and Laura Chrisman, 66–111. New York: Columbia Uni-
           versity Press.
Standing, Guy
    1989   Global Feminization through Flexible Labor. World Development 17 (7): 1077–95.
Stanner, William E.
    1953   The South Seas in Transition. London: Australasian.
Starr, June, and Jane F. Collier
    1989   Introduction: Dialogues in Legal Anthropology. In History and Power in the Study
           of Law, ed. J. Starr and J. F. Collier, 1–28. Ithaca, NY: Cornell University Press.
Steadman, Lyle B.
    1971   Neighbors and Killers: Residence and Dominance among the Hewa of New
           Guinea. Ph.D. diss., Department of Anthropology, Australian National Univer-
           sity, Canberra.

1975 Cannibal Witches in the Hewa. *Oceania* 46:114–21.

1985 The Killing of Witches. *Oceania* 56:106–23.

Steedly, Mary

1993 *Hanging without a Rope: Narrative Experience in Colonial and Postcolonial Karoland.* Princeton, NJ: Princeton University Press.

Steel, Robert

1880 *The New Hebrides and Christian Missions, with a Sketch of the Labour Trade.* London: Nisbet.

Steinbauer, Friedrich

1979 *Melanesian Cargo Cults: New Salvation Movements in the South Pacific,* trans. Max Wohlwill. St. Lucia: University of Queensland Press.

Stella, Regis, ed.

1994 *Moments in Melanesia.* Melbourne: Oxford University Press. [Collection of short stories by Melanesian authors.]

Stephen, Michele, ed.

1987 *Sorcerer and Witch in Melanesia.* New Brunswick, NJ: Rutgers University Press.

1994 *A'aisa's Gifts: A Study of Magic and the Self.* Berkeley: University of California Press.

Stocking, George W., Jr.

1987 *Victorian Anthropology.* New York: Free Press.

1989 Paradigmatic Traditions in the History of Anthropology. In *Companions to the History of Modern Science,* ed. R. C. Olby et al. London: Routledge.

1992 *The Ethnographer's Magic and Other Essays in the History of Anthropology.* Madison: University of Wisconsin Press.

1995 *After Tylor: British Social Anthropology, 1888–1951.* Madison: University of Wisconsin Press.

Stoler, Ann L.

1995 *Race and the Education of Desire: Foucault's History of Sexuality and the Colonial Order of Things.* Durham, NC: Duke University Press.

Strachan, John, Cpt.

1888 *Explorations and Adventures in New Guinea.* London: Sampson, Low, Marston, Searle, and Rivington.

Strathern, Andrew J.

1966 Despots and Directors in the New Guinea Highlands. *Man* (n.s.) 1:356–67.

1970 The Female and Male Spirit Cults in Mount Hagen. *Man* 5:571–85.

1971 *Rope of Moka: Big-Men and Ceremonial Exchange in Mount Hagen, New Guinea.* Cambridge: Cambridge University Press.

1972 *One Father, One Blood.* London: Tavistock.

1975 Why is Shame on the Skin? *Ethnology* 14:347–56.

1977 Contemporary Warfare in the New Guinea Highlands: Breakdown or Revival? *Yagl-Ambu* 4 (3): 135–46.

1979a Men's House, Women's House: The Efficacy of Opposition, Reversal, and Pairing in the Melpa *Amb Kor* Cult. *Journal of Polynesia* 88:37–51.

1979b Gender, Ideology, and Money in Mount Hagen. *Man* (n.s.) 14:530–48.

1979c *Ongka: A Self-Account by a New Guinea Big-Man.* New York: St. Martin's Press.

1982a Witchcraft, Greed, Cannibalism, and Death: Some Related Themes from the New Guinea Highlands. In *Death and the Regeneration of Life,* ed. Maurice Bloch and Jonathan Parry, 111–33. New York: Pergamon.

1982b Two Waves of African Models in the New Guinea Highlands. In *Inequality in New Guinea Highlands Societies,* ed. A. J. Strathern, 35–49. Cambridge: Cambridge University Press.

1982c The Division of Labor and Processes of Social Change in Mount Hagen. *American Ethnologist* 9:307–19.

1984 *A Line of Power*. London: Tavistock.

1988 Guns at Golke. Paper presented at the Annual Meetings of the American Anthropological Association, Phoenix, Arizona.

1990 Which Way to the Boundary? *American Ethnologist* 17:376–83.

1992 Let the Bow Go Down. In *War in the Tribal Zone: Expanding States and Indigenous Warfare*, ed. R. Brian Ferguson and Neil L. Whitehead, 229–50. Santa Fe: School of American Research Press.

1993a Violence and Political Change in Papua New Guinea. *Pacific Studies* 16 (4): 41–60.

1993b *Voices of Conflict*. Pittsburgh: University of Pittsburgh Press.

Strathern, Andrew J., ed.

1982d *Inequality in New Guinea Highland Societies*. Cambridge: Cambridge University Press.

Strathern, Andrew J., and Marilyn Strathern

1971 *Self-decoration in Mount Hagen*. Toronto: University of Toronto Press.

Strathern, Andrew J., and Gabriele Stürzenhofecker, eds.

1994 *Migration and Transformations: Regional Perspectives on New Guinea*. Pittsburgh: University of Pittsburgh Press.

Strathern, Marilyn

1972 *Women in Between: Female Roles in a Male World, Mount Hagen, New Guinea*. London: Seminar (Academic) Press.

1975 *No Money on Our Skins: Hagen Migrants in Port Moresby*. Port Moresby and Canberra: New Guinea Research Unit, Australian National University.

1979 The Self in Self-Decoration. *Oceania* 59:241–57.

1980 No Nature, No Culture: The Hagen Case. In *Nature, Culture and Gender*, ed. Carol MacCormack and Marilyn Strathern, 174–223. New York: Cambridge University Press.

1981 Self-interest and the Social Good: Some Implications of Hagen Gender Imagery. In *Sexual Meanings*, ed. Sherry B. Ortner and Harriet Whitehead, 166–91. Cambridge: Cambridge University Press.

1985 Discovering "Social Control." *Journal of Law and Society* 12:111–34.

1988 The Gender of the Gift: Problems with Women and Problems with Society in Melanesia. Berkeley: University of California Press.

1990 Negative Strategies in Melanesia. In *Localizing Strategies: Regional Traditions of Ethnographic Writing*, ed. Richard Fardon, 204–16. Washington: Smithsonian Institution Press.

1992 *Reproducing the Future: Essays on Anthropology, Kinship, and the New Reproductive Technologies*. New York: Routledge.

1996 Cutting the Network. *Journal of the Royal Anthropological Institute* (formerly *Man*) 2:517–35.

Strathern, Marilyn, ed.

1987 *Dealing with Inequality: Analysing Gender Relations in Melanesia and Beyond*. Cambridge: Cambridge University Press.

Strauss, Hermann, with Herbert Tischner

1990 *The Mi-Culture of the Mount Hagen People, Papua New Guinea*, trans. Brian Shields, ed. Gabriele Stürzenhofecker and Andrew J. Strathern. Pittsburgh Ethnology Monograph no. 13. Pittsburgh: University of Pittsburgh, Department of Anthropology.

Stürzenhofecker, Gabriele
  1994 Visions of a Landscape: Duna Premeditations on Ecological Change. *Canberra Anthropology* 17:27–47.
  1995 Dialectics of History: Female Witchcraft and Male Dominance in Aluni. In *Papuan Borderlands: Huli, Duna, and Ipili Perspectives on the Papua New Guinea Highlands*, ed. Aletta Biersack, 287–313. Ann Arbor: University of Michigan Press.
  1998 *Times Enmeshed: Gender, Space, and History among the Duna of Papua New Guinea.* Stanford: Stanford University Press.
Sullivan, Nancy
  1993 Film and Television Production in Papua New Guinea: How Media Become the Message. *Public Culture* 5:533–55.
Ta'unga, o te Tini
  1968 *The Works of Ta'unga,* ed. Ron and Marjorie Crocombe. Canberra: Australian National University Press.
  1982 Tuauru: The Cook Islands Mission to New Caledonia. In *Polynesian Missions in Melanesia,* 79–104. Suva, Fiji: University of the South Pacific.
Taussig, Michael
  1987 *Shamanism, Colonialism, and the Wild Man: A Study in Terror and Healing.* Chicago: University of Chicago Press.
  1992 *The Nervous System.* New York: Routledge.
  1993 *Mimesis and Alterity.* New York: Routledge.
Taylor, Anne-Christine
  1981 God-Wealth: The Achuar and the Missions. In *Cultural Transformations and Ethnicity in Modern Ecuador,* ed. Norman E. Whitten Jr., 647–76. Urbana: University of Illinois Press.
Thomas, Nicholas
  1989 The Force of Ethnology: Origins and Significance of the Melanesia/Polynesia Divide. *Current Anthropology* 30:27–41, 211–13.
  1991 *Entangled Objects: Exchanges, Material Culture, and Colonialism in the Pacific.* Cambridge: Harvard University Press.
  1994 *Colonialism's Culture: Anthropology, Travel, and Government.* Princeton, NJ: Princeton University Press.
  1997 *In Oceania: Visions, Artifacts, Histories.* Durham, NC: Duke University Press.
Thompson, Virginia, and Richard Adloff
  1971 *The French Pacific Islands: French Polynesia and New Caledonia.* Berkeley: University of California Press.
Thurnwald, B. Richard
  1910 *Im Bismarckarchipel und auf den Salomoinseln, 1906–1909.* Berlin.
  1916 *Banaro Society: Social Organization and Kinship System of a Tribe in the Interior of New Guinea. American Anthropological Association Memoirs* 3:253–391.
  1934 Adventures of a Tribe in New Guinea. In *Essays Presented to C. G. Seligman,* ed. E. E. Evans-Pritchard, Raymond Firth, Bronislaw Malinowski, and Isaac Schapera. London: Routledge and Kegan Paul.
  1965 *Economics in Primitive Communities.* Oosterhout, Netherlands: Anthropological Publications.
Tiano, Susan
  1994 *Patriarchy on the Line: Labor, Gender, and Ideology in the Mexican Maquila Industry.* Philadelphia: Temple University Press.

Tiffany, Sharon W., and Kathleen J. Adams
  1994 Anthropology's "Fierce" Yanomami: Narratives of Sexual Politics in the Amazon. *NWSA Journal [Journal of the National Womens Studies Association]* 6 (2): 169–96.

Tippett, Alan R.
  1956 *The Nineteenth Century Labour Trade in the South West Pacific: A Study of Slavery and Indenture as the Origin of Present-Day Racial Problems.* Unpublished M.A. thesis, American University, Washington, DC.

Tjibaou, Jean-Marie
  1978 *Kanaké: The Melanesian Way.* Pape'ete: Editions du Pacifique.

Toft, Susan, ed.
  1990 *Domestic Violence in Papua New Guinea.* Law Reform Commission of Papua New Guinea, Monograph no. 6. Port Moresby.

  1997 *Compensation for Resource Development in Papua New Guinea.* Papua New Guinea Law Reform Commission Monograph No. 6. Canberra: Resource Management in Asia and the Pacific, RSPAS, and National Centre for Development Studies, The Australian National University.

Townsley, Graham
  1987 The Outside Overwhelms: Yaminahua Dual Organization and Its Decline. In *Natives and Neighbors in South America: Anthropological Essays,* ed. Harald O. Skar and Frank Salomon, 355–76. Goteberg, Sweden: Ethnographic Museum. (Ethnological Studies no. 38.)

Trask, Haunani-Kay
  1991 Natives and Anthropologists: The Colonial Struggle. *The Contemporary Pacific* 3:159–67.

Trompf, Gary W.
  1991 *Melanesian Religion.* New York: Cambridge University Press.

Trouillot, Michel-Rolph
  1989 *Peasants and Capital: Dominica in the World Economy.* Baltimore: Johns Hopkins University Press.

  1991 Anthropology and the Savage Slot: The Poetics and Politics of Otherness. In *Recapturing Anthropology: Working in the Present,* ed. Richard G. Fox, 17–44. Santa Fe, NM: School of American Research Press.

  1997 "Between the Cracks" *Crosscurrents (Newsletter of the Institute for Global Studies in Culture, Power and History, Johns Hopkins University)* 6 (2): 1, 7–8.

Tsing, Anna L.
  1993 *In the Realm of the Diamond Queen: Marginality in an Out-of-the-Way Place.* Princeton, NJ: Princeton University Press.

  1994 From the Margins. *Cultural Anthropology* 9:279–97.

Turner, Ann
  1993 *Views from Interviews: The Changing Role of Women in Papua New Guinea.* Melbourne: Oxford University Press.

Turner, Terence S.
  1979a The Ge and Bororo Societies as Dialectical Systems: A General Model. In *Dialectical Societies: The Ge and Bororo of Central Brazil,* ed. David Maybury-Lewis, 147–78. Cambridge: Harvard University Press.

  1979b Kinship, Household, and Community Structure among the Kayapo. In *Dialectical Societies: The Ge and Bororo of Central Brazil,* ed. David Maybury-Lewis, 179–214. Cambridge: Harvard University Press.

1980 The Social Skin. In *Not Work Alone: A Cross-cultural View of Activities Superfluous to Survival,* ed. Jeremy Cherfas and Roger Lewin, 112–43. Beverly Hills, CA: Sage.

1992 Defiant Images: The Kayapo Appropriation of Video. *Anthropology Today* 8 (6): 5–16.

1993 Anthropology and Multiculturalism: What Is Anthropology That Multiculturalists Should Be Mindful of It? *Cultural Anthropology* 8:411–29.

Tuzin, Donald F.

1972 Yam Symbolism in the Sepik: An Interpretive Account. *Southwestern Journal of Anthropology* 28:230–54.

1974 Social Control and the Tambaran in the Sepik. In *Contention and Dispute: Aspects of Law and Social Control in Melanesia,* ed. A. L. Epstein. Canberra: Australian National University Press.

1976 *The Ilahita Arapesh: Dimensions of Unity.* Berkeley: University of California Press.

1980 *The Voice of the Tambaran: Truth and Illusion in Ilahita Arapesh Religion.* Berkeley: University of California Press.

1982 Ritual Violence among the Ilahita Arapesh: The Dynamics of Moral and Religious Uncertainty. In *Rituals of Manhood: Male Initiation in Papua New Guinea,* ed. Gilbert H. Herdt, 321–57. Berkeley: University of California Press.

1989 Visions, Prophecies, and the Rise of Christian Consciousness. In *The Religious Imagination in New Guinea,* ed. Gilbert Herdt and Michele Stephen, 187–208. Brunswick, NJ: Rutgers University Press.

1997 *The Cassowary's Revenge: The Life and Death of Masculinity in a New Guinea Society.* Chicago: University of Chicago Press.

Tuzin, Donald F., and Paula Brown

1983 Editor's Preface. In *The Ethnography of Cannibalism,* ed. Paula Brown and Donald F. Tuzin, 1–5. Washington, DC: Society for Psychological Anthropology.

Tyler, Stephen A.

1988 *The Unspeakable.* Madison: University of Wisconsin Press.

Urry, James

1993 *Before Social Anthropology: Essays on the History of British Anthropology.* Chur, Switzerland: Harwood Academic.

Van Baal, Jan

1966 *Dema: Description and Analysis of Marind-Anim Culture (South New Guinea).* The Hague: Martinus Nijhoff.

1982 *Jan Verschueren's Description of Yei-nan Culture.* The Hague: Martinus Nijhoff.

1984 The Dialectics of Sex in Marind-anim Culture. In *Ritualized Homosexuality in Melanesia,* ed. Gilbert H. Herdt, 128–67. Berkeley: University of California Press.

Van Baal, Jan, K. W. Galis, and R. M. Koentjaraningrat

1984 *West Irian: A Bibliography.* (Koninklijk Instituut voor Taal-, Land- en Volkenkunde, Bibliographic Series no. 15.) Dordrecht, Holland/Cinnaminson, NJ: Foris Publications.

van der Grijp, Paul, and Toon van Meijl, eds.

1993 *Politics, Tradition and Change in the Pacific. Bijdragen tot de Taal, Land- en Volkenkunde,* vol. 149, no. 4.

van der Kroef, Justus

1952 Some Head-hunting Traditions of Southern New Guinea. *American Anthropologist* 54:221–35.

van Velzen, H. U. E., and W. van Wetering
    1960   Residence, Power Groups, and Intra-Societal Aggression: An Enquiry into the Conditions Leading to Peacefulness within Non-stratified Societies. *Internal Archives of Ethnography* 49:169–200.
Vaughn, Tom
    1995   Feld Speaks on Freeport. *Daily Texan*, Dec. 7.
Vayda, Andrew
    1961   Expansion and Warfare among Swidden Agriculturalists. *American Anthropologist* 63:346–58.
    1971   Phases of the Process of War and Peace among the Maring of New Guinea. *Oceania* 42 (1): 1–24.
    1974   Warfare in Ecological Perspective. *Annual Review of Ecology and Systemics* 5:183–93.
    1976   *War in Ecological Perspective: Persistence, Change, and Adaptive Processes in Three Oceanian Societies.* New York: Plenum.
    1979   War and Coping. *Reviews in Anthropology* (spring): 191–98.
    1989   Explaining Why the Marings Fought. *Journal of Anthropological Research* 45:159–77.
Vicedom, G. F., and Herbert Tischner
    1943–48   *Die Mbowamb: Die Kultur der Hagenberg-stamme im Ostlichen Zentral-Neuguiney.* Museum für Volkerkunde und Voreschichte, Monographien zur Volkerkune, 3 vols. Hamburg: Friederichsen, de Gruyter.
Wagley, Charles
    1953   *Amazon Town: A Study of Man in the Tropics.* New York: Macmillan.
Wagner, Roy
    1967   *The Curse of Souw: Principles of Daribi Clan Definition and Alliance in New Guinea.* Chicago: University of Chicago Press.
    1972   *Habu: The Innovation of Meaning in Daribi Religion.* Chicago: University of Chicago Press.
    1975   *The Invention of Culture.* Chicago: University of Chicago Press.
    1978   *Lethal Speech: Daribi Myth as Symbolic Obviation.* Ithaca, NY: Cornell University Press.
    1981   *The Invention of Culture.* 2d ed. Chicago: University of Chicago Press.
    1983   The Ends of Innocence: Conception and Seduction Among the Daribi of Karimui and the Barok of New Ireland. *Mankind* 14:75–83.
    1986   *Asiwinarong: Ethos, Image, and Social Power among the Usen Barok of New Ireland.* Princeton, NJ: Princeton University Press.
    1988   Visible Sociality: The Daribi Community. In *Mountain Papuans: Historical and Comparative Perspectives from New Guinea Fringe Highlands Societies*, ed. James F. Weiner, 39–71. Ann Arbor: University of Michigan Press.
Waiko, John D.
    1992   *Tugata:* Culture, Identity, and Commitment. In *Confronting the Margaret Mead Legacy: Scholarship, Empire, and the South Pacific*, ed. Lenora Foerstel and Angela Gilliam, 233–66. Philadelphia: Temple University Press.
    1993   *A Short History of Papua New Guinea.* Melbourne: Oxford University Press.
Walker, Ranginui
    1990   *Ka Whawhai Tonu Matou: Struggle without End.* Auckland: Penguin.

Wallace, Michele
1990   *Invisibility Blues: From Pop to Theory.* London: Verso.
Wallerstein, Immanuel
1979   *The Capitalist World-Economy.* Cambridge: Cambridge University Press.
1980   *Mercantilism and the Consolidation of the European World Economy, 1600–1750.* New York: Academic.
1989   *The Second Era of Great Expansion of the Capitalistic World Economy, 1730–1840s.* San Diego, CA: Academic.
1991   *Geopolitics and Geoculture: Essays on the Changing World-System.* Cambridge: Cambridge University Press.
Wanek, Alexander
1996   *The State and Its Enemies in Papua New Guinea.* Nordic Institute of Asian Studies Monograph no. 68. Richmond: Curzon.
Wardlow, Holly
1992   "Women are Our Coffee": Historical Factors and Current Variables in Small-holder Coffee Production in Papua New Guinea. Harold K. Schneider Prize Paper, Society for Economic Anthropology.
1996   Bobby Teardrops: A Turkish Video in Papua New Guinea: Reflections on Cultural Studies, Feminism, and the Anthropology of Mass Media. *Visual Anthropology Review.* 12:1–17.
1997   The Tai Yunduga Python: Gendered Versions of Mt. Kare Myths. A paper presented at the conference "From Myth to Minerals: Narrative, Land, and Transformation in Australia and New Guinea." The Australian National University, Canberra, July 17–20.
1998   Changing Sexuality, Changing Self: The Huli *Dawe Anda* as Contemporary Male Ritual. Paper presented at the annual meetings of the Association for Social Anthropology in Oceania (ASAO), Pensacola, FL.
Warry, Wayne
1986   Kafaina: Wealth and Power in Chuave, Papua New Guinea. *Oceania* 57:4–21.
Watson, James B.
1971   Tairora: The Politics of Despotism in a Small Society. In *Politics in New Guinea,* ed. Ronald Berndt and Peter Lawrence, 224–75. Nedlands: University of Western Australia Press.
1977   Pigs, Fodder, and the Jones Effect in Post-Ipomoean New Guinea. *Ethnology* 16:57–70.
1983   *Tairora Culture: Contingency and Pragmatism.* Seattle: University of Washington Press.
Watson, James B., ed.
1964   *New Guinea: The Central Highlands. American Anthropologist* 66, special issue.
Watson, Virginia Drew
1997   *Anyan's Story: A New Guinea Woman in Two Worlds.* Seattle: University of Washington Press.
Wawn, William T.
1893   *The South Sea Islanders and the Queensland Labour Trade.* London: Sonnenschein. Reprint, ed. Peter Corris, Honolulu: University Press of Hawaii, 1973.
Weber, Max
1958   *The Protestant Ethic and the Spirit of Capitalism.* New York: Free Press.
1978   *Economy and Society: An Outline of Interpretive Sociology,* ed. Guenther Roth and Claus Wittich. Berkeley: University of California Press.

Webster, Elsie M.

1984 *The Moon Man: A Biography of Nikolai Miklouho-Maclay.* Berkeley: University of California Press.

Wedgwood, Camilla

1930 Some Aspects of Warfare in Melanesia. *Oceania* 1:5–33.

Weiner, Annette B.

1976 *Women of Value, Men of Renown: New Perspectives in Trobriand Exchange.* Austin: University of Texas Press.

1980 Reproduction: A Replacement for Reciprocity. *American Ethnologist* 7:71–85.

1987 *The Trobrianders of Papua New Guinea.* Fort Worth, TX: Holt, Rinehart, and Winston.

1992 *Inalienable Possessions: The Paradox of Keeping-While-Giving.* Berkeley: University of California Press.

Weiner, James F.

1982 Substance, Siblingship and Exchange: Aspects of Social Structure in New Guinea. *Social Analysis* 11:3–34.

1984 Sunset and Flowers: The Sexual Dimension of Foi Spatial Orientation. *Journal of Anthropological Research* 40:577–88.

1986 Blood and Skin: The Structural Implications of Sorcery and Procreation Beliefs among the Foi of Papua New Guinea. *Ethnos* 51:71–87.

1987 Diseases of the Soul: Sickness, Agency and the Men's Cult among the Foi of New Guinea. In *Dealing with Inequality: Analysing Gender Relations in Melanesia and Beyond,* ed. Marilyn Strathern, 255–77. Cambridge: Cambridge University Press.

1988a *The Heart of the Pearlshell: The Mythological Dimension of Foi Sociality.* Berkeley: University of California Press.

1988b Durkheim and the Papuan Male Cult: Whitehead's Views on Social Structure and Ritual in New Guinea. *American Ethnologist* 15:567–73.

1993 *The Empty Place: Poetry, Space, and Being among the Foi of Papua New Guinea.* Bloomington: Indiana University Press.

1994 The Origin of Petroleum at Lake Kutubu. *Cultural Anthropology* 9:37–57.

1995 *The Lost Drum.* Madison: University of Wisconsin Press.

Weiner, James F., ed.

1988c *Mountain Papuans: Historical and Comparative Perspectives from New Guinea Fringe Highlands Societies.* Ann Arbor: University of Michigan Press.

Weitzman, Marc, with Jean Guiart and Jean Chesneaux

1985 *Nouvelle-Calédonie: Un Siècle de balles perdues.* Paris: Vertige.

Werner, Dennis

1984 Paid Sex Specialists among the Mekranoti. *Journal of Anthropological Research* 40:394–405.

Wesley-Smith, Terence

1995 Melanesia in Review—Issues and Events, 1994: Papua New Guinea. *The Contemporary Pacific* 7:364–74.

Wesley-Smith, Terence, ed.

1992 *A Legacy of Development: Three Years of Crisis in Bougainville.* Contemporary Pacific, vol. 4, no. 2.

West, Cornel

1989 *The Ethical Dimensions of Marxist Thought.* New York: Monthly Review Press.

1993a *Keeping Faith: Philosophy and Race in America.* New York: Routledge.

1993b *Race Matters*. Boston: Beacon.

West, M. M., and M. J. Konner

1976 The Role of the Father: An Anthropological Perspective. In *The Role of the Father in Child Development*, ed. M. E. Lamb. New York: Wiley.

Westermark, George D.

1984 "Ol I Skulim Mipela": Contemporary Warfare in Papua New Guinea Eastern Highlands. *Anthropological Quarterly* 57:114–24.

1987 The Agarabi Moot. In *Customary Law and Legal Development in Papua New Guinea*. Special issue, guest-edited by Richard Scaglion. *Journal of Anthropology* 6 (1): 77–94.

White, Geoffrey M.

1983 War, Peace, and Piety in Santa Isabel, Solomon Islands. In *The Pacification of Melanesia*, ed. Margaret Rodman and Matthew Cooper, 109–39. ASAO Monograph No. 7. Lanham, NJ: University Press of America.

1991 *Identity through History: Living Stories in a Solomon Islands Society*. Cambridge: Cambridge University Press.

White, Geoffrey M., and Lamont Lindstrom, eds.

1989 *The Pacific Theater: Island Representations of World War II*. Honolulu: University of Hawaii Press.

1993 *Custom Today*. Special issue of *Anthropological Forum* 6 (4).

1997 *Chiefs Today: Traditional Pacific Leadership and the Postcolonial State*. Stanford: Stanford University Press.

White, J. P., and J. F. O'Connell

1982 *A Prehistory of Australia, New Guinea and Sahul*. New York: Academic Press.

Whitehead, Harriet

1986a The Varieties of Fertility Cultism in New Guinea: Part 1. *American Ethnologist* 13:80–99.

1986b The Varieties of Fertility Cultism in New Guinea: Part 2. *American Ethnologist* 13:271–89.

Whitehouse, Harvey

1995 *Inside the Cult: Religious Innovation and Transmission in Papua New Guinea*. Oxford: Clarendon.

Whiteman, Darrell L.

1983 *Melanesians and Missionaries: An Ethnohistorical Study of Social and Religious Change in the Southwest Pacific*. Pasadena, CA: William Carey.

Whiting, John W. M., and Beatrice B. Whiting

1975 Aloofness and Intimacy of Husbands and Wives: A Cross-Cultural Study. *Ethos* 3:183–207.

Whitten, Norman E., Jr.

1976 *Sacha Runa: Ethnicity and Adaptation of Ecuadorian Jungle Quichua*. Urbana: University of Illinois Press.

1985 *Sicuanga Runa: The Other Side of Development in Amazonian Ecuador*. Urbana: University of Illinois Press.

Whitten, Norman E., Jr., ed.

1981 *Cultural Transformations and Ethnicity in Modern Ecuador*. Urbana: University of Illinois Press.

Williams, Brackette F., ed.

1996 *Women Out of Place: The Gender of Agency and the Race of Nationality*. New York: Routledge.

Williams, Francis E.

1923a The Pairama Ceremony in the Purari Delta, Papua. *Journal of the Royal Anthropological Institute of Great Britain and Ireland* 53:361–87.

1923b *The Vailala Madness and the Destruction of Native Ceremonies in the Gulf Division.* Territory of Papua, Anthropology Report no. 4. Port Moresby: Government Printer.

1924 *The Natives of the Purari Delta.* Territory of Papua, Anthropology Report no. 5. Port Moresby: Government Printer.

1930 *Orokaiva Society.* London: Oxford University Press.

1936 *Papuans of the Trans-Fly.* Oxford: Clarendon Press.

1940 *Drama of Orokolo: The Social and Ceremonial Life of the Elema.* Oxford: Clarendon Press.

1977 Natives of Lake Kutubu, Papua. In *'The Vailala Madness' and Other Essays,* ed. Eric Schwimmer, 161–331. Honolulu: University Press of Hawaii.

Williams, Patrick, and Laura Chrisman, eds.

1994 *Colonial Discourse and Post-Colonial Theory: A Reader.* New York: Columbia University Press.

Williamson, Margaret Holmes

1983 Sex Relations and Gender Relations: Understanding Kwoma Conception. *Mankind* 14:13–23.

Williamson, Robert W.

1912 *The Mafulu, Mountain People of British New Guinea.* London: Macmillan.

Wilson, Monica

1963 *Good Company: A Study of Nyakusa Age-Villages.* Boston: Beacon.

Wingert, Paul S.

1962 *Primitive Art: Its Traditions and Styles.* New York: Oxford University Press.

Wirz, Paul

1922–25 *Die Marind-anim von Hollandisch-Sud-Neu-Guinea, I–IV.* 2 vols. Hamburg: Friederichsen.

1928 *Damonen und Wilde in Neuguinea.* Stuttgart: Strecker und Schroder.

1933 Headhunting Expeditions of the Tugeri into the Western Division of New Guinea. *Tijdschrift van de Instituut voor Taal-, Land-, en Volkenkunde* 73:105–22.

1959 *Kunst und Kult des Sepik-Gebietes (Neu-Guinea).* Koninklijk Instituut voor de Tropen Mededeling 133, Afdeling Culturele en Physische Anthropologie 62. Amsterdam.

Wolf, Eric

1982 *Europe and the People without History.* Berkeley: University of California Press.

1988 Inventing Society. *American Ethnologist* 15:752–61.

Wood, Michael

1995 "White Skins," "Real People," and "Chinese" in Some Spatial Transformations of the Western Province, P.N.G. *Oceania* 66:23–50.

1996 Logs, Long Socks and the "Tree Leaf" People: An Analysis of a Timber Project in the Western Province of Papua New Guinea. *Social Analysis* no. 39:83–117.

1997 The Makapa TRP as a Study in Project Failure in the Post-Barnett Era. In *The Political Economy of Forest Management in Papua New Guinea,* ed. Colin Filer. London: IIED; Boroko: NRI.

Wormsley, William E.

1987a Courts, Custom, and Tribal Warfare in Enga. In *Customary Law and Legal Development in Papua New Guinea.* Special issue, guest-edited by Richard Scaglion. *Journal of Anthropology* 6 (2): 55–108.

1987b Beer and Power in Enga. In *Drugs in Western Pacific Societies: Relations of Substance,* ed. Lamont Lindstrom, 197–217. Lanham, NJ: University Press of America.

Worsley, Peter

1968 *The Trumpet Shall Sound.* 2d ed. New York: Schocken.

1984 *The Three Worlds: Culture and World Development.* Chicago: University of Chicago Press.

Wright, Henry T.

1986 The Evolution of Civilizations. In *American Archaeology Past and Future,* ed. David J. Meltzer, Don D. Fowler, and Jeremy A. Sabloff, 323–65. Washington: Smithsonian Institution Press.

Wurm, Stephan A.

1982a The Linguistic Point of View. In *Melanesia: Beyond Diversity,* vol. 1, ed. R. J. May and Hank Nelson, 7–10. Canberra: Research School of Pacific Studies, The Australian National University.

1982b Papuan Languages. In *Melanesia: Beyond Diversity,* vol. 1. ed. R. J. May and Hank Nelson, 225–40. Canberra: Research School of Pacific Studies, The Australian National University.

1983 Linguistic Prehistory in the New Guinea Area. *Journal of Human Evolution* 12:25–35.

Wurm, Stephan A., and Shiro Hattori, eds.

1981 *Language Atlas of the Pacific Area.* (Pacific Linguistics Series C, no. 66) Canberra: Australian Academy of Humanities.

Yanagisako, Sylvia, and Carol Delaney, eds.

1995 *Naturalizing Power: Essays in Feminist Cultural Analysis.* New York: Routledge.

Young, Michael W.

1971 *Fighting with Food: Leadership, Values and Social Control in a Massim Society.* Cambridge: Cambridge University Press.

1977 Doctor Bromilow and the Bwaidoka Wars. *Journal of Pacific History* 12:130–53.

1980 A Tropology of the Dobu Mission. *Canberra Anthropology* 3:86–104.

1983a *Magicians of Manumanua: Living Myth in Kalauna.* Berkeley: University of California Press.

1983b Our Name Is Women; We Are Bought with Limesticks and Limepots: An Analysis of the Autobiographical Narrative of a Kalauna Woman. *Man* 18:478–501.

1986 The Worst Disease: The Cultural Definition of Hunger in Kalauna. In *Shared Wealth and Symbol: Food, Culture, and Society in Oceania and Southeast Asia,* ed. Lenore Manderson, 111–27. Cambridge: Cambridge University Press.

1989 Suffer the Children: Wesleyans in the D'Entrecasteaux. In *Family and Gender in the Pacific: Domestic Contradictions and the Colonial Impact,* ed. Margaret Jolly and Martha Macintyre, 108–34. Cambridge: Cambridge University Press.

Zavella, Patricia

1987 *Women's Work and Chicano Families: Cannery Workers of the Santa Clara Valley.* Ithaca: Cornell University Press.

Zegwaard, Gerard A.

1959 Headhunting Practices of the Asmat of West New Guinea. *American Anthropologist* 61:1020–41.

1982 An Asmat Mission History. Trans. Joseph de Louw. In *Asmat Sketch Book No. 2,* ed. Frank A. Trenkenschuh, 5–15. Hastings, NE: Crosier Missions.

Zegwaard, Gerard A., and J. H. M. C. Boelaars

1955 De Sociale Structuur van de Asmat-Bevolking. *Adatrechtbundel* 45:244–403.

Zelenietz, Martin
   1983   The End of Headhunting in New Georgia. In *The Pacification of Melanesia*, ed. Margaret Rodman and Matthew Cooper, 91–108. ASAO Monograph no. 7. Lanham, NJ: University Press of America.
Zelenietz, Marty, and Shirley Lindenbaum, eds.
   1981   *Sorcery and Social Change in Melanesia. Social Analysis*, no. 8. Adelaide.
Zimmer-Tamakoshi, Laura
   1993a Nationalism and Sexuality in Papua New Guinea. *Pacific Studies* 16:61–97.
   1993b Bachelors, Spinsters, and *Pamuk Meris*. In *The Business of Marriage: Transformations in Oceanic Matrimony*, ed. Richard A. Marksbury, 83–104. Pittsburgh: University of Pittsburgh Press.
   1995   Passion, Poetry, and Cultural Politics in the South Pacific. *Ethnology* 34:113–27.
Zuckerman, Steven
   1987   Vengeance and Mediation: The Incorporation of Village Courts into Kamano Society. In *Customary Law and Legal Development in Papua New Guinea*. Special issue, guest-edited by Richard Scaglion. *Journal of Anthropology* 6 (2): 1–34.

Index